THE GAMBIA

*Leading Political Personalities in the Decolonization
and Early Post-Independence Era*

The
VERY REVEREND
J. C. FAYE:
HIS LIFE AND TIMES

A Biography

JEGGAN C. SENGHOR

authorHOUSE®

AuthorHouse™ LLC
1663 Liberty Drive
Bloomington, IN 47403
www.authorhouse.com
Phone: 1-800-839-8640

Published by AuthorHouse 05/09/2014

ISBN: 978-1-4918-6954-3 (sc)
ISBN: 978-1-4918-6953-6 (hc)
ISBN: 978-1-4918-6981-9 (e)

Library of Congress Control Number: 2014904355

DEDICATION

In Eternal Memory of

The Very Reverend John Colley Faye,
Pioneer and Patriot

and

Cecilia Priscilla Faye,
A Tower of Support.

TABLE OF CONTENTS

ACKNOWLEDGEMENTS

In an undertaking such as the writing of the biography of a man like The Very Reverend (Rev.) John Colley Faye, a range of instruments and sources have to be used to pull together the vast amount of material required. One such source consists of interviews with individuals who, in one way or the other, were directly or indirectly involved in his life and work. Unfortunately, in this instance, very few of Faye's contemporaries are still alive—not even people in his age group who may not have been directly associated with him but were witnesses to the happenings in which he was involved.

Most in their generation, and that following, have passed on. In fact, as far as this project goes, the few I could identify included Sir Alieu Sulayman Jack, Alhaji Alieu E. Cham Joof, Sir Dawda Jawara and Alhaji Assan Musa Camara. Tragically, Sir Alieu Jack passed away two weeks before my departure from London for Banjul for a series of interviews with him, and Alhaji Cham Joof followed at the very hour my flight was taking off for Banjul. I acknowledge, posthumously, and with deep feelings of gratitude, the interest these two showed in this biography, their infectious excitement about it and their encouragement. How they looked forward to our exchanges and to sharing their knowledge! But this was not to be. Their deaths have deprived us of so much that is our collective inheritance. If only they could have been around to see the finished product! We recognize the inputs from Sir Dawda, particularly through his bold initiative to publish his autobiography.

Mary Ann Chapman (née Jarra-Owens), Rev. Faye's first cousin, also passed away whilst this biography was under preparation. Happily, though, in her case Marcel Thomasi had already recorded an extensive and in-depth series of interviews on Faye as seen from the inside. My thanks go to Aunty Mary, and credit to Marcel for his foresight and for a job very well done.

I am obliged to recognize the contributions of several other people, institutions, and people within institutions who played major roles in the course of preparing this work. First and foremost, there would have been no J. C. Faye biography if there was no Adele Faye-NJie. Adele, the only daughter of Rev. Faye, had long been committed to a true recording of the life of Rev. Faye for two main reasons: to document the numerous ways in which he contributed to his country, especially in the era of decolonization; and for posterity to learn about his experiences, benefit from the virtues and values he cherished, and from these gain guidance in moulding their own lives.

My own commitment to work on the biography was at a time when Adele had also embarked on other initiatives to get it done. Once I had taken the decision to give it a go, she threw her whole weight behind the project. She provided a wealth of information in many hours of formal interviews and informal chats, together with the few papers in the Faye collection that are still extant. In our discussions she impressed me with her incredible memory, especially for names and events. Further, Adele served as the point of coordination in Banjul and was particularly effective in searching through family records, trouble-shooting, participating in some interviews, and introducing the project and my good self to all and sundry—not to mention providing the sumptuous family meals at which I got to see the fun side of the NJie home. Daddy joins us all in thanking you, Adele.

Busy as they were with their multiple ventures, Rev. Faye's other children, Axel Faye and Colley Faye, gave moral support to the project. Three of Adele's own children—Michelle, Francis, and John Charles—provided background support. Their very genuine interest was a source of motivation, for I felt obliged to give them the opportunity to know their grandfather better, not in bits and pieces but in a full-length study. As Michelle confessed to me: "These days I find it difficult to read more than six pages; now you will compel me read hundreds of pages. Nevertheless, I promise you that I will finish reading the published book in two weeks maximum."

I acknowledge all the interviewees who, in one way or another, were involved with Rev. Faye in his many areas of work. Assan Musa Camara (previously named Andrew David Camara) a lifelong comrade-in-arms to Rev. Faye, gave many hours of his valuable time to answering my questions; at close to 90 years he had an amazingly retentive memory. There was no one around who knew more about Kristi-kunda than Assan Musa; he took as much credit for the rich material in the sections on the Kristi-kunda experiment as for Faye's politics. His affection for and loyalty to Rev. Faye were exemplary. How deeply do I regret that Assan Musa did not live to see the final publication for he departed this life in September 2013. How cruel the hand of Fate!

The discussions with The Most Reverend Dr. Solomon Tilewa Johnson were especially valuable in that, for Rev. Faye, life as a clergyman was such an important part of his being and his living. The late Bishop filled many gaps in the chapters dealing with this subject, for which I also offer my posthumous appreciations.

As indicated in the Preface, currently under implementation is a project titled "The Gambia: Leading Political Personalities in the Decolonization and Early Post-independence Era"; it is one of several projects under "The Gambia Leadership Programme" (*GamLeaP*). The project was born after I had committed myself to do this Faye biography. In many ways the team members influenced my thinking on issues and have generally been very supportive. The sharing of information, the location of sources, and the insightful comments when requested have been some of the hallmarks of our collaboration. With much respect to the other team members, I single out Ebrima Ceesay who was most useful in the conceptualization and operationalization of the *GamLeaP,* and unreservedly shared his vast reservoir of information on sources of material for this and other biographies in the series. An added bonus was that it was easy to bounce ideas off Ebrima and obtain useful responses; his support in the production phase of the book deserves separate acknowledgement. Abou Jeng was always fresh in his approach to research and innovative in his interpretation of events; his contributions made a difference. And, David Perfect not only facilitated access to the wealth of material at the National Archives in London but he was a dependable source of advice. To these and to other team members, Assan Sarr and Abdoulaye and Paula Saine, my indebtedness is here recorded. I look forward to reciprocating with the biographies in your charge.

Then there were some of those who had direct experience in working with Rev. Faye in his educational projects, namely, Delphine Carroll, Theophilus George, Wilmot John, Francis Jones and Femi Peters. They were privileged to see the business side of Rev. Faye, his dedication to education and his devotion to serving others. I honestly welcome your sharing your experiences of Rev. Faye and thereby making this a more worthwhile venture. In this regard, special words of appreciation go to Dr. Florence Mahoney, the doyen of Gambian historians, for a most stimulating exchange.

Quite a proportion of the material for this biography was obtained from archives, research and documentation institutions in Banjul and in England. I am much indebted to individuals in these places who went out of the way to search out relevant documentary information: Vera Minina Prom, head of the Anglican Diocesan Archives, ably assisted by Christopher Eber and Victor Johnson; Christopher Manley, the Diocesan Education Officer, who readily shared his abundant knowledge of the Anglican Vocational Training Centre; Baba Ceesay, Director General of the National Commission for Arts and Culture and Baba Saho, his former colleague; and Lamin Yarbo, Alieu Jawara and Nyangador of the Oral Archives Annex (alias The Mango Tree).

In the National Records Services (incorporating the archives) the prodigious Director, Elizabeth Bahoum, together with her colleagues—Adama Joof, Bashiru Manneh, Abdoulrahman Manka—were most efficient in meeting my varied requests. Conversations with Bakary Sanyang, the Director of Bibliographic Services at the Gambia National Library, and Bakary Sidibe, independent researcher and consultant, were very stimulating. I do not believe that there is anyone more familiar with the existing infrastructure for research in The Gambia than Hassoum Ceesay. I thank him for sharing his knowledge with me, for courtesies too numerous to attempt to enumerate, and for his dedication to research.

To these should be added the libraries and documentation centres where I was able to obtain a lot of secondary material. These include my own home institution, the Institute of Commonwealth Studies of the School of Advanced Study, University of London (David Clover); the School of Oriental and African Studies (SOAS), University of London; the National Archives in Kew, London; and Sheffield University Main Library.

In the process of producing a book an important role is played by the readers of the draft manuscript. My team of readers did a commendable job given, in particular, the length of the manuscript. St. George Ade Joiner, Baaba Sillah, Ebrima Ceesay, Ransford Cline-Thomas and John Charles NJie, each reviewed all or parts of the manuscript and commented on substantive issues, analysis and other areas. Here it behoves me to add that besides being one of my readers, Baaba Sillah went out his way to put at my disposal some of his rich material on family and other aspects of the life of Reverend Faye, his grand-uncle. I am sure he will agree that this book is definitely worth the cost of those countless Norway-England-Norway phone calls.

There is no way I can escape noting that Theophilus George was my "man on the ground". In addition to long structured interviews and many hours of open-ended dialogues, he took care of logistics, such as transportation and airport formalities, during my research trips to Banjul; he also helped in identifying potential interviewees and was an effective motivator. In general, he was a pillar of support in minding all the little things that lighten the burden of doing this type of research. How can I thank you, Pompy?

Turning to the production process, Jon Ashby was responsible for the copy-editing, proofreading, formatting and preparation of the draft index. Not only did he do an excellent professional job, but he demonstrated a very personal interest in the project. AuthorHouse Publishers were in charge of preparing the camera-ready manuscript, layout and graphic design (including the book cover), typesetting and final formatting, high-quality printing, and marketing, and much more. Both management and staff who were involved should be very proud of the end product.

Finally, there are my family members who provided moral and various types of support; even when tired of hearing me talk about the "bio project" they remained positive and encouraging. As in the past, the first line of attack comprised all members of my nuclear family. To these we now add a second line of defence: Gwendoline and (the late) Edmund Thomas, Karim and Ainsley Sagnia, Eve Forster, Herbert Bakary Sampson, and Saikou Jarju.

To all these individuals and institutions I extend my profound gratitude for joining me in celebrating the life and times of a great man—the Very Rev. John Colley Faye. But, for any omissions or commissions I exonerate you, and alone bear full responsibility.

Jeggan Colley Senghor   *December 2013*
University of London.

ACRONYMS

APC	African Presidential Centre (Boston University)
APARC	African Presidential Archives and Research Centre (Boston University)
AVTC	Anglican Vocational Training Centre
BATC	Bathurst Advisory Town Council
BTC	Bathurst Town Council
BYMS	Bathurst Young Muslims Society
CBE	Commander of the British Empire
CIDA	Canadian International Development Agency
CPE	Certificate of Proficiency in English
CPP	Convention Peoples' Party
DCA	Democratic Congress Alliance
ESOL	English for Speakers of Other Languages
(G)CP	(Gambia) Congress Party
(G)DP	(Gambia) Democratic Party
(G)MC	(Gambia) Muslim Congress
GMDMU	Gambia Motor Drivers and Mechanics Union
(G)NP	(Gambia) National Party
GOMB	Gambia Oilseeds Marketing Board
GSP	Gambia Solidarity Party
GTU	Gambia Teachers Union
GWU	Gambia Workers Union
JP	Justice of the Peace
KCMG	Knight Commander of the Order of St. Michael and St. George
H of T	House of Transfiguration
KK	Kristi-kunda

MBE	Member of the British Empire
MBHS	Methodist Boys' High School
MC	Military Cross
MRA	Moral Re-Armament
NCAC	National Council for Arts and Culture
NCBWA	National Congress of British West Africa
OAG	Officer Administering the Government
PEA	Prayer, Education, Action
PPS	Protectorate Peoples' Society
PPP	Peoples' Progressive Party
PWRDF	Primate's World Relief Development Fund
RPA	Rate Payers' Association
SOAS	School of Oriental and African Studies
SPG	Society for the Propagation of the Gospel
UAC	United Africa Company
UP	United Party
URD	Upper River Division
WAEC	West African Examinations Council
WASU	West African Students' Union
(W)MBHS	(Wesleyan) Methodist Boys' High School

PREFACE

In the 20th Century few equal, and surely none surpasses, the
Reverend John Colley Faye: in wisdom, in character, and in
achievements. History cannot proceed by in silence.

A. E. Cham Joof, funeral oration.

The Very Reverend John Colley Faye of The Gambia, West Africa,
was a man of many parts, a titan in various fields of endeavour—
education, politics, the Church and philanthropy. Through his work
he demonstrated an unusual sense of service to his countrymen and
countrywomen and to the improvement of their lot. For his day, he was
rare in that his field of operation was not exclusively in the Colony Area.
Rather, it extended to the Protectorate, the more underdeveloped and
deprived part of country.[1]

From the outset Faye was saddled with being a member of several
minorities: an ethnic Sereer (a group making up less than five percent of
the population); a Christian in a vastly Muslim society; an Anglican in
a Catholic-dominated community; and a well-educated and privileged
man (having had secondary schooling and university education in
Britain) in a largely illiterate population. Against this setting, to be
successful in public life one had to have very special qualities. Rev.
Faye had these in abundance. As noted in the quotation above from the
funeral oration by his staunch, faithful and life-long lieutenant, Alieu E.
Cham Joof, history just cannot be silent on the life and times of this icon.

To a great extent the fields of Faye's activities overlapped and, thus,
were mutually reinforcing, but the greater part was in local politics. The
period of his political activism (1949 to 1966) coincided with the most
turbulent era in politics in The Gambia. He was in the thick of things,

confronting the demands of shaping a political future in line with the expectations of the population. At different times he was leader of the team—a task appointed, assumed or self-imposed—and spearheaded bold initiatives in favour of the political emancipation of the Gambian people.

As he tried to execute his political mission, Faye's most powerful opponents were the colonial administration and other leading politicians, with their divergent versions of how things should be. But, throughout, Faye remained steadfast and focused on his personal ambitions for The Gambia. In this period of intense competition for political power and influence, he doggedly stood by his convictions and fearlessly defended them on any and all platforms; this distinguished him from many other politicians. He stubbornly held to his principles and, even where his positions were politically suicidal, rarely did he waver. In other words, opportunism, the hallmark of many a politician, was absolutely foreign to Faye. Hence his topsy-turvy political career and his unceremonious exit from the political stage.

Perhaps his Christian virtues had the better of him. Faye's politics were based on Christian principles and he did not see any contradiction in being a good Christian and a good politician at the same time. He was to find out that this was indeed possible. But, ironically, these same virtues were to come to his rescue as, on his retirement from active politics, he turned back to where his public service had begun in the first place, that is, to the school and the church.

Why this Biography?

The obvious motivation in undertaking this task is the imperative of putting on record the life of Rev. J. C. Faye, a distinguished son of The Gambia who has not been accorded the recognition he deserves. In general, posterity in The Gambia must be sensitized to and educated about the work of those who in various ways shaped the destiny of the country. Indeed, there is a very urgent need for researchers, both in The Gambia and in other African countries, to research and publish the biographies of the towering sons and daughters of yesteryear. Need we be reminded of Amadou Hampate Ba's warning that the physical death of one of these eminent characters means the disappearance of many rich libraries? Indeed, many greats, in all sectors, have passed on; their official and private papers have disappeared, mainly to private and public library collections outside the continent. In many instances their contemporaries are also no longer alive; so, obtaining the primary material required for befitting biographies has become really problematical.

These were some of the self-evident realities confronted in preparing this biography. Perhaps the fact that it has seen the light of day shows that it can be done. I have always been convinced that, at a minimum, the biographies of the political leaders, past and present, must be researched and published. Here, the message of the Wise One is loud and clear: "A nation that does not recognize its heroes is not worth dying for." A very feasible approach would be for the research to be undertaken by teams. As Rev. Faye reminded me on many occasions, there is safety in numbers; there is also a greater guarantee that the task will be successfully and satisfactorily completed.

The Preservation of Memories

Inspired by such thinking, in 2011 the Gambia Leadership Programme (*GamLeaP*) was launched by a team of researchers based in The Gambia, the United Kingdom, and the United States of America. Appendix 3 provides more detailed information on the programme, especially its background, justifications, objectives and implementation modalities.

A major project in this programme aims to promote research and document the biographies of some of the more prominent Gambian political personalities whose lives were dedicated to the country's pre— and post-independence nationhood. Two sets of outputs will be: first, an edited collection with chapters on each personality and, second, full-length, more detailed studies on each. The series will be published under the overall theme *The Gambia: Leading Political Personalities in the Decolonization and Early Post-Independence Era*. It is hoped that a separate set of portraits of other second-tier leading Gambians in different walks of life, past and present, will accompany the main project outputs. Altogether, the research will be exhaustive and produce new and previously unpublished material.

This present volume is a first product of this collaboration. It deals with both the "life" and the "times" of Rev. Faye. One is as vital as the other. In fact, the two are interlocking and interwoven. Thus, in places in the study, it may appear that too much attention is being devoted to the "times", but this is because Faye is best appreciated only when developments in the setting are in perspective. He had an impact on events just as much as events impacted on him. Much the same is applicable to the other figures whose biographies will be published in this project.

The project is confined to The Gambia. In the continent itself, perhaps it is because African researchers have not taken up the challenge of conducting research on the lives of their political leaders that some former Heads of State have turned to foreign universities in order to benefit from opportunities, and facilities, to put on record their experiences whilst in office, and even to house their presidential libraries. Well known in this regard is the African Presidential Center (APC) (originally the African Presidential Archives and Research Center (APARC), Boston University, United States of America.*

Based, among other concerns, on the need "to establish a forum for African leaders to engage other political, business, academic, and public sector leaders regarding Africa's relation to the world community of nations", the Center runs five programmes: the African Presidential Lecture Series (which superseded the African President-in-Residence Programme), the Public Papers/Private Conversations Project, the African Leaders State of Africa Report, the African Presidential Roundtable, and the APC American-African Universities Collaborative.

It is instructive to quote the main aims of some of these. First, the Lecture Series provides two-year residency:

---

* The material in what follows, including quotations, were obtained from: "The African Presidential Center, Boston University", http://www.bu.edu/apc.

for former democratically elected African heads of state. It provides access to former leaders . . . During his/her tenure the resident speaks at various venues throughout the United States, focusing on issues of political and economic development as they relate to Africa.

It offers an opportunity for African leaders "to transition to civilian status by providing a venue that will value and utilize the experience and expertise of these unique individuals". Holders give lectures and seminars and are encouraged to compose their reflections on their periods in office. These become useful for the preparation of their memoirs.

The Public Papers/Private Conversations:

is an oral and documentary history project focusing on current trends and development in Africa. It provides APC with an opportunity to chronicle the present period of dramatic change in Africa through the "eyes of the architects" of those changes—past and present heads of state and public and private sector leaders in Africa.

This particular project is an initial effort towards development of the archival activities of the Center. It would involve:

semi-annual visits to selected African countries to allow researchers to collect the public papers of democratically elected leaders, and to meet with them and conduct in-depth interviews regarding contemporary events in their countries and in the continent.

As concerns the intent, it is: "to digitize the materials collected and develop ways to make the information available to our collaborating institutions and the broader community". And, besides adding to the Centre's archives, the project also represents an opportunity to gather current information regarding developments in Africa, and would put the Center on the cutting-edge of policy debates and deliberations on Africa.

Turning to the African Leaders' State of Africa report:

[it] is an annual report presenting the perspectives of select African heads of state relative to their respective countries and regions. The report not only catalogues the "vision" and strategies of contemporary African heads of state for future generations of scholars, but it enables the dissemination of the "African point of view" to those presently involved in setting policy and shaping opinions about Africa.

African heads of state participating in these and associated programmes have been known to donate their official and private papers to the Center and the university. This, of course, deprives the present and coming generations of Africans easy access to what can only be seen as their heritage and inheritance. Also, the opportunity is missed to contribute significantly to strengthening African national universities and research institutions and bolster their standing.

Among heads of state who have been involved in one or other of these projects and programmes are the following: Rupiah Banda of Zambia, Festus Mogae of Botswana, Jakaya Kikwete of Tanzania, (the late) Bingu wa Mutharika of Malawi, Antonio Mascarenhas Monteiro of Cape Verde, Ketumile Masire of Botswana, Karl Offmann of Mauritius, Ruth Perry of Liberia, Amani Abeid Karume of Zanzibar, and Kenneth Kaunda of Zambia.

On the continent itself the Olusegun Obasanjo Presidential Library in Oke-Mosan, Abeokuta, Ogun State, Nigeria, should serve as a template for other former African heads of state; it deserves substantial support.

The rationale for setting up the library is equally applicable to other African cases:

> A primary concern for the establishment of a presidential library is first to acknowledge the contributions of, at any one time, the occupier of Nigeria's most important political office. It is also generally acknowledged that there is a gap in understanding the complex conditions that prevail or act upon important decision-makers when they occupy their positions. A presidential library, with documents and other archival materials, could avail to researchers important resources that would enable them to arrive at more accurate and objective analysis . . . It will clear up the myth and misconceptions of the office of the president and perhaps broker a much more pragmatic understanding of events and of the person.

Accordingly, the vision of the project is given as "to be an evergreen resource for inspiring the ideals of democracy and good governance". On the other hand, its mission is:

> to foster understanding of the life, career, and Presidential administration of Olusegun Obasanjo and through this exposition, promote the ideals of democracy, good governance and leadership; facilitate critical reflection on best practices in public service; and provide a clearer comprehension of developments in Nigeria, Africa, the Commonwealth and the rest of the world.

Some of the specific objectives of the library are:

- To make available for public study and research, such resources as documents, artefacts, personal items and memorabilia of President Olusegun Obasanjo, through research, exhibitions, public programmes, online services, documentary media, publications and outreach;
- To serve as a resource for inspiring African unity, democracy and good governance;

- To advance the standing of the Olusegun Obasanjo Presidential Library as a centre of intellectual activity and community leadership designed to meet the challenges of a changing world;
- To sponsor programmes and activities which will promote exemplary conduct in public service and good democratic governance.

The library holds the presidential files and papers which cover matters of public policy; the archive is a repository for the presidential papers and historical materials of President Obasanjo; and the museum exhibits significant documents, photographs, films, video tapes, sound recordings, etc., depicting stages in the public life of Obasanjo. To these is added a section for recreation, leisure activities, and housing and support facilities.

Following in the footsteps of some others, such as former Presidents Madiba Mandela and Obasanjo, the former President of Ghana, John A. Kufuor, launched the John A. Kufuor Foundation in September 2011. An innovative arrangement is that it consists of two components: the John A. Kufuor Centre for Leadership, Governance and Development based at the University of Ghana, Legon; and the John A. Kufuor Presidential Library and Museum at the Kwame Nkrumah University of Science and Technology in Kumasi. The former was launched on 20 September 2011 and the latter two days afterwards. Initial funding is from the proceeds of the World Food Prize awarded for halving hunger, which President Kufuor shared with President Lula of Brazil in 2011.

The vision of the foundation is: "To be an enabling vehicle for the continued development and consolidation of leadership and democratic governance in Africa". And the mission: "To advocate and promote leadership and democratic governance in Africa, providing a platform on which African states can build stable democracies and promote the common good of their citizens". Thus, the organization is built on the three pillars of leadership, governance and development, on the assumption that "the pursuit of these areas in tandem is critical to the development of the African continent".

It is hoped that all other African Heads of State and leaders in other spheres of life will emulate these examples for the benefit of present and future generations.

The Memory of Faye: The Personal Dimension

Writing the biography of Rev. Faye is a personal commitment which has been decades in fulfilling. During the period of my research on Senegambian integration in the early 1970s, I spent many hours discussing Gambia's political history with him and listening to reminiscences about his life experiences. I then made a commitment to do his biography—which pleased him immensely. He deeply regretted that he had given numerous interviews to non-Gambian and Gambian researchers and had parted with many of his private papers and records, against promises that they would be returned; most were never to be seen again. Thus, he warned, if the two of us did not make haste with his biography it was likely that he would lose many more.

A somewhat long sojourn outside the country prevented me from keeping my promise; but on my calls on Faye when I visited, we recalled the commitment and even worked on an outline. His death in 1985 rekindled the will to make time to take on the job. But it still remained a table-talk affair. Happily, Adele, his daughter, has inherited the qualities of stubbornness and determination from her father and, over the years, has initiated some bold moves to honour the memory of Rev. Faye with a biography. Happenstance brought us together again recently and the project was re-launched with vigour. Perseverance has seen it through.

To close this Preface, there is the culturally sensitive question of how to address the subject of this biography. Formally, he was known as "Rev. John Colley Faye". To his age-mates and many of his contemporaries, he was "J.C." To the vast majority of acquaintances, and for younger generations and most others, he was a generic "Uncle" or "Uncle J. C." This being the case, any and all of these are used in this biography, as thought appropriate.

Jeggan Colley Senghor   *December 2013*
University of London

INTRODUCTION
THE FOUNDATIONS

Family and Genealogical Roots

John Colley Faye was born on Tuesday 25 February 1908 to John Charles Faye, a Sereer, and Gracée Jarra-Owens, a Wolof, at the family home at 24 Hagan Street in Bathurst.* Upon the death of his father the family moved to the residence at 82 Dobson Street, the compound next to the former Methodist Boys' High School. Gracée was a celebrated Christian lady known in town for her *haute couture* which she modelled on Queen Mary's and Queen Victoria's.

According to family records Faye's genealogy on his mother's side can be traced to three brothers, Omadi Jarra, Sambu Jarra, and Ansuman Jarra, who in the mid nineteenth century migrated from Segu, French Soudan (Mali) to The Gambia; they belonged to the Bambara ethnic group. The brothers had a long line of descendants in The Gambia. Faye's grandfather was the second brother, Sambu Jarra, who upon conversion to Christianity was baptized Samuel Owens. Omadi's baptismal name was William Owens and Ansumaan's was Joseph Owens. Sambu was married to Lisa Ndella Chaw, a high-class Wolof; the marriage produced five children, namely, Mame Begay, John, William, Gorée and Gracée. The last girl, Gracée, married John Charles Faye.

---

* The capital was named Bathurst, after Henry Bathurst, 3rd Earl Bathurst, Secretary of State for the British Colonies, in 1816, when it was founded. The name was changed to Banjul, its original African name, on 24 April 1973. In this study the old appellation is retained in the pre-1973 period.

On his father's side, Faye was a descendant of Salmon Faye, king of Siin, who was followed as *bur* by his kin, Kumba Ndofen Diouf. Family history has it that Faye's great-grandfather came to Bathurst to purchase firearms to defend the Kingdom of Siin against enemy troops who were on the verge of taking it over. However, when he arrived, instead of pursuing his mission he was convinced by his sister—who was married to the manager of Maurel and Prom, a French firm—not to return but to stay and start a new life. He agreed, and laid the roots for his descendants, of whom John Colley Faye was one.[1]

John Charles Faye was a storekeeper and one of the first trained Gambian draftsmen in the Public Works Department (PWD), Bathurst; among his duties was that of roads rehabilitation. He was a prominent member of the St Mary's Anglican Church and was known for his many contributions to the institution, among which was putting the finishing touches to the structure; for his contributions he was allocated a special pew in the church.

Unofficially, John Charles was recognized as a spokesman for the inhabitants of Bathurst. Around 1900 fire broke out in Bathurst and destroyed many houses, the majority of which had thatched roofs. After a public demonstration John Charles led a delegation to see the Governor and requested that the administration provide corrugated iron sheets to every affected house. The request was granted and implemented after protracted negotiations.

The son, John Colley Faye, was the second of four boys, the others being Thomas, Ivan, and August. The eldest, Thomas, served for a long time as a lawyer's clerk in a local firm whilst Ivan was a certified mason, tiler and bricklayer trained in the Gold Coast (Ghana). From an early age August was poor in health and he died early. John Faye missed not having any sisters and this led him to develop a "soft spot" and protective attitude towards women, particularly Cecilia, his wife, and the females in the extended family. As admitted by one of them: "The love that he should have lavished on his sisters he passed on to us the other females in the extended family."[2]

Indeed, Faye demonstrated this warmth in several ways, but especially in his readiness to provide financial and other forms of support to widows and women in need, both within and outside of the family; his objective was that women should ensure that they were independent in life to the greatest extent possible. An example of his concern that women should have greater confidence in themselves and be self-reliant was the case of the young daughters of his cousin (who died young) whom Faye saw through school, afterwards providing opportunities for them to train as teachers. As noted by Adele, the daughter:

> The wife of Rev. Canon Mensah once told me that she and all the women whose lives my father had touched, through teaching or supporting them professionally or by helping their husbands in their careers, were deeply grateful to him. Many excelled in life or their husbands were encouraged to reach the highest levels in their careers. Daddy always said 'Get a career. If you have a good husband then, *tant pis,* but if not nobody will know because you will be able to look after yourself.' So if you have knowledge it will stay with you up to the grave; knowledge is strength, knowledge is independence.[3]

Ethnicity

As has already been noted, Faye's father was Sereer and his mother Wolof, but he considered himself to be Sereer and not Wolof, and definitely not a "Wolofized Sereer". The Sereer have always been a small minority in the Gambian population compared to the situation in Senegal, where they have been among the top three. For Bathurst, they ranged from 2 percent to 7 percent in the period from 1911 to 1963 and comprised an even smaller percentage in the country as a whole. In the period 1963-1993, they never made up more than 2 percent of the total population.[4] The Wolofs, on the other hand, have, in the twentieth century, been the third largest group in The Gambia—at least 15 percent of the total population at any point in time. In the Colony Area they predominated, making up about half the population through the decades.

Faye never forgot his origins and maintained close ties with his extended Sereer family in Senegal; he had strong interest in preserving

Chosani Sereer and in keeping the kith and kin together. In turn, many in the family in Senegal stayed close to him and were frequent visitors to the Faye home in Bathurst. Not only were his origins Sereer but being Sereer was a source of great pride to him and he made frequent references to his Sereer origins.

Though Faye had a profound knowledge of Wolof culture, this did not make him Wolof. Arguably, if his Sereer people had had a greater prominence and were more concentrated in The Gambia he would have had greater possibilities of displaying his "Sereer-ness". In other words, the fact that his people, the Sereer, were a small minority and dispersed in The Gambia prevented him from interacting with them as intensely as with members of other ethnic groups especially the Wolof.

Faye had a rather restricted command of his father-tongue, again because of its relatively limited use in Bathurst. He had very impressive expertise in the Wolof language; he spoke some Mandinka and enough Fula to help him interact with members of this ethnic group. In displaying his depth of knowledge of Wolof he was fond of testing the vocabulary of young people; for instance he would ask for the Wolof word for 'chair' and when he got the answer *'chaise'*, he would laugh and explain that this was French and not the authentic Wolof usage. These vocabulary-testing sessions would last many hours.

All this was quite typical for many Sereers, especially those in mixed-marriage situations. This biographer is himself aware of the case of his own father, a Sereer also married into a Krio/Aku* family. The father resolved the problem by organizing frequent weekend get-togethers with indigenous Sereer compatriots at his home at 26, John Forster Street (formerly Fitzgerald Street), and by going all out to speak the language, partake of Sereer cuisine and engage in Sereer drumming and dancing till the wee hours of the morning. These encounters he cherished, for they enabled him to maintain his fluency in the Sereer language and stay close to his roots. Like Faye, the old man was very fluent in Wolof but he resisted being absorbed into Wolof culture at the expense of his own Sereer language and culture. At the same time, not keen on speaking Aku he adopted Wolof as his "maternal" language.

---

*   See footnote 4 in Chapter 1.

In any case, the Sereer and Wolof are closely related in terms of ancestry, history, culture and customs, and in traditional social structures. Of particular importance are the parallel modes of social organization, marked by distinct status and functional groups and sub-groups of which there were broadly five. First, the ruling noble class and their relatives who were the holders of royal power; they were headed by the ruler (*bur*). Second, the warriors or soldiers (*tyeddo*) who constituted the entourage of the nobles and their senior chiefs. Next there were the free-born commoners (*jambur*) who were the largest status group; they participated actively in the political systems and their assent was required before any major decisions were adopted. Then there was a series of castes based on occupations (artisans) such as *griots*, smiths, and leather workers; caste status was inherited and related to an economic or social activity. Lastly, there were the slaves who were categorized into domestic slaves and those captured in battle.[5]

Boyhood

Faye grew up around Hagan Street in the Half Die area in Bathurst. His group of intimate friends comprised Jeremiah Mboge, Jose Harris, Sam Forster, and Simeon Robinson; together they formed an exclusive club named "The Indomitables". So close was Faye to Mboge, in particular, that on learning of Faye's death in 1985, Mboge observed to his family that there was now no one competent enough to write his (Mboge's) biography as Faye knew him better than any living person. According to Mboge's wife, from that day on he lost his memory!

Wrestling was a favourite pastime; Faye's sharp skills scared away even much older competitors. He had a particular dislike of bullies and never hesitated to use his wrestling skills in favour of weaker and more vulnerable boys; it brought him popularity and renown. This passion continued even later in life. At weekends he would travel from Bathurst to Serekunda, Bakau and another arena in Kombo St Mary in search of wrestling competitions; often there was none and he had to go home disappointed. Football was another favourite team sport followed by cricket; Faye would do anything not to miss the local and inter-colonial cricket competitions between teams from the British West African colonies. He also participated actively in local cycling and athletics competitions. Throughout his life Faye never drank alcoholic drinks or smoked cigarettes.

Though a born Anglican, the young Faye frequently attended the Methodist Church where he had friends in the choir and he loved the Methodist hymns and liturgy. With the location of his home just opposite the Wesley Church on Dobson Street he had a much shorter distance to cover than to St Mary's Anglican Church, to which he belonged. In the latter, as will be seen in later chapters, he was very active in all types of religious activities which must have influenced his decision to go into the priesthood.

Education

Faye had his primary school education at the Anglican Day School of St Mary's (King's School) in Bathurst, up to Standard IV; this church school was opened in 1876. Armed with the required grades, he then proceeded to the (Wesleyan) Methodist Boys' High School (MBHS) in 1921. Here he excelled and passed the Junior Cambridge School Certificate in December 1924. He was also successful at the Senior Cambridge School Certificate examinations, in December 1926, achieving the following grades: 2 *alphas* in art and religious knowledge; 1 *beta* in geography; 3 credits in English language and literature, health science, and history; and 2 passes in Latin and mathematics. Based on this performance, Faye was granted exemption to university entrance examinations.[6]

By any standards these results were attainable only by very few students in The Gambia. In actuality, many did not even have the opportunity to have a secondary education; in 1921 only 16 percent of the potential students in his age group benefited from this level of education, and even in 1951 only 27 percent of the Bathurst population was literate in English—compared to 0.2 percent of the Protectorate population.[7] Nonetheless, the senior school certificate and the matriculation certificate were basic requirements for admission to degree programmes in universities in Britain and in the British Empire. Geography and mathematics were Faye's favourite subjects even though he did not do well in either in the school certificate examinations. Later in life he took great delight in his ability accurately to forecast the weather for his family, based on knowledge acquired long before in his geography lessons at school.

Faye was awarded a scholarship to read for a Bachelor of Arts degree at Fourah Bay College in Freetown, Sierra Leone, along with Louis Valentine and Jacob Mahoney, his high school classmates and friends. The College was founded in 1827, and from 1876 it was chartered to award degrees of Durham University, England. Most regrettably, Faye could not take up the scholarship, ostensibly because there was a serious shortage of teaching staff at the MBHS and he could not be released. In fact, he was in charge of the senior forms of the school and was preparing students for the Junior and Senior Cambridge Local Examinations; he was also the art and games master. The scholarship was therefore awarded to another student and Faye continued his private studies under the supervision of Mr. Eburne, his Principal. A secondary reason for foregoing the scholarship was that Faye's family members were themselves not very keen on his going to Freetown, about which they had heard many horrendous stories.

As compensation for his not being able to take up the scholarship, and given his obvious intellectual prowess, it was arranged for Faye to take an overseas correspondence course with Wolsey Hall Correspondence College in Oxford, England; he was also provided with a reasonably well-stocked library of educational books. Studying privately, in 1927 he added to his laurels by obtaining a Local Government First Class Certified Teacher's Certificate and a First Class Teacher's Certificate in hygiene (health science); other papers set for this examination included school management and teaching methods.[8]

Early in 1930, Faye passed the examinations for Part 1 of the Associate of the College of Preceptors in the United Kingdom; this examination was then equated with the Intermediate Bachelor of Arts degree, University of London. His passes were in Latin, English language and literature, geography, and history. Later that year he was again successful in the professional part of the examinations and obtained passes in the principles of education, educational psychology, methods of teaching and school organization, the history of education, and school hygiene.[9]

The College of Preceptors was established in 1849 by the granting of a Royal Charter of Incorporation by Queen Victoria; the name was changed to The College of Teachers in 1998 by Supplemental Charter. It is essentially an institution supporting teacher education in all areas; and its qualifications are more professional than academic in nature, "allowing everyone involved in education to have their professional achievement and expertise recognized and rewarded". The qualifications are granted under the Royal Charter which means that "they benefit from international recognition allowing their holders to move schools, local authorities and even countries safe in the knowledge that their qualifications will be recognized."[10]

Faye then won a British Council scholarship to the University College of Southampton (England) in 1937, for a refresher course in education and English; he was one of the earliest Gambians to win such a scholarship for study in a British university. The college was a successor to Hartley University College (1902) and a degree-granting branch of the University of London. Its further development was stalled by the bombing and destruction of much of Southampton during the Second World War but in 1952 it was granted a Royal Charter with authority to award its own degrees.

On completing his studies at Southampton, Faye was awarded the Cambridge Certificate of Proficiency in English (CPE), First Class, Special Mention, endorsed by the United Kingdom Board of Education (1938). This qualification is still offered by universities and other academic institutions in England and is recognized world-wide; the written papers are assessed and the certificate awarded by the University of Cambridge, which describes it as:

> the most advanced general English exam provided by the University of Cambridge ESOL (English for Speakers of Other Languages) examinations. The English level of those who have passed the CPE is supposed to be similar to that of a well-educated native speaker of English.[11]

Clearly, Faye distinguished himself in his academic work and won awards. He was never in the same age group as many of his classmates; most were much older and physically mature. Going beyond that, he was much respected at both St Mary's and the Boys' High School; at the latter he was appointed Prefect in 1923 and 1924 and Senior Prefect in 1925. Faye was also a devoted scout and rose from Scout (1921) to Patrol Leader (1923), Assistant Cub-Master (1925), and Cub-Master (1926-1928). Later, he was to develop strong interest in watercolour painting and in animal husbandry.

Obviously, Faye must have demonstrated high standards of comportment and such distinctive leadership qualities as tact, perseverance, tolerance, strength of character and diplomacy, some of the qualities required for effectiveness in performance. The fact that in any and every sport Faye was outstanding and a prize-winner made him very popular; it also made it easier for him to execute his leadership responsibilities.

Summary Observations

From the above it can be concluded that solid foundations had been laid for Faye to function successfully in any field of endeavour. First, his minority status afforded a lot of scope for effective performance without him being seen as a threat; it made him easily acceptable in all communities. His academic credentials were impeccable for his day; this was to have positive implications in whatever career he chose to follow and, definitely, in the teaching, pastoring, and political careers. Given the high value attached to quality education in Gambian society Faye's academic achievements accorded him instant recognition in society; and no doubt this qualified him for leadership in any profession he chose to enter.

Besides his academic distinctions, the fact that Faye actively participated in a diverse range of sporting activities, and excelled in many, enabled him to develop qualities which would stand him in good stead in any career. Among others, it made him a good mixer, able to transcend social class and ethnicity. All in all, with these foundations Faye was well-prepared for an active and progressive professional and personal life, and this started off with that of an educationist.

CHAPTER 1
EDUCATIONIST: PLANTING INSTITUTIONS

As in the colonies throughout Africa and beyond, Christian missionaries played a leading role in the introduction and implantation of Western education in The Gambia. Soon after their establishment in the country, the Wesleyan Methodists turned to education.[1] In the 1920s they had elementary schools in Banjul, the Ceded Mile and MacCarthy Island (in the Protectorate); in terms of rolls they outnumbered both the Anglicans and the Catholics. For example, the Blue Book Report for 1862 recorded that the Wesleyans had 403 children in their schools (223 boys and 180 girls); the Roman Catholics had 105 pupils (55 boys and 50 girls); while the Garrison School, under a civilian headmaster, showed 40 children on its register (26 boys and 14 girls) plus a special class of 20 Congo boys newly liberated from slavery.[2] But, by 1918 the situation had changed somewhat: the Methodists had a total of 592 pupils compared to 538 for the Catholics and 235 for the Anglicans. The Mohammedan School, opened in 1903, had 186 pupils on roll.[3]

Concerning secondary-level education, there was the (Wesleyan) Methodist Boys' High School (MBHS) in Bathurst. It was founded mainly for training local missionary assistants and for the education of children of the Krio/Aku community.[4] Registration at the MBHS stood at 15 at its foundation, 39 in 1918 and 140 in 1955.[5] The (Wesleyan) Girls' High School was principally for girls with backgrounds similar to the boys at the MBHS. The Roman Catholics followed the Methodists in 1847 and, besides primary schools in Bathurst and the Protectorate, established a secondary school, St Augustine's High School, in Bathurst. Thus, by the 1930s there were two boys' and two girls' secondary

1

schools, one of each run by the Methodists and the Catholics. Secondary education was highly competitive, given the limited possibilities students had to demonstrate excellent academic abilities.

As noted, the Anglicans had no high schools, so most qualified students from St Mary's School had to go to the MBHS. It may not have been policy but the practice was that the Catholics gave preference to students of their own denomination and relatively few Anglican or Methodist students studied at the Catholic high schools. Though the primary recruits for these schools were from the Christian community, Muslims, not having their own secondary schools, made use of both Catholic and Methodist high schools. For example, it has been estimated that in 1955, out of the 140 pupils registered at the MBHS, 29 were Methodists, 24 Anglicans and 87 Muslims—that is, more than one-half were from the Muslim community.[6] Particularly in relation to inter-ethnic and inter-faith relations among the future elites this was a very healthy situation.

As in other sectors, the rest of the country outside the capital was very much deprived as regards education: in 1918 there were only two elementary schools, and by 1938 there had been an increase to six. The fact that these early educational institutions were run by missionaries discouraged some Protectorate families from patronizing them, on the strong suspicion that their children would be converted to Christianity.

Early Teaching Career

It was in this context that Faye opted to join the teaching profession. At the MBHS it was usual practice to retain the boys with the best results in the Junior and Senior Cambridge School Certificates to teach in the junior forms in the school, in expectation that they would proceed for further professional training and return to teach at the school.

In line with this policy, Faye was appointed a pupil teacher and tutor at the school a year before taking the Senior Certificate examination. His assignments included teaching geography, fine art, Commonwealth history, and games to the school as a whole; he was form master initially in the Junior Section, from 1925 to 1927, and tutor in charge of the third, fourth, and fifth forms, in turn, from 1927 to 1931. In addition to his specialist subjects, Faye also taught religious knowledge, mathematics, and English language and literature to the forms for which he was responsible.[7]

Faye moved to the Methodist Central Junior High School as guinea-pig Headmaster from 1932 to 1934. It was a new school and the first junior high school in The Gambia. Within three academic years, by dint of the hard work by Faye and his staff, it became one of the best middle schools in the country; it was under his leadership that the school attained "A" status—the only school to attain this ranking in The Gambia. In 1934, Faye was compelled to resign and return to St Mary's, the school of his denomination, as Assistant Headmaster. Indeed, the Anglicans were not broad-minded enough to permit one of their numbers to make a success of the school of another denomination whilst their own had need of his services. The fact that Faye accepted a demotion speaks volumes about his commitment to education.

After completing his programme at University College of Southampton, Faye was promoted to Headmaster at the same St Mary's in July 1938; his immediate predecessor was the distinguished Reverend H. N. Hunter who moved to Nigeria to become Chaplain to the Bishop of Lagos and, subsequently, Lt. Col. Chaplain-in-charge for the Nigerian Army.

Kristi-kunda, Upper River Division

The Diocese of Gambia and Rio Pongas was created in 1935 and John Charles Sydney Daly consecrated its first Bishop by the Archbishop of Canterbury on 1 May 1935; he had been ordained deacon and priest only 12 years earlier in 1923, at the tender age of 22 years. At 34 years he became the youngest bishop in the Anglican Communion. Before the creation of the diocese the church in The Gambia was administered from Freetown.

On Ascension Day, 31 May 1935, Bishop Daly landed in Bathurst and assumed his functions at St Mary's Pro-Cathedral. The church inherited by Daly was small, as was the staffing. In fact, there were only two staff members. Father During, the Chaplain at St Mary's, came from Freetown, Sierra Leone, and had volunteered to serve in Bathurst in 1931; he stayed on till 1937 when he retired to his home country. Then there was Henry Newman Hunter, a Gambian deacon, who, as noted above, was Headmaster of St Mary's School and an assistant to Rev. During; he was "priested" by the Bishop in his first year *en poste*. Besides these, there were no other clergy. Of the two catechists, one ran a mission church in the North Bank of the Gambia River and the second was in charge of St Cuthbert's Church at Basse in the Upper River Province.

A man with a strong sense of mission, Bishop Daly was clear from the outset as to his "Vision" for his ministry and his operational plan. He wrote in a report to the Missionary Council in London at the end of 1935:

> As far as I can see my best policy will be as follows: to find an unworked area in the Protectorate and there to establish a central station with as big a staff as I can afford. At that station I shall hope to have a Central Boarding School for boys and girls, a Dispensary and Hospital, a Model Farm, a Training College for Catechists and 'Bush School' teachers and a Church.[8]

The Bishop's clear and manifest objective was to spread Christianity (Anglicanism) to all parts of The Gambia, Guinea and the Rio Pongas. At his enthronement ceremony at St Mary's he himself had declared his first mission to be: "To provide a spiritual home for those who had left England to live awhile in Africa". The second was: "To unite into one Church people of the Diocese." And, significantly, the third mission objective was: "To extend Christ's kingdom throughout the diocese".[9] It was in tune with this that the editor of the *Gambia Pongas Magazine* (Autumn 1935), in his turn, also stated three great tasks that the Bishop and his staff should have before them at the commencement of his mission, to wit:

1. To strengthen and make real the faith of the Christians in their care.

4

2. To maintain a stand against the zealous and effective missionary spirit of the Muhammedans.
3. To win to the faith those pagans who have as yet withstood the call of Islam.[10]

Daly's Plan of Action

Daly's overall timeframe was that from 1935 to 1940 resources would be focused on building foundations from which to launch the new missionary work. The years 1940 to 1945 would see the steady growth of that work under wartime conditions. And 1945 to 1951 would be a period of consolidation; this is what he termed THE GREAT PUSH FORWARD.[11] By 1938 two more priests had arrived from England to man the Pro-Cathedral, after Pastor During had retired. This increased staffing gave the Bishop some leeway so he could concentrate on concrete missionary activities.

Within this project framework, one of the pillars of Bishop Daly's mission was the setting up of a station far into the interior of the country, "to establish a community of Christians amongst the Mohammedans so that they could not fail to see the life".[12] As noted above, an educational establishment would be at the centre of the mission's plan of action; after all the Anglican Church only had St Mary's School in Bathurst but none in the Protectorate, whereas the Catholics had one at Basse Santa Su and the Methodists one at Georgetown.

Thus, the three *volets* of Daly's grand scheme were for all efforts to be focused on the spiritual through evangelism, the mind through education, and the body through medical services.

The project evolved in two phases. In the first, just before the beginning of the Second World War, it was decided that the Bishop, accompanied by young volunteers of the youth group known as Prayer, Education and Action (PEA), should proceed with the "plan for mission", though it was very limited in actual or anticipated funding; "to serve the people in the Name of Christ and to that end a school, a clinic, a model farm and a church" would be set up. The group included a hospital dispenser, an agriculturalist, a laundryman and a cook; they received no pecuniary reward but only food, clothing, and pocket money of five shillings a month.

The Bishop had also invited Faye to join the mission:

"John, I would like you to accompany me on a survey mission to select an appropriate site for the school we are planning; we would also have consultations with the local traditional leaders and government officials."

Faye replied: "My Lord, I do appreciate your kind invitation. However, I believe your mission will be more productive if you are accompanied by someone who is much more familiar with the terrain and is a son of the soil, as it were."

"Who do you have in mind, John?" the Bishop asked.

"There could be nobody better than Andrew," he said, meaning Andrew Camara [whose name was changed later to Assan Musa Camara on his re-conversion to Islam]," who is here with us at school."

"Good idea. I shall take Andrew with me," Bishop Daly concluded.

Thus, Andrew Camara, who was then in Standard Four at St Mary's, joined the team. They visited a number of sites considered as fit for purpose but the inhabitants were reluctant to risk having anything new in their locality. In February 1940 the team identified another suitable Fula village in the Kantora District, a few miles from Jawo-kunda. They were warmly welcomed by the chief and elders who made arrangements for them to be lodged in the Government Rest House. The chief later mobilized the young men from the thirty villages within his jurisdiction to build a small village for the missionaries, according to their requirements.

It was usual for villages to be named after the headman, with his name preceding the word "kunda" meaning "small town" in Mandinka, the predominant language in the country. Thus it was decided that the name of their settlement should be "Kristi-kunda" or "Christ town" as Jesus was the headman. Besides Jawo-kunda, other planned sister-villages in the area were Saare Yesu in Kumbul and Bishop-kunda. Saare Yesu was to be a centre for European missionaries working in evangelism, in conjunction with Kristi-kunda (KK), while also providing administrative support until such time as African priests were identified for KK. Basse was the nearest river-town and Fatoto the commercial centre.

The mission received support from the trading companies such as the United African Company, and individual local and foreign traders, especially in the transportation of personal effects and construction material. The Bishop also contributed personally in cash and kind; for much of the early days he was "on the ground" with the other pioneers, local and non-local. Support was also to be forthcoming from the government but this was conditional; the Governor, in early 1942, inspected KK and concluded that:

> It could, in his opinion, be usefully correlated with the Government development programme and it would supplement what is likely to be found practicable in that programme in the near future. The Governor did, however, add provisos, to the effect that there should be adequate financial provision for development as well as initiation, without recourse to Government funds, and that there should be European supervision by someone with financial and business acumen, able to maintain friendly relations with the Muslim population and prepared to respect their religious feelings.[13]

But, the teething problems at this new village were countless and the challenges overwhelming; the most serious of these was the lack of water. When the Bishop was on leave in England the new village found itself in a state of "dissolution". He then recognized that the task was daunting, especially for the workers: "It had been too much to expect men who were untrained to the religious life to live with all things in common like Franciscans. However, there had been no other way when the challenge came to start the mission."[14]

In August 1941, Faye was commissioned by the Bishop to visit KK and report to him on the cause of the dissension that was threatening the future of the young mission station. Faye managed to resolve the problems and restore normality; he was convinced that the absence of African leadership was a source of difficulties. But, in addition, the water problem grew more severe as activities began to increase and as the population grew; it was therefore decided to move on to a new site.

After further consultations, both within the Church and with other interested parties, new land and basic facilities were obtained from the chief and local authorities and from the colonial administration. This was all to the good as, before then, excellent relations had been maintained with the Fula of Jawo-kunda and new wells at the new KK village brought the two communities much closer than they had been before.

The mission was granted legal permission to the land by the chief of the District of Kantora, with the consent of the elders and people, on the following terms and conditions:

> [that they were] to erect and establish on a site nearer the river and near the native town of Jawo-kunda, a mission station, on the understanding that this land is not to be held by you on native customary tenure and that the premises are subject to usual conditions governing a yard in a native town.
>
> This means that, inter alia, you are liable to yard tax, extra houses tax, and lodgers tax annually to be paid to the Alkali of the village on demand; and also should the Seyfu and village elders at any time wish to terminate your occupancy of the land they shall give you six months notice and on the expiration of such notice you will be liable to ejection without further reason given and without any compensation for any improvements effected to the land or for any buildings you may have erected.[15]

This marked the beginning of the second phase of the KK project. With these exciting developments, perhaps it was not unexpected that Faye volunteered, in September 1942, to take on the task of being Headmaster of the school; he succeeded the Reverend H. Tekyi-Mensah who returned to Bathurst to assume the Headship of St Mary's School vacated by Faye. Befittingly, in 1944, Faye was put in charge of the whole mission station in addition to his Headship of the school; this appointment as administrative head of KK left Archdeacon Mumford, a British missionary, with more time to concentrate on the proselytizing work of the mission among the Fulas.

During Faye's stay he was also to serve as Alkali (Village Head) as well as Supervisor of Anglican Schools in the Upper River Division and member of the Kantora Local District Authority (1943-1949). Barely one year after his arrival he was able to gain extensive popularity among the people of the area. His colleague, Mudford, reporting to Bishop Daly, observed:

> There is no doubt whatever that they (the villagers) feel the warmest friendship towards the people of Kristi-kunda, especially its Headman, John Faye, and its teacher, Cates. The houses of Faye and Cates are crowded most days with Mohammedans and very often these friends and visitors lead the conversation to religion and ask questions and seek knowledge of our Christian beliefs.[16]

For the much wider community, KK was to become the focal point of attention in the Upper River Division. Many times the chief would hold court and local authority meetings there.

Establishing Roots

This new village life was very difficult for the Faye family, especially for Faye's wife, Cecilia, who joined him in 1943. This was particularly so given their previous lifestyle and their social status in Bathurst. Cecilia came from an established Krio/Aku family and had had a cloistered middle-class life at the family home at No. 7 Hope Street, Bathurst. One day she said to her husband:

"J. C. You know as headmaster you were earning four pounds a month and, as a result of the militancy of your Teachers Union, the salary has been increased to five pounds. Now, here we are with you getting no salary at all; even though accommodation, food etc. are provided by the mission this is still a big difference."

"Yes, my dear, I agree," he retorted. "As you know, even the Bishop is supporting the work from his own pocket; in any case, we are doing the work of the Almighty God and helping to uplift those who are less privileged than us. Nothing is more important than that."

"I see that, and you have my fullest support," she confirmed. "But, you know, this place is too dead. We don't even have birds singing to enliven the place. It is so lonely that even the birds are avoiding the village."

"Such thoughts have also crossed my mind, my dear," came back the reply. "But some day when we start pounding the rice, millet, *findi*, corn etc. they will come in large numbers."

Cecilia became a birdwatcher and had much joy when, months later, the first birds appeared. They looked so heavenly!

In the early years, the school was experimental and mainly attended by local day students. By 1945 there were two schools. The St John's "Tots" School was a small infants/primary section for boys and girls who spoke the vernacular and were mainly from local families in KK and adjoining villages. The House of Transfiguration School, commonly known as the H of T, was the senior stream following an elementary and, later, a standard secondary school curriculum. Originally it was hoped that the H of T would develop into a Diocesan Secondary School to train future Church workers such as catechists, teachers, priests, dispensers, and veterinary workers.

Faye saw the need for further growth and the boarding and other facilities were upgraded. Policy then shifted and boys from Bathurst were admitted in large numbers. The first cohort came from the Church-sponsored House of Transfiguration which had been set up on Pignard Street in Bathurst as a foster home for boys, under the "parentage" of Faye and Cecilia (see Chapter 10 below for more on this).

Recruitment of other students was mainly through parents approaching Faye or any member of the clergy directly; he had ultimate responsibility to assess whether or not to accept the candidate based on such factors as the level of education, comportment, character, and potential to contribute to life in the community. Other candidates were from among the large number of Faye's wards and, in some instances, recalcitrant boys whose parents could no longer handle them. Of course, there were also those who could not afford to pay for their education in Bathurst. Lastly, Faye brought to KK youngsters who had demonstrated their academic talents and needed to be in an environment which would enable them realize their potential under closer supervision. Thus the student population was a mixed bag.

With this expansion, the whole Faye "clan" had to move to the new settlement to join Cecilia and her small team of locals. In the party were ladies such as Constance Sarr, Fannie Cates, Winifred Thomas, and Yai Marie; they constituted the support staff and teachers who were responsible for such matters as supplies, maternal care to the young ones, sewing, and boarding school operations. The toddlers who lived with the team in the main house included Winston Joiner, Farsaraba, Paul Sajaw, and this author. Also in the same location were the girls, that is, Adele Faye, Clara Johnson, and Mary Lewis. Betty Cates lived with her parents, Arthur and Fannie Cates.

Besides Faye and his wife, the complement of teaching staff was skeletal. Arthur Cates was the Headmaster of the Tots and Faye headed the H of T. Cates was educated at Dobson Street Methodist School and MBHS; he began teaching at St Mary's School in 1940. Previously, for 14 years he worked with Maurel Frères, a French establishment headquartered in Dakar, Senegal; on behalf of this company he traded at Bathurst, Kombo, Jawarra, Kaur and Basse. Whilst heading the junior school Cates also gave classes in the senior H of T.

Willie Macauley was trained in animal husbandry in Tamale (Gold Coast), in 1941-1942, and gave lessons in this subject, hygiene, and physical training in both schools. He was Guinean by birth and was educated at the local Anglican School in Conakry, St Mary's and MBHS. John Stapleton had also undergone the same training as Willie Macauley at the same institution and had also attended St Mary's. Mamadou Camara, locally recruited, taught basket weaving, mat-making, fan-making, and fencing, three times a week. Jean Batiste Macauley (Willie's brother), Matarr Sillah and Winifed Thomas were among those who also served on the staff. Of course, some of the expatriate clergy and missionaries gave lessons in various subjects when the need arose.

The manner in which some of the staff were recruited was unconventional by any standards. Cates, as cited above, left trading for a French company to enter the teaching profession and to become a pioneer teacher in the outback. The case of Matarr Sillah is of even greater interest partly because he was a Muslim and partly because of how he was recruited and retained. Sillah was an ex-student of Faye's at St Mary's who, on completing his education, joined the Standard Bank. A year or so later, Faye visited the bank on business and was surprised to see Sillah at the counter. Instantly, he invited him aside for a chat:

"Matarr, what are you doing here. I taught you over many years and know you very well. This is not your calling. Your calling is to serve humanity. So I want you to come with me to Kristi-kunda where you are going to be a teacher."

Immediately, Sillah, out of respect for his former teacher, decided to resign; he was offered a promising teaching position by the government but opted to join the group at KK. This was the beginning of a long and very distinguished career for Sillah in the teaching profession.

Circumstances ensured that retaining Sillah in the job would not be a problem. On one of his visits to Basse, the river town closest to KK, he bumped into a young lady whom he had never seen before and, on enquiring, was given her name and told that she was from Banjul. He was much attracted to her. He undertook careful research about her background and, based on evidence accrued, concluded that she would be a good wife. After further reflection he approached Faye, his boss:

"Sir, I have seen this young lady in Basse whom I want to marry. Her name is Sabel Jarra. Can you please help get her for me?"

Faye went into hysterics. "Sillah," he said, "you are right, that girl's name is Mam Sabel Jarra. Don't you know we belong to the same Jarra family? She lives at the home of my first cousin in Bathurst, Mary Owens, who had informed me that the young girl was coming to Basse to spend the holidays with her father. I did not know that she is already in the vicinity. You see, she came to Basse on holidays and now she has found a husband in Kristi-kunda."

In fact, Sabel was one of the great grand-daughters of Ansuman Jarra, who, as earlier noted, was a brother to Sambu (Samuel) Jarra, the father of Faye's mother.

Faye ungrudgingly gave his approval and served as a go-between with the rest of the family. Eventually Sabel and Sillah were married. With this Sillah had an extra debt of gratitude to Faye, now his in-law, and had little choice than to stay on the KK teaching staff, be loyal and execute his responsibilities to the best of his abilities.

The dispensary was headed by Mark Thomas, an experienced medic, and William Hathornwaite, a British missionary, fondly known as *Kottoh Bill*; they were assisted by Nelson Camara, a local, and some of the older boys from the school and men from the villages. Its services were very much in demand for it was estimated that within three months of its opening over 900 patients had been seen.[17]

Generating Funds: The Hawkes Mission Trust

The greater proportion of the funding for the KK project came from British philanthropists who became patrons of the school; some of the school houses were named after them. Such funding was secured at a time when all seemed lost because of the poor finances. Luckily, through his contacts, Bishop Daly was informed that the Society for the Propagation of the Gospel (SPG) had been requested to administer a substantial bequest from the Hawkes Mission Trust, established by the Hawkes sisters, and supporting daring initiatives in spreading the word of God. The Bishop applied. As fate would have it, the Society decided that KK would be one of its first beneficiaries; it would receive a grant of 2,000 pounds annually, backdated to 1 January 1943.

One reason why the bequest had been granted is that a former retired Governor, Sir Thomas Southern (1936-1942), now back in England, strongly supported Bishop Daly's application, as he was sure that since John and Cecilia Faye, whom he had known well in Bathurst, had "condescended" to go to live and work in KK, the mission was guaranteed to be a success. Therefore, he had argued, funding from the Hawkes bequest would surely boost the chances of such success.[18] As viewed by the SPG, the ideals and objectives of the KK mission were parallel to those of Daly, that is, "the mission is to found a Christian settlement . . . There is to be a hospital, industrial farm school giving vocational training; and the settlement, living a communal life and engaged in agriculture, is to be a centre of service to the surrounding district."[19]

With these fresh funds it was possible to build a more substantial African village. St John's Church was transformed, with a fine thatched roof, and the new sanctuary was more beautiful, dignified and reverend. Besides this primary funding source, occasional donations were forthcoming from time to time. For example, the Kantora District, on its own volition, granted an annual amount of 50 pounds whilst the then Governor of the Gambia, Sir Hilary Blood (1942-1947), having made a visit, also pledged a personal annual grant of 50 pounds.[20]

In accordance with the Hawkes bequest, the funds were to be administered only by European personnel; thus, for this purpose, the Bishop had to keep a European priest in the area, initially at Bishop-kunda and later at Kumbul; he had to sign the cheques and manage the funds overall. According to the first budget, an annual subvention of only 600.00 pounds was allocated for the school, the running of the village, and staff wages and salaries; this even though three-quarters of the work in the whole area was under Faye's responsibility. An amount of 600.00 pounds was allocated to the hospital and yet another 600.00 pounds for paying the salaries of the European missionaries, Archdeacon Cyril Mudford and Rev. M. Carey.

The Ups of the New Life

Conventional wisdom of the day, especially in Bathurst, was that KK School was primarily for recalcitrant and rebellious boys who were beyond parental control. No doubt, some were. However, the attraction was more the high moral and educational standards offered to the students. Indeed, the hallmark of KK School was character-building. Inputs to the process included the following: the highest levels of academic performance; respect for elders and those in authority; strict discipline, with the expectation that the boys should be obedient, dedicated, and dependable; no discrimination either on the basis of ethnicity, family background, place of origin, or intelligence; and service to the local communities. The boys who were transferred from the House of Transfiguration in Bathurst were the pace-setters, especially in terms of discipline and good behaviour.

Besides the regular academic work, vocational pursuits were undertaken at the senior school; students were taught to value all types of work and not look down on any productive activity, especially agriculture, animal husbandry, carpentry, broad-cloth weaving, poultry keeping, gardening in the dry season and groundnut and guinea corn farming in the rainy season, and many other trades. For these purposes the school had farms, workshops, football and sports fields, and other appropriate facilities; the school itself benefited from the products of these facilities.

Character-building included achieving excellence in one or other of the competitive extra-curricular activities for which the school was divided into houses such as Mary Hawkes and St Mary's. There was intense competition between the houses particularly in athletics and all sports disciplines, academic performance, gardening, and football; wrestling was a particularly enjoyable pastime and weekly contests were organized on campus.

The school produced outstanding sportsmen and participated and won prizes in competitions in places like Tambacounda and Wulikunda in nearby Casamance (Senegal), and Basse and Bathurst.

The day began at 05:30 hours with the sound of the school siren, and a roll call was made at 06:00 hours in the church grounds. This was followed by the morning service, after which students went back to their houses to clean up the premises and tidy their own possessions. Breakfast followed at 08:30 hours, after which all classes began, lasting till 14:00 hours when lunch meals were served. After lunch, and up to 16:00 hours, students had to have compulsory rest in their dormitories. The period from 16:00 hours to 18:00 hours was devoted to studies and homework; at 18:00 hours students went to the field for sports, scouting, gardening, firewood collection and other outdoor activities. An assembly was held in front of the church at 19:30 hours, when there was another roll call. A church Evensong service and dinner followed, and students retired to their rooms. At weekends there were extra-curricular programmes such as scouting, camp fires, and concerts.

The twice-daily roll calls were important as, at times, some of the older students would opt to visit ladies in the nearby villages as far away as Fatoto, and even spend the night. Apart from the roll calls, the housemasters would check the beds at bed-time to make sure that they were occupied. The story is told of one of the senior students who, having planned to spend the evening at nearby Jawo-kunda, put his pillows in the middle of the bed pretending that he himself was under the sheets. His house master, Matarr Sillah, discovered the prank during his inspection rounds and decided to substitute himself for the pillows. The trickster, on his return quite late in the night, quietly opened the mosquito net of his bed and was gobsmacked to find the house master snuggled in. Of course, he was fittingly punished the next day.

One notable observation is that the deportment of "KK boys" reflected the values and standards they had imbibed. For example, spoken English was compulsory at all times; indigenous languages were permitted but not ones that had the potential effect of causing confusion with English—that is, *Krio* or *Aku* ("Broken English"). Anyone (student or staff) caught communicating in this language was severely penalized. As a result, a good command of spoken English became one of the distinguishing features of KK boys. Long after returning to Bathurst they continued to address each other in English; old habits do indeed die hard. Non-KK boys and girls found this to be comical.

A former KK student narrated that on the return of the students to Bathurst in 1949, he just could not fathom in what language his mother and siblings were trying to communicate to him; to all intents and purposes they were from Mars! In his class lessons at St Mary's School, he had a distinct advantage over the other boys because of the solid background acquired in KK, both in terms of academic performance and comportment. He was highly favoured and loved by the teachers, especially Teacher Phini and Miss Brown. But he also experienced many problems making friends, partly because he only spoke English and tended to look down on the "ignorant and uncivilized Bathurst boys".

The regimented life at KK was broken on the Feast of the Transfiguration when the founding of the school was commemorated. The holiday was enlivened with drumming, dancing, masquerades, and sporting competition. Champion wrestlers came from Casamance and surrounding villages; some students did not hesitate to challenge them. Many are the stories of the outcomes of these combats. Several animals were slaughtered and food and non-alcoholic drinks were available a-plenty. People from neighbouring villages actively participated in the celebrations as did guests from the mother church in Bathurst.

KK afforded its graduates an opportunity to build lifelong relationships and belong to an old-boy network which served very useful purposes. It made them more independent and self-reliant, able to interact easily among peoples of different backgrounds. Among the former students at the school are many who went on to be leaders in different spheres of life in The Gambia and beyond; many middle-level positions in departments in the public sector and the teaching service were manned by KK boys. In politics, Andrew D. Camara after his education at KK, became a teacher and then Headmaster at the school (1948-1959). In his subsequent political career he served in six different ministerial portfolios from 1960 to 1982 (Labour and Health, Education, Works and Communications, External Affairs, Finance, and Local Government); from 1972 to 1982 he was Vice-President of the Republic. As put later by Bishop Olufosoye (1965-1970):

> KK had produced Christian leaders like Revd. Fr. J. J. Williams, Hon. A. D. Camara, our Minister of Works and Communications, many policemen, teachers, and many hospital workers. In the olden days boys came from Bathurst and some from Conakry about 900 miles away and returned to their own homes when they finished in KK, and so the effect of the community was not felt only in Kantora District where the community is situated and perhaps meant to serve more.[21]

Some of the *alumni* were: Kissima O. Janneh, Momodou O. Janneh, Edward Boyen, Edward Leigh, Malick Lowe, Momodou NJie, the twins Jacob and Esau Williams, Dodou NJie, Nelson Foster, Joseph Bokossa Goswell and his brother Melville Menseh Goswell, James Campbell, Kenneth Richards, Rudolf Allen, Charles Turner, John Jawo, Arthur Senghore, Paul Sajaw, Bokarie Fofana, Modou NJie, George Sagnia, William Colley, Henry Grey-Johnson, Solomon NJie, Silas George, Randolf George, Charles Fowlis, Eric Tunde Janneh, Jeremiah Allen,

Sammy Palmer, Nathaniel Davies, Lexi Davies, Dan Macauley, Stanley Lusack, Denham Jones, Lamin Jarra, Chernor Jarra, Dawda NJie, Abraham Sylva, Henry James, Louis Lightbon, Ednie Tebbs, John and James Baker ("the sons of Zebedee"), Simeon Jallow, Ebrima NJie, D. E. Faal, Willie Cates, Harry Cates, Alex Phillott, Ernest Biodu Davies, Edward Bankole Ceesay, Francis Mbacke NJie, Solomon Othman, Michael Jones, Louis Mendy, Amang Kanyi, Saer Gaye, Sulay Jarra, Dodou Faal, Andrew (Dentist) NJie, Modou Samba, Sammy Johnson (from Conakry), Pa Sarai Ba, Femi Peters, and Gambia Williams.

Things Falling Apart—The Process

Sadly, but as was to be expected in a venture of this genre, and in the unique circumstances in the village, there were a variety of problems confronting the mission, especially inter-personal relationships and management issues. All was not always smooth among the team of personnel. Eventually, Faye himself became a victim. At the end of 1948 he was suspended from his duties and asked to move back to Bathurst. Further, based on information provided by a staff member and one of the English priests, he was charged with failure to balance the accounts in September 1948 because he knew that they were in deficit.

However, when, under the supervision of the Bishop, the accounts were audited it was found that, in actuality, it was the mission that owed Faye 350.00 pounds. In part, this was money due to him as unpaid salary, and unpaid advances he had made to the mission from incomes from his farms which enabled it to purchase food at a time when funds were running low. Bishop Daly then arranged for the repayment to be made to Faye in instalments of 50.00 pounds per quarter in 1949 and 1950. Faye was vindicated.[22]

Actually, Faye's failure to balance the accounts in September was due to the fact that he had received a cable from the Governor's office to leave the next day for Bathurst and then London for the African Conference (see Chapter 3), so he had no time to close the accounts. Faye intimated as much to the colleague who was to manage the accounts in his absence; he recommended that during the period of his absence separate accounts should be kept and the two sets of accounts would be balanced on his return.[23]

Besides such distractions the KK experiment, in its larger ambitions, was not really sustainable after 1949. The huge costs involved and the investments in maintenance and personnel turned out to be too heavy. In some church circles Faye was criticized for having overspent the annual budget and for wanton waste. But he was exonerated by Bishop Daly on the grounds that the large size of the student and staff population and the wide range of expenditure items were the main reasons for the huge expenditures incurred in running the project. For example, the village population rose from 10 in September 1942 to 175 in 1948, of which 148 boys and five girls were school boarders and the rest were workers, teachers and their families.

In fact, the worsening financial situation went back many years, as explained in the Bishop's letter of appeal in January 1949. He also indicated that in 1945 the Anglican mission as a whole spent over 1,200.00 pounds on the H of T and over 500.00 pounds on St John's School. The small mission could definitely not be expected to continue to contribute so heavily to these schools at the expense of its other schools in the country and other mission programmes.

An appeal for a grant was made to the government, which accorded amounts of 100.00 pounds to each school. At the end of 1946 the accounts were balanced with great difficulty. The school continued to expand, as pointed out above, and the recurrent costs rose proportionately; by the end of 1947 the deficit was huge. Again, assistance was sought from the government, but none was forthcoming; the Bishop's efforts to raise funds whilst on leave in England did not produce significant results. The only conclusion for the Bishop then was that "the deficit at the end of 1948 is so big that I cannot allow the school to continue". As he further reasoned:

> I do not think that it has been run extravagantly; it is simply
> that the mission without substantial help is unable to run such
> a school. The closing of the House of Transfiguration School
> will seem a catastrophe to the mission and many cherished
> hopes will die with it, but I cannot expect those responsible

for education in Gambia to regard it as more than a minor
set-back.[24]

With hindsight, the fact is that, among the benefactors, it had been
expected that over time the project would become independent and self-
financing. But this objective had not been achieved. No doubt, halting
efforts had been made towards self-sufficiency. For example, spinning
looms were bought from the Gold Coast (Ghana) and two of the boys
were taught the techniques of weaving; they developed enough expertise
to weave the uniforms for most of the other students. Both the extra
cloth and produce from the farms were sold in markets in neighbouring
towns and villages, and even in Bathurst. But, such bold efforts were
inadequate.

From the viewpoint of Rev. Faye, an important factor leading to
his separation from the KK project was jealousy, not only on the part
of some senior members of his staff and of the Church in Bathurst but
also the management of Armitage School led by a colonial educationist
named Holloran. KK School was indeed a model for Armitage but,
in actuality, it was perceived as a strong rival by Holloran and his ilk.
In competitions of whatever type, invariably Armitage lost to KK.
Allegedly, after the demise of KK, the Principal at Armitage adopted
many of the innovations that Faye had introduced further up the river.

Just about a year after Faye left, attempts were made to interest
him in going back to help in picking up the pieces. One day, as he was
preparing to travel to KK, Bishop Daly said to Faye:

"John, if only I could put you in my suitcase I would take you back
to Kristi-kunda."

This angered Faye as never before, for he felt gravely insulted; after
all the sacrifices he and his family had made to make something out
of a virgin village he was now confronted with damning allegations as
regards use of the funds.

"Good morning, my Lord," he retorted, and marched out of the
room.

The Verdict: Unanimous or Not?

This was the official end of Faye's involvement in the KK project, to which he had dedicated a huge portion of his life as an educationist. Observers and participant observers have given their verdicts on the project when in its heyday. Bishop Daly, writing in 1949, in an update to the book by John Laughton, a missionary priest who had also served in KK, was clearly of the opinion that to all intents and purposes the original vision sketched out by him in his report to the Missionary Society of London (1935) had been actualized. He says:

> A beautiful church is in the centre of the town and at the very heart of its life. There are two schools: one with 27 boarders, studies in the vernacular; and another, with 90 boys and a few girls, studies in English. There are Girl Guides and Scouts and Wolf Cubs. Two looms produce cloth for the school uniforms and also fancy cloth for sale in Bathurst. There is a little herd of cattle: donkeys, poultry, sheep, goats and dogs have their home there. There are many acres of farm land. The dispensary has grown into a little hospital . . . [25]
>
> The Head of Kristi-kunda, the Headmaster of the vernacular school, their wives and many others, have made real sacrifices for Christ's sake in order to settle at Kristi-kunda. They are quietly living out the Gospel and it is that which tells. The chief has invited the two leaders to join his Council. Headmen and others come to Kristi-kunda to seek advice in their villages and to settle family disputes. Ex-servicemen take their lead from Kristi-kunda in cooperative farming . . . [26]
>
> Kristi-kunda is not perfect but there is the germ of something worthwhile, something that God can use and is using. It is the witness, however faulty, of the life which is African and Christian. Their motto is: Love one another.[27]

And, as seen by another contemporary, KK was:

> An African Christian settlement on a community basis,
> living a normal village life illuminated and transfigured by
> the light of Christ. It farms for the purpose of approaching
> self-support; it tries to improve local animal industry,
> experimenting for this purpose with a herd of its own; it
> aims at improving local arts and crafts and in initiating new
> village industries.
>
> In its schools, it tries to give a sound elementary
> education to all who are willing to learn. It hopes to teach
> the Gospel without preaching it and by friendliness and
> charity to all comers to break ground for the sowing of the
> word. It is, in short, an experiment for the social, ethical
> and cultural improvement of the people of the bush with
> the strongest Christian basis. It is an inspired effort towards
> indirect evangelization.[28]

Yet another visitor is reported to have added:

> When you see Kristi-kunda—with its cosy little round mud-
> thatched houses; a weaver under fine shade trees weaving
> locally grown cotton; herds of cows, working bulls, sheep,
> goats, donkey, horses and fowls—you cannot help loving the
> place; it is a feast for tired eyes.[29]

Perhaps no other assessment was more consequential than that of
the Commissioner of the Upper River Division (URD) reporting to the
Honourable Colonial Secretary on the vast changes that had taken place
at KK within a few years of Faye's takeover. He observed that from "the
inefficiency of it all, and particularly the indescribable squalor of the
buildings" there was now real transformation, notably in the following
areas: old dilapidated buildings had been demolished and new ones
constructed, these were of better craftsmanship and design; there had
been some resignations and dismissals; the station was no longer to be
run on the lines of early Christian communism, which had given rise to

"a great deal of trouble (including a few appearances in the native Court for debts and so on)"; a new missionary priest (Archdeacon Mudford) had been appointed to take charge of overall administration; the mission was now "enormously wealthy" with an annual income much higher than the total government budget for the whole of the URD including all its staff and development programmes; thereafter there would still be a balance.[30]

The Commissioner heaped accolades on Faye [whose name he spelt as 'Fye']; for example:

> At a time when it is obvious that Africans will be expected to take over an increasingly large number of jobs previously reserved for Europeans, Mr Fye's career is of considerable importance to this very small colony. I am most anxious to see how he settles down in the alien environment of Kantora and it can be said so far that he is an almost unqualified success. He has practically taken over the entire control of Kristi-kunda and its administration.
>
> Mr. Fye seems to be so popular everywhere. It has been so distasteful to see the usual Bathurst intelligentsia, on the strength of a Cambridge Local, patronizing the headmen and scholars of the Protectorate. There is nothing of this in Mr. Fye; he appears genuinely to get on well with them and to respect them; and he has had the tact to go on gently in religious matters where they are likely to cause friction. A remarkable phenomenon he has started is night classes for the local Fulas, where fifty-two adults attend to get a mixture of religion and education. Several adults are struggling with the difficulties of the alphabet. He has once arbitrated in the question of a disputed headmanship without, so far as I know, interfering in the bad sense of the word. In fact, so far as my present knowledge goes, he is doing all that might be hoped and nothing that might be feared.
>
> Of course, it is early days. He may get a swollen head; he may get unjustifiably involved in local politics;

the proselytizing fervour of Mr. Mulford may cause local friction.

. . . [But] on balance, however, I have been impressed with the remarkable change that has come over the settlement since Messrs Fye and Mudford took over, and I have far better hopes of its developing into a useful institution than ever I thought I should.[31]

The Commissioner proceeded to speak very positively about specific areas such as animal husbandry, farm crops, adult evening classes, fees, record keeping, school subjects, buildings, handwork, books, and general cleanliness.

KK: The Beginning of the End

It was accepted that in the immediate post-Faye era it would be necessary to have a considerably scaled-down version of the original KK. The church and school remained but only a skeleton of the vibrant and promising Christian village of the late 1940s. An Irishman, Father Pike (later to become Bishop of The Gambia, 1960-1963) took over the management. Able Thomas became Headmaster of the KK School, comprising a house for boys from Bathurst and a house for local boys; Arthur Cates continued as the Second Master of the whole school and House Master of the junior local boys. Andrew Camara joined the staff in January 1949 after obtaining his Cambridge School Certificate; he was appointed Assistant House Master and put in charge of the stores. Later, on graduating from the Georgetown Teacher Training College, he returned to KK and rose to become its Headmaster.

The KK project continued to be very seriously bedevilled with the problem of finance. By the end of the 1940s the colonial government intensified the debate on a Protectorate Education Policy which, inter alia, included issues such as the following: What role for central government and for the Christian missions? How can the government's interference and likely control in the running of mission schools be prevented? What role for the government as compared to the district authorities? Who was to take responsibility for funding what? If the government was to pay the salaries and other emoluments of teachers, which category was it to cover? Were the students to be offered scholarships and who would take responsibility for this?

Naturally, KK benefited from the outcomes of this debate and the policies adopted subsequently. For example, in May 1949 the government decided to give the school a grant of 200 pounds, "on a year to year basis and the school will be inspected, in order that Government may be satisfied about the organization, later this year as soon as inspection staff is available".[32] But this was mere temporary relief, for the decline both in the school, the farms and in medical services to the local community seemed unstoppable.

A visit in 1955 by Sam H. M. Jones, a senior member of the Anglican Church and reputable educationist, about six years after Faye had departed, painted a not-too-glowing picture of the situation. First among his comments was that those who knew the place in the 1940s would be "bound to experience a sense of disappointment". Second, after 15 years since the mission was started, the results were "somewhat meagre": the school had 40 pupils of whom 23 were boarders and among these only three were Fula and they were not from the neighbourhood either. Third, and following from this, the mission to the Fulas had failed; church services and other religious activities were right in their midst but they were totally indifferent. To quote the report: "Thus, two communities exist side by side but exert very little noticeable influence on each other. The policy of 'peaceful co-existence' is relevant in the Great World outside; however in the field of missionary enterprise it is fatal."[33] Regrettably, many of the *personae* on the missionary side had come to accept all of the above and were resigned to their fate.

Quite the contrary for Jones, who was not as pessimistic about the future of the settlement. He argued vehemently for a revival, maintaining that "a full-scale and sustained attack is called for; it should be many-sided in nature and carefully planned". The overall aim would be "to make greater and more vital contacts with the people so as to convince them that their cooperation is for their own benefit."[34] He listed the elements of this onslaught as: work through children; work with the women; house-to-house visitation; closer links with the native authorities; and a total reorientation of the existing educational system and the philosophy behind it. Jones, from his vast reservoir of quality experience in the field of education, then offered a number of substantive ideas for transforming education not only in Kristi-kunda but in the division as a whole.

At the beginning of 1960 the SPG decided to undertake its own comprehensive review of the project with a view to determining what approach to adopt regarding continued support from the Hawkes Mission Trust. One reason for this particular timing was that:

> To the difficulty of finding European staff who could maintain the original inspiration, and put the 'objects and ideals' into full effect, there had been gradually added the difficulty of the falling value of money, which has now reached such proportions that even if the staff could be found, it would be impossible to implement the scheme for a hospital, and for extension of agricultural work, from the Hawkes Mission Trust, the income from which has not increased proportionately since 1942.[35]

In May 1961 the Secretary of the SPG visited Bathurst to have direct consultations with the Bishop and officials of the medical and education services. At the end of the consultations the Secretary concluded as follows:

(a) That the Society as Trustees of the Hawkes Mission Trust, does not consider that the object and ideals of the Mission at Kristi-kunda are now capable of achievement with the resources at the disposal of the Trust, and it has therefore regretfully come to the conclusion that the Trust can no longer be used at Kristi-kunda.

(b) Whether or not the withdrawal of the Hawkes Trust will entail the closure of Kristi-kunda school and the dispensaries must depend to a large extent upon Government policy in the area.

(c) The Society might be able to assist the Diocese to some extent to maintain these institutions, but it is very doubtful whether it could provide from its General Funds a sum approaching that available from the Trust (i.e. approximately 3,000.00 pounds per annum) and it would need to be assured that help was coming from other sources adequate to make the work worthwhile, both as a social service and as an opportunity for evangelism. [36]

The Society terminated all it's funding to the KK project in April 1966.

Rapid decline followed. A medical officer, C. O. S. Blyth Brooke, after an informal private visit in March 1966 had noted, with remorse: "I found it very sad to see the dilapidated state of the buildings, including the church, but much more the decay of what must have been at one time a very valuable Christian enterprise." [37]

With the new term in September 1966, Alex Yorke, the Headteacher, reported to Bishop Olufosoye that there were no entry pupils, compared to the previous year when the new intake was 17 pupils, one of the highest in recent years. But, even then, a week after, 12 had dropped out and only five children were still in Primary One, the first year class, by the end of the school year. This was in marked contrast to the government-run neighbouring school in Fatoto where 80 pupils applied, though it could only enrol 40. The 40 who did not get in were advised to go to the KK School, but none of them applied. The total enrolment for the whole KK School was 30 pupils.

In the circumstances, the only word of caution the Headteacher could give the Bishop was that the school could not continue.[38] To this communication the Bishop admitted: "it means that there will be no school there in another five years. The root is cut. Please do all you can to save the situation." [39]

This sorry situation was confirmed by A. C. Andrews, Education Officer, Primary, in his inspection report, 17-18 October 1966. He pointed out that there were only two teachers employed in the school and that "this school is likely to die within the next five years. It is a disturbing situation and one that calls for urgent but careful consideration."[40] The reasons for the withdrawal of the pupils, as presented in a meeting between Andrews, the chief, and representatives of eleven villages in the Kantora District were noted. Amongst other failings:

- They noted the lack of a Koranic teacher, which the school had had some years earlier.
- They complained that there was no organized School Committee and Parent/Teacher Association, where members could speak freely on matters educational affecting their district, as was the practice in most government schools.
- They blamed the staff for not being vigilant in the service they were supposed to be rendering. They recalled with joy the happy days they had with Rev. J. C. Faye and the late Mr. Arthur Cates.
- They felt quite strongly that the children at Kristi-Kunda School were not being properly handled. They were given impossible manual tasks to perform.
- They explained that Mr. James Baker (the Assistant Headteacher) did not live at Kristi-kunda and was not fully interested in the life of the community there.
- They criticized the teachers for not associating themselves with the villagers.

Andrews concluded: "It was forcefully pointed out to me that it is the wish of parents to transfer all pupils from Kristi-kunda if there were places elsewhere to accommodate them." And, he lamented: "This is a sad comment on a school that has offered such valuable services in the past."

It is not surprising that soon after this visit the Deputy Headteacher, James F. Baker, asked for a transfer from the mission service to the government teaching service. Writing to Honourable Andrew D. Camara, his former boss at the school and now the Minister of Education, Baker argued that he had spent five years in KK but "with the present condition of the school I cannot do my work properly as I ought to do it." He continued:

> This is all due to the long period I have had in the school
> without seeing any progress as a whole. The roll of the school

has not even reached the roll required for a full class, and above all, the people living around the school have very little interest in the school as if not they would have sent their children to the school.[41]

The report of the Director of Education on the school the year following merely repeated what was clear for all to see. It quoted the record of Alex Yorke in the Log Book on 19 September, in which he lamented:

> School re-opened today. The attendance was poor. There's no new intake. It appears to me that Kristi-kunda School has had its day. The Glory of KK has gone, and now the people of Kantora are not worried whether we are here or not.

The Director's report warned that the two teachers had no intention of returning to the school in the following school year: Yorke was due to retire on pension and Baker would transfer to another school. As with others before him, the Director concluded:

> With the opening of the school at Fatoto, the noticeable lack of support from the people of Kantora, the low morale of the present staff, and the unlikely prospect of suitable replacement being found, the days of Kristi-kunda are numbered. Already the station has the appearance of a ghost settlement and an air of decay hangs heavily on the remaining buildings. It would be kindest for the Bishop of The Gambia and Rio Pongas to arrange for the transfer of the children at this school to Fatoto School.[42]

Faye to the Rescue? Not Again!

Bishop John Daly, under whose watch the KK project had been initiated in 1940, paid a courtesy visit to the diocese in early July 1968. On being informed about the fate of his pet KK project, he encouraged the presiding Bishop Olufosoye to set up an ad hoc committee on its future.

Besides Daly himself, the committee comprised Rev. J. C. Faye, Dr. S. J. Palmer, Dr. Florence Mahoney, the Honourable Andrew D. Camara, Dr. Fred Oldfield, and the Venerable M. C. George. Faye's membership was logical, given the fact that from the outset he had worked very closely with Daly in starting the school and, together, they had taken it to its zenith in the 1940s; to this must be added the strong mutual respect and empathy between Daly and Faye.

The committee met on 12 July 1968 and, after a thorough assessment of all aspects of the situation, recommended as follows:

1. That the mission should retain the primary school at KK and make all efforts to expand it. It was felt that in time the Fatoto School would not be able to accommodate the high demand for places, and parents would have no choice but to benefit from the opportunities at KK.

2. That the Anglican mission should explore the possibility of starting a post-primary school in KK which would cater for pupils from Bathurst and its environs as well; boarding facilities would be made available for those from outside the area. Such a school would not only absorb primary school leavers from Fatoto but would receive government support, as there were no plans by government to set up such a school in the district in the future.

3. The mission should try to find a "pushful" person—Gambian or expatriate—who would serve in the area immediately.

4. The primary school must be kept functioning at all costs. School fees should be kept at 10 shillings annually; the mission must now provide books free, as done in government schools. Careful forward planning must be embarked on for the post-primary school, especially for the boarding school for students from Bathurst.[43]

The third recommendation was considered critical to the relaunch of KK. Amazingly, Faye informed the meeting that "he would have very much liked to offer himself for this challenging work but was not in a position to make that offer at the moment because of pressing commitments here in Bathurst". The record of the meeting continued:

> He (Fye) told us that when he was [recently] up-River with Bishop Daly, the Seyfo (Chief) of Kantora had called him apart and invited him to return among them. [At the present meeting] Mr. Andrew Camara assured us that only Rev. Faye would be able to re-establish the confidence of the people of Kantora. If we couldn't get him, he [Camara] strongly recommended that an expatriate should be found for KK.

The report then noted that: "Rev. Faye proposed that if it were acceptable he would be willing to go to KK once a month and spend a few days there, until such time as a suitable person could be found to run the station."

In the light of the treatment meted out to him in the past, this was the height of selflessness and generosity of spirit on the part of Faye. It captured all that was Christian and virtuous in him—qualities so rare among men in general. Some saw him as having been a victim at the crucifixion; now, he was to engineer the resurrection.

In any case, Faye's offer could not be entertained as, at that juncture, Daly had other plans for Faye which he had outlined to Bishop Olufosoye. This was that Faye's next move would be formal training for the priesthood. For this, a period of quiet study was necessary. KK was proposed as a venue but later thought to be inappropriate: not only would Faye not have the time for study and worship but he would not be seen as having given up politics. Instead, Daly's preferred option was for Faye to go out of the country. He, Daly, was ready to assist in getting Faye into an institution such as the College of the Ascension at Selly Oak, Birmingham, England, which offered non-residential theological courses for mature students. Daly further offered free accommodation at his home in Coventry from which Faye could commute by train to Birmingham which was only twenty minutes away.

This plan was reminiscent of a proposal first advanced by the same Bishop in the late 1940s in an effort to bring Faye to the mainstream of his profession as a clergyman. At the time Faye had not been enthusiastic.

Now, however, he agreed that Daly should go ahead and submit the plan to his Bishop, Olufosoye, on his return from the Lambeth Conference of Anglican Bishops in London. The fact that, at the time, Faye had officially resigned from politics and was inclined towards a future as a full-time clergyman was, undoubtedly, a favourable factor. Regrettably, none of this was to be.

Sinking to the Depths—Never to Be Again

Despite these very noble and commendable efforts at regeneration, sustenance and, possibly, growth, the downhill trend at KK continued, as again demonstrated in the report of Gabriel J. Roberts, Assistant Director of Education, of 7-11 January 1969.[44] As regards staffing, Yorke retired and Peter Jawo proceeded to the Yundum Teacher Training College. Only Baker was left at the school and he repeatedly requested a transfer to another school. Eventually, he moved to St Mary's in Bathurst.

Enrolment continued to decline, as did the staff complement; and the leadership was unstable, as shown below: [45]

Enrolment

1961/2	80
1962/3	68
1963/4	50
1965/6 and 1966/7	36
1967/8	25
1968/9	18

Turnover in Headteachers

1961/2	Rev. Jacob Williams
1962/3	M. Macauley
1963/4	J. B. Jawo
1965/6 and 1966/7	A. S. Yorke
1967/8	J. Baker (Acting)
1968/9	J. Baker

Number of teachers

1961/2	4
1962/3	4
1963/4	4
1965/6 and 1966/7	3
1967/8	1
1968/9	1

At the end of the 1968/69 school year, 8 of the 18 pupils requested transfers to the Fatoto school; the remaining 10 made similar requests and as these were not granted by the KK Headteacher they decided to stay away from school altogether. Eventually, Baker had no alternative but to accede to their requests and all the pupils moved to the Fatoto School. Against the protestations of Bishop Olufosoye, the pupils never returned.

January 1970 marked the official closure of the KK School. Today the site and the few buildings are in ruins. The local inhabitants have encroached on the land and it is likely that ownership may eventually be transferred to other interested parties.

Summary Observations

Education was the first career of choice for Faye. Even before completing his secondary schooling he had been exposed to the profession and, obviously, he developed a passion for it; hence, in a sense, his rapid rise to senior teaching and management positions in the leading schools of the day. No doubt, Faye's own credentials, both academic and professional, had prepared him for such responsibilities.

KK brought all these qualities together and Faye benefited considerably from his previous experience in the educational field. But, it put a heavy strain on the young professional and on his family. The challenges were enormous, both in terms of the external environment and within the leadership team, which had its own share of in-fighting. Yet, the overall verdict is that most of the objectives in this venture were realized. The variety of visible results attests to this, whether in relation to personal growth and development of the students or the spread of Christianity and western education among the locals. It was a unique experience which was never to be replicated in the country through the work of any religious or secular group.

CHAPTER 2

EDUCATIONIST: PLANTING INSTITUTIONS—THE SEED MULTIPLIES

The Parsonage Nursery School/Rev. J. C. Faye Memorial School, Banjul

Whereas the seeds planted in Kristi-kunda germinated, flowered for a while and then withered, those planted at the Parsonage Nursery School and at the Anglican Vocational Training Centre (Farafenni) blossomed and bore fruit.

Responding to a Need

Ten years after leaving politics and over 25 years after KK, Faye turned to his old dream of establishing an institution at No. 2 Clarkson Street to cater for the needs of different categories of the population. First, there was the project of a nursery school in Banjul which was to be named after his great grandmother, the Ndella Chaw Memorial School. When the Gambia government decided to raise the school entry age from six to eight years he strongly disagreed, arguing that this would stifle the intellectual growth of the child and that it was imperative that educational systems be built from the base upwards. He then proposed to the church that a nursery school/play group be set up at the Anglican Parsonage in Banjul with the entry age at five years; the project would also be a means of generating revenue. As it happened, the Bethel Methodist Nursery School was experiencing a major boom in pupil registration and income and it even planned an expansion of its operations; for Faye this was proof of the viability of his own project.

Undeterred by opposition from some church leaders, Faye proceeded with the project and founded the Parsonage Nursery School in February 1976 as a private school.

As confirmed by Bishop Tilewa Johnson in June 1992:

> This [school] was embarked upon in response to what the Rev. J. C. Faye saw as a national need. The nursery school was to help in satisfying the then great demand for nursery schooling in the city of Banjul in the mid-1970s. Rev, J. C. Faye believed it would also strengthen moral upbringing at its roots.[1]

The Bishop has also noted that Rev. Faye, as the then incumbent of St Mary's Pro-Cathedral, was generous enough to give up the whole of the Parsonage, his official residence, so it could be used by the school and, thus, generate additional rental income for the Church. In fact, the rent was fixed at 12,000 Dalasi per annum, a massive boost to the dwindling financial resources of the Church. Faye reasoned that he was already living comfortably at Gloucester Street and, through the benevolence of the owner, Mr. Secka of the Public Health Department, was not paying any rent. If he had to move out of this house into the Parsonage then he would have to move out when he retired from his Church position; he would then have to start searching for another private residence. He simply pointed out:

> I have lived in England. I have lived in mansions. I have been driven in a Rolls Royce. So I have had so many things. I have seen a lot. So, not living in the Parsonage does not take anything away from me.[2]

This was therefore a win-win situation for all parties concerned.

Faye went beyond this. He decided that the greater proportion of his monthly salary would go towards the starting of the school; he would be repaid when the school was able to stand on its feet. His first recruit as a teacher was Winifred Thomas, a loyalist from the KK days.

The overarching intention of the school was "to develop the health, spiritual, nutritional, intellectual, social, moral and physical needs [of the children] . . . and thereby assist in satisfying the need to constitute a potent factor in The Gambia's educational system". Its specific objectives were:[3]

1. To strengthen Christian upbringing at its roots in this time of stresses and strains.
2. To bring together, during the formative 3-plus to 7-year stage of life, Christian and Muslim children from different ethnic groups under the umbrella of the Church and thus not only help in strengthening the existing understanding among religious and ethnic groups for which The Gambia is well known, but also promote the same.
3. To assist in the all-round development of children 3 to 7 years in a healthy environment; train the children for life rather than merely for examination success.

Officially, the school was owned by the Cathedral Parish of St Mary's. The executive Management Board comprised Rev. Faye, the Priest-in-Charge, as Chairman (ex-officio), the Parish Treasurer (ex-officio), a member of the Parent Teachers Association, a staff member, and four people nominated by the Church Body. The Board reported to the Church Body on a monthly basis and to the Vestry Meeting annually.

The Limit is the Sky

Initially, the school followed a pre-primary school curriculum. It grew rapidly, well beyond expectations. The new Priest-in-Charge reclaimed the top floor of the building and the space in use by the school was limited only to the ground floor. It was therefore necessary to have it re-sited to the Bishop's Court, at the entrance to Banjul, in January 1991. One year later, the Board and the Parent Teachers Association agreed that the successful results from the nursery school, with its emphasis on small classes and use of qualified teachers, were enough evidence of the need to establish a primary stream. An application for permission was made to the Ministry of Education which granted its approval, with the proviso that any request for financial assistance from the government would only be considered after a period of five years.

Meanwhile the groundbreaking ceremony for the primary school took place on 24 June 1992, on the same occasion as the official opening of the new nursery school buildings. As was proper, Bishop Johnson paid tribute to the late Reverend Faye in his address and gave credit to him for his singular effort in the establishment and development of the school. He declared:

> Today you have been invited to this very special occasion that honours a true Gambian who served selflessly for the enlightenment, through education, of people in this country. A personality of rare talent who can be described as one of the fathers of independent Gambia, through his activities in the political life in the 1950s and 1960s. Perhaps most important of all, he was a priest and a pastor of all God's people, no matter what class, creed or station in life. I refer, of course, to no less a person than the late Very Reverend J. C. Faye.[4]

In April 1986, a few months after Faye's death, and at the instigation of Rev. Johnson as Manager of the school, the board decided to change the name of the school to The Rev. J. C. Faye Memorial School. The letter from Rev. Johnson informing the Faye family of this decision states:

> I write to inform you that at my first meeting with the Board of Management of the Parsonage Nursery School the suggestion to change the Nursery School's name to the Rev. John C. Faye Nursery School was warmly accepted and endorsed by all the members of the Board present.

The Nursery School owes a lot to the late great man; he spent time and energy to establish the school in spite of all colossal odds. The children, the Community and indeed the Cathedral Parish are all reaping the fruits of his labour. We cannot repay him for all he has done for us in founding our Nursery School. As a mark of our deep gratitude to him, therefore, we shall name the Nursery School after him at the school's Tenth Anniversary Thanksgiving Service to be held on Sunday 27th April 1986 at the Cathedral.

We shall be grateful if a member of the family will be at the service to unveil the new school signboard.[5]

Indeed, Johnson was well-acquainted with Faye. He had served his tutelage under Faye, as a candidate for ordination, when Faye was Priest-in-Charge, and then Provost of the Cathedral. It was after this period of preparation that Johnson proceeded for his theological training. He was to rise to the position of Bishop of the Diocese (1990) and Primate, Archbishop of the Church of the Province of West Africa (2012).

Concerning resource mobilization, assistance was forthcoming from the World Vision International and the Canadian Fund for Local Initiatives. The latter, through the Canadian High Commission, Dakar, contributed an amount of CAN$25,000.00 for the project "Completion works to J. C. Faye Memorial Nursery School" (1990); this was mainly for the construction of the ground and first floors of the building for the nursery school. Among other things, the project funded by World Vision International (1991) paid the rent for the Parsonage, salaries of the project manager and the correspondence assistant, and provided some stationery and other items, etc. School uniforms and overall sponsorship for some children were also provided by the organization.

With the government's introduction of a new educational system in The Gambia a four tier structure now exists in the J. C. Faye Memorial School, namely, Nursery, Lower Basic (Primary, grades 1-6, 7-13 years), Upper Basic (Junior Secondary, grades 7-9, 13-16 years), and Senior Secondary (High, grades 10-12, 16-19 years). But it could not develop into a private school, going from primary up to the General Certificate of Education Advanced levels, for which Faye and some members of the Board would have opted. Faye had envisaged that it would be a quality school that competed with the local elite Marina School, but also support the work of the Church among Christian children, very much like St Joseph's and St Augustine's of the Roman Catholic Mission. It would produce the choristers, servers, and young workers for the Church, teach music, classical subjects, and musical instruments such as the violin, piano, etc. Faye himself looked forward to the day when the school would stage operettas. All this was very much along the lines of exclusive Cathedral Schools in England. The beneficiaries would definitely stand out in society.

The Anglican Vocational Training Centre, Farafenni, North Bank Division

The second project close to Faye's heart was the Anglican Vocational Training Centre (AVTC) in Farafenni, North Bank Division, which is sited on a 78-acre plot leased by the Gambia government to the Anglican Diocese in The Gambia through the Kerewan Area Council. At the same time as he was conceiving the nursery school, Faye came up with the idea of a technical skills-development institution for students in the rural areas who did not have the aptitude for secondary education and found themselves unemployable drop-outs. In fact, as was typical of the man, he sowed the two sets of seeds (the nursery school and the vocational centre) at the same time and nurtured them simultaneously.

Faye shared this new idea with the Bishop, Rigal Elisee (1972-1986), who embraced it enthusiastically. Over time, there were further consultations and the concept matured into a full-blown project. It was said, rather unkindly, that the Bishop was actually motivated by an interest in leaving behind a legacy when his term of office expired just as it had been for Bishop Daly and KK!

The AVTC became the pet project of these two gentlemen. Elisee concentrated on external relations. Faye, on the other hand, was the local operator who took on such tasks as negotiating with the government and the traditional authorities on matters such as the land; with his wide network of local contacts he was able to produce quick results. This broad division of labour made for rapid advance in the infant stages of project design and networking.

The Issue of Location

There was unanimity that the centre should be based in the Protectorate; if for no other reason than that, with KK closed down, there was no substantial Anglican educational presence in this part of the country.

From the inception of the project-idea, it had been assumed that Banjul N'ding (near Yundum Airport) was the natural home; all project activities and negotiations with the overseas partners were based on this assumption. But there were those not too enthusiastic about this choice. In the first place, it was argued that it would not be politic to have St Peter's Technical School (Roman Catholic) on one side of the road and the (Anglican) Vocational Training Centre on the other. Then also, Banjul'Nding was too close to Banjul; if the school was to be rural then logic demanded that it should be situated in a truly rural part of the country. And, actually, if plans were still afoot for a theological centre to be established in Banjul'Nding then the two institutions could not be located in the same place. The old KK site was also advanced as a possibility. But, it was a non-starter: it had hosted a failed project and the experience had left a lingering bad taste in the mouth. Anyway, it was too far away!

It was the government that came up with Farafenni as an option, together with Basse and Georgetown as other possibilities. In early July 1974, the Bishop had officially presented the project to the Gambia government with a request for financial participation. Replying almost a year later, the Ministry of Education sought explanations and justifications on a number of aspects of the project. Among these was why the centre should not be in a "more deserving provincial centre with good communications, water and electricity supplies such as Farafenni, Basse or Georgetown". Faye, in his capacity as Chairman of the Diocesan Education Committee and project prime-mover, responded to these three possible sites but, obviously, his responses were inadequate and further explanations were solicited from the Church hierarchy by the ministry.[6]

For both Basse and Georgetown a number of constraints were identified, as follows: the construction and operational costs would increase as it would be necessary to transport materials from Banjul; attracting staff would be more problematical because of the remoteness of these places; provision for a four-wheel vehicle would also increase costs; malaria and other health problems would be prevalent; supervision would be more demanding, especially for the Bishop and Rev. Faye; and food and other domestic needs would have to come all the way from Banjul.[7]

Whether or not having Farafenni as the location of the institution was a condition for Gambia government assistance, it was interpreted as such by the local and external stakeholders. Farafenni was in a strategic junction and the new centre would be one of the few vocational schools in the rural areas and in the most deprived division in the country, the North Bank Division. Potentially, this location could also contribute to slowing down the rural-urban drift from this and neighbouring divisions. With these additional *atouts* the proposed site was soon changed from Banjul N'Ding to Farafenni.

The conception of the type of institution that was required also changed over time; that which lasted the longest was of a centre with three components, that is, a mixed junior secondary boarding school which would offer two-year courses in agriculture, trades (radio mechanics, painting, plumbing, carpentry and motor engineering), secretarial studies, hotel management, tourism, and domestic science; a theological seminary (offering a three-year course for ordinands for the Anglican priesthood, and a six-month course for catechists, evangelists, lay readers etc.); and all-purpose facilities (camps, seminars, conferences, retreats, retirement and vacation site). In time, this conception was refined; the last two components were eliminated and the scope of the first considerably reduced. It was to be purely a vocational and technical institution.

Action on All Fronts

On 7 August 1976 the Centre was registered at the Government Registrar's Office and, thus, legally established. The stated rationale for the institution was that:

> Instead of duplicating what already exists in the national education plan, the Anglican Church thought it better to propose to the Government and people of the Gambia a pilot educational scheme, the aim being to educate and equip the rural youth of the country for their effective participation in the nation-building programme of the Government . . .

It was further maintained that the institution would be the best contribution the Anglican Church could make towards the implementation of both the government's Ten Year Plan for Education and the Five Year Development Plan. The Bishop explained:

> [The Centre] should be directed towards enabling young people to become more self-reliant and more self-sufficient. And the best way to inculcate this self-reliance and this self-sufficiency is to provide opportunities for them to practice and experience it under qualified supervision. That is precisely the aim and purpose of the Anglican Vocational Training Centre.[8]

By the end of 1976 the first Board of Governors of the AVTC was composed by the Bishop in close consultation with Faye. Six leading Church personalities were to be the founding members: Rev. J. C. Faye himself, Sam A. Bidwell, Delphine E. S. Carrol, Christian A. Dawodu, Malcolm E. Millard, and Sam. J. Oldfield; each had specialized experience to contribute to this major initiative. The list was presented to an emergency meeting of the Gambia District Church Council which approved it. Some others who were to join the Board over the years included Wilmot John, William E. Hydara-Colley, Theophilus W. George, Francis Jones, Rev. Jacob Williams, and Rev. Fred George.

At the time of the constitution of the Management Board a decision was taken by the Church authorities that the Chairman should be a member of the clergy. Given his unquestionable dedication and commitment to the project since the conception stage, and his undisputed experience in education and in the planting of educational institutions, Rev. Faye was the natural choice; he remained Chairman until his health began to deteriorate. It was also in respect of this decision that Malcolm Millard, after his ordination as deacon, assumed the position as Vice Chairman; as Millard was already Secretary to the Board it became necessary for an Assistant Secretary to be appointed.

Given the wide range of decisions it had to take in the early phase of project implementation, the Board met regularly and at least once a month, it also held several emergency meetings. Almost every other month members actually travelled to Farafenni for meetings; this enabled them to see for themselves what was happening on the ground and to raise questions.

A ceremony for groundbreaking and the laying of the foundation stone of AVTC was held on Sunday, 27 March 1977, graced by His Excellency the President of the Republic, Sir Dawda K. Jawara. Among those in attendance were: Sir Alieu Jack, Minister of Works and Communications (deputizing for the Minister of Education); the Seyfu of Upper Baddibu; Hon. Kebba Jammeh; the Deputy Imam of Farafenni; and the Chairman and Board members of the Centre. Bishop Elisee presided.

In his statement President Jawara noted that this was "a significant milestone in the contribution of the Anglican Church to this country, and it dovetails into the general strategy of our five-year plan and ten-year education policy." The location of the centre in Farafenni was ideal, he noted, as it is:

> one of the two growth centres in the government five-year
> plan, the other being Basse . . . The population drift from
> rural to urban areas has been considerable, so our strategy
> is to provide growth centres with more of the bright lights,
> providing them with electricity, running water, transport,

health and educational facilities comparable to those in the urban areas.[9]

More specifically, the Centre "would provide skills to the rural community and self-reliance, the basic skills to obtain a higher standard of life and productivity, to modernize agriculture, a lot of skills".

The Bishop seized the opportunity to explain that the development of the Centre was based on a five-year plan which began in 1976; in September 1978 there would be an initial intake of 80 boys and girls. The formal opening was scheduled for 1 January 1979 and the boarders were expected to join by September 1979.[10] At the end of the fifth year it was projected that the student body would be about 300 students, with half as boarders and the other half as day students.[11]

Action was soon initiated to recruit a Principal both through advertising in the local *Gambia News Bulletin* and in *West Africa Magazine*; preference was to be given to suitably qualified Gambians and then West Africans, in that order. Two applications from Gambians were received but neither applicant was considered qualified for the post. Much interest was then directed at attracting candidates from Ghana, given the wider pool of experts in areas to be covered in the Centre's curriculum. In the process, much use was made of contacts such as in the offices of the West African Examinations Council (WAEC) in Accra, the Ghana Educational Service and the Ghana Polytechnique. A selection committee was set up in Accra, with members from the WAEC, Holy Trinity Cathedral, and Accra Technical College. Out of 27 applicants, 15 were shortlisted and 11 interviewed; four were eventually subjected to a second interview.[12]

The successful candidate recommended by the panel was Joseph A. King-Adu, who was then a senior official in the Ghana Education Service; the recommendation was endorsed by the AVTC Board at its 12th meeting on 10 November 1977. King-Adu's reporting date was fixed for 1 September 1978. Others who were to hold the position included William Forster, Rev. Millard, Rev. Fred George, and John Jatta.

Faye was very influential in the choice of a Ghanaian to head the Centre. Going by his own criteria, Ghana had long experience in technical and vocational education and, overall, the educational system was considered by him to be of a higher standard than elsewhere in West Africa. Much of the correspondence with Accra on the subject involved Faye personally and, obviously, the persons involved in the process on the other end were well known to him. The donors themselves were keen that a good candidate should be appointed; they were very impressed by the objectivity of the selection process and by the qualifications and experience of the successful candidate.

Resource Mobilization

Substantial investments were required for the buildings, equipment, tools and other infrastructural needs. For their financing and for the establishment of the Centre it was necessary to attract external assistance.

At the early stage of project conception and design, the immediate problem confronted was the lack of capacity and technical know-how; experience in this field in the diocese as a whole was very limited. Conscious of this lacuna, in January 1973, Bishop Elisee appealed to Christian Aid in London to identify and finance an experienced person who would advise on how to proceed; the duration would be a maximum period of two months. Christian Aid lacked the mandate and, perhaps more important, the funds.

The mission also attempted to raise funds from within the Province of West Africa through Bishop Olufosoye (1965-1970) who had preceded Bishop Elisee in the diocese and had now returned to Nigeria. Specifically, the former Bishop encouraged Anglican churches in his country to designate a "Gambia Day" during which information would be circulated on the training centre project and donations collected.[13]

In addition, Bishop Elisee met with President Jawara late in the same January 1973 to brief him on the project and to solicit the support of the government. In a follow-up letter to the Minister of Education the Bishop specifically requested assistance in the form of grant aid. In reply, very strong support was promised, seeing that this venture was much in line with government policy and that it would fill a huge gap in the provision of educational service in the country, as the Head of State was to note at the ground breaking ceremony years later. At the same time, the ministry requested information on how much money had been reserved by the Mission for implementing the project and what funding was anticipated from external sources.[14]

Faye supervised the drafting of a project document for a massive resource mobilization campaign. It was first submitted by Bishop Elisee to the Anglican Church of Canada through its Primate World Relief and Development Fund (PWRDF), in early February 1973; attached to it were endorsement documents from the Ministry of Education and other interested parties. In April, a visit was made by Reverend R. D. MacRae of the Fund to Banjul during which he held discussions with key stakeholders. Subsequently, in September, he formally presented the project to the Fund's allocations committee and to the Canadian International Development Agency (CIDA). After a thorough study of the proposal and extensive exchanges by CIDA and the other parties, a Programme Development Mission to Banjul was organized; this was in response to the already-noted concern about the limited technical competence in planning and programme development available locally.

In April 1974 the mission was mounted by a senior CIDA official, its purpose was:

> to assist the Gambian Diocesan Education Committee to pull together all aspects of the thinking on the project to date, evaluate it in terms of the needs and priorities of the country from educational, labour and social perspectives, and synthesize a workable, technically feasible, operational revision of the project which would be submitted to the Diocesan Education Committee for approval and possible submission to their overseas' partners for consideration of funding assistance.[15]

Rev. Faye was one of the three members, the others being a CIDA technical education consultant (W. D. Cooper) and a Development Projects Officer from the Anglican Church of Canada (George Cram). Faye's specific responsibilities were defined as:

> [to] provide knowledge of the history of the project, the
> planning process to date, and the hopes and expectations of
> the impact on the various segments of Gambian society with
> regard to the proposed project.[16]

The team submitted its report in June 1974, detailing the stages through which the project had gone, the personnel requirements, costs estimates, and other related issues. Among the recommendations the most critical related to the need for a written commitment from the Gambia government indicating its support and its willingness to pay the salaries of all qualified teachers after an initial period; according to the plan this would involve 13 teachers and begin in the fifth year when the Centre became viable and reached its full operational potential.

Satisfied with the overall findings of this team, the Fund decided to assist in mobilizing resources for the project in addition to its own inputs. Though for about one year there was no contact between the two parties, the Primate's Fund used this period to enter into negotiations with members of its Projects Committee, CIDA officials, and other interested groups in order to ascertain that there was all-round commitment to the project. This was finally secured.

At the Banjul end, during this period of a lull in communications, Faye and members of the Diocesan Education Committee worked hard, on all fronts, to keep the project on the front burner. One notable area of concentration was that of obtaining a commitment from the government in the form noted above. This was a delicate task, but it was the minimum the funding agencies, including CIDA, expected, before they would ratify their participation in the project. To demonstrate their sincerity the donors were even disposed to accept a broad and conditional agreement and not one that was "iron-clad and unchangeable".[17]

Why was the government's formal agreement not easily forthcoming? From the viewpoints of Faye and Elisee this was due to two things: (a) the difficulty of trust; and (b) the approach adopted was different from that normally followed by bodies such as the Catholic Church. In these cases, their own resources were first invested in the project so as to demonstrate its viability and anticipated impact before the government was approached for a subsidy.

Another ground for the foot-dragging in issuing the letter requested by the Canadian donors was that in some civil service circles it was feared that any such commitment would be seen as binding on the government and involve a *carte blanche* subsidy. On the other hand, there was always the possibility that the venture would turn out to be unfeasible and unworkable; the resulting loss to the government would be huge.[18]

Finally, there was always the suspicion among the Christian missions that the growing presence of Islamic non-governmental organizations in the country at this time, and the more active role of Arab governments in Gambia's development, could be influencing the position of the government.

In January 1976 the written commitment of the Gambia government was finally obtained; it offered to begin paying salaries of qualified teachers from the third year of the successful operation of the institution.

This development was soon followed by the organization of another review commission from the PWRDF, which visited Banjul from 22 to 29 May 1976. Its main remit was "to update and revise the original assumptions, costs and plans of the 1974 Planning Commission".[19] The output, the first Review Commission Report, was approved by the Diocesan Education Committee, the PWRDF and all parties involved; it was later dubbed "the Yellow Paper" and became the basic document and reference point for project management.[20]

Among other things, the Yellow Paper defined more sharply the objectives of the Centre, thus:

a) To provide post-primary students with the basic life skills that will fit them [the students] for a more productive and useful role in Gambian society.

b) To develop in all students specific manual skills in the fields of agriculture, handicrafts and home science, so that they will be self-reliant and prepared for self-employment, and to provide the minimum academic education for those students that are able and wish to obtain higher education after leaving the Centre.[21]

On funding, it proposed a six year timetable for self-support consisting of a first phase of three years which was also to be mainly a construction period, and with an intake of 80 students. The second phase would be one of growth and secondary construction; this would lead to self-support.

Based on the findings and recommendations of this review, the Church of Canada submitted a request for funding to the Canadian International Development Agency (CIDA) of the Government of Canada and other donors. CIDA was positive and approved a contribution of US$235,000—almost fifty percent of the total budget. It was to be disbursed in *tranches* over three years, in the amounts of US$94,715 (fiscal year 1976-1977), US$110,000 (fiscal year 1977-1978), and US$30,000 (fiscal year 1978-1979).[22] At this point, the procedures for overall management of the project, particularly the reporting and accounting systems, were agreed upon.[23] In December 1976, Peter Hawkins was sent out by the Church of Canada to act as Vice-Principal of the Centre and to be fully responsible for technical aspects of the construction phase of the project; up until the recruitment of a Principal he also assisted in institution-building activities.

The Church of Canada itself donated various amounts over a period, with US$50,000 as mobilization fee (January 1977). An agreement was entered into with the Anglican Church of The Gambia spelling out future relationships and the nature of support to come from the Church of Canada. As from the 1981/82 financial year, after the initial period of Canadian support, funds from the government of The Gambia constituted the core support for the project, as agreed in principle in 1976—particularly teachers' salaries. Finally, the Diocese of The Gambia and Rio Pongas made a contribution to the annual budget of about 48,000 Dalasi in the early 1980s. So also did the SPG which made available an amount of 4,000 Dalasi annually up to 1994.

Project Operationalization

In April 1977, Faye, in consultation with the Management Board, set up a special Tender Board, basically for handling matters pertaining to the first phase of the construction of the 13 buildings of the Centre.

A problem that arose immediately was that there were four bids but the lowest (1,017,000 Dalasi) was almost double the amount budgeted (489,000 Dalasi). In conjunction with an expert sent by the PWRDF three possibilities were examined. First, for a budget line increase to be renegotiated with the donor; it was thought that this would be difficult and it would incur a delay of at least six months. Second, for the number of buildings to be reduced so that the total costs would be within the tenders' amounts; here the risk was that the other buildings might not be constructed at all in the future and that the donors might not even agree to this option.

The third possibility was for the buildings to be constructed on a *tesito*/self-help basis rather than on a contract basis with a single firm. This meant that the works would be done on a private basis with each *tranche* contracted locally under the overall management and supervision of the Vice-Principal and a Supervisor of Works. The advantages of this option, as recognized by the Board, were as follows: work would be started immediately; there would be greater flexibility; equipment purchased would be retained as property of the Centre; and the total cost would be reduced by about 40 percent of the offer by the lowest tender.

The Board adopted the third option and requested that a concrete action plan be drawn up.[24] According to the "order of construction", the initial set of buildings would be the staff house, teachers' residence, Principal's house and the classrooms. Then the next phase would be the vocational workshops, home economics rooms, and the arts and crafts centre. And this would then be followed by the boys' dormitory, Vice-Principal's house, dining and assembly hall, the administrative building, and the girls' dormitory. In the original plan, the construction of the Phase II buildings was to be part of the training for the students; this, however, turned out to be idealistic as after a two-year or even four-year training period students would be qualified to assist, but not be in charge of, the construction of buildings.

Not unexpectedly, overall project implementation did not go as projected; for example, the first phase extended over four academic years instead of the projected three. Thus, a second review was commissioned in 1979, mainly to work on modifications of the 1976 plan. This, and many other "settling down" difficulties, led to the conclusion that a more radical review and planning system in the Centre was what was needed. The third Review Commission (July 1981) was subsequently organized "to review the original assumptions of the Centre and to suggest policies and technical recommendations for the implementation of Phase II." It confirmed the relevance of the original operating principles and the objectives of the Centre and made recommendations on the administration, staffing, financing and curriculum of the institution.

It came as no surprise when in February 1982 the Anglican Church of Canada, through its PWRDF, announced that it was to phase out its financing of the Centre. It proceeded to design a three-year phase-out budget which would lead to the complete termination of its funding and the assumption of all project operating costs by the Gambia government, the diocese, school fees, and other domestic and external sources. PWRDF/CIDA funding was to terminate at the end of the 1985/86 academic year. By then, the total investment was 1,851,369 Dalasi, made up of 1,224,351 Dalasi in capital costs and 627,018 Dalasi in operating costs.

With this development, it was decided to set up a fourth Review Commission which had to undertake two tasks, namely, a thorough evaluation of the project and, based on the findings, a plan for the future of the Centre in the post-1986 era. This left the institution with a budget deficit which no external donor was ready to cover. Drastic actions, such as the phasing out of the boarding element of the school at the end of the 1987/88 school year, and an urgent appeal to the PWRDF/Anglican Church of Canada for a two-year extension of the phase-out in 1985/86, were recommended by the fourth Review Commission.[25]

All these notwithstanding, a terminal project evaluation was conducted in 1988; its purpose was "to establish what has been achieved [since 1974]; to critique the decisions and implementation that have been made and to suggest how they might have been avoided; and to make specific recommendations for the future".[26] Its findings were quite comprehensive, as were its recommendations.

AVTC: Outlines of a Balance Sheet?

The performance of the Centre has been mixed. AVTC started off as a vocational boarding/day school, mainly for students who did not qualify for entrance into secondary schools. As such, and as a vocational and technical institution, its curriculum offered training in skills to prepare students for contributing to the national economy; these, as noted, included carpentry and joinery, building construction, masonry, woodwork, agriculture, home economics, metal work, horticulture, animal husbandry, and arts and crafts. However, in the 1980s its curriculum expanded and the "vocational" emphasis shifted to make way for more "academic" subjects; new subjects such as English, mathematics, geography, history, and social sciences were introduced.

This change in emphasis was in line with the preference of many local parents and students for courses which would prepare individuals for another attempt at the entrance examinations leading to a secondary-level education. With this, the government and all parties agreed that the requirements for a "vocational" institution were no longer being met and the name of the Centre was changed to "Anglican Training Centre."

Soon after this, when the external funding began to dry up, consideration was given to closing the Centre. The diocese could not contribute counterpart funds to what was being provided by the government; and total dependence on government was thought to be unwise and unsustainable. The "Yellow Paper" had projected that the diocese would be contributing about 25,000 Dalasi by 1983; but because of certain difficulties it could only afford 15,000 Dalasi (or 4 percent of the operating costs) by 1987. These operating costs had skyrocketed due to unexpectedly high inflation, particularly boarding costs, and in the latter days profits from the farm declined noticeably. One saving grace was that after negotiations between the Mission and the government, which resulted in the latter agreeing to resume its funding, the World Bank provided some funds for infrastructures.

It was expected that funding would be attracted from United States sources but this was not forthcoming in any significant amount. To make this particular project appealing to religious non-governmental organizations in the United States and Europe it was decided to bring back the "religious" dimension—the name of the institution was changed again, this time to the "Anglican Mission Institute." The three constituent units were the Upper Basic School, the Home Economics Department, and the Agriculture Department.

From the point of view of the original Board, it was preferred that the government classify the Centre as a Local Agreement School, under the following terms and conditions: there would be partial ownership of the school by the Mission and the government; there should be no interference by the government in the daily administration of the school; the school would be free to recruit students and to appoint the teachers and the Principal, without any government involvement; and the salaries were to be paid directly to the school and not to the Church. The Ministry of Education was granted a seat on the Board of the institution.

On another subject, the geographic distribution of the student population was problematical for much of the period, as illustrated below:

1979/80 Academic Year

		Boys	Girls	Total
1.	Banjul and Kombos	45	5	50
2.	North Bank Division	14	3	17
3.	MacCarthy Island Division	7	4	11
4.	Lower River Division	4	0	4
5.	Upper River Division	2	0	2
		72	12	84

Among the boys, 60 were boarders and there were 12 day students; as for the girls, eight were boarders and four were day students.[27] The predominance of students from the capital and other urban areas was of concern, as the original concept was to take children from the rural areas. The reason for this was that the fees were a deterrent to parents from rural areas; some could not afford even five Dalasi. If the Centre had been free of charge then more students would have been recruited from the rural areas. The day students were indeed all from the rural areas but they were mostly in arrears in school fees. Much depended on whether or not education was a priority for the parents—for the

1980 academic year out of 160 places at the neighbouring Farafenni Secondary School (where education was free) only 98 were taken up.

Nevertheless, many benefited from the existence of the Centre. By the end of 1987, 108 students had graduated from the institution; it is not likely that many of these would have been employed if they had not been trained at the AVTC. Workers had gainful employment during the different phases of the evolution of the Centre; then also the business community in Farafenni and environs gained through the custom of the many people associated with the Centre, and many benefited also from the services offered to the community and the produce from the Centre's farms. For many years there were bountiful and significant profits gained from sales to hotels, retail outlets and private individuals. As regards the workshops, the furniture from the production centre was sold mainly to schools and government departments. But poor management and other problems were to set in which resulted in a massive slump as from the second half of the 1980s.

Faye and the AVTC: A Labour of Love

Faye was passionate about this enterprise just as he had been with the KK project and the Parsonage School. As noted by Bishop Johnson: "He was the brain, the live-wire behind the project",[28] its leading light. He did not hesitate to do anything that he perceived as contributing to the advancement of the project. As Chairman of the Board, he hardly ever missed a meeting or failed in following up on decisions taken at meetings. Outside of on-site Board meetings, he frequently travelled to Farafenni on his own to obtain first-hand information on developments, so he could provide his Board with authentic and not hearsay information. In interviews with past Board members, there was a consensus that Faye went well beyond the call of duty in executing the functions of Chairman.

Faye was deeply involved in all the activities discussed above and, on the Gambian side, he was actually in charge at every stage in the evolution of the Centre. As an example of the extent he was ready to go to see the project take off and grow, when Peter Hawkins, the Canadian technician and Vice Principal, first arrived in Banjul, Faye travelled with him to Farafenni to inspect the site. This was on 17 December 1976; three days later they were in Sibanor to negotiate with the landlord of a house for Hawkins. Early the next month, Faye accompanied Hawkins to St Peter's Roman Catholic School to order furniture for the house and to the law courts to settle legal matters pertaining to the project; they also held discussions at the United States Peace Corps Office to associate its Director with the planned project for the Centre.[29] In short, Faye made himself fully available to settle in the young man so the work could begin at the earliest opportunity and so that the seriousness of the Gambian side in seeing the project launched would be clear. Though occupying the high position of Chairman of the Board, he did not consider it too condescending to run errands and organize meetings with all and sundry in an effort to promote the project.

It was because of this incredibly strong determination to make a success of the project in the shortest time possible, that difficulties quite often arose in Faye's relationships with some team members. He had a visceral reaction to anything he saw as bureaucratic and "red-tapism", and which had the consequence of slowing things down. Here, financial rules and regulations were Faye's nemesis and his attempts to by-pass them only resulted in tension, and even open conflicts, with some of the collaborators and partners. Similarly, he was intolerant of proposals and suggestions from others which appeared to him not to be in line with what he saw as best for the project. Peter Hawkins was a victim of his impatience on both counts.

In appreciation of Faye unflinching determination and hard work Bishop Elisee wrote to him, in October 1979:

> I wish to seize this opportunity to express my thanks and gratitude to you for your unfailing support to me and the Diocese during the last seven years . . .
> I think that the programmes for the dedication and official opening of the Anglican Vocational Training Centre have been very successful under your chairmanship. We hope and pray that under your care and supervision the project will continue until its completion to the glory of God

and the betterment of the people of Farafenni and the Gambia
as a whole.

Later, on his part, Bishop Johnson decided that as a mark of profound
appreciation for the hard work and significant contributions of Faye to
the establishment of the Centre, the main hall should be named after
him. In fact, some Board members were of the view that the whole
Centre should bear his name; however, this was not likely as he already
had one Anglican educational institution named after him, the Rev. J.
C. Faye Memorial School in Banjul.

Faye on Educational Policy

In the 1950s, in the course of Faye's tenure in the Executive Council/
Cabinet, he demonstrated special interest in educational subjects.
Indeed, as explained in another chapter, in deciding what ministry
to assign to him Governor Wyn-Harris had initially preferred the
Education portfolio. However, he changed his mind as he considered
that a more demanding office would be more suitable.

From the outset, as Executive Council member, Faye demonstrated a
profound knowledge of and commitment to the sector. An example is that
in 1951 the government proposed the introduction of a co-educational and
non-denominational secondary school and commissioned the Baldwin
report to look into requirements for secondary education in The Gambia.
Among the recommendations was the merger of all existing secondary
schools into one common institution. This was acceptable to Faye and
his political party, on condition that additional secondary schools should
also be built in the Protectorate; Armitage School was oversubscribed
and incapable of meeting existing demand. The government turned
down this recommendation and decided instead to build Crab Island
Secondary Modern School as a feeder to the amalgamated high schools.

Faye as Careers Guide and Advisor.

Faye had a knack for identifying appropriate career choices for his
"boys" and preparing them for their careers. In this regard, there is

the example of him having once raised the matter with four of the young men housed at the House of Transfiguration in Bathurst which he supervised.

"Boys," he said, "What would you like to be when you complete your schooling?"

Sam Palmer, the first, replied, "My father spent some time in the medical services and I would like to follow his footsteps and become a medical doctor."

Andrew (Abdoulie) NJie, said, "I would like to be a dentist."

Willie Macauley admitted, "My own father was a catechist and I would like to be a full priest and go back to work in my country, Guinea."

"As for me," said Amang Kanyi, "like Palmer, I would like to be a medical doctor."

Faye thought these to be lofty ambitions. Nevertheless, he proceeded to assist each with books and other reading materials and encouraged them at every opportunity. Eventually, each, excepting Kanyi, did achieve his career ambition. Palmer was among the first batch of Gambian doctors, NJie was the first Gambian dentist, and Macauley the first Bishop of Conakry. Kanyi's father suspected that with his son's continued residence at the House and his close association with Christians he would, in time, be converted; he therefore decided to withdraw the young man on successful completion of his secondary school education. Kanyi was to go into politics and to hold several state ministerial offices.

Faye had such high esteem for the teaching profession that he encouraged young people to adopt it as a career choice. Here, this biographer had his own share of influence from Faye. On graduating from the MBHS with a Cambridge School Certificate he was approached by an official from the Accountant General's Department with a job offer that had attractive prospects, including overseas training and rapid promotion. This was very tempting but first he had to seek approval from Faye. His response was unequivocal:

"My indefatigable son," his usual form of address, "Your father was a teacher. I was a teacher. Your mother was a teacher. Your aunty was a teacher. Therefore, you will also be a teacher."

He concurred. In fact, he had no choice. Faye subsequently arranged for him to be appointed a pupil teacher at St Mary's, and teaching turned out to be a vocation. Indeed, it became a passionate vocation.

In an interview, Faye proudly elaborated on how he discouraged aspirants to chieftaincy positions in the Protectorate not to go for training in the Commissioners Office after their education but to go into teaching. He argued that, as chiefs, all they would do is:

> oppress the people for taxes, sell gunpowder, pocket some of the money, and witness all sorts of corruption. So I told the chiefs to let their children become teachers so they will get enlightenment as well as love of humanity, those who have capacity to teach. But you send them to the office and those who had the potential to be good teachers would become exploiters.[30]

Summary Observations.

Undeterred by the eventual fate of the KK project, Faye's burning preoccupation with education led to his dynamic pioneering role in the planting of the Parsonage Nursery School/Rev. J. C. Faye Memorial School, and the Anglican Vocational Training Centre. The fact that to some extent they have fulfilled their purposes is a massive credit to the man. In each area there was a vacuum which, for whatever reasons, had not been filled by the government or any other organization.

Both institutions were not static and, over time, grew in directions different from their foundation missions, to the extent that they are now unrecognizable in the forms originally conceived by Faye. For these two, just as it was for KK, heavy dependence on external sources turned out to be a debilitating factor and, indisputably, termination of funding ushered in periods of uncertainty and instability. But, both have survived—to the credit of Faye, the seed-sower!

CHAPTER 3

POLITICIAN: BLAZING THE PATH

The political landscape in The Gambia in the pre-1950 period was characterized by the following. First, there were no organized political parties and, as such, political demands were ad hoc and not necessarily linked to the interests of the population at large, political or otherwise; the "political" agenda was broad-based and non-threatening. Second, the activities of the National Congress of British West Africa (NCBWA) and attempts to form a Bathurst Branch dominated the public space, especially in the period from 1920 to 1935; to a large extent "politics" revolved around this movement. Third, the colonial government was all-dominant in policy making; it ensured that it was in full control and that it called the shots. It paid particular attention to anything that smelt like demands for change in the status quo, and constitutional change in particular. One blatant item of evidence was to be seen in the process of composition of the legislative and executive organs, membership of which was highly valued.

Fourth, personality, social class, and family background played dominant roles in decisions as to who to involve in "government". The end result was what Hughes and Perfect call "patrician politics"[1] which gave rise to personal competition and conflicts. Fifth, the majority of the "patricians" originated from other West African British settlements, especially from among the Krio of Sierra Leone. Sixth, politics was concentrated in the Colony Area and completely left out of the Protectorate.

There had been a host of organizations of a political or trade union character before Faye's entry into politics, many of them revolving around Edward Francis Small. To name a few, besides the Bathurst Chapter of the NCBWA there were the Native Defence Union (1919), the Gambia Planters' Syndicate, the Carpenters' and Shipwrights' Society, the Bathurst Trade Union (1929), the Gambia Farmers Cooperative Marketing Association (1929), the Bathurst Rate Payers' Association (1932), the Committee of Citizens, the Gambia Representative Committee (1926), the Bathurst Urban District Council, the Gambia Labour Union (1935) and the Amalgamated Trade Union. Involved in the creation and management of these organizations was a small number of "politicians" from different ethnic and religious backgrounds with whom Faye was to work later or compete for access to the legislative and executive arms of government.

In the late 1940s and 1950s the political system opened up, in tandem with constitutional changes introduced by the colonial government, sometimes in collaboration with indigenous political forces. Most significant, there was the rise of organized political parties with defined structures, manifestos articulating policies to be advocated if elected to office, membership drives, formal political rallies and all the trappings of a political system. This diverged considerably from the informal and diffused "programmes" and fire-fighting strategies that the various interest groups and associations had previously used in pursuing their goals.

This was the overall environment in which Faye's political career was to be launched and in which he was to be a very active player. The dying days of his stay in KK witnessed an unanticipated but major turning point in his life. It involved a re-entry into politics, no longer at the low level of local government but at the highest levels of colonial governance. Here again, as in the education field, Faye was to take a huge leap into the unknown.

Appointment to the Legislative Council, 1947

In the framework of the policy of decolonization adopted by the British colonial administration after World War II, political advancement in the colonies was measured by the representation of locals in the Legislative and Executive Councils, that is, "unofficials" as opposed to "officials."

The principal function of the Legislative Council was "to make and establish all such laws, institutions and ordinances as may from time to time be necessary for the peace, order and good government of our subjects and others within the said present or future settlements in the River Gambia and its dependencies".[2] In its early days the Council had no powers to initiate legislation and the colonial authorities could veto any laws or ordinances adopted by this body.

The first major action to put the Gambia on the road of decolonization was The Gambia (Constitution) Order-in-Council, 1947, which saw a re-composition of the Legislative Council, as for the Executive Council. It now comprised three ex-officio members, three nominated officials, six nominated unofficial members; one more nominated unofficial member represented the commercial houses.

There was provision also for one elected member even though the franchise was limited to the Colony Area. The election to the Council was won by Edward Francis Small who polled 1,491 votes. For the four other candidates the results were: Sheikh Omar Fye—1,018 votes, Ibrahima M. Garba-Jahumpa—679 votes, J. Finden Dailey—4 votes, and Richard S. Rendall who obtained a mere 3 votes.[3]

Small then joined the legislature, the first Gambian to be directly elected to that body. He was a rebel with causes to which he dedicated his life, the overarching mission being to fight against colonialism in all its manifestations, in The Gambia, in West Africa and in the African continent as a whole; and to attack injustice, exploitation, inequality and discrimination in whatever form. For fighting his causes Small set up and led a range of political and professional organizations, political pressure groups, trade unions, and newspapers, most of which are listed above. He had served on the Legislative Council from November 1941 as a nominee of the Bathurst Advisory Town Council (BATC).

In the new order arising from the 1947 Constitution, representation of nominated unofficial members was increased to seven compared to six officials, meaning that for the first time there was a majority of unofficials over officials in the legislature; this had the effect of expanding the base for broader local representation in this organ. For the very first time also the Protectorate was granted a presence in the legislature. Up till then, the form of indirect rule introduced in this part of the country made for little disruption of the traditional ways of life of the people; it was assumed that the system catered for their interests, and definitely insofar as administration was concerned.

But, as will be amply demonstrated in chapters following, notably Chapter 6, this was at the cost of socio-economic development and the involvement of the population in the management of affairs pertaining to their future. It is also of interest to add that the indigenous populations were "British protected" and not "British subjects", which meant that they were denied some of the legal and constitutional rights applicable to the Colony subjects until the late 1950s.[4]

When the issue of Protectorate representation in the legislature arose, the original intention was to divide the area into four constituencies; each would name four persons who were literate in English and of good standing. From these, the Governor would nominate one to represent each of these constituencies. In March 1946, the Divisional Commissioners were requested to hold consultations on the matter during their Conferences of Native Authorities. In June, the Senior Commissioner advised that so new were the issues involved in such representation that the chiefs would accept whatever the Commissioner decided.

The fundamental problem was that there were not sufficient candidates in the Protectorate with a good command of English and who could contribute meaningfully to the work of the legislature. The exception was in the Central River Division which had three chiefs (Tamba Jammeh, Karamo Kabba Sanneh and Matarr Sise) who were sufficiently literate in English, so their names were forwarded to the Governor. The concept of representation on a divisional basis was not rejected but was held in abeyance.[5]

Concerning the URD the local authorities met under their chiefs in Basse and agreed on Faye as the only person whom they trusted to represent them. The Commissioner in the Division conveyed this to the Senior Commissioner who also "supported the recommendation and recorded his full confidence in Mr. Faye". The Governor in his own correspondence with the Colonial Office added that:

> The recommendation has, indeed, been supported by all
> whom I have been able to consult; Mr. Faye is well-known
> here for his unselfishness and devotion to duty and for his
> outstanding work as an Anglican Mission teacher, formerly
> in Bathurst but now in Kristi-kunda in the Upper River
> Division. I am satisfied that this would be an excellent
> appointment if Mr. Faye felt able to accept it.[6]

The Commissioner directed that this decision should be treated with the utmost secrecy; in no circumstances was Faye to be informed as, if so, it was likely that he would turn down the offer given the magnitude of the challenges he was grappling with at KK. It was Governor Andrew Barkworth Wright (1947-1949) himself who visited KK and broke the news to Faye. Though appreciative, Faye pointed out that he would first have to seek the approval of his Bishop. But any such consultation had been pre-empted by the Governor who had already obtained the Bishop's consent. In fact, according to the Governor, the Bishop had added: "Now I can see the Gambia shot up like a rocket as the people of this most backward area can choose so well."[7]

The Bishop's pride in this development was also reflected in the fact that after a subsequent visit to Conakry, Guinea, he recounted to Faye that the Roman Catholic Vicar-General (there was no Roman Catholic Bishop in Conakry then) had congratulated him on the selection of Faye; the Vicar-General saw this as a compliment to the whole Christian community, given that the constituents who had chosen him as their one and only nominee were all Muslims.[8]

Thus, the Protectorate was represented in the Legislative Council by four legislators composed of three Chiefs (Jammeh, Sanneh, and Sise) and Reverend J.C. Faye.

It is noteworthy that, in the process of selecting these nominees two other constituencies had been considered by the Governor. The trade union movement, though embryonic, was deserving of its own representation but the Governor observed that at least two of the candidates for the planned Legislative Council elections (E.F. Small and I. M. Garba-Jahumpa) were involved in trade unionism. The second constituency, the women, were considered by the Governor for appointment in order to represent their own special interests; already two or three names had been submitted to the Governor. The decision of the Governor, then, was that ". . . if Mr. John Faye should decline to serve, and no other suitable candidate be forthcoming to represent Protectorate interests, I should be disposed, on general grounds, to appoint a woman."[9]

Appointment to the Executive Council, 1947

The Executive Council had a history going back to the founding of the Colony. Following its divestiture from the administration from Sierra Leone in 1843 The Gambia became a Crown Colony with its own Governor, Executive Council, and Legislative Council, both answerable to the Governor. However this was not to last, as 23 years later, in 1866, administration of the British territories in West Africa was again centralized in Freetown. The Executive Council was abolished. This arrangement was confirmed when in 1874 the four settlements (The Gambia, Gold Coast, Lagos, and Sierra Leone) were consolidated into two, with The Gambia continuing under Sierra Leone jurisdiction. Not till 1888 was there a final separation and the legislative and executive bodies in The Gambia restored.

The appointment of African unofficials to the Executive Council began in the Gold Coast (later Ghana) and Nigeria, with Sierra Leone following. In The Gambia, few unofficials had served on the Executive Council throughout the decades. Governor Hilary Blood (1942-1947) accepted the idea in principle but could not implement it as there were no suitable candidates. But, at least he was able to ensure the passage of The Gambia (Constitution) Order-in-Council, 1947, according to which two of the nominated unofficial members and the one elected member would become unofficial Members of the Executive Council.

The primary function of the Executive Council was "to advise and assist the Governor . . . in the administration of the Government".[10] The Governor consulted with the members in the execution of his official duties except where these involved matters adjudged to be sensitive, minor, or too urgent. He was not obliged to accept the Council's advice but was expected to inform the Colonial Office in London in instances where he acted against the views of the Council.

The Executive Council enjoyed high status in the colonial set-up and membership was coveted both by the colonial officials and the local elites. It confirmed one's position at the highest level of society and afforded access to the corridors of policy-making. Membership was in the two categories of "officials" and "unofficials" and, as indicated above, one means of denoting progress in constitutional development was the proportion of one to the other. Essentially, representation of unofficials was from the non-public sector and "civil society" compared to representation of officials from within the colonial administration.

Faye was appointed by Governor Andrew Barkworth Wright in November 1947 to serve on the Council. He was joined by Seyfo (Chief) Tamba Jammeh—also representing Protectorate interests—and Edward F. Small, the elected member.[11] Thus, Faye, like Tamba Jammeh, was a member of both the legislature and the executive simultaneously.

This was a singular honour and a deserved recognition of Faye's sterling personal qualities and outstanding competences. It was even more telling in that such recognition came from the colonial administration with which Faye was to be at great odds in the decade or so following. As noted above, though a thoroughbred Colony man, Faye was one of the few who knew the Protectorate well, was widely respected by the inhabitants and the traditional leadership, and was ready to make sacrifices for the benefit of the less privileged members of Gambian society. All these were to be of consequence in his later political life.

Member of the British Empire

Faye was said to be much respected by both Governors Hilary Blood and Andrew Barkworth Wright. It was Governor Blood who before his departure from The Gambia nominated Faye to the Secretary of State for the Colonies for the award of the insignia of Member of the Order of the British Empire (MBE) by His Majesty King George VI; it was bestowed on him in January 1947. This honour is still given to individuals who have provided outstanding and dedicated service in and to their communities, or undertaken local practical activities which stand out as examples to others. There was no one better placed than the Governor himself who had visited KK and seen the massive transformation that had taken place over a relatively short period of time, due primarily to the leadership, hard work and dedication of Faye. He was convinced that by any standards Faye had met all the requirements for the honour and was a deserving candidate.

The African Conference 1948

In his turn, in January 1948, Governor Wright received an invitation from the Secretary of State for the Colonies for the Gambia to send delegates to an African Conference, in London, from 29 September to 13 October 1948. The matter was referred to the Legislative Council which unanimously adopted a resolution empowering its President (that is, the Governor) to select one official and two unofficial members to attend. After further consultations with the Legislative Council, the Governor decided that Edward F. Small and Faye should represent the Council; the delegation would be led by the Attorney General, an official member.

To illustrate what a great privilege it was for Faye to be selected to attend this conference, the Governor had expressed interest in increasing Gambian representation to accommodate one more person, C. L. Page, the local manager of the United Africa Company (UAC) and a nominated member of the Legislative Council. Wright argued:

> Page has been in The Gambia for so many years, knows its problems and people so well and is so good natured and sensible that I feel he would be a valuable addition not just from our local point of view but from that of the general mixing of types and pooling of views which must be important features of the event.[12]

Wright further argued that the Attorney General, though well qualified to "be the mouthpiece and sponsor of our delegation", lacked experience of the country and familiarity with the type of problems to be discussed at the conference. But, "with the two Africans on the one hand and with Page on the other he should do very well and derive much personal benefit from the opportunity."

Page requested, and the Governor concurred, that even if he was not selected as a full member of the delegation, he should be permitted to attend at his own expense, as he would be on leave in England during the conference period. In principle, the Colonial Office welcomed the suggestion of Page's membership of the delegation and saw no objection to increasing it to four. But, there was the likelihood that "in the present circumstance" representation of one of the African territories by an employee of the UAC would result in criticism. Any such criticism could only be blunted if Page were to attend as a full member of the delegation and of the Legislative Council, and selected according to the same procedures as the other delegation members. If, in addition, the unofficial members of the Council were also in agreement, then Whitehall would go along.[13]

After further reflection and consultations, the Governor decided not to pursue the matter. He recognized that including Page on the delegation would entail bringing another resolution to Council to accommodate one more unofficial member and this would be "a political mistake".[14]

The Conference assembled members of the legislatures of British colonies in East, Central and West Africa to exchange views on a diverse range of subjects especially on constitutional matters as they related to the colonies. It dealt, in depth, with current economic problems and development strategies, agriculture issues, public relations, medical and education policy, and local government.[15] All in all, it:

> provided a public demonstration both of Africa's prominent position within a redefined post-War Empire and of the Labour Government's new Africa policy. This policy, responding to an increasing African political consciousness and to Britain's own declining international standing, is most succinctly described as one of 'political advancement and community development'.[16]

Of especial interest to the delegates was the statement by the Secretary of State for the Colonies outlining his government's policy on the African territories, including political developments. It was in this context that he laid out basic elements of policy:

> Certain broad lines of policy are accepted by all sections of the House of Commons as being above party-politics, two of these are fundamental. First, we all aim at helping the colonial territories to attain self-government within the Commonwealth. To that end, secondly, we are seeking, as rapidly as possible, to build up in each territory the institutions which circumstances require.[17]

This must have been inspirational to Faye and it influenced his politics in the years to come. As he observed, it was at this conference "that the ball of independence started to be rolled and London was convinced that British West Africa at least was mature and worthy of greater autonomy".[18] On his return to Bathurst, Faye confided to some close associates that he had met Dr. Hastings Banda of Malawi at the conference; Banda had been very impressed by Faye's performance and even invited him to go to southern Africa to assist the stillborn pro-independence movement.

Governor Wright's Transfer—Faye on the Attack

In the prevailing environment of Bathurst, Faye's relationship with the Governor and his exposure to international audiences must have earned him the enmity of others. This was to worsen in the months to come, after Governor Wright's tenure. Perhaps the main reason for the affinity between the two men was that, by all accounts, Wright was progressive and had a plan for decolonization which would see a programmed take-over by the Gambians in all sectors of society, particularly governmental organs, the civil service, the judiciary and the private sector.

At the personal level, Wright had trust and confidence in and respect for the emergent Gambian political class, particularly Faye.* He was very relaxed with them and on a first name basis with people like Faye. He consulted with Faye on an informal basis as and when he thought necessary and, quite frequently, would request his fellow colonial administrators to leave the room when he had private matters to raise with Faye. Wright directed that a government vehicle should be sent to KK every month to bring Faye to meetings of the Executive Council, just as for the chiefs. In addition, he had arranged for all matters pertaining to education, agriculture and of general Protectorate interest to be put on the agenda of meetings at the beginning of the month so as to enable Faye and the chiefs to contribute to policymaking processes in these sectors.

All this was deeply appreciated by Faye and the other leaders. But, both among many of the Governor's collaborators in Bathurst and some officials in London this type of relationship was wholly repugnant. For the likes of Faye, there was no doubt that it was a primary reason why Wright was recalled after only two years of service (1947-1949) instead of at the conclusion of the usual four/five years. Since 1930, no other Governor had served for such a short period; by contrast, his successor, Wyn-Harris, was in office for a record nine years.

The announcement of the transfer of Governor Barkworth Wright to Cyprus was made by the Colonial Office in early May 1949. The official reason for this decision was that the political situation in Cyprus was getting more and more complex and Barkworth Wright would be a suitable replacement to the outgoing Governor because of his previous experience there.

This sudden and unexpected development was unacceptable to members of the Legislative and Executive Councils, and Faye, supported by Small, took on the leadership role in handling the response. Following consultations, he decided to adopt a seven-pronged strategy whose basic

---

* Each of the colonial Governors was said to have a favourite among the political leaders: for Barkworth Wright (1947-49) it was Faye; for Percy Wyn-Harris (1949-58) it was Garba-Jahumpa; for Edward Windley (1958-62) it was NJie; and for John Paul (1962-66), Jawara.

goal was to put maximum pressure on the Colonial Office to reconsider and, possibly, rescind its decision—or at least, delay Wright's departure for as long as was feasible.

The strategy also aimed at demonstrating how widespread was the opposition to the Governor's transfer. That is, opposition was not personal to Faye and Small, but inclusive of a wide spectrum of society. Telegrams, petitions, resolutions, and letters addressed to Arthur Creech Jones, the Secretary of State for the Colonies, were the means of communicating their grievances; a protest demonstration in Bathurst was the ultimate weapon to be used if it became necessary.

First, a telegram from African members of the Legislative and Executive Councils was despatched to London, in which they noted that the announcement of the transfer:

> has caused widespread feelings of disappointment and frustration in this country. All communities here wholeheartedly support the Governor's policy and are apprehensive that the sudden change of his administration would have an adverse effect on the country's welfare.

They requested an extension of his term of office so he could continue the "healthy policy he has only had two years to outline and pursue". They further assured the powers that be that provision could be made for the extra costs involved, in that:

> the African majority of the Standing Finance Committee is prepared to support the grant of an extra personal allowance to His Excellency to offset any financial loss the proposed extension of his term may entail.

The message was signed by E. F. Small, J. C. Faye and Abdu Wally Mbye on behalf of the group.[19]

The second prong was a resolution adopted unanimously at an extraordinary meeting of the Bathurst Town Council on 16 May 1949 for the attention of the Secretary of State. Besides highlighting the virtues of the Governor and the plans he had spearheaded, the Council members expressed full ratification of the text of the telegram addressed to Creech Jones, the Colony Secretary, by Small, Faye, and A. W. Mbye.[20]

Third, another telegram conveyed a resolution addressed to the Secretary of State on behalf of a mass meeting attended by people from all sections of the community; it was signed by Faye as the convenor and Rene Valentine as Chairman. This resolution was supported by a petition which elaborated on most of the arguments that had been made, or were to be made, by all the other interested parties. It opened on the note that the news of the transfer had been received "with great dismay and much perturbation". The grounds for the petition were that "Sir Andrew has proved himself to be a very liberal and progressive administrator whose interest in the welfare of the peoples under his administration has been of a nature truly well-meaning and deeply-abiding."

Other qualities were that Wright was amiable, accessible, had a positive and confident outlook and was devoted to duty, which "endeared himself to all classes of the Colony and Protectorate". In particular, the petitioners singled out the Africanization policy, which was a model for other West African colonies: "the smooth and peaceable introduction of this policy is due to the personal initiative and persuasion of Sir Andrew who has been able to avoid any friction and upheaval in the process." Finally, the meeting suspected that the transfer of Governor Wright would lead to "a retardation on the part of his successor, of the policy of liberal advance, and a frustration of the prospects of the African inhabitants of the small, but loyal, Colony of The Gambia".

Based on all these arguments, the request was that the term of office of the Governor be continued for the next three years "in order that he will bring to complete fruition the policies he has so ably initiated with such good will towards the peoples of this place". The petition was first signed by Faye, followed by such luminaries as R. Valentine, the Almami of Bathurst, Lenrie Peters, C. R. L. Page, Ousman Jeng, Sam Sylva, Matarr Silla, Lucy Joiner, Erskine Richards, Judith Mensah, Ebrima Samba, and at least 25 other persons; more would have signed but could not because of the limited time available before the transmittal of the message to London.[21]

Fourth, Faye followed this petition with a personal letter to Creech Jones, in which he repeated, in very strong language, some of the above, and related, points. He recalled that, just a few months earlier at the African Conference in September/October 1948, he, Faye, had warned that:

> the advancement of the smaller colonies is always hampered and retarded by the quick transfers of deserving officers who have set their minds on their work and are doing excellently at their posts. The sooner good officials are left to serve longer at places where their work is appreciated by the peoples with whom—and for whom—they work, the better shall it be for the countries concerned, and the better shall it make for solidarity and greater understanding in the Commonwealth and Empire.[22]

Faye concluded by noting that movement of expatriate officers "who are proved to be misfits" is understandable, but "it is always upsetting so to do in the case of energetic and progressive officials whose hasty and sudden removal would not ensure the execution of the plans they have studied and mastered."[23]

Fifth, the Gambia Teachers Union, as an organized special interest group, sent a terse telegram to Creech Jones also reiterating its regret at the sudden transfer of the Governor and appealing for an extension of his term. Its petition, which followed the telegram, reiterated many of the positions expressed by other bodies and individuals, especially "the robust and progressive" policies promoted by the Governor which were beneficial to the people. [24]

As regards its own professional interests, the Union noted that Sir Andrew had instituted a Whitley Council for Teachers and appointed committees to review the salaries and emoluments of the teachers. Hence: "We leave it to Your Excellency to imagine the sense of apprehension we feel and/or fear that these matters may be allowed to languish and perish through inattention and lack of interest." The petitioners were realistic enough to know that the request for retention for another three years would not see the light of day. They therefore pleaded that the successor would be advised to follow in the footsteps of Sir Andrew "in order that the feelings of loyalty and confidence in the

Administration may be enhanced to a degree greater than ever before". The petition was signed by E. F. N. Asamoah, the President, and the other 11 members of the Executive Committee.

Sixth, there were petitions from prominent individuals. An example was that of Lucy Elizabeth Joiner, a successful Krio/Aku businesswoman and a staunch and loyal supporter of Faye.[25] On this occasion, she sent a very touching and sentimental appeal for the Secretary of State's "kind and sympathetic consideration toward myself and the members of my sex who inhabit this remote corner of His Majesty's Empire". She pleaded for a reconsideration of "your decision in removing from our midst one who has fully represented the very high principles of British rule and administration and without fear or favour, and with ill will to no one, has held the reins of Government of this Ancient and Loyal country, with unparalleled discretion and ambidexterity". The announcement of Governor Wright's transfer had presented "a dark and gloomy cloud all over Gambia today and which registers a red-letter day never before in the annals of this most Ancient and Loyal country".

Joiner spoke glowingly of Wright's development programmes for the country which were long overdue and which, with his transfer, "will die un-natural death and the humane objects for which Sir Andrew has laid them will be frustrated." Concluding, she pleaded:

> In the name of Gambia's womanhood, in the name of the time-honoured and pristine justice of Good Old England I pray you to let and permit us to reap the harvest of peace for which our brave sons have died and laid down their precious lives.

Seventh, there was a threat to mount a "No Wright, No Groundnuts" campaign but this was nipped in the bud by the government. Faye and his supporters then organized a mass demonstration which received only token support from die-hard Faye devotees. This may have been because people were largely unaware of their right to this means of protest; it had not been established as part of the political culture in the country.

In response to these varied actions, the Secretary of State and his colleagues warmly welcomed the profound appreciations of the character and good works of Governor Barkworth Wright, on the part of the Gambian subjects. He considered the offer to provide extra allowance to offset any financial loss that an extension of his tenure might entail as particularly thoughtful. But, while not belittling the problems of The Gambia and its special needs, Creech Jones noted to Wright that: "in the present circumstances, Cyprus, of which you have such long experience, has an even greater need for your services." He explained generally that it was strictly "on grounds of highest public interest that I recommended to His Majesty that Sir Andrew Wright should go to Cyprus and should take up his duties there as soon as possible."[26]

Nonetheless, he assured all concerned that:

> I much regret that these considerations have caused the public of The Gambia to lose a Governor who enjoyed their confidence so greatly, and I repeat that when I come to advise on the selection of a successor the representations which have been made to me will be kept most sympathetically in mind. [27]

In the end, Sir Andrew did leave the shores of The Gambia in December 1949, moving on to Cyprus. Faye's last gesture of goodwill was the presentation of what he titled "An Illuminated Address to Sir Andrew Barkworth Wright, K. C. M. G., C. B. E., M. C. From the Peoples of The Gambia". It was copied to the Officer Administering the Government and the Secretary of State for the Colonies.

The "tribute of gratitude" recorded the appreciation of the people for Wright's "unswerving attention to all matters relating to the progress and advancement of this country". Africanization and other afore-mentioned achievements of the previous two years were raised again. A mass meeting at St Augustine School convened by Faye and chaired by R. C. Valentine endorsed the Illuminated Address; it also advised that henceforth machinery for consultation with the African members of the Councils should be set up in cases where the exigencies of the service required the transfer of a Governor. This the Colonial Office turned down.

No other Governor's departure had given rise to so much anxiety in The Gambia and treated as an opportunity for Gambians to demonstrate their gratitude and affection. The experience was the first of such magnitude, scope, and intensity, and one of the first that involved direct access to London for redress. In the years following more such direct representations were to follow on many other matters. Though the overall aim was not realized the experience was to be of great value in the future, especially for Faye and the new politicians of the coming years.

Formation of the Gambia Democratic Party (DP), 1951

It seems that Faye started to develop a serious interest in politics when he was approached by Eustace Richards, on behalf of E. F. Small, to stand as a candidate of the Rate Payers' Association (RPA) in the elections to the BATC in 1940. The RPA was made up of prominent elders in the town who made representations to government on matters of interest to the people. Officially, it was not a political party but had some of the characteristics of one. Richards himself had been a founding member of the NCBWA in 1920 and was close to Small.

Faye was reluctant, but could not afford to turn down a request from Richards, a close family friend and someone he considered an elder to be respected. Some other leading members of the RPA added their pressure on Faye and he eventually stood in the Jolof and Portuguese Town ward in the local government elections; he was unopposed. He subsequently moved to the Soldier Town ward in 1941 and 1942, which also returned him unopposed in the elections. With Faye's move to KK he had to resign from the BATC in November 1942.

Even in these early days it was useful for Faye to be an active member of public organizations. In most of the colonies throughout both "British" and "French" West Africa, involvement in trade unionism was a passport to a career in politics. In many cases, unionism served as a bridgehead to politics; either unionists metamorphosed into politicians or politicians "used" unionism to further their own ends. Unions afforded an opportunity to build the constituencies and core support bases needed in the pursuit of political ambitions.

One reason for this was that trade unions were among the few organizations to have legal rights to exist and, though they were often banned by the authorities, the right to organize to protect workers' interests was more or less inviolable. The fact that there were strong international networks able to "protect" the fragile African national unions was beneficial. It was partly for these and related reasons that trade unions proliferated in the colonies. Gambia was no exception.[28]

Faye was involved in the Ship-Wrights' Union. More for professional than political reasons, he was also an active foundation member of the Gambia Teachers Union (GTU). The Union was founded on 9 February 1937 and its Rules and Regulations were approved on 19 March 1937, signed by M. K. Hunter, J. Emanuel Mahoney, J. H. Bolingbroke Fowlis and C. W. Downes-Thomas. Downes-Thomas was its first Honorary Secretary. Up to the time of his departure for KK, Faye was its Liaison Officer and negotiator with the Gambia government.

Essentially, the GTU aimed to protect the rights and benefits of its members and bargain for fair terms and conditions of service. As stated in its Rules and Regulations, the aims and objectives were to be:

> (a) The development of the intellectual, social, physical and moral standard of teachers; (b) the promotion of good fellowship among teachers; (c) the maintenance of better relationships between teachers and local education authorities.[29]

Despite the similarities, the GTU was officially seen as more of a trade association than a trade union; the colonial authorities admitted that "it did not require registration as it does not fall within the definition of either a Trade Union or a Friendly Society."[30] Though it devoted its resources predominantly to its stated objectives and had no direct political ambitions, it served as a model for other civil groups pursuing their own rights. Faye represented the union on the committee set up by government (1941-1942) to study the status of teachers and the mode of granting subventions to schools. As a result of its work, a new salary scale for teachers was adopted by the government; also, payment of grants to missions was to be based on the salaries of teachers and not on "per capita" passage by pupils as before.

But, like some others before and after him, Faye also ventured into trade unionism as a means of building his own base and mobilizing popular support for his political ends. Thus, he engineered the creation of the Gambia Motor Drivers' and Mechanics' Union (GMDMU) a few months before the 1951 elections. The union was mainly for taxi drivers and, at the height of its popularity, claimed its membership to be as many as 600, of whom more than half paid their dues. Their votes might have been decisive in the elections—just as Faye had anticipated.

After the elections, Faye appears to have lost interest in unionism; even though he was blessed with many competences, trade unionism was a domain beyond his reach. The GMDMU drifted from 1952 to 1962, when attempts were made to inject new life into it. However, in 1970 it wound up and many of its members formed a new Gambia Motor Drivers and Allied Workers' Union, which continued to operate through the 1980s.[31]

On the political front, Faye spearheaded attempts to establish the Bathurst branch of the West African Youth League. He started off as the Bathurst distributor of the League's newspaper and subsequently embarked on recruiting members; this was problematical as most of the target group of educated Gambians were civil servants who, in general, were prohibited from participating in political activities, holding political offices or addressing political meetings. Besides, professionals in areas such as the law frowned on simple schoolmasters like Faye in their desire to challenge the status quo. On the other hand, independent citizens such as Pa Henry Jones supported Faye's initiative.

The League was founded in Accra in June 1935 by I. T. A. Wallace-Johnson of Sierra Leone and was one of the most radical organizations of the times. Its motto was "Liberty or Death" and its manifesto pledge read as follows:

> We the Youth of [Name of Country] and of West Africa
> in general, in order to form a more united body to watch
> carefully and sincerely affairs political, educational,

economical and otherwise, that may be to the interest of the masses of the motherland, to sacrifice, if need be, all we have for the progress and liberty of our Country, and to ensure happiness to ourselves and our prosperity.[32]

The paramount objective of the movement was to secure greater African "parliamentary" representation in the colonies so as to increase Africans' say in the running of their affairs. Like the NCBWA it sought to protect natural and constitutional rights, liberties and privileges for the African peoples. It was closely allied to Communist parties in Europe and Wallace-Johnson himself was well-schooled in socialist ideology.

The movement was intended to be pan-West Africa, incorporating English, French and Portuguese colonies. In Ghana, Nigeria, and in Johnson's own Sierra Leone, it organized strikes in various industries; in fact, Johnson, an articulate and formidable agitator, worked with Small in organizing the workers' strikes in The Gambia in 1929. From its Marxist-Leninist perspective, the League was scathingly opposed to colonialism and its inherent injustices. Through political meetings and its newspapers, the *African Standard* and *Dawn*, it campaigned for better conditions for workers, for national unity and for a greater role for the masses in political and civic affairs.

On his return to Bathurst from KK in February 1949, Faye plunged actively into local politics, taking up from where he had left off in 1942. This was now easier for him, firstly because he was getting familiar with the world of government and politics since his appointment to the Executive and Legislative Councils, and secondly because his role in the KK project was now virtually at an end and his services no longer required. He was a relatively free agent—except for his minor duties in the Church.

Surprisingly, Faye was not prevented by Bishop Daly from going into politics; instead, the Bishop permitted him to combine his politics with his Church functions. Then again, though Faye and his family were Christians, he was also encouraged to become active in politics by the Muslim leadership in Bathurst. Imam Mama Tumaneh Ba, the Imam Ratib of Bathurst, visited him at his home in Fitzgerald Street with seven Muslim elders, including Omar Jallow (the Imam's secretary), Ousman

NJie Moji, Ibrahima Ndow, Demba Ndow, and others. Faye recalled that, after the usual salutations, Ousman Moji stood up and informed him of their appreciation of all he was doing in the Executive Council and that, though his work had been concentrated in the URD, he was actually benefiting the whole country. This, they observed, was nothing strange as they could see that Faye was wearing the shoes of his father.

The delegation then requested Faye to form a political party to contest the (1951) elections as, for one thing, there was no guarantee that the new Governor, Wyn-Harris, would nominate Faye again to the Council, and the chiefs themselves might nominate someone else instead. The surest way of guaranteeing Faye's presence on Council was for him to be a candidate in the elections.[33]

Faye requested them to give him a week or so to consult with other parties such as the Church, selected chiefs, and his old KK community. In these extensive consultations, some warned that the Bathurst population was fickle-minded and undependable and would let Faye down. But the majority consulted were in support, as they saw this as another opportunity for Faye to continue to serve the country. Indeed, this was very much in line with Faye's own thinking; so he informed the Imam and party of his readiness to accede to what they had asked.[34] A few weeks later, another nine-member multi-ethnic multi-religious Bathurst delegation also visited Faye with the same request.

Strong opposition came from within Faye's family. Some members argued forcefully that the risks involved were too high and that he would soon find himself in the jaws of the lion; in time, they warned, the people would let him down, just as they had done to Edward Small. Faye's first cousin, Samuel Owens Jarra (Modou Jarra), wrote a long letter to him mainly cautioning that politics was a dirty business in which people from respectable families should not participate. To all these Faye responded comprehensively, stressing, in particular, that he had an obligation to answer the call of the people to go and serve them. He was very convincing in his arguments, and Jarra, for one, relented. Out of courtesy, Faye also consulted Governor Wyn-Harris for his opinion on the formation of a political party. The Governor advised against it. He cautioned that the country was too small and peaceful for one and advised that Faye should form an "all-comers committee" or some such organization but not call it a political party.

Faye convened a meeting at the Catholic Mission Schoolroom on Hagan Street on Thursday 22 February 1951, which he chaired. It was attended by about 200 persons, "representative of all classes of the African community". The purpose, as stated by him, was to discuss the formation of a new political party to canvass for the next Legislative Council elections; it was also to promote unity of political purpose among the people and promote unity among the trade unions. A committee of five (S. E. NJie, Pa Henry M. Jones, Koto Richards, Idrissa Samba, and Gormac NJie) was appointed to work out the details. These were to be considered at another meeting, to be held in the near future, at which the party would be formed and a name adopted. [35]

Backed by the Committee of Union and Progress, Faye organized other meetings, bringing together a variety of multi-purpose groups to debate his ideas on future political directions for the country.[36] These became very popular rallies and attracted broad support. It therefore came as no surprise when, after a meeting of a cross-section of the Bathurst community at the Information Bureau on Allen Street in Bathurst, a decision was taken on 25 February 1951 (Faye's birthday) to form the Gambia Democratic Party (DP).

Faye and his team devoted the next few months to strengthening the foundations of the party. In June 1951 the birth of the DP was confirmed by him at a public meeting at McCarthy Square in the centre of Bathurst. The fundamental objective of the party was to work for unity between the Colony and Protectorate and agitate for a continuance of the policy of Africanization; the party was also to sensitize government of "the desire of the electorate for two of its representatives to be appointed as Ministers without portfolio".[37] Key guiding principles of the party were:

- It was always to have a united front; the country was one and it should not be divided.
- Bathurst did not have a monopoly of leadership; leaders of the party could come from any part of the country.
- The party must endeavour to improve the lot of the population in general: workers in town and farmers in the rural areas.

- It would fight for a better constitution for the country so that representation would be more elective than by nomination.

Among the foundation members attending the February meeting were the following: Councillor Hannah Forster; Ousman NJie Keen, Ousman NJie Moji, Mamanding Dampha; Mustapha Colley; Crispin R. Grey-Johnson; Crispin Jones (Koni Bagbey); H. M. Jones; L. C. Cherry; Momodou Jagne (Benda); H. R. Noah (Priding); Modou Ceesay; Kumba NJie (Lysa); Alieu Gibril; Koto Richards; M. E. Ndure; Ferguson Mahoney; Jones Lewis; and A. E. Cham-Joof. According to sources, I. M. Garba-Jahumpa was also in attendance and, in fact, he it was who proposed that the name of the party should be the Gambia Democratic Party, a proposal that was unanimously accepted.

This, indeed, was a diverse group of persons if ever there was one. The same was true of the office holders and the Executive Committee which included Faye as Leader, and others such as Alhaji Basiru Jagne, Henry Jones, Koto Richards, Crispin Grey-Johnson, Alieu E. Cham-Joof, Louis Cherry, Dawda NJie, and Saihou NJie.

Grass-roots support for the DP came from mixed constituencies but at the core were Krio Christians (Protestants). In the policy-making bodies Krio representation was out of proportion to their numbers in the Bathurst or Gambian population. Historically, the Krio had migrated to The Gambia from Sierra Leone and Nigeria either for trade purposes or to staff the lower echelons of the colonial civil service and the more specialized positions in the public service, for which they could be released by the administrations in the other colonies. They dominated the social and political life of Colony society, the professions (particularly law, medicine, accountancy, and teaching) and business. They were also accorded special recognition and privileged positions by the colonial government. It was their kith and kin who in the nineteenth and twentieth centuries had led the struggle against the merger of the Gambian and Sierra Leonean administrations with Freetown as the headquarters, especially during the second merger from 1866 to 1888. They had also fought against the control of the governance of the Colony by the mercantile class; against an educational system that was second-class compared to that in Freetown; and against the merger of English Gambia with French Senegal.

The Krio were known for their pride in their British connections, which was manifested in their glorification of British education, their devotion to Protestantism and British names, and in their dress, eating habits and residential patterns. Among the African population they constituted an elite and set standards for other ethnicities.[38]

"Krio" is the name by which the group identifies itself, its language and culture; authorities on the subject, such as Florence Mahoney, have used the terms "Liberated Africans" or "recaptives". The related "Creole" is used interchangeably with "Krio" in other West African countries in which they settled, stretching from The Gambia to Cameroun. Only in The Gambia is the group also known as "Aku". It was more widely used in the capital and particularly among the Wolofs; over time it gained popular currency and spread to other ethnic groups. As regards officialdom, from the early days of settlement in the 1820s the name "Aku" was also used in official colonial communications and regular correspondence. In particular, the group was identified as "Aku" in official population and other censuses.

Given the need to accommodate these realities, in this biography "Krio/Aku" is used for this population cohort.

DP supporters also came from the evolving indigenous broad-based class of professionals, businessmen, civil servants, traders, teachers and the like. Some backers of E. F. Small supported the new organization. Given the character of Gambian society, both Christians and Muslims and an admixture of ethnicities featured among both the leadership and the followership. At one point, Faye even had members of the St Mary's (Anglican) Group, the Catholic Young Men's Group, and the Bathurst Young Muslims Society (BYMS) on his side. The support of many of the constituents in his old Jolof and Portuguese Town Ward and Soldier Town Ward, which Faye had represented in the BATC, was assured.

Of interest is the steady support Faye and his DP received from the relatively small Oku-Marabout community, made up of Krio/Aku who were Muslims. One reason was that, like the Christian Krio/Aku, they mostly hailed from Sierra Leone where the two groups maintained close communal relationships; this to the extent of inter-marriages and the sharing of cultural assets. Also, they spoke the same language (Krio) and there were bonds of lineage between the two groups traceable to the Yorubas of south-western Nigeria.

A case in point is that of Moulie Alieu Gibril (Long Street, Bathurst) who loyally and faithfully stood by Faye and his DP through thick and thin. He was a founder member of the party and a signatory to various petitions sent at different times to the Secretary of State for the Colonies pleading the case of the party. Gibril contributed to the party substantially, in cash and kind, throughout the years. He regularly attended party meetings across the capital and ensured that the party's message was spread in the various trading stations in the Protectorate where he worked. Other Oku-Marabout loyalists of the DP were from the Abdul Fatah Betts, Othman, Denton, and Mamadou Cole families.

Without this strategy of recruiting the leadership and support groups from different communities, especially Muslim and Wolof, there is no way the DP would have survived. As put by Cham-Joof, one of the DP main organizers, "Faye . . . advocated a non-denominational, secular party and preached for the coalition of a broad-based all-embracing mass organization that espoused the principle of unity and freedom for the Gambian people."[39] In many respects, Faye himself was a composite of his support base; in terms of ethnic origins, language competences, family background and religious affinities, he easily identified with the different components of his followership.

Elections to the Legislative Council, 1951

Under the Gambia (Constitution) Order in Council, 1951, the number of elected members to the Legislative Council was increased to three; of these two were to come from Bathurst and one from the neighbouring Kombo St Mary. Protectorate representation remained the same, at four chiefs, as recommended by chiefs at Divisional Chiefs' Conference. There was also a re-composition of the Executive Council in which there were to be four unofficials, selected from among both the unofficial and elected members of the Legislative Council. Two of the four unofficial Executive Council members were to be appointed "members of the government", which meant that they could provide advice to the Governor on specific subjects as required but were not allocated "ministerial" portfolios—i.e. this was more of an advisory arrangement and definitely not a full ministerial system.[40] They were also expected to support any matter within their purview introduced in the Legislative Council; if they could not support the administration on any major issue they would be compelled to resign.

As the law-making bodies had well passed the mid-point of their existence, the administration decided to conduct new elections under the new Constitution. Before then, at the Legislative Council meeting of 8 May 1951, Faye was selected to travel to London, from 9 to 30 July 1951, to be the sole delegate of the country at the Festival of Britain. The Festival, which started in May 1951, was a national architectural exhibition with the principal site on the South Bank in London; local and travelling exhibitions and festival ships toured cities and towns throughout Britain. It was an occasion for the British to celebrate their artistic, industrial and scientific achievements and the country's recovery and progress after the devastating Second World War, and to promote better quality design in the rebuilding of towns and cities. It also commemorated the centenary of the 1851 Great Exhibition. The delegations met with representatives of the British Government in Church House, London.

The second elections to the Legislative Council were held on 25 October 1951. Faye (DP) was one of the seven candidates; the others were P. S. NJie (Independent), Edward F. Small (Gambia National League), I. M. Garba-Jahumpa (Bathurst Young Muslim Society), J. Finden Dailey (Common People's Party), Mustapha Colley (Common People's Party), and J. Francis Senegal (Independent).[41] For the Kombo seat the contestants were: Howsoon Semega-Janneh, John Williamson Kuye, and Henry A. Madi (a very wealthy Lebanese businessman with family roots in The Gambia going back decades).

Concerning campaign issues, Faye and his DP were strong critics of the Constitution. Of highest priority for them was:

> political advance within the British Commonwealth of
> nations, particularly by the appointment of Gambian
> ministers-without-portfolios, to increase responsibility of

African members, and to ensure closer association of the
Government with the people.

The party manifesto vigorously opposed the constitutional provision
that each voter should have only a single vote in a dual-member
constituency.

Another issue which pitted the administration against the DP and
helped it project a radical anti-colonial image in the manifesto were
the strictures imposed on the "members of the government", which,
the DP argued, should be replaced by a full ministerial system. It also
demanded "a speeding up of Africanization of the civil service, to be
followed by the mercantile community". The cooperative movement
should be further developed and Gambian participation in commerce
increased. As regards education, the party advocated improvements in
educational facilities and the introduction of civic rights and duties in
the school curriculum. Finally, the DP manifesto promised to promote
unity among different sections of the Gambian community.[42]

The programmes of most of the other candidates overlapped with
those of the DP, though there were variations for some. Small, for
example, pressed for "social improvements including old-age pensions
and unemployment benefits". Garba-Jahumpa stated as his primary aim:

> To raise the status of Islam and to secure for Moslems equality
> in public life with their Christian brethren. In demonstration
> of this aim of equality, to contest only one of the Bathurst
> seats allowing the Christian element the other.

Finden Dailey considered religious ministers and barristers as:

> unsuitable as representatives . . . The only profession that
> qualifies its members for politics is journalism . . . Former
> members [of the legislature and executive] have done little
> for the general welfare of The Gambia but Finden Dailey, if
> he were elected, guarantees to work miracles.

P. S. NJie sought massive reforms in the legal system, including repeal of the Criminal Code and revision of the Workmen Compensation Ordinance; in addition to infrastructural development he advocated "greater facilities for technical and higher education, including a university college and more scholarships to the United Kingdom".[43]

The DP made use of members of the GMDMU to transport supporters to the public meetings and to the polling stations on Election Day. The reality of Faye being from the small ethnic and religious minority dictated that he should be nominated to stand for the elections by a prominent non-Christian, non-Krio/Aku member of Bathurst society; this he found in Momodou Musa NJie (Fula/Protectorate), a very wealthy and highly respected Muslim who was mainly in the import/export and real estate business.[44] The other sponsors were Sigismund Gibbs and Hannah Forster; of course the party symbol, a snake, was adopted by Faye.

Election Results (1951)—Performance Assessment

The results of the elections gave a majority to Faye who obtained 905 of votes cast (40 percent), closely followed by Garba-Jahumpa with 828 votes (36.6 percent) and NJie with 463 votes (20.6 percent). For the others, Edward Small obtained 45 votes (2.0 percent), Mustapha Colley got 10 votes, J. Francis Senegal a paltry 6 votes and J. Finden Dailey came at the rear with 5 votes. In Kombo St Mary, Henry Madi attracted 813 votes compared to 255 for Howsoon O. Semega-Janneh and 7 votes for John W. Kuye.

The assessment of the performance of the three main candidates in the elections undertaken by the colonial administration is insightful. On Faye, E. R. Ward, the Colonial Secretary, argued that his victory was not unexpected, given the groundwork undertaken by himself and his party supporters and the advantages of a relatively well-oiled party machine. Ward also observed that Faye had "the support of many Christians and quite a number of educated Muslims (Wolofs)"; also that Faye and his party "had cornered all the drummers in Bathurst so that when the Young Muslim Association entered the field they had to obtain permits for drummers to enter Gambia from Senegal".[45]

To these observations the administration rightly added the fact noted above, that Faye was able to get Momodou Musa NJie to be one of his official nominators. No doubt, the virulent and sustained attacks by Faye and the DP on the Wyn-Harris Constitution, and on the unpopular Wyn-Harris himself, contributed to his winning the votes of sectors of the electorate. Garba-Jahumpa's backing from the Muslim population was solid. NJie was relatively new to the political scene and, to some extent, his constituency overlapped with that of Faye.

To the colonial officials, the defeat of Small was most perplexing but explainable: he seemed to have lost interest in radical politics and was preparing to opt out of active politics—the fire had gone out of his belly! Whilst the other candidates had started their campaigns at least three months earlier, Small joined in only a few weeks before the polls. Whereas the others were on the hustings with their numerous mass meetings, drummers and praise-singers and sloganeering, Small was "quite a recluse who rarely leaves his house but is accessible there, was indecisive and reluctant to enter the hurly-burly of an election campaign which was more intense than any in the past". He was eventually convinced "by some of his moderate and rather out-moved supporters" to run, "but he gave the impression of being a tired man and of not trying very hard."[46] As put by R.H. Rowland, a senior staff member in the Colonial Office: "It is distressing when the march of time reaches a speed that the loyal and steady supporter of many years can't keep up with it, and our sympathies go to Mr. Small."[47]

On the basis of the results of the elections, Faye, Garba-Jahumpa and Madi took their seats in the Legislative Council. The first two were subsequently appointed to the Executive Council to serve as "members of the government without portfolio". In this capacity they would be asked to advise on policy at the early stages of formation in areas of special concern to each. For Faye the selected areas were: natural resources, transport (water, land and air), posts and telegraphs, and cooperation. There was also the provision that the members of government without portfolio could be consulted on other key issues; and one of their most important responsibilities would be to participate in the preparation of the government's annual Estimates. Madi had no specific tasks assigned to him but, given the problems faced by

Protectorate members in attending Council meetings, he was asked to hold a watching brief for this part of the country.

Other terms and conditions were:[48]

- That they would be paid an amount of 500.00 pounds per annum for three years or until they ceased to be members of the legislature, whichever was earlier.
- The appointment would be terminated by the Governor if he considered it desirable.
- They would be expected to resign if they found themselves at odds with other members on a serious issue or continually at loggerheads on smaller issues.
- With regards to the agreed-upon areas of jurisdiction, when necessary they would have access to files on the subjects on which advice was sought; but they would not initiate policy on Government files unasked. Staff matters were outside their purview.
- If it was decided that certain matters were to be referred to the Legislative Council, then they would be subject to the Government Whip, if applied, or should resign.

Summary Observations

The 1947-1951 period ushered in a new phase in the political development of The Gambia—just as it did in the other British West African colonies. Faye was invited to take centre stage and, given the backgrounds of the other participants, he easily assumed dominance of the political scene. All this was confirmed with the formation of the DP. Was it a coincidence that these developments took place at the same time that KK was confronted with mounting problems and Faye's eventual withdrawal?

A related observation is that the period witnessed a convergence of the four fields in which Faye was to devote the rest of his life: education, politics, the Church, and philanthropy. These years saw a coming-together of these roles, all rolled up in one person. In this sense, it was both a turning point and a pointer for the future.

CHAPTER 4

POLITICIAN: BEGINNINGS OF THE STRUGGLE FOR POWER

Formation of the Gambia Muslim Congress (MC), 1952

From the 1951 elections and the politicking surrounding them two other personalities emerged to challenge Faye, namely, I. M. Garba-Jahumpa and P. S. NJie. Both were originally associated with the DP; in fact, as indicated above, Garba-Jahumpa was one of the founding members.

The 1951 elections showed that there were constituencies whose loyalties to Faye and the DP were weak; they did not have much in common with the rump of his support and could easily be attracted away from the DP. For Garba-Jahumpa this was mainly the Muslim population which also constituted the majority of the Bathurst population. He was conscious of the need to protect their interests and to use politics to solve their grievances, "particularly with respect to the dominance of the smaller Christian community in public life and modern employment".[1]

Garba-Jahumpa was emboldened by a statement made by A. J. Senghore, a senior member of the Muslim community, at a public meeting at the junction of Haddington Street and Mosque Road. Senghore had argued that, in the past, ever since the Legislative Council was established, local representation was drawn from the two religious groups; it was thus that Sheikh Umar Faye and Ousman Jeng had served as the Muslim representatives whilst Sir Samuel Forster represented the Christian community. This was the tradition; but now (in 1951) there were two parties (the DP and the Gambia National League) each led by a Christian. It was therefore time, Senghore argued, for the Muslims to break away from the DP and form their own party.

Accordingly, Garba-Jahumpa and his backers formed the Muslim Congress (MC) party in January 1952, bringing together about 40 Muslim societies in one organization. For much of its life the MC was sectarian and exclusive; only adherents to the Islamic faith were accepted as members. As starkly stated in its first manifesto, the Congress was to serve "the political aspirations, traditions and political circumstances of the Muslim community".[2] As a "revised and joint edition" of the Bathurst Young Muslims Society (BYMS, 1936) and other Muslim groupings its support base was guaranteed. The Society itself was originally a cultural organization, but was converted into a political association by Garba-Jahumpa. In the BTC elections (1946) it won three seats, but unsuccessfully sponsored him in the 1951 elections, as noted above.[3]

Clearly, religion was key to Garba-Jahumpa's politics, and he was to exploit the ethno-religious factor in the competition for popular support. This use of Islam was unanticipated in that Garba-Jahumpa had for many years been an assistant to E. F. Small, a Christian, and was closely involved in the latter's radical politics and diverse trade union activities. As maintained by Cham Joof, one of the ever-loyal Muslim faithful of the DP:

> The lines were now drawn in the sand and ever since then party loyalty became dependent on one's religion, ones ethnicity and so on . . . You see! Religion was a key player in what obtained in the period and both NJie and Garba-Jahumpa had no problems using it for their political advantage.[4]

Formation of the United Party (UP), 1954

The dominant personality in the UP was Pierre Sarr NJie. He was born in Casamance (Senegal) into a Wolof commercial family and traced his ancestry to Semou Joof, the last king of Saloum. After a turbulent career in the civil service, he proceeded to England in 1943 to read law at Lincoln's Inn and was called to the bar in 1948. He returned to Bathurst the year following and set up a legal practice which flourished in the early 1950s, mainly on conveyance and land cases.

Apparently, on deciding to enter politics and contest the 1951 elections, NJie joined the DP. But, as the party already had Faye as candidate he stood as an Independent. After his loss in these elections he, like Garba-Jahumpa, concluded that he would not make any headway in politics if he stayed in the DP playing second, or even third, fiddle to Faye and other leaders. It also appears that NJie joined the MC when it was formed in 1952; even though he had converted from Islam to Roman Catholicism decades earlier, he was not only a member of the BYMS but, in 1937, was selected its honorary secretary.

NJie spent much of the time after the 1951 elections consulting with his advisers and laying the groundwork for a new party; at the same time he busied himself with several legal suits against the colonial administration. Not until about six months before the 1954 elections was the formation of the UP announced, with NJie as its leader. The UP's power base was built around the Roman Catholic Church and community and sections of the Wolofs, particularly those from Saloum Saloum. Ethnicity was central to his politics.

As the first Wolof high-status lawyer in the country, NJie won the respect and admiration of many; he was seen as the common man's lawyer and, in line with this image, did not hesitate to offer his legal services to his supporters free of charge. By any standards, the UP had much greater access to funds compared to the other two political parties. It had significant support from the traders and rich businessmen, many of whom were Lebanese, Moroccans, and other North Africans and Arab moneybags. His claim to royalty was a card that he played very wisely and effectively.[5]

Features of the Party System in Gestation

These three parties (DP, MC, and UP) were to dominate the political scene throughout the 1950s until the emergence of the Peoples' Progressive Party (PPP) at the end of the decade. The names of the leaders, Faye, Garba-Jahumpa and NJie, came to be coterminous with the parties they led, and the identities of party and leader were inseparable. Personality mattered more than ideology, policies or programme; as each of the three individuals had recognizable charismatic qualities, personality-cult politics came to be the order of the day.

In terms of organizational structures each party had a central committee made up of most of the leadership, and committees in each of the wards into which the Colony Area and Kombo were divided for municipal elections. Whatever programmes existed they barely touched on issues beyond the most immediate one of what should be the next stage in the process of constitutional advance.[6]

An important element in the party structure was the women's wing which had the *yai-kompins* as the mothers of the local branches; the DP went further and had a mother of the party as a whole, the *Yai-partibi*. These *yai-kompins* included women such as Sira Jobe, Lily Mama, Cecilia Moore, Elizabeth Buxton-Wright, Mbahe Bajan, Mam Fatou Mane, Harriet Mboge and Oumie Samba; they mobilized the women for political rallies and during elections made sure that party members were registered and that they did cast their votes.

Each party had its own particular dress code, the *ashobi*, for women and men; it was worn mainly on special occasions and at party events. The common material was usually synthetic silk and ordinary prints (*fanti*) and wax prints. Each also had a party colour, symbol and motto; for the DP the colour was yellow, the symbol was a snake (Faye's clan totem) and the motto was "Upward and Forward". Members paid monthly subscriptions which were mostly used for financing party activities, especially election campaigns.

Another feature of the political scene in these early years was that because of the dominance of one "big man", personal insults and abuse, slander and character assassinations were directed more at the three leaders. The principal purveyors were seasoned specialist propagandists who, led by drummers, traversed the town spreading filth about the opponents of the party they supported. It was not uncommon either for the families and close associates of the political leaders to be included in their insults.

The same propagandists had the responsibility of announcing details of scheduled meetings of their parties and, in the course of public meetings, they played prominent praise singing and sloganeering roles. The party colours were widely displayed, songs praising the virtues of the leaders were loudly chanted, and venom hurled at the other parties and their leaderships. Some of the DP propagandists were Binta Nyang, Marie Samuel NJie, Sosseh Jagne, Dodou Matarr NJie, Sulay Mbaye, Mustapha NJie, Ousman Secka, Putty Samba and Sergeant Gaye. In the course of time, some, such as Dodou Matarr NJie, Sulay Mbaye and Marie Samuel NJie, left for the UP and MC, just as others moved from these parties to join the DP.

Some of the lyrics and guitar music for the popular songs of the DP were composed by party members such as R. K. O. Joiner, Wilson, Chiki Chaka Cummings, Francis Savage and Moses Saidy. One such was:

> Demo . . . Democratic
> If not, If not, Why not?
> I received a telegram
> Say na Demo go cam first.

At political rallies, street broadcasts and other festivities, chants and praises sang for Faye in Sereer were: *Dugu dugu Wagaan, Biram Penda Wagaan, Hanjis Wagaan and Hanjarr Wagan*; these were reminders of Faye's immortal ancestry and for a man of enduring fame. There were battle cries and vocalizations that the *griots* of the Faye clan sang, to praise and strengthen him as a warrior proceeding into battle. These songs were accompanied by the clattering, clanging and ringing of bells and other instruments intended to put the fear of God in the enemies. Songs also carried messages, such as "One must not thump a porcupine as if you do the erectile bristles will sting you"; or "Faye, you are the lurking elephant by the fence."[7]

So potentially explosive were these competitions between parties, leaders and supporters that, on one occasion, the Muslim elders convened a meeting with the party leaders and their propagandists at the Ritz Cinema on Fitzgerald Street in Bathurst and advised them to cease using obscene language in the campaigns. As they cautioned: "Politics ought to be viewed as a game. It is, however, a game that is to be played with fairness, it is a game that ought to unite and not divide."[8]

In such an environment, it is small wonder that the election campaigns did not lead to open, large-scale physical violence. Of the 1960 elections one observer was compelled to remark:

> . . . We have attended and have heard in these meetings acrimonious, abusive and defamatory language used against candidates; in some cases speakers pried into the personal private business of a candidate. Most of these statements have been known to be incorrect and just fabrications but the person attacked gets someone else to retaliate on his behalf and so the vicious circle proceeds until the elections are over.
>
> We take this opportunity of counselling our party leaders and soliciting their aid to prohibit abusive remarks and uncouth actions . . . It should be remembered that in these mass meetings women, who deserve honour and courtesy, the aged who demand the utmost respect, and young people who easily emulate, are always present, and abusive and insulting expressions do exhibit the traits of those making those statements. We implore our leaders to see that such is stamped out.[9]

Sourcing Constitutional Inputs from the Colonized

Hardly had the dust settled after the constitution of the legislative bodies in 1951 before voices criticizing the new order arose from among the political class. In responding to these, the colonial administration decided to adopt a more participative approach to constitution-making: rather than impose from Government House and the Colonial Office in London, local inputs were to be actively solicited. The Governor, Sir Percy Wyn-Harris, embarked on extensive consultations with a large number of persons of different shades of opinion, including Garba-Jahumpa and Madi. Faye was out of the country, in Accra, on one of his absences-without-permission, during these consultations but, apparently, had informed the other two that he was prepared to accept whatever was agreed.

In April 1953, a 34-member Consultative Committee to the Governor on Constitutional Reform was set up, with a mandate "to examine with the Governor the existing constitution, to consider what the aims of constitutional policy should be and to frame proposals for a constitution suited to the needs of The Gambia".[10] The membership was quite diverse, even if lopsided. There were 10 Muslims and 24 Christians; of the latter, ten each were Anglicans or Methodists and four Roman Catholics. There were also five women, namely, Rachel Carrol, Gwendoline Forster, Hannah Forster, Rosamond Fowlis, and Louise NJie.

Of course, the elected and other unofficial members of the legislature were part of the team. The consultants to the committee were the Colonial Secretary, the Attorney General, and the Financial Secretary. The four members of the Legislative Council representing the Protectorate (Tamba Jammeh, Matarr Sise, Omar Mbacke, and Sulayman Ndure) attended the first two organizational meetings as observers.[11]

The DP and the MC each prepared and presented memoranda to the committee. Though differing on some issues, they were united in their intention that The Gambia should remain part of the British Commonwealth. To consolidate positions on issues on which they agreed, an initiative was launched by the MC in January 1953 to combine forces or even to merge the two parties. The DP responded positively and proposed that a joint committee be set up to work out the modalities. However, no such action was taken, and Faye did not insist, perhaps because he was suspicious of the move and, for this reason, did not favour having the collaboration in a formal written agreement, as desired by the MC.[12]

The Governor had five meetings with the committee and a sixth, on 28 May, at which the draft report was submitted for consideration. It is interesting to note that in his own report on the work of the Committee, addressed to the Secretary of State, the Governor anticipated that it would be signed by "an overwhelming majority, very possibly unanimously".[13] Neither did he have any doubts as concerns the approval by the Protectorate members of Council. His only apprehensions were about Faye. To quote from his confidential report to the Secretary of State:

> The only dissent likely is the Rev. J. C. Faye who made counter-proposals which have been rejected. It is quite possible that he will fall in with the majority but, on the other hand, he may claim that he has the support of the Democratic Party, of which he is the founder and which now seems to have no single person of standing on it. You are aware of his position, and it seems very likely that he may have to disappear from Executive Council. As he probably realises this is possible, he may attempt to whip up illiterates in Bathurst against the proposals but informed opinion is very doubtful of success along such a line.[14]

The committee recommended that in the Legislative Council representation of unofficials should be increased to 16 composed as follows: three directly elected in Bathurst and one in Kombo St Mary; seven indirectly elected to represent the Protectorate; three would come from a pool of candidates from the Bathurst Town Council and the Kombo Rural Authority. Of the two remaining, one would come from the commercial sector and be appointed by the Governor "after consultation with" the Legislative Council; the last would be appointed "after approval" by the Council. As regards the three members from Bathurst, they would be elected in a single constituency and on the principle of "one voter, one vote". A Speaker of the Legislative Council should also be appointed "after approval" by the same Council.

Concerning the Executive Council the recommendation was that it should have a majority of unofficials and at least two of the unofficial members should be appointed ministers and be assigned specific departments over which they would have full responsibility. Advisory committees to the ministers should be set up only at the request of the minister concerned or by a member of the Executive Council.[15]

For Wyn-Harris and the Colonial Office, some of these proposals were acceptable whilst others—which were, in fact, the critical ones—were considered premature or inapplicable. On the issue of a full ministerial system the Governor was stridently opposed for various reasons. Most important among his arguments was that there were very few persons outside the civil service who were suitable to be appointed ministers but, even among these, none was qualified. Besides, all of the likely candidates would be from Bathurst and would therefore not give the attention required to the needs of the Protectorate population. This was because the Protectorate, which had the majority of the population, could not produce even one person of ministerial calibre.

Over and above these arguments was the Governor's conviction that the Colony's finances could be better used for other purposes than for setting up ministries and paying ministerial emoluments; in fact, for him, the cost of establishing ministries, apart from the ministerial salaries, was beyond the capacity of The Gambia.[16] Very importantly, on the advisory committees the position of the colonial administration was that it would be obligatory for ministers to work with these committees and that they would in no way undermine the authority and status of the ministers.

Wyn-Harris was, at the same time, conscious of the necessity to come up with some form of constitutional progress in order to contain the pressures from corners such as Faye's. Nevertheless, given the peculiarities of the Gambian situation it was not altogether imperative to proceed along the same route as the other West African colonies. In Wyn-Harris's own words:

> My own view is that we have come to the parting of the ways as far as constitutional advance is concerned in West Africa, and that The Gambia has got to look elsewhere than southward for its constitutional objectives . . . The premise on which I would like to base any discussions are:
>
> (i) That any union of The Gambia as a political entity in future with Sierra Leone or even French territories is out of the question.
> (ii) That, although small, The Gambia from historical and political reasons has got to be a separate entity.

(iii) That the wish of The Gambia is to be part, and a very close part, of the British Empire and that self-government is an economic and political impossibility.

(iv) That a ministerial system is not a practical policy here.[17]

Hence, Wyn-Harris came up with the proposal of a "River State" first mooted in the "Report of the Committee Appointed to Consider the Constitutional Development of the Smaller Colonial territories", 1951.[18] The River State would have a State Council and an array of committees dealing with different subject areas, somewhat akin to the committee system in the Channel Islands constitution.

If anything different from the Westminster model was unacceptable to Gambians, then the Executive and Legislative Council could continue with identical membership. Wyn-Harris saw some distinct advantages in establishing an equivalent to the Protectorate Chiefs' Conference in the Colony Area. It could begin as a temporary advisory body such as the Consultative Committee he was to set up to consider changes to the constitution and which, it was intended, would evolve into a permanent institution. Its membership would include representatives from bodies such as the religious missions, political parties, the town council and rural councils.

The State Council would comprise five official members and four members each from the Colony and Protectorate; representation from the latter would be increased as more qualified persons became available. Membership would also be extended to the chairman of each of the above-mentioned committees and external persons could also be appointed. Further, for the Governor, some committees would have official chairmen, such as Faye and Garba-Jahumpa.

The Executive Committee would be the principal committee, with the same membership as for the State Council; however, the Protectorate members would not be expected to attend, given the inconveniences of travel and other logistics. In the event that both the State Council and Executive Council schemas were rejected, the Governor anticipated that the same committee system discussed above would be adopted, similar to the Development Committee he had introduced in the Executive Council. Finally, the Governor should preside when the State Council was in executive session and the Vice-President when in ordinary session.[19]

Happily, by the time the Consultative Committee was established and started its work Wyn-Harris had abandoned such thinking and was ready to conceptualized change within the overall context of the Westminster model; and more-or-less along the lines of constitutionalism in the other British West African colonies

Faye's Critique of the Committee of 34 and its Recommendations

As it turned out, Faye was not pleased about the composition of the Committee. He argued, rightly, that half of the members were current or former civil servants, which meant that they could undercut the political class. Many who had worked in the colonial administration or were currently in service, he added, were colonial in their mentalities and outlooks and moderate in their recommendations. Faye quoted from their report to demonstrate how "non-leftist" was the group:

> We have carefully surveyed every point and now put forward proposals which we believe . . . will give The Gambia a stable and workable form of government . . . We consider that in order to ensure that our policy is successful we must consider by all means to encourage our pride in The Gambia and the privileges that citizenship of The Gambia carries with it. With that pride must go our ancient loyalty and pride in our close links with the United Kingdom.[20]

For Faye, rather than civil servants, old age pensioners and others who had no knowledge of or experience in constitutional issues, the Governor should have asked each political party to nominate an equal number of representatives to the committee.

Faye was not pleased with the work of the Committee either; he considered the recommendations to be very "tame" and to diverge from what any other body, if elected by the people, would have demanded. They were "very elementary compared with the demands of the other British West African colonies which have been receiving more respectful attention".[21] On the other hand. Faye welcomed proposals such as the appointment of a Speaker, enlargement of membership of both legislative and executive bodies, appointment of full ministers, and the holding of party-based elections in the Colony Area.

As expected, the Governor separately submitted to the Secretary of State his own comments on the report of the Committee. This Faye did not appreciate as, he maintained, the comments constituted a minority report and were all but final. He further pointed out that the recommendations of the Committee, even if "tame", should have been treated "with respect and understanding and regarded as an irreducible minimum".[22] After all, this group of busy prominent citizens had worked hard on their assigned tasks, held six sessions and examined in detail every document submitted to them; in every case agreement was reached after thorough deliberations. Faye observed also that the Committee's report had been signed by all the members except the Governor and other top-level officers, who were not expected to sign it; thus, it was inappropriate for anyone to tamper with the final product. For him, then, the question that arose was: why set up the Committee in the first place?

Faye was also dissatisfied with the manner in which the Protectorate was brought into the equation by the Governor. He challenged the latter's position that "I have no reason to believe that there would be any dissident voice in the Protectorate to the proposals of the Consultative Committee . . . The report is unanimous and I have no doubt that it would receive overwhelming support throughout the territory."[23]

In the light of all of the above—and more—Faye maintained that the Governor should have submitted the Committee's report in its entirety. Rather, the counter-suggestions in his "minority" report had "emasculated the Committee recommendations, thereby making null and void the devoted hours of thirty-four persons whom he himself called "a cross-section of all shades of opinion in Bathurst". A report which the Governor himself described as "acceptable to the people" should not by any means be superseded by the wish of the Governor.[24]

More than those of any of the other party leaders, Faye's criticisms were very virulent and were sustained over many months. In particular, he came down heavily on the Colonial Office's views on the status of the ministers and the role of the advisory committees. Faye not only articulated his opposition during several political rallies of the DP but went further and organized a committee of like-minded opponents (November 1953) to prepare counter-proposals and to maintain pressure on the colonial administration. The counter-proposals he despatched to the Secretary of State.[25]

Elements of the New Constitution (1954)

The final terms of the new constitution were worked out after a visit by the Governor to London in August 1953 and consultations with the Protectorate District Councils and the Chiefs' Conference in January 1954.[26] The final Constitution partially responded to the demands of Faye and other political leaders. It again expanded the composition of the two arms of government, the Executive and Legislative Councils. Seven members of the Legislative Council were to be elected from the Colony Area and seven from the Protectorate, chosen indirectly. In the Executive Council there was to be no less than six unofficial members appointed by the Governor after consultation with the elected Legislative Council members. Not more than three, and not less than two, were to head specific ministries and be involved in policy making and coordination. The life of the new Constitution would be extended from the current three to five years.[27]

A summary of major elements in the new Constitution is as follows:[28]

Legislative Council   21 members
President   Governor
Speaker   Appointed by Governor
                        "after approval by
                        Legislative Council"

5 Officials	4 ex-officio	Colonial Secretary
		Financial Secretary
		Attorney General
		Senior Commissioner
	1 Gambian public officer, appointed	
	by office	

16 Unofficials	3 elected from Bathurst	
	1 elected from Kombo	
	7 Protectorate	4 elected by
		Division Councils
		3 elected by Chiefs
	3 elected by above 11 from:	
		6 names submitted by
		Bathurst Council
		3 names submitted by
		Kombo Council
	1 Unofficial appointed by Governor	
		"after approval by
		Unofficial members of
		Legislative Council"
	1 Commerce member appointed by	
	Governor	
		"after consultation with
		Legislative Council"

Executive Council   11 members

| President | Governor |

5 Officials	4 ex-officio	Colonial Secretary
		Financial Secretary
		Attorney General
		Senior Commissioner
	1 Gambian public officer, appointed	
	by office	

6 Unofficials	Appointed by Governor "after consultation with Unofficial members of Legislative Council"

Ministers —

Not less than 2 and not more than 3	Appointed by Governor "after consultation with Unofficial members of Legislative Council"

Others	Other ministers may become "Ministers without portfolio".

Advisory Committee —

At the request of a Minister with portfolio or of an ex-officio member with executive functions, the Executive Council may appoint an Advisory Committee to assist him.

This was to be the first instance of the new constitutional order being officially determined on the basis of recommendations by representatives of the Gambian peoples. It was also the first occurrence of broad-based Protectorate representation in central government, even if the selection was indirect. Yet a third first was that elected members of the Legislative Council were to be given the opportunity to run ministries—though their powers were somewhat circumscribed. It seemed very likely that this would only lead to greater opening-up in the future.

One of the highly controversial issues still retained in the new Constitution was the appointment of advisory committees to assist the ministers in the execution of their responsibilities; if there was disagreement between a minister and the head of department the matter could be taken to the Executive Council for decision. On this the Governor was adamant: he maintained that the committees should be part of "the fabric of the Constitution".[29] In addition to the arguments presented earlier, for him the committees would be necessary for two new reasons: first, there would not be other staff available in the ministries to advise the ministers; and second, the committees would be in line with the desire of the Consultative Committee to have all major interests included in the government. But, for Faye and for like-minded members, even if the idea was acceptable in principle a paramount objection was that, as admitted by the Governor, in practice only heads of departments (colonial officials) would be members of the committees. And, given the composition of Council, it was not likely that any resort to the Executive Council, in cases of disagreement between minister and head of department, would be resolved in favour of the minister.

Election Campaign (1954)

The assumption was that another election would be held after the new Constitution had been promulgated; in any case, the three-year mandate of the government had elapsed. The date for the elections was fixed for 19 October 1954.

Under the banner of the DP, Faye contested the third elections to the Legislative Council. Once again, he stood in one of the three seats in Bathurst, joined by NJie, Garba-Jahumpa and George St. Clair Joof, a new entrant to electoral politics. Henry Madi and Samuel Jonathan Oldfield (an industrialist originally from Sierra Leone) were the candidates for the Kombo constituency. The competition for Kombo was likely to be stiff. Faye was approached to express his support for Madi publicly; this he did rather reluctantly, being suspicious that Madi would use his wealth for purposes not in the interest of the country. Madi, on the other hand, was convinced that Faye was the only person who could get him elected to the House, and offered to put money into the DP and its election campaign. Elders such as Pa Henry Jones, Pa Chernor Jagne and Alhaji Ousman Jeng, for whom Faye had the highest respect, prevailed on him to relent. Later, Faye felt vindicated in that, as he had predicted, Madi, once elected, ingratiated himself to Wyn-Harris and became one of the Governor's personal friends and allies.

Campaigning was intense and mainly revolved around the modifications made by the Governor to the recommendations of the Consultative Committee of 34.[30] As in the 1951 elections campaign, Faye continued to be especially critical of the lack of meaningful authority for the "ministers" as there was no provision for collective responsibility on their part and they had no power to implement their manifestos. On this and other issues Faye's position was very clear, as detailed in the DP manifesto. In his usual picturesque manner he dismissed the whole constitution as:

> one in which Gambians were the horse and rider but the Governor had the reins firmly in his hands; if you ask for anything he would say he is not on the horseback and if you ask us we would reply that we do not have the means (reins) of control.[31]

Election Results, 1954

With vastly improved electoral registers and a new system of voters' cards, based on the recommendations of the Revision of Electoral Machinery Committee (1952), the election results were now more dependable than for the previous two elections to the legislative body. NJie led the pack with 2,123 votes (UP, 36 percent), Faye came second garnering 1,979 votes (DP, 33 percent), while Garba-Jahumpa had 1,569 votes (MC, 26 percent). Joof of the new and short-lived Gambia People's Party (GPP) secured a miserable 252 votes (4 percent). In Kombo, again Henry Madi (Independent) won the polls with 904 votes and his rival Samuel J. Oldfield (Independent) obtained 650 votes.[32]

Faye lost to NJie by only three percent of the votes cast. One reason for this decline in performance was that he had faced financial difficulties due to the failure of his several business ventures, particularly the Pilot Produce Syndicate.[33] It can also be argued that Faye's performance was due less to weaknesses in the DP and his personal problems than to the fact that his opponents had grown in strength. They now had behind them well-organized political parties, strong core support bases, guaranteed funding sources, and, in general, they had better mastered the art of politics and of winning elections. This was particularly so in the case of NJie.[34]

Appointment of Faye to the Executive Council, 1954

For the appointment of members of the Executive Council after the 1954 elections the elected members, together with the nominated unofficial members, were requested by the Governor to propose three candidates and two potential ministers. This was at variance with the constitutional provision that not more than three and not less than two would be appointed. It was rumoured that Faye, though the second elected member for Bathurst, was to be by-passed by the Governor. On hearing this, the Women's Wing of the DP, animated by their leader and party financier, Councillor Hannah Forster, staged a demonstration and went up to Government House to express their dissatisfaction with the rumoured decision that was to be announced by the Governor.

Initially, the Governor was reluctant to see the delegation, but he was prevailed upon by Commissioner of Police Mayden. He then met them at the foot of the building housing the Executive Council and directed the demonstrators to select six from among themselves to discuss their grievances. After that meeting it was clear that the rumour was baseless. Subsequently, Wyn-Harris offered the three leaders ministerial positions. The appointments were subject to review after one year. Total annual salary was 7,500 pounds each; this was very generous compared to Gold Coast Ministers who received 3,500 pounds and 2,500 pounds for Nigerian Federal Ministers.[35]

Faye was made Minister of Works and Communications, whilst NJie went to Education and Social Welfare and Garba-Jahumpa to Agriculture and Natural Resources. It is not far-fetched to conclude that, after the protest by the women, the Governor was aware of the possible reactions of Faye's many supporters and sympathizers if he had not been granted a ministerial portfolio. The fact that Faye had defeated Garba-Jahumpa in the elections meant that the Governor could not give any thought to selecting Garba-Jahumpa over Faye.[36]

Interestingly, because of his background and experience, Faye had been offered the Education portfolio but he turned it down. Apparently, this was primarily because he considered that the extensive transformation required in this sector would not be possible under the colonial administration. He was also convinced that his "radical" views on educational reform would only lead to greater friction between him and the Governor and this was best avoided; as Faye put it: "if further clashes between himself and me would be avoided 'education' should be far from me."[37]

The fledgling Ministry of Works and Communication had seven departments initially (post and telecommunications, public works, water works, electricity, transport, air communications, and marine); three others were subsequently added (surveys, meteorology, and printing) in acknowledgement of the Governor's satisfaction with Faye's performance.

It was during Faye's tenure that the following were achieved or plans laid out for their execution. Water services, originally pumped at public standpipes and from 140 dug water wells in the country, were augmented by the government and the Abuko station was constructed to provide pipe water in the country. A new Bathurst power station was built at Half-Die with bigger engines, to cope with increased water consumption in the capital area; the water tank at Fajara was enlarged. Funding for a new Ports Authority building was secured in the form of a grant from the Colonial Development Fund, which also provided resources for the construction of a number of school buildings (Crab Island Secondary Modern School, and Malfa School) and the renovation of the General Post Office in Bathurst.

Bridge-building was a top priority for Faye's department. Among others, the second Oyster Creek Bridge (Denton Bridge) connecting Bathurst to the Africa mainland and the Brumen Bridge were constructed during Faye's tenure as was the Pakali-Ba bridge; a hand-drawn ferry was available at Sankulay-kunda. Bathurst was drained, several roads were macadamized and re-surfaced and new ones were laid out. Georgetown had a laterite road and electricity was expanded to some parts of the town. In Basse, the three-mile "rainy season road" was redone as was the Brikama-Mansakonko stretch up to Sibanor. Very

High Frequency (VHF) communications were established during this period to facilitate communications across the country. Old wharves were reconstructed and new ones built in many of the major towns along the river. It was also during this time that the Trans-Gambia Road was completed and opened by Faye and Alieu Badara Mbengue, his counterpart from Senegal.

Faye reported that the Governor was of the opinion that Works and Communications was the most complex and "heavy" ministry, but after three months the Governor revealed in a private communication to a colleague in Whitehall that his scepticism had disappeared and that the ministry was as efficient as any in England. Later, he, the Governor, invited Faye to his office, shook his hand and declared: "You have achieved more than I ever achieved with the civil engineers." The Governor then gave Faye the key to the back gate of Government House with an open invitation to "come to see me whenever you like".[38]

It was due to this very high-level performance that, during the visit of the Duke of Edinburgh to The Gambia in 1957, Faye was put in charge of all functions outside the sphere of action of Government House; he then set up specialized committees to assist. The visit was indeed very successful and, on departure, the Duke said to Faye: "The Queen must come back with me and see The Gambia as I have seen her. Thank you."[39]

Summary Observations

The main observation arising from the above discussion is that the contours of politics in The Gambia in the decades to come were sketched out during this period. Faye was at the centre, actively engaged in shaping the future. His earlier experience in the legislative and executive arms of the colonial administration served him well; in this respect, he had a distinct advantage over his political competitors. With these advantages, Faye assumed a leadership role in the major events of the day, such as the formation of organized political parties, the 1951 elections, the debates on the next stage of constitutional advance and the 1954 elections.

But Faye did not have it all his way. Opposing forces could only strengthen their presence as they familiarized themselves with the intricacies of local politics and acquired skills to compete. But, at the same time, there was the behemoth of the colonial administration with which Faye had to contend, in the person of the Governor, the most senior representative of Britain, the colonizer.

CHAPTER 5

POLITICIAN: CONTENDING WITH THE COLONIAL ORDER

Rev. John Colley Faye versus Governor Percy Wyn-Harris

In an interview in 1982 Faye graphically summarized the relationship he had had with Wyn-Harris, as follows:

> An egg should not play with a rock as if you knock it against the rock it will break. But who is the rock and who is the egg? What is of benefit to the Gambian masses is of God and if what I say is true, and in their interest, then it is of God. And what is of God is the rock. He who opposes it is the egg. I am here on my rock standing as a rock; it is the Governor who came all the way from England to meet us so he is the egg. If he hits himself against us it is he who will be smashed to pieces.[1]

It was common knowledge in both political and non-political circles that there was no love lost between the Rev. J. C. Faye and Governor Percy Wyn-Harris, almost from the day the latter assumed office in 1949. Illustrative of this is the fact that, in 1951, Fourah Bay University College (then affiliated to Durham University, England) in Freetown, Sierra Leone, nominated Lettie Forster (later to be Principal of Annie Walsh Memorial School in Freetown) and Faye (though not an alumnus of the College) to represent The Gambia on its Council. The Governor turned down the nominations; many believed it was because Faye was one of the nominees.[2]

Many and varied were the 'problems' that Faye created for Wyn-Harris and his colleagues in Bathurst and for the Colonial Office in London; these give insights into how the colonial system operated and into Faye's own personality and character. The differences between the two gentlemen were manifested in a number of areas, particularly from 1951 to 1954.

Private Business and/or Public Politics?

An initial matter of preoccupation on the part of the colonial administration was Faye's activities overseas, which gave rise to strong suspicions that he was building alliances with radical organizations and individuals. In August 1952, he was selected by members of the Legislative Council to represent them at the conference of the Commonwealth Parliamentary Association in Ottawa, Canada, to be held that September; he was a founding member of the Gambia branch of the association. The theme of Faye's address to the conference was "Defence in West Africa".

En route to Canada, Faye first attended a meeting of the Moral Re-armament Movement (MRA), in Caux, Switzerland. Essentially:

> the movement had Christian roots, but grew into an informal,
> international network of people of all faiths and backgrounds.
> It was based around what it called "the Four Absolutes"
> (absolute honesty, absolute purity, absolute unselfishness
> and absolute love) and encouraged its members to be actively
> involved in political and social issues. One of the movement's
> core ideas was that changing the world starts with seeking
> change in oneself.[3]

A main reason for accepting the invitation was that Faye was attracted by the MRA avowed principle which favoured "what is right and not who is right". During the Second World War, MRA members gave their unflinching support to the Allied forces and fought in several theatres of war with distinction. Others worked in war-related industries and built up reputations for selfless service to humankind and in defence of freedom and liberty. As characterized by a leading United States politician of the day: "where others have stood back and criticized, they [MRA members] have rolled up their sleeves and gone to work. This is where the Moral Re-Armament group comes in." The words are those of Senator (later President) Harry Truman, Chair of the Senate Committee investigating war contracts.[4]

With the end of the War, the group turned to the business of achieving lasting peace in the world. This also involved expanding to other geographic areas in Asia and Africa, particularly to support countries in transition to independence from colonial rule. It was in this context that Faye was invited to Caux. On his side, he wanted to learn more about the movement and to see how The Gambia could benefit from its activities. It was reported by Pa Henry Jones, the DP press agent, that Faye "gave a good account of himself and of The Gambia to the great admiration and satisfaction of the other delegates".

After the MRA conference Faye travelled to London. One business he had to attend to was a meeting with the Secretary of State, which had been arranged with some difficulties originating from Bathurst. According to a report by the Superintendent of Police, Special Branch, Banjul, Faye was also actively engaged in reviving the Gambia Students' Union under the auspices of the West African Students' Union (WASU).[5] Through a WASU activist, H. L. O. George, Faye had approached the Students' Liaison Officer (British Government) for funds for launching the Gambia Students' Union but none was forthcoming. Nonetheless, on 1 November 1952 the inaugural meeting of the Union was held at the premises of WASU.[6]

WASU was anti-colonial and nationalistic. In the 1930s, like the NCBWA, it launched a campaign for Dominion status and universal suffrage in the British West African colonies. Particularly in the 1940s, it strongly advocated internal self-government for these countries leading to independence within five years after the war. WASU had a following in West Africa, primarily through associate student organizations in Ghana, Sierra Leone and Nigeria. It subsequently worked closely with Kwame Nkrumah's West African National Secretariat; a jointly organized conference came up with a platform on anti-imperialism and socialism (1946). In the months following, Nkrumah became WASU's Vice-President and consolidated the organization's radical, pro-independence and anti-colonial orientation.

Faye was known by the colonial administration to have travelled to Paris after the Ottawa conference, but it was unclear as to the purpose of his visit. Also, it was known that he had been trying to raise funds for the Pilot Produce Syndicate (see below). Besides this, no information was available on the date of his return to Bathurst, not even from his wife; he had made airline reservations to travel to Bathurst six times and cancelled all—some without notification and others just without showing up. For the police, one possible explanation for this silence was that "Faye has been in financial difficulties for some time and it is known that some of his creditors have been pressing him and are likely to bring action against him."[7] The Colonial Secretary added to this:

> We are rather worried about what is happening to Faye who, as you know, left here in August to attend the Commonwealth Parliamentary Association Conference in Ottawa . . .
>
> I will not bore you with local rumours as to the reasons for his non-return but I should be most grateful if you could find out what he is up to and when he would be expected back. I am sorry for giving you what may be a difficult task but his absence is worrying and his activities abroad even more so.[8]

Thus, the secrecy was also worrying to the authorities in Bathurst in case any activities he was involved had a bearing on politics in The Gambia. To the relief of Bathurst and the Colonial Office, Faye finally travelled from London on 11 December 1952 with many questions hanging over his head. The Colonial Office reflected this relief when it noted in an internal memorandum: "Confirm that Faye checked in at Victoria Station this morning and joined the bus for the airport. We can take it that he has embarked and is on his way."[9]

First Suspension from the Executive Council: Confidence in Me or No Confidence in You?

Primarily because of his uncompromising attitudes towards the colonial government Faye had the distinction of being the first and only member of the Executive Council in Gambian history ever to be suspended three times. On the first occasion, barely nine months after his victory at the polls in 1951 and his accession to the position of member of the Executive Council, Faye had an open and direct brush with the Governor. This was connected with the visit of Oliver Lyttleton, the Secretary of State for the Colonies, to Bathurst in June 1952. Among his scheduled engagements was a meeting on 12 June, with the unofficial members of the Legislative and Executive Councils (J. A. Mahoney, Faye, Madi, Garba Jahumpa, Tamba Jammeh, Matarr Sise, Omar Mbacke, Suleiman Ndure and T. D. Mallinson).

Taking the lead, as First Elected member of Council, Faye presented a document covering major elements of a new constitution which had been formulated by a high-powered group comprising representatives from existing parties, commerce, traditional rulers, and independent politicians. Faye delved directly into the burning constitutional issues contained therein. For one, he argued that the unofficial majority of one in the legislature was too small. Bathurst should have three elected members and the Protectorate eight members, of whom four should come from the divisions and four from the Chiefs' Conference. All unofficial members should be elected.

For the Executive Council the view was that the majority of ex-officio members should be reduced to only three; this also applied to the Legislative Council. The other members of the executive should be six unofficials nominated by the unofficial members of the legislature and three of these should be appointed ministers without portfolio.

Faye also made a case for a more rapid pace of Africanization of the public service; already, he argued, there were suitable Gambian candidates for the posts of Chief Justice and Director of Medical Services. Finally, he criticized the method of appointing chiefs, preferring that it should be by hereditary criteria as "under any other system the Chiefs became mere puppets".[10]

Garba-Jahumpa strongly supported Faye's views, especially the need for unofficial majorities on the Executive and Legislative Councils, the granting of portfolios to ministers, and representation of the Chiefs' Conference in the Legislative Council. He advocated improved liaison with the French authorities in Senegal so that the difficulties experienced by families divided by the artificial frontiers could be minimized. Madi also expressed full agreement with what had been said by Faye, particularly the need for unofficial majorities in both legislative and executive organs and increased pace of Africanization. Mallinson made a pitch for continued representation of commercial and economic interests in Faye's scheme of things through representation by a nominated member from the Chamber of Commerce.

Lyttleton, in reply, expressed regret that neither he nor the Governor had been forewarned of the demands for constitutional change about which Faye had spoken; he found it "a little odd that nothing should have been heard of this until immediately before [my] arrival in the country".[11] He neither believed that there was widespread demand for constitutional change nor could he accept that The Gambia was ready for any such change. Rather, the present constitution should first be tried out before its success or otherwise could be assessed; any advances must first be demonstrated and consolidated before further changes would be introduced. Or, as captured by the Secretary of State: "It was a great mistake to pull up the flowers to see how they were growing."

Lyttleton was also convinced that the country could not yet sustain a system of ministers with portfolios.[12] This position was shared by the Governor who had noted in an earlier communication:

> We have not available sufficient men able and willing to enter politics for a ministerial system to work effectively. The only Gambians who have the time for politics and have sufficient facility in English are for the most part unsuccessful in the Civil Service, or the unsuccessful in trade or from the professions . . . The cost of a ministerial system in a colony of this size is unjustified, and I see no way in which under such

a system a virtual dictatorship could be avoided. Already nepotism is a problem.[13]

The Secretary of State concluded that those who felt strongly on these matters should provide him with proposals, in writing, and he would give them the careful study they deserved.

On another matter, though supporting Africanization in the civil service in principle, Lyttleton argued that this should not be only for its own sake, as "much damage would be done not only to the public service but to the cause of Africanization".[14] The post of Chief Justice had been filled and he promised to look into the possibility of appointing an African to the post of Director of Medical Services.

At a subsequent meeting between Sir Gorell Barnes, a highly-placed official in the Colonial Office accompanying the Secretary of State, constitutional matters were raised again by Faye, Jahumpa and Madi. According to the report on the meeting, Faye repeated his view that the constitution was unsatisfactory and was now far behind that of Sierra Leone. His main interest was that there should be unofficial majorities in both Councils.

Garba-Jahumpa began by explaining that constitutional issues had been raised with the Secretary of State without first discussing them with the Governor because the delegation did not wish to miss the opportunity of the Secretary of State's visit; it was not every day that such an opportunity presented itself. Moving away from Faye's position, Garba-Jahumpa added that:

> he and his party were not thinking of immediate changes to the Constitution but were concerned that the question should be considered in good time so that any changes which seemed desirable could be made at the end of the lifetime of the present Legislative Council in about two-and-a-half years' time.[15]

Madi was particularly interested in a system for election of representatives from the Protectorate and raised this with Barnes. The question of Africanization of the civil service and trade issues were also raised.

Barnes, like his superior, disabused the minds of the three gentlemen of any possibility of an early change of constitution. For any such change to take place the Governor must be fully consulted and be in full agreement; this also applied to any communications on constitutional affairs which were to be sent to London. Furthermore, any communications must be "as a result of careful enquiries regarding the views of the people of the territory as a whole".[16] For certain, during his tour of the Protectorate it was clear to Gorell Barnes that the priorities of the people in the Protectorate diverged considerably from what he was hearing from the (Bathurst) legislators: "the question which was occupying the minds of the people of the Protectorate was not anything concerned with the Constitution but the price of rice."[17]

The Secretary of State, after his meeting with the unofficials, gave the Governor a brief verbal account of what had transpired. Wyn-Harris was infuriated. He immediately convened a meeting with three of the chiefs who were the unofficial members representing the Protectorate. From the discussions with them he concluded that the chiefs were not supportive of the demands presented to the Secretary of State, that they were unaware of the proposals before they arrived in Bathurst to meet the Secretary of State, and that they had not had any consultations with the people of the Protectorate on the matter. They assured the Governor that they had indeed attended a meeting on the subject and sat on the platform; but, they had left early without signing any statement. They, in any case, had no intention of signing a petition for constitutional reform.

The Governor then summoned the three Executive Council members (Faye, Garba-Jahumpa, and Madi) to his office and castigated them for having embarrassed him by not having first raised the matter of constitutional reform with him, and for failing to seek his permission to discuss the matter with the Secretary of State. He informed them that he had travelled across the country and was convinced that there was no popular demand for further constitutional progress. Even if so, the three, as members of the Executive Council, should have first brought the matter to his attention. Rather, "they had attempted to jockey Protectorate members into agreement by appearance on a public platform when they knew that there had been no opportunity for them to consult their people in the Protectorate."[18]

The Governor reminded the three that before the visit they had been requested by the Colonial Secretary, at his direction, to present a list of subjects they would like to discuss with the Secretary of State during the visit but they had preferred not to do so. By their action, according to Wyn-Harris, the three had been disloyal to him and their conduct was not in the best interest of the country. He then informed them that his confidence in them had been badly shaken. He further demonstrated his dissatisfaction with Faye, the ringleader, and Garba-Jahumpa, by citing other specific instances when they had stepped beyond their executive powers in dealing with the chiefs and senior European government officials.

Faye had established the routine of briefing his rank-and-file party supporters of any major discussions he had had with the Governor and/ or his senior officials. This was an effective tactic for it demonstrated that he was in close touch with the generality of the Bathurst population and that the process of decision-making had popular groundings. This "people's man" image was not altogether welcomed by the colonialists.

Thus, in line with practice, two weeks afterwards, on Thursday 26 June 1952, a political meeting was convened by the parties at the Mohammedan School. According to Faye's own version of events, he informed the gathering:

> I am sure you must have heard about my recent differences
> with the Governor. Well, he was livid that, together with
> Garba-Jahumpa and Madi, I had had a private meeting with
> the Honourable Secretary of State for the Colonies, at which
> we briefed him on our demands for constitutional advance.
> The Governor had ended his diatribe with the statement that
> his confidence in us had been badly shaken by this incident.
> Well, my people, I know that he has agents in our midst. But,
> if he has no confidence in us then I, I, I, (three times) J. C.
> Faye, have no confidence in the Governor.[19]

This was translated into two major local languages, Wolof and Mandinka, so that the whole house would fully understand what was happening.

"I want to ask you: Do you have confidence in me?" Faye bellowed. The crowd, in turn, responded, "Yes, we do."

"No, that is not loud enough. I want the Governor in Government House to hear you."

To which there was a thunderous roar "Y . . . E . . . S".

The meeting then took on an atmosphere of self-congratulation—because their representatives had confronted the lion in its own den. Not surprisingly, this was reported to Wyn-Harris both by unofficial agents and in an official police intelligence report. The paragraph in the report relating to Faye's performance at the meeting reads thus:

> Going on to describe their interview with His Excellency he (Faye) became irate and appeared at pains to display his emotions. He stated that the Governor had been vexed and that they too had been vexed. Indeed they had good reason to be vexed because of the Governor's attitude towards them. Referring to the accusation that their action in approaching the Secretary of State directly had been unconstitutional he claimed that they had in fact disclosed to the Colonial Secretary that they intended to speak to the Secretary of State on the subject of the constitution. As for the Governor's statement that he had lost confidence in them, had he not interviewed the Chiefs separately before he had spoken to them? Was not this procedure unconstitutional? They also, therefore, had lost confidence in the Governor.[20]

Flustered, the Governor again invited Faye, Garba-Jahumpa and Madi to his office and gave them a dressing down for their deportment at the political meeting. Subsequently, in a letter dated 28 June 1952, he asked Faye to confirm or deny that at the meeting he had made the statement about not having confidence in the Governor; he further demanded that Faye should publish an apology in the *Gambia News Bulletin*, the government information newsletter. Faye refused on both counts. Defiantly, he requested that the Governor should first publish all that he had told the three of them and then he, Faye, would present his version to the country. To quote Faye himself:

> I am not in a position to repeat, either in writing or otherwise, any statement I might have made at the public meeting under reference, not until you, Sir, have confirmed in writing what Your Excellency had vehemently declared to us, the three elected members, regarding your confidence in us.
>
> I may add that I regret my total inability of satisfying Your Excellency's request at this juncture, as any statement made by me or my colleagues at that meeting was very conditional to your pronouncement to us during the last interview we had with Your Excellency.[21]

Following this exchange, the Governor requested Faye to resign as a member of government and of the Executive Council:

> In accordance with established constitutional practice it is not possible . . . for a member of the Executive Council to make the public statement which I am satisfied you made last Thursday, or indeed to take up the attitude you have chosen to adopt in your letter, of refusing to repeat to the Governor what you said at a public meeting and at the same time continue to be a member of Executive Council.[22]

The Governor informed Faye that the constitutional line of action to take was for him to send in a letter of resignation both as a member of Government without portfolio and also from the Executive Council; the Governor would then send a reply and both letters would be published. At the same time, the Governor explained that Faye's membership of the Legislative Council would not be affected by these developments; he would remain the Senior Elected member and not be responsible to the Governor for any opinions he may wish to express in that Chamber.

Again, Faye refused to respond by the deadline the Governor had stipulated, i.e. the next meeting of the Executive Council scheduled two days hence. Faye's stated ground for this was that:

> I feel in duty bound to consult with my constituents and to be advised by them before taking such an important step as requested by Your Excellency.
>
> ... In the circumstances I am compelled to ask for some little time and much as I feel loath to dislocate the machinery of Government, yet I must ask for time longer than the noon of 3 July.[23]

Faye asked for an extension of five more days. This the Governor rejected; he proceeded to convene a meeting of the Council. Even on the day of the said meeting, the Governor invited Faye to his office so he could review the situation with him, in the presence of the Colonial Secretary and the Attorney General. Faye still refused to resign.

The Governor then went to the Council meeting and, in the presence of Faye, officially reminded members of recent developments and of Faye having been granted the option of resigning but he had chosen not to do so. Therefore, and as a consequence, he was removing Faye from the office of a member of government without portfolio and, in accordance with the Royal Instructions, was suspending him as a member of Executive Council.[24] This was to take effect from 4 July 1952. In line with practice in the House of Commons in Britain, Faye was informed that he was at liberty to make a personal statement before the Governor suspended him. Faye declined the invitation and Wyn-Harris signed the Instrument.

As for Garba-Jahumpa and Madi, their reactions, and their fates, were different. The former, in a letter dated 1 July 1952, wrote:

> Further to our interview yesterday, I write to inform you after consultation with the Inner Council of the Gambia Muslim Congress, the majority of whom were at the mass meeting of the 26 June, I cannot associate myself with the personal loss of confidence in the Governor expressed by my

> Honourable friend, the Hon. and Rev. J. C. Faye, M. B. E.,
> at that mass meeting when he said, "If the Governor says he
> has no confidence in us I—I have no confidence in him."[25]

In the case of Madi, two days after the Mohammedan School meeting, he had gone to see the Governor privately and reported to him what Faye had said and all that had transpired. He promptly followed this visit with a formal letter assuring the Governor that "I dissociate myself from the views expressed by the Rev. Faye in so far as the loss of confidence in you is concerned."[26] Both Garba-Jahumpa and Madi retained their membership of the Executive and Legislative Councils and Garba-Jahumpa continued in his position as a minister without portfolio.

The repercussions of Faye's suspension were not unanticipated. In the House of Commons in London, some members of parliament who were friends of Faye raised the matter. They were led by Hon. R. Sorenson, MP.

Locally in Bathurst, the reaction was much more dramatic. The Executive Council of the DP convened an emergency meeting and a telegram was instantly despatched to the Secretary of State; it announced: "Bathurst community strongly deprecates action of Governor in suspending Rev. John Faye from Executive Council and will petition accordingly." Some of the signatories were: Ousman Jeng, President, Muslim Elders; Imam Mamah Ba; L. F. Mendy; Councillor J. F. Senegal; Alhaji Momadou Jagne; E. Lloyd Evans, MBE, J.P; Badara Cham; M. A. Gibril; and Elizabeth Cherry.

Though it was not known publicly, on advice from the Colonial Office, the Governor was keen that the matter should be resolved at the earliest opportunity. He was ready to reinstate Faye on the following terms: that Faye apologize publicly; that he admit that the whole matter had been wrongly handled; and, in addition, admit that, if his statement at the political rally had conveyed the impression that he had no confidence in the Governor, then that was not the intention, but that, in fact, he had *every* confidence in the Governor. The final condition was that Faye should promise that, in the future, he would fully collaborate with the colonial administration in the operation of the constitution.

The Governor had to do everything to save face and adopt a no-nonsense stance; as he said:

> [Faye's reinstatement] will have to be done in such a way to
> make it clear to the whole of Bathurst that the reinstatement
> is not the result of the cries of the rabble, but due to the proper
> approach by responsible citizens who have called Mr. Faye
> to reason and to see the error of his ways.[27]

Wyn-Harris was also aware that the longer the saga continued, the more people would become sympathetic to Faye, including his opponents, and even see him as a martyr. It was also anticipated by the colonial officials that Faye would exploit the event to increase his popularity. As it was noted: "It was evident on that occasion that however small might be the merits of Mr. Faye's case he was capable of whipping up a very considerable degree of support among the more irresponsible elements of the Bathurst community."[28] And, it was later admitted that "He [Faye] has gained in popularity because of his suspension particularly on the grounds that he was not the only sinner."[29]

As if to give substance to this apprehension, the DP convened a mass rally not only to protest against the way and manner in which their leader had been treated, but to plan a march to Government House, and even attack it. The meeting attracted large crowds of party militants and sympathizers. However, proceedings were interrupted by a heavy rainfall and the meeting was called off till the next day. As it turned out, plans were afoot for negotiations with the Governor and his officials to begin on the same day so the rally was postponed *sine die* by Faye himself.

The Governor then held long consultations on the crisis with the Anglican Bishop, Roderick N. Coote (1951-1957), and they agreed on the setting up of a committee of twenty-five responsible and highly-regarded citizens, from all denominations and across the Bathurst community, to assume responsibility to resolve the matter. As the principals had mellowed over time, the negotiations turned out to be both cordial and fruitful.

The committee came up with a well-argued petition in which it appealed to the Governor for Faye's reinstatement:

> on the grounds that there had been a misunderstanding about what was actually said at the public meeting on the 26 June, and that they had confidence that on the present misunderstanding being cleared up, Mr. Faye could perform with benefit to the Gambia the duties of a member of Executive Council. It is fair to state that Mr. Faye is also of the opinion that his suspension was due to a misunderstanding and was not due to any default on his part, but has also independently assured the Governor that he did not intend to give the impression at the public meeting on the 26 June that he had lost confidence in the Governor and has expressed willingness to cooperate in the Government of The Gambia.[30]

According to the Governor, after meeting with him the committee consulted with Faye and convinced him to write to Wyn-Harris assuring him that he, Faye, "did not intend to convey loss of confidence in the Governor and offered to cooperate whenever and wherever his cooperation was sought".[31] The Governor recognized that this was not the type of apology he expected but one which would serve as a basis for reinstating Faye. He also believed that:

> Faye was in an awkward position with his more hot-headed followers, and I early realized that sympathy of even the moderates was with him, after he had called off the public meeting . . . To insist on an apology which Faye found too humiliating to give, and which I would not get, was merely to create permanently in Bathurst a majority dissident party with Faye a martyr at its head. [32]

Wyn-Harris was also of the view that Faye was anxious "to come back into the fold" and would not in the future repeat the type of action that had led to his suspension. Furthermore, the Governor was said to have been very appreciative of the sincerity and goodwill of the deputation and promised to reconsider his decision, on the assumption that he would be assured of the loyal and friendly cooperation of Mr. Faye after he had been reinstated.

Through the Bishop, Faye was informed that the Governor was ready to reinstate him but that he, the Governor, would have a free hand in drafting the public announcement to be issued on the latest happenings. In the event, objections raised by Faye on the draft of the announcement were accepted by the Governor and sealed at a meeting between the Governor, Faye and the Bishop. It was followed by a letter to Faye, dated 25 July 1952, in which Wyn-Harris informed him that he:

> had signed the Instrument removing your suspension from sitting in Executive Council as from Monday July 28, and at the same time I would inform you that I am reappointing you as member of Government without portfolio on the same terms as your original letter of appointment.[33]

Faye accepted both the reinstatement and the reappointment, confirmed in a letter expressing his gratitude for the removal of his suspension; he pledged his "whole-hearted co-operation in anything that will establish the good government, and enhance the progress of this territory".[34]

No doubt, the way in which Faye had stood up to the Governor and eventually won his reinstatement, increased his popularity. The news was received with joy by the hierarchy and the generality of the DP, who instantly sent a telegram to the Secretary of State, in which they expressed their satisfaction and informed him that the petition mentioned in the earlier telegram was now cancelled. The telegram was signed by A. E. Cham Joof, Alhaji Ousman Jeng, J. Koto Richards, S. Lloyd Evans, and Alhaji M. A. Jobe.[35] As put by a witness: "The heart of the community heaved a deep sigh of relief."[36]

Faye's supporters were jubilant; a procession of cars and other means of transport went round the town hooting and singing, and drummers provided rousing music to add more life to the party, all the way to Government House. This "Goodwill Demonstration" was intended "to convey to the Governor their relief and to pledge their collaboration and friendly cooperation in all affecting the welfare of The Gambia".[37]

In Government House, there was also much relief. The Governor observed that this was a most historic day in his life and that he was very proud to be Governor of The Gambia. This satisfaction with the turn of events was seen in his report to the Secretary of State:

> On the afternoon of August 2nd a deputation of about 30 came to Government House, accompanied by a crowd of about one thousand and four African bands.
>
> The deputation, which consisted of men and women of all walks of life, and representatives of both the Christian faith and also of Islam were invited into Government House, while the crowd danced and sang outside. The spokesman of the delegation in a few words expressed his thanks for Mr. Faye's reinstatement and their full confidence that he would co-operate with the Government for the good government of the Gambia, and wished to reaffirm their intense loyalty to the Crown. To this I replied and the deputation, after being entertained to tea, then led the crowd away in procession to the accompaniment of drums. While there is no doubt that the demonstration was aimed at strengthening Mr. Faye's position, it was clear that the general wish of Bathurst is for the unofficial members to work with Government.[38]

Second Suspension: First Absence Without Permission

The second occasion of Faye's suspension from the Executive Council was in April 1953. Actually, he had left for Accra on 23 March 1953. Before his departure he prepared a note to the Clerk to the Executive Council, O. C. NJie, informing him of his travel to Accra for a few days and requesting that the Governor and Kennedy (Coronation Committee Secretary) should be informed; he promised to be back "as soon as my business is consummated."[39] However, Faye specifically requested his family to deliver the letter only after his departure.

Though Faye had (deliberately) left no address in Accra, the Colonial Secretary was able to trace his main contact to Honourable Casely Hayford, Minister of Agriculture and Natural Resources in Kwame Nkrumah's government. Through him the Colonial Secretary informed Faye that his absence was causing difficulties in the handling of some vital matters currently under discussion and for which the Governor intended to seek the advice of all unofficial members of Council. The Colonial Secretary, at this stage, brought to Faye's attention the relevant provisions of the Royal Instructions on the matter in hand, and spelt out the possible ramifications of Faye's omissions.[40]

In reply, Faye sent a telegram, and then a letter, in which he explained that he had earlier despatched another letter to the Officer Administering the Government (OAG) and the Clerk of Councils, indicating that he could not obtain a flight from Ghana earlier than 16 April. He apologized for any inconveniences caused by his action and promised that "should I have recourse to leave Bathurst at a short notice on any future occasion, as happened in this, I shall not fail to have a direct contact with His Excellency" and closely follow the stipulated procedures. With tongue in cheek Faye also informed the officials that he had been using the time spent in waiting for his flight visiting educational and agricultural institutions "so as to widen my knowledge in these fields in so far as West Africa is concerned".[41]

In actual fact, Faye's real agenda was mainly to consult with senior members of the Convention People's Party (CPP) of Prime Minister Kwame Nkrumah on their struggle against colonialism and its applicability to the Gambian situation; he sought advice on strategy and modalities for ensuring that independence would be achieved in the shortest possible time. Forms of collaboration between the two countries and with the other British colonies were also on Faye's agenda.

The colonial administration in Bathurst had other views as to Faye's intentions for the unauthorized visit to Accra:

> It is reasonable to suppose that he was trying to gain C.
> P. P . . . support, both financially and otherwise, with the
> long-term plan of finding a seat for himself on the dominion
> government in Accra [for all West African British colonies,

as favoured by the CPP]. He certainly requires financial support as the interpleader proceedings . . . have gone against his interest and certain of his property has been attached.[42]

On returning home after a period of absence of 24 days—during which the Executive Council had sat three times—Faye met with the Governor; on this occasion the Governor had been advised by the Colonial Office to be flexible, given the financial and other difficulties Faye was experiencing. The Governor merely informed Faye that, in accordance with clause 4 (1) (d) of the Royal Instructions, and by his own action, he had automatically vacated his seat on the Executive Council; an appointed member of the Executive Council shall vacate his seat if, without permission of the Governor, he shall be absent from The Gambia. Nevertheless, "in view of Mr. Faye's written undertaking to the Colonial Secretary, and on the definite understanding that absence without proper permission would not occur again, the Governor reinstated Faye."[43]

This was not a benevolent act but, in a sense, it was calculating, as garnered from a letter from the Governor to the Secretary of State. He reported that:

> At the same time I told him (Faye) that his pecuniary embarrassment was giving Government serious anxiety and had made it difficult for me to reinstate him but I was doing so because I did not wish to take advantage of the situation which he had created by being absent without leave, particularly as leave of absence for a short period is never normally refused.
>
> At the moment Faye is, I think, steadily losing ground with most people of any standing and I am anxious to do nothing which would enable him to divert into a channel of martyrdom the steam which is carrying him along. This would be particularly embarrassing at this stage when we are about to start talks on the constitution.[44]

Third Suspension: Second Absence Without Permission

The second occasion of Faye's absence without permission and his third suspension from the Executive Council was a few months later, in August/September 1953. On this occasion, however, it was handled somewhat differently by Waddell, the OAG, who was in charge of the Colony in the absence of the Governor on official leave.

A day before Faye departed Bathurst for Senegal on 28 August 1953 he had telephoned the Acting Clerk of Council, his old friend Louis F. Valentine, to inform him that, as he would be away, he would not be able to attend the meeting of the Standing Finance Committee scheduled for the day following, and hoped to be back for the next meeting of the Executive Council. Faye did not show up for this meeting. After some days, on 7 September, his wife telephoned on his behalf to say that her husband had been compelled to stay longer than anticipated. Days later, on 19 September, Faye sent a letter to the Clerk offering an apology for his unexpected long absence.

Naturally, the purpose of this trip was not made public, but the colonial administration had reports to the effect that Faye had gone to Kaolack in Senegal to buy groundnut cake and castor seed for an unknown businessman in London; he was accompanied by his close associate, Pa Henry M. Jones.[45]

On Faye's eventual return, on 21 September, he met with the OAG, basically to express his regrets for his absence. This visit, he explained, was originally meant to be for a few days but was delayed due to urgent unanticipated personal business; he also explained what efforts he had made to keep the administration informed of his travel plans.

All this was to fall on deaf ears, for the OAG had already made up his mind. He informed Faye that, in accordance with Section 4 (1) (d) of the Royal Instructions, Faye had vacated his seat on the Executive Council. This time, however, "I do not (repeat not) propose to reappoint him," the OAG made plain in a telegram to the Colonial Office.[46] The Governor (who was on official leave in England) was informed of this action and gave it his "entire support". As surmised by the Colonial Office: "This somewhat fortuitous development seemed to solve the Governor's difficulties over what to do about the increasingly embarrassing financial position of the Rev. Faye."[47]

The gravity of the situation was not lost on Faye and his supporters; they instantly submitted to the Secretary of State for the Colonies one letter each from Faye and the DP, one memorial from Faye, and one petition from the DP. In Faye's letter he argued that in the first instance of absence without permission he had promised to cooperate with the government officials and this he had done faithfully: "but I do not translate cooperation to mean a servile 'Yes' to every question, even should I know that thus saying would in the end bring complications between my people and the Government." He had then rendered service in Council "based on truth and sincerity" but this had now led to a misunderstanding and he "is now viewed with suspicion and labelled as reactionary or something bordering same".[48]

Faye took to the warpath. He declared that both to himself and to most of his people the prompt application of the Instructions "is taken to mean good riddance of a person whom officialdom here views, with no true justification whatsoever, as a thorn in the flesh". For him, this characterization was based on his having opposed or questioned actions taken or intended by the administration on a number of subjects, some of which he detailed as: introduction and purchase of tear gas; transfer of four villages, against their will, from Kombo East to Kombo Central; immigration regulations limiting entry of Indians (managers in the Chellarams' business ventures) into the Colony to compete against the British and French commercial houses.

Other issues on which Faye had challenged the administration's position were as follows: the raising of aid or a loan to meet augmented salary scales, as higher salaries would automatically lead to increased prices of goods, and the money would eventually find its way into European hands; the dismissal of a competent productive master-fisherman; Bathurst as a free port which would serve French interests; and the new Constitution which, inter alia, would provide for full ministerial posts for unofficial members of the Executive. On these and other matters Faye's views were drastically different from those of the colonial officials; naturally, for this, many did not like him. Regardless of their antagonism, Faye maintained that he merely saw himself as carrying out his duty to his country and to England and nothing would stop him from doing so.

The letter was followed by an articulate memorial sent by Faye to the Secretary of State criticizing the rigid application of the Royal Instructions. Among other questions raised was that of whether from a technical point of view the Royal Instructions were applicable to Executive Council members who were without portfolios.

As regards the DP, a protest telegram was directed to the Secretary of State by Alieu Cham Joof, followed by a letter and petition signed by no fewer than 45 citizens. As Cham Joof pointed out, many more would have signed the petition were it not for the fact that the party leadership had decided to exclude "all civil servants in order to avoid complications and were it not for the fact that mail day is quite near". Surprisingly, among the signatories were Rev. E. Ben Stafford of the Methodist Church and Rev. Willie Macauley, Curate at St Mary's Anglican Pro-Cathedral.[49]

The petition reiterated some of the argumentation in Faye's submissions, particularly the charge of victimization and that his contravention of the Instructions was unintentional. As it said, "we feel that the constant and unshaken efforts of the Hon. and Rev. J. C. Faye in representing us in Council have earned him no little victimization, a phase of which the present situation marks." For over five years Faye had offered "yeoman and highly appreciated service for his country, people and the Commonwealth"; without his presence in Council their representation would not only be "weakened but also ineffective".

In the correspondence between the OAG and the Colonial Office three major grounds for rejection of these and other arguments were emphasized. First, that the Instructions must be seen to be observed not just because of its mandatory wording but also "because it is an important safeguard to good government, as breaches of its observance can make it difficult if not impossible for the Governor to make suitable arrangements for the conduct of public business".[50]

Next, this was the second time in the year that Faye had been absent without permission and, after the experience of the first he should have known the likely consequences if he repeated the same thing. Faye, the

THE VERY REVEREND J. C. FAYE: HIS LIFE AND TIMES

OAG argued, had not been suspended or deprived of his seat by the OAG or by any other official but by himself through his own action.

Third, the absence of Faye had "caused prejudice to the proper despatch of public business". More plainly put by the Secretary of State himself:

> as both [Faye's] unauthorized absences this year have been due to urgent private business, it appears to me that the demands of his business interests have proved to be incompatible with those of his membership of the Executive Council and the growing public duties entailed, and I would not feel justified in these circumstances in directing that he should now be reappointed to Executive Council.[51]

As if wilfully to obfuscate the issue in hand the Governor decided to introduce a fourth, i.e., "a more serious—and to my mind—overriding difficulty of which Mr. Faye is aware, but which he has not chosen to refer either in his memorial to you or when meeting his supporters."[52] This was Faye's financial burdens which, for Wyn-Harris, were a background factor in determining the official response to the reactions of Faye and his group. Arguably, this should not have been a relevant factor as the matter had been thrashed out at the time of Faye's reinstatement after the second suspension.

Faye had explained then that his financial problems were caused by his being a trustee of the Pilot Produce Syndicate. But he had recently entered into a number of contracts which would straighten the affairs of the business; he would sever his business connections after this had been achieved. Despite this, for the Governor: "Mr. Faye's affairs are still inextricably mixed up with those of the Pilot Produce Syndicate and both he and the firm are insolvent." To buttress his preoccupation with Faye's finances Wyn-Harris enumerated other judgements against Faye, some of which are discussed below.

Notwithstanding all of these exchanges within and between both sides, the suspension of Faye from the Executive Council was effected. Importantly, the Secretary of State took a more radical position on the subject than the Governor. The latter had advised his superiors that when Faye could satisfy him that his business interests would no longer interfere with his public duties he would be willing to recommend that Faye be reappointed. The Secretary, on the other hand, strongly opposed anything that would leave Faye with the impression of a promise of reinstatement under certain conditions.[53] The decision was final. Faye was suspended and was not appointed again as a member of the Executive Council till after the Legislative Council elections in October 1954.[54]

Governor Percy Wyn-Harris versus Rev. John Colley Faye

Court Litigations against Faye.

As indicated in the preceding section, a critical area that was a source of tension between Faye and the colonial administration was that of Faye's finances and his court cases. No other leading politician of the day was so deeply embroiled in legal battles as Faye. As shown in Chapter 9, this also reverberated on Faye's work in the Church.

Perhaps the case involving the Pilot Produce Syndicate was the most threatening. On his return to Bathurst from Kristi-kunda, Faye set up the syndicate, as a trustee, partly to provide employment for unemployed traders, and also to counter the exploitative methods of the European trading firms, particularly the UAC, which were buying groundnuts at cheap prices. Faye mobilized the traders who were members of the syndicate and sent them to buy the nuts at competitive prices and resell them directly to the Gambia Oilseeds Marketing Board, which enjoyed a monopoly of exporting Gambian groundnuts.

Faye worked very hard to ensure the organization's success. During his visit to London after attending the conference of the Commonwealth Parliamentary Association in Canada, in September 1952 (see above), he devoted much time to fund-raising, not only locally but also in Europe. In a meeting with Colonial Office officials he reported that the syndicate owned two cutters, four lorries, six properly constructed buying stations with retail stores, and some 2,000 pounds worth of consumer goods, mainly textiles. He added that the syndicate had paid out 10 percent dividends to its investors in the two previous years; lack of capital was the major bottleneck. He further revealed that his visit to Europe had been successful in that he secured financial backing in Holland. In London the Syndicate had found a representative and the company was to be registered as a private company known as the Gambia Produce Syndicate.[55]

This report, whether real or imaginary, merely increased apprehension among colonial officialdom: "Current rumour has it that his [Faye's] Pilot Produce Syndicate is in debt to the tune of some 15,000 pounds and his new found business friends in England and Holland whom he has met on his overseas visit, may well regret their connection."[56]

The Syndicate's modus operandi was not to the satisfaction of the Bathurst Chamber of Commerce—dominated by Europeans in the employment of multinationals—which proceeded to undermine its operations; one technique employed was to get their agents to offer to the syndicate's traders higher prices for their produce than the syndicate could. Another tactic, used this time by the government, was to withhold financial payments due to the syndicate; with this it was unable to pay the traders who in turn could not pay the farmers for their produce.

Eventually, the syndicate was unable to raise capital to sustain the project and it collapsed. A successful court action was brought against trustee Faye in January 1953 for an amount of 1,150.00 pounds and another suit for 700.00 pounds was pending. A *garnishee* order was obtained against the expected payments to the syndicate from the Gambia Oilseeds Marketing Board. Altogether, it was estimated that the syndicate was in debt to the tune of 10,000.00 pounds or more.[57] At the same time, its delivery of groundnuts dropped considerably, from over 600 tons in 1952 to 80 tons in 1953.[58] Some of the traders made losses but rather than retain the landed properties which they had deposited as collateral, Faye returned the title deeds to them and disposed of his own properties to settle the debts outstanding.

Other Financial Woes.

It cannot be overemphasized that the debts involved were not necessarily for Faye's personal use, but he was accountable as they were in his name or in his trust. This was particularly so for the amounts used for the benefit of the syndicate and other business and political ventures. For the 1951-1952 period alone a list composed by the Colonial Secretary included the following: [59]

- The judgement writ by C. R. L. Page, the Chairman of the Gambia Oilseeds Marketing Board (GOMB)—of which Faye was a member—for recovery of the sum of 1,150.00 pounds and 17 guineas costs.

- Another suit of 2,000.00 pounds filed against Faye as a trustee of the Syndicate by an African trader.

- Unrevealed but substantial amounts (between 10,000.00 pounds and 20,000.00 pounds) owed to Henry Madi, a fellow Council member; Madi had not pressed for payment.

- A debt of 160.00 pounds for seed nuts supplied by the GOMB in 1951.

- Seed nuts valued at 1,200.00 pounds issued to the Syndicate (1951) but written off by the GOMB.

- An amount of 300.00 pounds owed to the GOMB by the Syndicate for a rice credit scheme administered by the Syndicate as agents of the Board.

- A judgement for the United Africa Company for 400.00 pounds in respect of goods advanced to the Junior Civil Service Co-operative Association which Faye administered. No writ of execution was issued because of unavailability of assets.

Of great interest to the colonial administration was a credit of 10,000.00 pounds remitted from the head office of the Bank of British West Africa to Faye's account in Bathurst at the end of January 1953. The Colonial Office was determined to trace the source, mainly due to their suspicion that the money was to be used for purposes not related to Faye's business activities. It made enquiries at the Bank of England which, after exhaustive investigations, concluded that without more precise information, such as the date of the transaction, it could not be of much help. It was speculated that the creditor may have been the London representative of the Syndicate—a Mr. Smith, from New Zealand, who had earlier accompanied Faye to his appointment at the Colonial Office. Or it may have originated from the financier in Holland referred to by Faye at the same meeting.[60]

Faye's dealings with the courts deteriorated to the extent that, in one case, the bailiffs were instructed to attach his landed and personal property unless the money was paid. A claim was made for the release of the property from attachment as specific items belonged to other claimants; these included personal effects but also real estate in Serre-kunda with a building on it. In this last, evidence was adduced to support the claim that the property had been sold to the claimant for 200.00 pounds. Despite other legal arguments the final judgement was that such moves had been made with the intention of defeating the creditors.

Much the same happened with regards to another property which had been attached and on which one of the brothers of Faye resided; judgement was that Faye, as judgement-debtor, "possesses an interest in the property and his interest can be attached." Thus, the two claims were dismissed.[61] A writ of execution resulted in 266.00 pounds for the Dobson Street house and 199 pounds 9 shillings for his Serre-kunda property, leaving a balance of 710 pounds 8 shillings still outstanding but with no further major disposable assets available. Thus, the *berceau* at Dobson Street was lost, not to mention family and household property attached by the courts at various points in time.

The Sam Sylva Drama

Yet another event that involved a suit against Faye was the civil case brought by Sam Sylva. As observed earlier in the previous chapter, personal abuse and character assassinations of political leaders were the order of the day, particularly during election campaigns. During the campaign for the 1954 elections this degenerated considerably. Sam Sylva, a senior official in the government's Labour Department, had been on the side of Faye in his earlier disputes with the colonial system but, especially since the emergence of the UP, he had become a vicious critic of Faye. He went to the extent of writing untruths about Faye in flyers and handouts, but Faye chose to ignore them. Sylva then decided on another strategy for attracting Faye's attention. Every morning for four days, on his way to work, he would take a strategic position by the large drain opposite the residence of Faye on Grant Street and rain insults on him, his wife, his party-mates, and his family.

This drama attracted a crowd, mainly of persons on their way to work or school. Sylva would not cease his diatribes even when the reverend gentleman, who had been at the morning Church mass, appeared, slowly riding his bicycle, and was about to alight and enter his home. Indeed, the abuse would reach a crescendo and be more biting when Faye appeared on the scene. Faye would ignore him and quietly continue. On the fifth day, Sylva chose to direct his insults at Faye' mother who, in fact, had had a hand in Sylva's upbringing and had been very generous towards his own mother. Faye's patience was challenged to the limit as he had so much respect for women in general and insulting them to be totally repugnant. Incensed, he parked his bicycle by his gate and rushed for Sylva. He wrestled him to the ground, picked him up again and threw him headlong into the drain; he had generously applied wrestling techniques reminiscent of his younger days. Sylva was rescued by members of the growing crowd. He suffered wounds in various places and a broken leg.

Faye was sued to court by Sylva and the UP. In his evidence, he described and demonstrated how he *"gal-gal"* Sylva, *"busulu"* him, and landed him in the drain; that is, Faye wrapped his right foot around Sylva's left foot, lifted and settled the little man on his shoulder before delivering him into the drain, head-first. The court audience broke into rapturous laughter. For the colonial administration, though, this was a big blot on Faye's character.

Options for the Colonial Administration

One possible consequence for the administration was the impact of Faye's worries, particularly over his financial situation, on his official duties and responsibilities. This was well articulated by the Colonial Secretary on Faye's return from his extended trip overseas after participating in the Commonwealth Parliamentary Conference in September 1952. He opined:

Faye duly returned and does not appear to be quite his own self, and it may be that his business matters are very much on his mind. Certainly, he has shown very little political or "ministerial" activity since his return and spends much of his time in the Ex. Co. in somewhat of a dream. Perhaps he is dreaming of the cutters, lorries and buying stations to which you refer in your letter.[62]

This was repeated one year later in the context of Faye's third suspension from the Executive Council:

Mr. Faye has twice found it necessary during this year to absent himself from The Gambia on private business, and it appears to me that the nature of his business affairs makes it impossible for him to perform adequately the growing public duties attached to membership of Executive Council. I am not therefore prepared to direct that he should now be reappointed thereto.[63]

Needless to note the concern among officials about how all this affected the image and standing of the Executive Council in society. This is what led the Colonial Secretary to argue:

While we can only go on the proved facts it is clear that Faye's position as a member of Government and of the Executive Council is rapidly becoming impossible, but having regard to the events of last June it is unlikely that he will resign of his own accord. If the Governor had to suspend him from Executive Council there is little doubt that there would be a rallying of Faye's standard and that there would be a cry of "political persecution". There is a real danger that the impropriety of his commercial actions could become a political issue which might have far-reaching effects as on this occasion there could be no reinstatement until he had completely cleared his indebtedness which appears unlikely.[64]

A major difficulty for the Governor and his advisers was what line of action to adopt towards Faye "when Judgement debts running into some thousands of pounds have been proved against him". There was the possibility of bankruptcy. The Legal Library in the Colonial Office looked into this, but it seemed that there was no Bankruptcy Ordinance in force in the territory. But, as the Supreme Court Ordinance (1889) provided that the laws of England in force on 1 November 1888 were in force in the Colony, then the Metropolitan Bankruptcy Act 1883 was thought to be applicable. It was recognized, though, that this approach would prove unproductive, as a bankruptcy petition could only be presented by the creditors or by the debtor himself, and "it is most unlikely that any creditor would file bankruptcy proceedings against Mr. Faye." This being so, the office of the Secretary of State itself reasoned:

> We assume that there is unfortunately little likelihood of evidence becoming available which might lead to conviction for dishonesty or criminal negligence . . . If other creditors are unwilling to do so, might not the Marketing Board be discreetly persuaded, perhaps in the interest of producers, to institute proceedings, in spite of Faye's membership of the Board.[65]

It also appeared likely that Faye would keep his seat on the Legislative Council, as the prospects of his being prosecuted successfully for fraud or other similar offences and of his being imprisoned for over six months were quite remote, going by section 13 (1) (e) of the Gambia (Leg. Co.) Order in Council, 1946 to 1951.[66] Concerning the Executive Council, it was felt by the administration that although bankruptcy did not explicitly debar Faye from being a member "even the most misguided of Mr. Faye's followers could not protest very vehemently against the termination of his appointment as a member of the Executive Council once he had vacated his seat on account of bankruptcy in the Legislative Council."[67] Furthermore, Article 4 (1) of the Royal Instructions was not a basis for termination of a member's appointment if he refused to resign; he could only be suspended under Article 4 (6).

This being the situation, the setting up of a commission of enquiry, in camera, to look into Faye's activities as a "trustee" of the syndicate was proposed. Such an approach was thought not to be the right way to establish that Faye's connection with the syndicate and its mismanagement had been the cause of his suspension from the Executive Council. Therefore:

> unless evidence is forthcoming sufficient to warrant a prosecution either for fraud or some other offence, then I very much fear that the Governor of The Gambia will be stuck with Mr. Faye, in spite of his mounting debts, until the period of his appointment expires.[68]

In a letter to the Colonial Office, the Colonial Secretary once cautioned, very perceptively, that "as Faye has an aptitude for wriggling out of financial troubles it is not at all certain whether he will yet crash, but the indications are not too promising."[69] At the end of the day, Faye did not crash; rather, it was the hopes and expectations of the colonial set-up that were dashed. Faye lived to continue his political struggles for the political advancement of his country and peoples. As if by design, the drama was soon overtaken by the instances of absence without permission and by his second and third suspensions from the Executive Council recounted above.

Freed from the strictures of membership of the apex executive body, Faye felt at liberty to attack the colonial system without any qualms. As had been feared by the administration on other occasions, Faye took advantage of his expulsion to present himself to the population as a political martyr. The Governor expressed his apprehensions thus:

> He has been holding public meetings and he is using every weapon on which he can lay his hands to incite dissatisfaction with every activity of the Government and, not unnaturally, one of his main fields is the question of the proposed new Constitution. It is impossible to assess at the moment what his success will be, but clearly he can gain a great deal of sympathy over this particular attack. In a public speech he

has described the whole Constitution as spurious and bogus and I know he is putting it about that he signed the Committee [of 34]'s Report in the interest of a peaceful solution and not because he believed in it.[70]

Even a cursory reading of the voluminous correspondence between the Colonial Office, London, and Government House, Bathurst, leads to the conclusion that they were both out to "kick him [Faye] out" of the legislative bodies and destroy his political career. At different times he was labelled "irresponsible", "leader of hooligans", "a fool", and the like. Faye's mischievous hands were seen in anything that smelt of destabilization or seemed inimical to the interest of the established authority. Cases in point were the organized strike of sanitary workers in Bathurst in June 1952, when it was asserted that "there is suspicion that Faye supported, if not encouraged, the strike".[71] Then again, at about the same time, Faye was suspected of being behind the hotly-disputed candidacy of the Chernor Bande family in the chieftaincy dispute in the Fulladu West District in February 1952. Perhaps, aside from Edward F. Small, no other Gambian politician of the colonial era was pursued with such doggedness and determination by the British colonial administration.

As has been noted in several places, Wyn-Harris was one of the longest serving Governors (1949 to 1958) but, altogether, he and his administration were far from popular. In January 1956 he also dismissed NJie, as he had done Faye before him, from the same Executive Council. In this instance, early in October 1955, there had been a fracas between supporters of the UP and the MC in Bathurst near the home of Garba-Jahumpa. A number of UP backers were arrested, which caused NJie to accuse Garba-Jahumpa of having instigated the dispute and of having imported whips from Senegal to flog UP supporters. NJie invited the Attorney General to charge Garba-Jahumpa and, when this was refused, he accused the police superintendent of condoning violence and treating people's lives with laxity.

The Governor mounted a commission of inquiry under F. H. Baker, a former senior judge in the Nigerian government, who did not find sufficient evidence to support NJie's charges; his report was also very critical of NJie's reactions. The Governor considered this enough grounds to instruct NJie to resign as a member of the Executive Council and as Minister of Education and Social Welfare. In a move, reminiscent of the Faye case in 1952, NJie refused. Wyn-Harris first suspended and then dismissed him in January 1956. He was never to be reinstated.

The root of the problem between Faye and Wyn-Harris was that the former totally rejected what he saw as racism and a superiority complex on the part of the latter. This Faye termed "negrophobism". For him, such attitudes of Wyn-Harris had been nurtured in Kenya where he had joined the colonial service in 1929 at the age of 23; he subsequently served for 20 years and rose to the position of Chief Native Commissioner. Faye interpreted some of Wyn-Harris's policies as being derived from prejudices brought over from Kenya; he therefore seized every opportunity to show that Gambians were not Kenyans and that the high-handedness of British colonialism in Kenya would not be tolerated in The Gambia. As history would have it, Wyn-Harris's successor, Edward Windley (1958 to 1962), also joined the colonial service in Kenya as a district officer (1931), two years after Wyn-Harris; he also held the position of Chief Native Commissioner and Minister for African Affairs (1953). As Faye put it:

> Wyn-Harris laid the egg of the Mau Mau [freedom-fighters] and it was Windley who minded the egg until it hatched Mau Mau. It was the same man, Windley, who took over from Wyn-Harris in Kenya and who also succeeded him as Governor here.[72]

For Faye, Wyn-Harris compared very unfavourably with Barkworth Wright. The latter was aware of what was happening in South Africa with the accession of the National Party to power in 1948 and the beginnings of the process of institutionalizing *apartheid*; he was determined that any trace of racism and segregation in public affairs in The Gambia should be instantly uprooted. Concretely, this was reflected in Barkworth Wright's directives that the "European Club" in Fajara should be de-Europeanized and open to all who could afford the membership and other fees; this was followed by the change of name to "Bathurst Club". Similarly, at the Royal Victoria Hospital the "European Block" was changed to "Private Block" and was also open to anyone who could afford the charges. Hence the affection Gambians had for Wright and their resistance to his premature transfer to Cyprus, as discussed at length in Chapter 3.

Wyn-Harris was seen in many places as tyrannical, contemptuous of his subjects, and intolerant of any locals who appeared to challenge his authority. Besides, there was sufficient evidence to show that he was opposed to rapid constitutional progress, just because he saw Gambians as unfit to make a success of parliamentary democracy. For Faye, the DP stalwarts and the Governor's "enemies", nothing could be more fitting for this obdurate and opinionated enemy of African progress than his departure from the Colony which he had ruled for nine long years. Apparently, on the due date, in April 1958, he returned to England from Dakar without much protocol after crossing the border in the upper reaches of the River Gambia into Senegal; no doubt this was in an effort to avoid farewell demonstrations that had been planned by Faye's party. How vastly different from the departure of his immediate predecessor![73]

One of the leading weekly newspapers, *The Vanguard*, endorsed this perspective.[74] It argued that after nine years the outgoing Governor had realized little:

> He has been an obstacle to us instead, a big obstacle too. As soon as he came here everything became stagnant . . . Urgent schemes that were to work, such as the Bathurst Reclaimed Area, were suspended indefinitely.

After enumerating the various areas in which there had been retardation during the period the article concluded:

> He is exactly the opposite of our sincere Sir Andrew Barkworth Wright . . . Sir Percy has really wasted our time, money and energy but we should not be discouraged. There is still a chance to prove ourselves capable of facing the struggle for freedom. We do not know the man who comes next but there is still cause to hope that the Colonial

Office will not allow him to come here as another Sir Percy Wyn-Harris.[75]

Summary Observations

All of the problematic episodes discussed in this chapter occurred almost concurrently; that is, Faye's rebellious attitude towards Wyn-Harris over Lyttleton's visit overlapped somewhat with the incidences of his absences without permission. For the administration these were burdensome and time-consuming; but they had to be squarely confronted because of their potentially explosive character and because of the personality in question. Faye never hesitated to remind the authorities, before the 1954 elections, that he was the First Elected Member from the Colony and that he had strong support in whichever party was in power in London. The all-inclusive character of his party and of his primary constituency provided him with added clout.

CHAPTER 6

POLITICIAN: A BUMPY POLITICAL TERRAIN

New Actors on an Expanded Political Stage

The 1954-1962 period was, by all accounts, one of the most difficult in the political life of Rev. J. C. Faye. It was a period of multidimensional struggles, a period of challenges which were separate but yet interrelated, both in their nature and in their consequences. Within the DP, though rank and file support was always guaranteed, occasionally internecine tensions raised their ugly heads.

Just as for the other politicians, the struggles confronting Faye fell into four interlocking categories, namely: (a) the colonial administration headed by the Governor; (b) new potentially contending political forces in the Colony Area; (c) the emergence of the Protectorate juggernaut in the form of a "politicized" traditional leadership; and (d) the birth of a rural-based political party.

(a) As regards the colonial administration, for the most part, as in the preceding years, the all-dominant subject was constitutional advance—its form, its pace, its implications, and its long-term impact. Constitutional advance was also a basis for forming alliances between parties and political forces (e.g. trade unions), for dissolving them, and constructing new associations with others. Faye was to confirm this as late as 1962 when talking about "the bold front we have hitherto shown against any measure that has been derogatory to the progress of The Gambia." Specifically, the first of these was:

the struggle for better constitutions and other steps in our political progress . . . since 1951; so too, the enlightenment of the public given by us in that connection . . . against every oppressive measure introduced by government in the past.[1]

On the ensuing confrontations with the administration, Faye and the DP took the lead in agitating for more drastic changes to the constitution, knowing how sensitive the colonial administrators were on this matter and the risks involved. They were accompanied by NJie and the UP; for the BTC elections in October 1955 the DP and the UP formed a loose alliance mainly against the MC, which was entrenched throughout the town; each concentrated on one ward.

As seen by the Governor, the overall objective of these two parties was "to place effective political control of The Gambia into their joint hands".[2] In 1957, the DP and UP came up with new constitutional proposals. Among others, they challenged the allocation of one vote per voter in a three-member constituency, which meant that parties could not have more than one candidate; they also continued to be vehemently opposed to the advisory committees.

Furthermore, these new partners demanded the following: direct elections in Bathurst and the Protectorate; an increased number of seats for the Legislative Council; Bathurst to have five single-member constituencies; the establishment of a Council of Ministers to replace the Executive Council; and the appointment of a Chief Minister (by the DP) or a cabinet with a Prime Minister (UP). In April 1958 Faye and NJie also signed a resolution that Gambia should be granted self-government status in 1959. Neither the MC nor the Protectorate chiefs supported this resolution.

Before his departure from the country, Wyn-Harris invited Faye and NJie to a meeting to discuss the general subject of constitutional change and their specific proposals, but they both refused to attend.[3] As it had already been announced that he was to go on retirement in mid 1958, the two politicians opted to wait for the next Governor. Coincidentally, these were the only two politicians who had been subjected to the humiliation of dismissals from the Executive Council by the same Governor Wyn-Harris. Perhaps their intransigence was understandable.

Having had such difficult times with Wyn-Harris, Faye welcomed Edward Windley, the successor, whom he assumed could not be worse than his predecessor. But then new forces which had the potential of challenging Faye and the political system in which he was one of the leading architects appeared on the scene. They were in the form of a new political party, a revived trade union movement, and the rise of organized political forces firmly rooted in the Protectorate.

(b) The Gambia National Party (NP) emerged from the "Committee of Gentlemen", a team of four independent-minded political analysts and critics set up in 1957. Its leaders were: Ebrima J. Samba, a radicalized businessman; Melville Senami Benoni Jones, an articulate and unrepentant anti-colonialist; John W. Bidwell-Bright, a prominent businessman; and Kebba Wally Foon, an accountant and titular party head. From the outset the NP adopted a rabid anti-colonialist stance on any and all issues. They attacked the personality-based politics of the day and argued for a shifting of the political discourse to issue-based ideological politics. They were closely familiar with anti-colonial politics elsewhere in West Africa (particularly in Nkrumah's Ghana) and in the continent at large. Their newspaper, *The Vanguard*, became an avant-garde voice of the colonized and was very popular.

Altogether, the NP attracted the attention of young radicals and the budding intellectual class. As confirmed by a contemporary observer:

> It is distinct from the others, not by its policies, which seem at present to be obscure, but by its organization. It shuns the one-man-party-leader organization of the others and entrusts all its decisions to committees. As yet it cannot be construed as a serious rival to the other three but it has voiced loudly its criticisms of the government and the other parties. It does not restrain its abuse from private individuals outside these two spheres . . . It certainly has attracted local malcontents and a number of young men, disheartened by the seeming inability of the other three parties to 'get anything done' are joining it.[4]

It was to be expected that the NP would align itself with Faye in the battle for a more progressive constitution for the country. Instead, Faye, in particular, was the butt of criticisms by the NP and many of their once-weekly night meetings were held in Fitzgerald Street within earshot of Faye's family residence. This may have been because the DP was already well established on the leftist ground from which the NP attempted to have it dislodged. The NP contested a number of local government elections but failed to make a real dent in the support-base of the other parties.

The trade unions were an equally big source of concern. Faye and the other leaders knew the value of trade unions in that, in the 1930s and 1940s, Edward Small, Garba-Jahumpa and Faye himself had attempted to use them as Trojan Horses to pursue their professional and electoral ambitions. As noted in Chapter 3, Faye had set up the Motor Drivers' and Mechanics' Union and had also been very active in the Gambia Teachers' Union. Thereafter, up to the early 1950s, trade unionism lapsed into a comatose condition, to be revived at the end of 1956 when the Gambia Workers' Union (GWU) was founded. Unlike some of its predecessors which were crafts/trades unions, the GWU was a general workers union which gave it a larger catchment area. By 1959 it represented a huge proportion of organized labour.[5]

The GWU was led by Momodou Ebrima Jallow, a charismatic and articulate unionist, together with Henry Joof and other like-minded activists. Jallow started his career in the civil service and then, encouraged by friends, moved on to form the Gambia Construction Employees' Society followed by the GWU. Though a novice in the field he was able to negotiate some attractive contracts with some employers, such as Gambia Minerals Limited. The GWU's clout was demonstrated in the one-day general strike of unskilled workers in February 1960 in which it gained a 25 percent increase in the minimum wage for the workers.[6] Its popularity skyrocketed, and by the mid-1960s it declared its membership at 1,100 paid-up members. In January 1961, the union called a two-day strike, seeking a much larger pay increase. A massive public demonstration was convened to support the workers, which was dispersed by the police, using tear gas and batons. Jallow was arrested and charged with incitement to riot; he was subsequently tried and asked to pay a nominal fine. After further negotiations with the employers an acceptable pay increase was agreed upon.

The public was incensed by the reactions of the administration to the strikes, which were linked by many to the struggle against continued British colonialism. Jallow's support base expanded outside the movement to include the youth, left-leaning activists, the "intellectual" class, and junior civil servants and professionals. His standing in these circles was boosted with his visit to Ghana in early 1959 and his discussions with ministers and senior advisers to Prime Minister Kwame Nkrumah. As in the case of the NP, this was the same constituency that Faye had worked hard to secure.

Neither Faye nor any of the other political leaders was able to win the endorsement of the GWU, not only because it did not want to be involved in the murkiness that had been created in the debates over constitutional change but also because both leaders and followers of the union were already active in one or other of the old parties. Jallow and the union leadership vociferously criticized the politicians as being ineffective, due to their "failure to explain what they are trying to do— so that they have never evoked strong loyalties". Jallow also saw the politicians as having been "twisted by the government, and [to have] simply caused confusion".[7] Thus, in contrast to the unionist stance in many other African countries, the GWU insisted on its neutrality.[8] This afforded it some leeway to make vicious attacks on the status quo, especially the performance of existing parties and the machinations of the colonial administration. They demanded an even more rapid political change than the political parties.

(c) The third development, the emergence of the Protectorate as a major political actor, was of a magnitude that was unexpected; it was to have the greatest impact not only on that era but also on the future of the country as a whole. At the fifteenth Annual Conference of Protectorate Chiefs, held in Brikama in February 1958, the chiefs, led by Tamba Jammeh, presented a letter to Wyn-Harris (it was his last such conference before his departure on retirement) on behalf of all the other chiefs. In it they stressed that:[9]

(1) All Seyfolu (chiefs) of the Gambia Protectorate desired the Senior Commissioner and the Divisional Commissioners to be with them as usual and work together through the channel of the Governor to the Senior Commissioner, the Commissioners, and the Seyfolu.
(2) There should be no changes to the duties and responsibilities of the Senior Commissioner and the Divisional Commissioners.
(3) There should be no changes of the duties and responsibilities of the ministers in The Gambia.
(4) They desired more Legislative and Executive Council members.
(5) They wanted more Protectorate-born candidates to represent the Protectorate in the Legislative and Executive Councils.
(6) If there were any likelihood of a further change in the present Constitution, they, the Seyfolu of the Protectorate, would like to be consulted first.

Several chiefs spoke in support of the Chief Tamba Jammeh whilst others indicated that the views expressed by him were unanimous.[10] Clearly, all was not well. The chiefs had grievances, constitutional and non-constitutional, which they were ready to bring into the open. Within months of his assumption of duty, the new Governor, Sir Edward Windley, having been advised about the sensitivities in Protectorate/Colony relations, announced an orderly plan of action for constitutional change as a priority field for action.

In the first place, the plan stressed the urgency of convening a meeting with the chiefs to obtain their views on the nature and form of any envisaged constitutional progress; some of the sessions would be open to the Colony politicians. Windley proposed that if the Bathurst political parties themselves agreed on proposals for revision of the Constitution, then a follow-up meeting would be convened between a small committee of chiefs, selected by the chiefs themselves, and representatives of the major parties, in an attempt to reconcile any points of differences. The outcomes of these two meetings would be fed into a major Constitutional Conference in Bathurst. The Governor would then submit to the Secretary of State for the Colonies both the proposals on which there was agreement and those on which there were disagreements, together with his own views, for final decision on a new Constitution for The Gambia.

In accordance with this plan the committee of chiefs met with representatives of the political parties in Brikama in October 1958.[11] But, unfortunately, this became a platform for the chiefs to air their multiple grievances against the Colony parties; it brought out the huge gaps in outlooks between the two, and the intense hostility borne by the chiefs towards the Colony.

Three proposals were presented, again by Tamba Jammeh, in the form of a petition. First, in any future constitutional changes, the status quo in Protectorate administration should be maintained, i.e., it should not be in the schedule of any ministerial departments that might be established. Second, there should be increased Protectorate representation in the Legislative and Executive Councils, through elections based on the prevailing system of indirect selection. Third, three of the Protectorate members of the legislature should be appointed to positions of ministers without portfolio. The petition was presented to the Governor for onward transmission to the Colonial Office, with detailed arguments demonstrating that the interests of the Protectorate were markedly divergent from those of the Colony Area.

Though stunned by the gravity of this development, Faye nonetheless pleaded for unity—particularly if the goal of self-government was to be realized in the near future. In his intervention he also urged the Colony parties to accept that in the legislature there should be 20 seats for the Protectorate compared to seven seats for the Colony, even if this would mean dismantling the political domination of the Colony Area. He added: "We do not fear you. You are larger than us and you must have more seats."[12] Faye then vehemently rejected the announced plan of the chiefs to form a Gambia Protectorate Party, because it would divide the country. Immediately the Chairman (Chief Karamo Sanneh) reassured Faye that this project had long been abandoned. Faye ended by appealing to the chiefs to accept universal adult suffrage and direct elections in their part of the country.

There appeared to be some appeasement and the chiefs toned down their criticisms; some even expressed appreciation of what had been said by Faye and the other Colony political leaders. Tempers flared again, however, when Chief Moriba Krubaly resumed the attack on the politicians, arguing that "the Bathurst proposals give us little, our children get little education, all the good jobs and places go to the children of the Bathurst people". This unleashed a flow of invectives. Chief Tamba Jammeh led the cavalry. He and other senior chiefs berated the Colony people for having "sat on them"; this would no longer be the case as the Protectorate people now had their own young men who were educated and could run their affairs. He stressed that:

> We are the farmers and you the Bathurst peoples are literate. Literate and illiterate cannot argue. The literate pays little attention to the views of the illiterate or his opinions . . . At the next elections we want to elect some of our young men who can read and write English and are prepared to travel in the Protectorate and see our works. But at the last elections not one of our people who are ministers came to see our work. I saw nothing done by them to improve our farming methods. None of them knows good farming from bad. We want our own young men who are literate as ministers, who can go into the mud and climb the hills . . .
>
> We farmers work with our physical strength, the Bathurst people work with their heads. That is why we want our children who are literate to be Ministers who can travel in the Protectorate. If the Protectorate man chosen to be our minister is unwilling to travel then we can curse him. There is no palaver between the Bathurst people and us but I would point out that the majority of the people in the Protectorate are Mandinka, but there are none in the Bathurst parties.[13]

This speech was loudly acclaimed by the other chiefs and several tried to take the floor in support of Jammeh. Faye, on his part, was equally uncompromising. He was particularly angered by the accusation that the Colony was responsible for the relatively backward state of the Protectorate; in this allegation he saw the ugly hands of the colonialists at work:

Three hundred years of maladministration cannot be rectified in three or four years. Besides, the constitution is not correct as the reins of government are still in the hands of the Governor and officialdom. Until we have general elections and we have collective responsibility you must not say the town is in power. The town is NEVER in power. The power is with the government. Don't be fooled. It is the government that did not make the country. It is the government that did not develop the Protectorate. The blame should not be put on the heads of the Colony people but it is the colonial government that is at fault not Banjul [Bathurst] people. You people were left in the dark, without education and it was I, Banjul-born, that went there and I was persecuted for your sake.[14]

Faye's rejoinder may have been valid, but the evidence did clearly reveal that there was a massive gap in socio-economic development between the Protectorate and Colony.[15] In size, the former was much larger—10,303 square kilometres as compared to 78 square kilometres. So also for the population—263,000 in the Protectorate as compared to 21,000 inhabitants in the Colony (1959). In terms of distribution of ethnic groups, in 1959 the Mandinka were 40 percent of the total population and 29 percent of the Colony population; the Wolof made up 14 percent of the total and 57 percent of the Colony population. The Aku were one percent of the total population and 13 percent of the Colony population. Thus, the Wolof and Aku constituted 70 percent of the capital's population whilst the Mandinka—close to half of the total population—were predominantly rural.

Socially and economically "the situation that obtained in the Protectorate could, in one word, only be summed up as dismal. Actually, for most of the Protectorate people the period up to 1959 was largely some dark ages in terms of living conditions."[16] As regards the education sector, in 1959 none of the four secondary schools providing education up to the Cambridge School Certificate was in the Protectorate. Armitage School, the only post-primary establishment had a five-year system from which graduates moved on to one of the secondary schools in

Bathurst. Of 51 primary schools in the country, 15 were in the Colony Area with two-thirds of the total student enrolment. The 36 in the Protectorate had an enrolment of 2,097 and were staffed mainly by unqualified and untrained teachers. In sum, whilst there was almost universal demand for primary education in the Colony Area, in the Protectorate it averaged about 10-20 percent.[17]

Much the same pattern existed in all other areas, such as medical and health facilities, the road system, transportation and communications, and even the legal systems. Briefly, as illustrations: for medical facilities the modern Royal Victoria Hospital in Bathurst had 175 beds, four doctors and a full complement of nurses and support staff, while Bansang Hospital, which served the whole of the Protectorate, had only 65 beds and one doctor. Small rural medical units were dispersed throughout the Protectorate comprising seven health centres, 15 dispensaries, 23 sub-dispensaries; resident trained personnel for manning these facilities were few and far between. For roads, of 121 kilometres of all-weather roads in the country 64 kilometres were in Bathurst and its vicinity; most of the roads in the Protectorate were impassable during the rainy season.

As far as the political arrangements were concerned, and as noted above, in the pre-1960 era the franchise was restricted to the Colony Area. In both the 1947 and 1951 constitutions Protectorate representation in the legislative bodies was indirect; the 1954 constitution, on the other hand, increased representation, but not by direct voting by the population. Besides, the level of representation was not proportional to the population and size of both entities. In the executive, in 1947 and 1951, there was one from the Protectorate compared to two from the Colony; in 1954 there were three each for Colony and Protectorate but no single minister came from the latter.

These differences gave to the Colony and the Protectorate distinctive identities; the two were dramatically different even if there was not much development in the country as a whole. In other words, the Protectorate gained only a tiny proportion of whatever "development" the colonial system offered The Gambia. Obviously, this distinctiveness was to be attributable to the colonial administration but the Protectorate leadership were led to blame the Colony politicians and people.

True to character, the colonial administration emphasized, in policy and in practice, the differences between the two parts of the country and, in political and constitutional terms, saw no reason why they should not be treated as such. This was very much in tandem with the "divide and rule" policy of the British colonialist as practised throughout the Empire.

The next meeting of the committee of chiefs and the Colony parties took place in Georgetown on 23 January 1959; it pronounced on a wide range of constitutional questions.[18] First, though, it agreed that the portfolio of Minister of Finance should be created together with that of Financial Adviser; the incumbent of the latter post should not be a member of either of the Councils. After extensive debate it was also resolved that the franchise should be extended to every man and woman over 21 years of age—in other words, universal adult franchise. On the question of whether Colony-born persons should be allowed to stand for elections in the Protectorate, the meeting decided to leave it to the full Chiefs Conference to decide; the subsequent decision of this body was in the negative.

The Georgetown meeting also agreed that the Senior Commissioner should continue to execute his functions in both Legislative and Executive Councils.[19] The chiefs jealously guarded their right to speak for themselves on matters pertaining to the Protectorate and to be responsible for organizing Protectorate affairs. And, any meetings on constitutional matters held in the Protectorate should be under the chairmanship of the Commissioner in whose division it was being held. Obviously, the chiefs had greater confidence in the Commissioners than in their own Colony kith and kin.

On most of the other issues the different sides failed to reach any compromises. Again, the chiefs repeated their positions as at the Brikama meeting.[20] Faye, supported by NJie and opposed by Garba-Jahumpa, also remained adamant; he was particularly critical of the position that Bathurst residents should not be allowed to stand for elections in the Protectorate.[21] As with the others, he did not waver at any time and forcefully defended his opposition at every opportunity.

Broadly, as far as the constitutional order was concerned the topics of interest and the initial positions of the two sides can be summarized as below:

Political parties	Chiefs
1. Universal adult suffrage to be extended to the Protectorate.	The franchise should be restricted to every male yard owner and his younger brother, ex-servicemen, village self-help society leaders and their assistants.
2. Candidates for the Legislative Council elections could be from any part of the country; this was particularly applicable to seats in the Protectorate. Similarly Protectorate-born candidates could stand anywhere.	Candidates for Protectorate seats must have been born in this part of the country, be on the Protectorate electoral registers or be recognized as coming from a Protectorate family.
3. Legislative Council seats to be increased to 27, with 20 going to the Protectorate.	Agreed on 20 seats for the Protectorate but that 12 should fall under the restricted franchise and 8 be reserved for chiefs nominated at the Chiefs' Conference.
4. There should be 9 ministers in the Executive Council.	Of the proposed 9 ministers, 6 should be reserved for the Protectorate.
5. All political parties should be free to operate in any part of the country, including the Protectorate.	Bathurst political parties should not be permitted in the Protectorate

6. The next elections should be held as soon as feasible and not later than October 1959.	The elections should be postponed to May 1960, so as to give all time to organize.

The challenge was how to bridge the gaps in these and related areas over time, and between the leaderships in the two parts of the country. Needless to note, there was no unanimity among the political parties themselves: not all were of one voice on each and every issue. For instance, the MC supported the chiefs on the issue of the franchise whereas the DP, UP and NP were opposed. Faye and his DP assumed the leadership role and, backed by the NP, were more constant in their positions; this was clearly unlike the other leaders who aligned themselves with other political parties on some issues and with the chiefs on others.

Disturbed by happenings at the meetings in Brikama and Georgetown, Faye devoted the months following to mobilizing opinion to counter the divisive forces, and to continue agitating for speedy advance to self-government and independence. He became the flag-bearer of the political class ready to challenge the conservative views of the rural leadership.[22] He was devastated, as it was clear that a power shift was on the horizon and that all the Colony parties would be likely victims.

Faye then initiated action to form a common front of all the parties and other political forces with the aim of formulating a joint front on the country's constitutional future. A commendable strategic move by him was to leave the door open for the chiefs to participate if they so desired. However, each political party saw matters differently; as often in the politics of decolonization, each was preoccupied with its own survival and with how to benefit from the new dispensation. This partly explains why Faye's attempt to hold a joint rally of all parties to discuss the chiefs' petition did not materialize.

Given his strong commitment to confronting the new situation Faye was not totally discouraged by the responses of the other leaders. He and his party resorted to a gradualist approach in which the initial move was to form an ad hoc committee which would prepare a roadmap for fusion of all parties. Several planning meetings were organized by the DP. Regrettably, the UP failed to attend any of them. The MC did send participants but under strict instructions that they should oppose any proposal for fusion. The NP also attended, but its participation was low-key; they were not as loud as was characteristic of its leadership.

Still undeterred, Faye and his DP again instigated the formation of an All-Party Committee in March 1958. It organized several meetings and, at one of these, a resolution was adopted which declared that as the 1954 constitution was "outmoded and inadequate to meet the needs of this territory, a new and advanced constitution granting internal self-government to The Gambia in 1959" should be introduced.[23] For whatever reasons, the MC dissociated itself from the resolution and withdrew its involvement. The UP had shown a nonchalant attitude to the work of the group. Thus, as before, the DP and the newly formed NP were left to carry the can.

A new Inter-Party Select Committee was set up in late May 1958 to make another attempt at getting a consensus on the earlier resolution. Unlike the previous approach, however, it attempted actively to involve the Protectorate leadership in the drafting of the resolution from the outset rather than present it with a *fait accompli*. However, as they were not in opposition to the overall approach the committee presented the resolution to a mass rally which endorsed it. Subsequently, a drafting committee was formed with the responsibility to prepare a draft constitution.

Within the following weeks agreement had been reached among the parties on many issues, some rather thorny. These included: the electoral system, the composition of the Legislative and Executive Councils, powers of ministers, and the role of the Public Service Commission. As in previous instances, however, both the UP and MC were lukewarm to the whole exercise and their attendance at meetings was infrequent. As for the chiefs they withdrew altogether. Determined, Faye and the DP and NP pushed on. In September 1958 the drafting committee convened a public rally in the name of all political parties and the Memorandum on Proposed Constitutional Changes was adopted.[24]

Faye, with his usual penchant for unanimity, pleaded for a united common front. He was sensitive about any delaying tactics up the sleeves of the Governor and his advisers. He singularly focused on rapid constitutional advance in the form of self-government and ultimately independence, the goal to which he had devoted much attention in the preceding months.[25] Faye was joined by the Deputy Leader of the UP, in particular, who attacked specific issues coming from the chiefs, such as their refusal to allow Colony political parties to ply their trade in the Protectorate.[26] The chiefs reacted in kind, again emphasizing the massive socio-economic chasm between the two parts of the country and the desire that no attempts should be made to bring them together. They bemoaned the lack of interest in Protectorate development on the part of the parties and their ignorance of the conditions in that part of the country.[27]

(d) It was in this context of turbulence in relations between the political leaderships in the Colony Area and the Protectorate that a new political party appeared on the scene. It had evolved from such social welfare associations as the Protectorate People's Society, the Kombo and Niumi Progressive Society, the Mandinka Society and the Jangjang Bureh, Fankanta and Kambeng Kaffos (age-set groups). The leadership of these associations was essentially rural but it was equipped with Western education and modern political skills. Though born in the Protectorate, many had lived, and were educated and employed, in the Colony Area. Some had also horned in their political skills through "apprenticeship" in one or other of the established political parties. In the course of 1957 and 1958 the Protectorate People's Society and the associations were consolidated into a political party, and on 14 February 1959 the Protectorate People's Party was launched. To reflect its aspiration for a national identity it was soon to be re-baptized the People's Progressive Party (PPP).

Dawda Kairaba Jawara was elected its leader. After completing his undergraduate and post-graduate studies in veterinary science in Scotland, he had returned to The Gambia in 1954 and joined the veterinary department. He was appointed Chief Veterinary Officer and, in 1958, promoted to Principal Veterinary Officer. Jawara entered politics at about the same time and played an active role in the founding of the PPP. As one of the two Protectorate (Mandinka) university graduates, he soon rose to prominence in the party and did not confront much competition for the leadership.

The PPP had distinct advantages over the other parties: its roots were firmly embedded in the Protectorate, where it could rapidly spread because of the rural affinities of its leadership; it received overt and covert support from the colonial administration; and it was determined to build a strong political party with the single aim of winning political power and using it for the uplift of the bulk of the population. Unlike the established parties, the PPP had a distinct identity and stronger ties binding the leadership together. It anchored its structures on traditional Mandinka social organizations, thus facilitating communication and socialization of the bulk of its membership.

Intensification of Demands for Rapid Political Advancement

The Bathurst Constitutional Conference was convened by the Governor, in March 1959, to provide another opportunity to the competing political forces to market their ideas on the next phase of constitutional development. It was chaired by the Colonial Secretary, and the Speaker and Attorney General were in attendance. Participating were members of the nine-man Committee of the Chiefs (Karamo Sanneh, Landing Sonko, Muhammadou Krubally, Koba Leigh, Moriba Krubally, Matarr Sise, Tamba Jammeh, Yugo Drammeh, and Fabakari Sanyang), Independents (Henry Madi and John L. Mahoney), United Party (Rene A. Blain and James E. Mahoney), National Party (Henry Joof and Kebba W. Foon), Muslim Congress (Sulayman Beran Gaye and I. M. Garba-Jahumpa), and the Democratic Party (John C. Faye and Crispin R. Grey Johnson).[28]

Agreement was reached on such agenda items as the composition of the legislature, universal adult suffrage, electoral units, qualification and disqualification of candidates, procedure in the legislature, President and Speaker, title and life of the legislature, procedures for ministerial appointments, summoning of the executive and related matters, titles of the Executive, and the public service.

There were also miscellaneous subjects that had previously been controversial but on which there was now agreement: the advisory committees for ministers were to be abandoned; departmental officers would no longer be able to appeal to the Governor against a minister's decision but the minister should inform the Governor of the disagreement without delay; and that the Leader of the Opposition should be constitutionally recognized through payment of a salary and a place in the official Order of Precedence.

Naturally, there remained areas of differences. For instance, on remuneration of members of the new House of Representatives the chiefs and the DP agreed that this should be based on the principle that politics was a career and, as such, should attract full-time remuneration. The MC consented that remuneration should be adequate but not necessarily in terms of politics being a career. The UP favoured generous payment on the basis of actual expenses or losses suffered whilst attending to the business of the legislature. The NP abstained.

Other areas of disagreement were as follows. On qualifications of candidates, contrary to the view of other participants, the chiefs proposed that candidates for the 12 universal suffrage constituencies in the Protectorate should not be required to be registered voters but that they should be born in the Division or "belong to the Division" in which the concerned constituency was located. On the language(s) to be used in the legislature the chiefs preferred that this be left to the future Legislative Council to decide through its Standing Rules and Orders; on the other hand, the political parties and Independents favoured English as the only language. For them this was important enough to feature in the constitutional instruments.

Concerning the composition, powers and duties of the Executive Council there were differences among all parties and also the Independents; however, these differences were not on principles but more on matters of practical details. For example, between the chiefs and the DP/UP there was agreement that the Governor should serve as Chairman of the House. But whereas the chiefs supported a total of nine ministers with or without portfolio, the DP/UP went for the same number but maintained that at least six should have portfolios; between the two sides the fields covered for portfolios also overlapped.

The chiefs proposed that there be three ex-officio members (Colonial Secretary, Attorney General, Senior Commissioner) who would continue with their present responsibilities, but these should now be regarded as ministerial portfolios. The DP, in full agreement with the UP, proposed that the following subjects would be reserved for the Governor: external affairs, defence, public services, and security. In addition, they requested that provision be made for a Deputy Governor who would preside over Council in the absence of the Governor.[29]

Increased animosity among some of the parties towards the administration and its trenchant positions on some of these issues led to an intensification of the campaign against the Governor. By the time of the visit of Alan Lennox-Boyd, Secretary of State for the Colonies, in June 1959, such antagonism had reached explosion point. For Faye and his supporters the visit by the man who was ultimately responsible for policy was an opportunity to demonstrate their opposition to many things, but particularly constitutional matters.

Lennox-Boyd decided to meet with the delegates to the Bathurst Conference first. Faye and his party did not favour the idea but decided not to make much of their disagreement.[30] In opening the meeting, the Secretary of State congratulated those who had participated in the Bathurst Conference and promised that their views, as recorded, would be carefully considered in London and Bathurst. The purpose of the meeting was to find out if the delegates to the March conference had anything to add, or had comments to make, on any particular features of the report of which the Secretary of State should take special note.

Faye, in his statement, highlighted four issues. First, on the composition of the Executive Council the number of ex-officio members should be reduced: while chiefs could stay there was no place for the Senior Commissioner. Second, salaries should be paid for members of the new legislative assembly and should be enough for them to "step out of their jobs and get into the country's business". Third, he further urged that the special qualifications proposed by the chiefs for candidates for Protectorate seats would divide the country—which was already too small anyway. As he had emphasized at the earlier Georgetown Constitutional Conference:

Anyone born under the British flag whether he was born in
Bathurst or England has a right to vote (in England). A black
man who was not born in England but was a British subject
is allowed not only to vote in England but to stand there as a
candidate, provided he fulfils the residential qualifications.[31]

Fourth, on the proposal agreed to at the March Conference, that
the position of Deputy Chairman of the Public Service Commission
should be filled by the Deputy Governor, Faye and his party now held
the view that it should be filled by an independent person from outside
the civil service. On each of these issues the Secretary of State raised
questions and attempted to show different sides of the issue. He did not
expressly agree with Faye's position on any of the critical issues, such
as the suffrage or competency in the English language as a qualification
for membership of the legislature.

The next day, the DP and NP convened a public rally at Albion Place
in Bathurst to inform their supporters about the discussions with the
Secretary of State. In fact, Faye was not involved in its planning which
had been done by DP party bigwigs, A. E. Cham Joof and Crispin R.
Grey-Johnson, and Melville Jones of the NP. As concerns the leaders of
the other parties, P. S. NJie was not interested in participating in any such
initiative mooted by other parties. And, as it happened, Garba-Jahumpa
could not attend, as he was chairing a meeting of his party's Executive
Committee, convened to review the outcomes of the deliberations with
the Secretary of State the previous day; he could not delegate any senior
members of his party to attend, as their presence was required at his
committee meeting.

At the rally two speeches were made by Cham-Joof, and one each
by Faye and Jones. Cham-Joof, in his introduction, said that he had
heard that only a few of the recommendations of the March conference
had been accepted by the Secretary of State; this being the case, the
gathering should listen to Faye and, if not satisfied with the situation,
they would move to Government House.

Faye gave an account of what had transpired at the meeting with
Lennox-Boyd and agreed with Cham Joof that 75 percent of the March
recommendations were not accepted by him. He declared that it was

up to those present to decide as to what to do next. Jones then followed and, after castigating Faye and other ministers as "wolves in the skin of lambs" and "too tame and mild", he urged the crowd to advance to Government House. Cham-Joof gave his support to this appeal to move on to the Governor's office.

The other members of the DP and NP leadership then asked Faye to leave the scene and, led by Cham Joof, Grey-Johnson and Jones, the menacing crowd headed for Government House. They chanted loudly "We want Rights and Justice" and, later, "We want Bread and Butter"— slogans that made this event historic and memorable in the annals of Gambian history. When the crowd reached the Governor's office, they were confronted by Superintendent of Police, John Bray, who informed them that Lennox-Boyd was out on official duties and that they could select six individuals who could meet with him the next day. This the protesters rejected, preferring to wait for Lennox-Boyd's return no matter how long it took. When sections of the crowd appeared threatening, Bray read out the Riot Act twice; after a third reading armed units of the police were called in and they charged on the protesters. They, in turn, attacked the police with whatever missiles they could lay hands on and many were injured. For the first time in Gambia's history physical force was used by the police in a purely political event.[32]

The Secretary of State again met with some members of the group he had seen the day before and others. He first summarized what had transpired at their previous meeting which, for him, had been conducted in a mature and balanced manner. He noted that all he had done at the earlier meeting was to present arguments for and against various proposals made at the March Conference, or made directly to him. At the end he had openly declared that no door was closed.

In the opinion of the Secretary of State, the demonstration, which he characterized as "irresponsible and un-Gambian", was premeditated in that an announcement of the mass meeting at Albion Place had been made in the *Gambia News Bulletin* even before the meeting he had had with the delegates to the Bathurst Conference. He then gave a blow-by-blow account of all that had transpired at the public meeting, stressing that most of the persons attending were supporters of the DP and the NP. His summary of the flow of events, the role of each of the leaders and their interventions, was outstanding—a credit to his agents who had prepared the report. He concluded:

> All I have wanted to do here [during the visit] was to listen patiently to any views, and I cannot understand why people who call themselves responsible should behave in this way. But as the Democratic Party and the National Party apparently have things they want to say, I have taken the initiative of asking you all to come (and I am sorry for the short notice) in order that they can here and now say what they wish to do in a more seemly and proper manner than that in which certain things were said last night.[33]

Faye, in his submission on what role he had played and what he had said at the meeting first observed that, in terms of sequence, the Secretary's narration was accurate but not in terms of facts. As to the announcement about the meeting in the newspaper, he informed the gathering that he was not aware of the meeting until summoned from his home to attend. He further explained that in his statement he had focused both on issues on which he was in agreement with the "constructive and unifying" views of the Secretary of State, and on others on which there was disagreement. For example, on qualifications of candidates he agreed that it would not be proper for them to be limited only to place of birth; residency should be added, so that if a Colony man were resident in the Protectorate he could qualify to contest for a local seat.

Again, on the post of Chief Minister, Faye also recognized that there was always the possibility of no party having a majority in the legislature, which would lead to a stalemate. However, Faye reiterated that he remained in disagreement with the government's positions on several old and new issues, especially literacy requirements for candidates (on which the Secretary of State seemed to favour "illiteracy"), salaries for members of the legislature (on which seating allowances seemed to be preferred by the other side), and composition of the legislature (which would mean that there would be many more ex-officio members if the administration's position prevailed).

Faye concluded that, after having repeated to the audience his positions on these topics, he was asked to leave the scene whilst the convenors organized the supporters to march on to the Governor's residence and let their voices be heard. If he had been consulted by the organizers of the meeting, it appears that Faye's preferred line of action would have been that a petition should be drawn up and sent to the Secretary of State as there was no chance of seeing him before his departure.

In the rest of the discussions with the Secretary of State these issues raised by Faye became reference points in the interventions of other speakers, namely, Kebba Foon (President of the NP and secretary of the All-Party Committee), Crispin Grey—Johnson (DP), H. Madi (Independent and Chairman of the Committee), Melville B. Jones (NP), Garba-Jahumpa (MC), Chief Tamba Jammeh, Chief Matarr Sise, Chief Koba Leigh, Chief Moriba Krubally and Alhaji Momodou Krubally.

Given the gravity of what had transpired the previous day and the possible repercussions, the leaders of the parties present at this second meeting, other than the DP, explained that they had not attended the Albion Place public rally and had not taken part in the demonstrations. They did not deny, though, that their parties may have been represented unofficially. In fact, Grey-Johnson, who admitted to having made the announcement in the *Gambia News Bulletin* in the first place, did confirm that the UP and MC were, indeed, represented and that this was not a purely DP and NP affair. On the substantive subjects raised by Faye, each participant, including the chiefs, expressed a position very much in line with long-held views.

Lennox-Boyd was very conciliatory and diplomatic. Cautioning that this was not "an inquest into what had happened", he emphasized that:

> I am always more interested in the future than in the past and, though I think what happened last night was a great pity I shall continue to behave in the complete belief that the people of The Gambia are a mature and sensible people. It is to the future I shall be looking . . . I am not going away with any door closed, but when so many differing opinions are expressed, I am bound to take note of them and pray for

God's wisdom in making the right decision when I am asked
to do so many different things.[34]

But on the most burning issue of the type of Constitution planned
for the country, the Secretary of State was vague and non-committal:

In my view the constitution should clearly provide for
increased association of Gambians in running their own
affairs. That will be my firm intention, but you have heard
yourselves on questions of literacy and matters of that kind,
very strongly expressed views, and I do not think you could
fairly expect me, in a visit of three days, to weigh up the
various arguments for and against and come to a decision.[35]

Without a doubt Faye's image as a rabid anti-colonialist—and a
similar image for his party—were boosted. The "Bread and Butter
Demonstration" (as it was subsequently named) was epoch-making both
for the 5,000 citizens the DP claimed had taken part, and in the political
history of the country. Quite early the next morning, Cham-Joof, Grey-
Johnson and Jones took to the streets distributing leaflets calling for
another meeting at the same Albion Place venue. There and then, the
police arrested and charged them with incitement. Their case was taken
up by the versatile, if sometimes melodramatic, lawyer S. Bamba Saho,
who got the three released on bail. Later in court, Saho's main defence
was that the three were exercising their constitutional and human rights,
both when they peacefully marched to meet the Secretary of State at
Government House and when they convened the follow-up meeting. He
won the case and the three were released.

The last stage in the constitutional reform plan of Governor Windley
was that he would submit to the Secretary of State his own views on the
issues arising from the Brikama, Georgetown and Bathurst conclaves
and from other sources.[36] These were to be the foundation provisions of
the 1960 Constitution.

A first point related to universal adult suffrage for every voter above
the age of 21 years throughout the country, which of course received
his full support. The Governor pointed out that after a long struggle

this fundamental principle was now acceptable to the chiefs, but it took some time for the sceptical ones to be brought round. Under the existing Constitution universal suffrage was applied only to the Colony Area and to voters of 25 years and above.

Second, there was the sensitive subject of the qualification of candidates for universal suffrage seats in the Protectorate. Windley was convinced that:

> it would be wrong to under-estimate the strength of feeling
> behind the Protectorate insistence on this provision. There is
> real apprehension felt that the more politically experienced
> Colony may unduly influence a rural electorate new to the
> mysteries of the ballot box.[37]

He therefore accepted the position of the chiefs that for these seats, in addition to being a voter, candidates must be registered in the Protectorate, OR have been born in the Protectorate, OR be recognized by native law and custom as being a member of a Protectorate family. Third, the distribution of seats in the Legislative Council between Colony and Protectorate—5 seats for Bathurst, 2 seats for Kombo St Mary, and 12 seats for the Protectorate—was acceptable, even though there was much greater weight granted to the Colony.

Fourth, the Governor agreed that the single constituency arrangement should be replaced with single member constituencies; this was a welcome advance which was not opposed by the chiefs. Fifth, the proposal that there should be ex-officio members (four) and nominated unofficial members (three) in the legislature was acceptable to all sides; in principle, though, the Governor was of the opinion that they should be open and not restricted only to Gambians, as preferred by the March Conference.

Sixth, surprisingly, as concerns the proposal that English should be the language of communication in the legislature (because there was no other written local language), the Governor supported the chiefs. He opined:

> On balance, I consider it best that a constituency should not be prevented, if it so wishes, from returning a candidate who wins his election on merits other than knowledge of written English . . . I believe that the new legislature can safely be left to decide whether, if candidates are returned lacking fluency in English or the ability to read it, it is desirable to provide translation facilities in the House. It is pertinent to record that the volume of documents which members of the present legislature are required to digest is not excessive and I have little reason to believe it will become much greater.[38]

Seventh, on the subject of remuneration to be paid to members of the House of Representatives, views diverged. The Governor pointed out that Faye had argued that all members should be paid salaries that were enough for them to "step out of their jobs and into the country's business",[38] specifically, a minimum amount of five hundred pounds annually. The Governor strongly counter-argued that "it was undesirable to turn membership of the legislature into a salaried career".[39] His "firm" recommendation was that "members should receive, as at present, generous allowances to cover the costs incurred in attending to the business of the legislature".[40]

As regards the constitution and functions of the Executive Council, for Windley the guiding principles were that "an over-elaborate executive machinery for government should be avoided", that "possibilities of unnecessary conflict between peoples of different persuasions, whether religious or political, should be reduced to the minimum", and "the executive should broadly represent the balance of forces among the peoples as a whole as this emerges from the process of elections to the legislature."[41]

Based on these principles the aim should be to have:

> an effective but small Executive Council truly representative of the interests of the country as a whole and designed to give within the Government a voice to all representative elements so as to enable them to have the opportunity to serve in their country's affairs.[42]

Against these principles, therefore, the Governor opposed the recommendation of the March Conference for a Chief Minister who was appointed on the strength of his having "an effective majority" in the legislature, given that such a person may not have the general support of the community. This would be of consequence particularly in instances where there were serious differences between the Protectorate and the Colony.

Besides this issue, the Governor proposed the retention in the Council of four ex-officio members—namely, the Civil Secretary (formerly Colonial Secretary), the Attorney General, the Financial Secretary, and the Commissioner for Local Government (formerly Senior Commissioner). A maximum of six ministers was seen as appropriate, given the costs involved; it was advantageous to have fewer, efficient, and effective ministries rather than to have posts that are "functional in name only and in practice nothing more than political sinecures".[43] It would be up to the Governor to determine the sectors and the allocation of functions to each ministry.

Very significant, Windley agreed with the Bathurst Conference that the advisory committees should be discontinued as "it has not in practice proved possible to associate the committees with the day-to-day work of government and they have languished."[44]

The Secretary of State reacted positively to the views of Governor Windley, especially after his many discussions during his brief visit to Bathurst. As he put it:

> I agree unreservedly with the basic principles which Sir Edward Windley feels should govern the establishment of a system of government designed to take account of the special circumstances of The Gambia and I welcome the detailed changes to the constitution proposed in his despatch.[45]

The instruments for the new Constitution, as agreed upon by the colonial authorities in Bathurst and Whitehall, were duly published as a Sessional Paper three months later in September 1959. This gave Faye another opportunity to bolster his standing. Clearly, some of the recommendations of the Bathurst Conference (March) were diluted extensively and, in places, rejected out of hand. Some of these proposals, including universal adult suffrage in the Protectorate, the elimination of the Advisory Council, and increased membership of the Legislative Council were accepted by the Governor.

But, for Faye and the other leaders the proposals rejected were equally crucial. These included the introduction of the post of Chief Minister, on which the counter argument of the colonial order was that there was no guarantee that the elections would produce someone with a dependable majority behind him, or that if there was some such person he would be qualified to head the government, a leader of one of the parties or a group of them.[46] There was also disagreement on the number of ministers: whereas the conference had recommended nine, the colonial administration preferred a maximum of six. Similarly, offices such as those of Attorney General and Financial Secretary should be manned by colonial officials as it was not likely that the elections to the House of Representatives, which were to follow, would produce persons qualified to hold these posts.

Another provision that was rejected was on the qualifications of candidates contesting Protectorate constituencies, on which the administration insisted on some discriminatory conditions not favourable to candidates from the Colony Area. In like manner, the administration strongly opposed the payment of salaries to members of the House, given that it would meet only a few times every session; this, it added, could, conceivably give rise to a class of professional parliamentarians wholly dependent on the salaries. On one more point, that of English as compulsory in the House, there was also soft opposition by the colonial authorities.[47] This subject was left to the House which, at its first meeting, decided to retain English as its official and working language.[48]

When the Gambia (Constitution) Order in Council, 1960, was published attempts were made by the Colony parties to close ranks. Again, Faye sought to mobilize opposition to the Constitution through a newly-formed Committee of Citizens (1959) made up of representatives from the DP, a pro-DP wing of the NP, the MC and organized labour; significantly the UP and an anti-DP wing of the NP were not represented throughout.[49]

The Committee prepared and presented a petition to the Governor and then to the Secretary of State criticizing the proposed constitution which, in many areas, coincided with the views of the chiefs.[50]

The contestations continued in the weeks following, with the Colony parties in a tenuous coalition against the colonial system. They were given a new lease of life with the announcement in October that new Legislative Council elections would be held in May 1960. This accelerated the need for rebranding, for new alignments among the parties, and for a clearer specification of where one stood on Gambia's Constitutional trajectory. For the DP this was not much of a problem. It had a long-standing radical orientation. Faye, the leader, had a profound distaste for the colonial order; from an early age, as noted in earlier chapters, he challenged established authority and was always ready to face the consequences.[51]

In this respect, Faye was seen in some circles as the leader who had inherited the mantle of Edward Small. Actually, since the 1951 elections, which Small had lost to Faye, his interest in politics seemed to have been on the wane. As afore-noted, even before then, he did not participate as actively as before in the preceding heated constitutional debates on the 1951 constitution and, surprisingly, he accepted it without much criticism. On the other hand, Faye and Garba-Jahumpa were vociferous in their attacks.[52] In the two Councils, Small was less inclined to raise political issues, in contrast to his practice in earlier years.

Indeed, there had been signs that Small had intended to hand over to Faye at the end of his term in the Legislative Council in 1951. However, it appears that he was irked by the decision of the colonial administration, just before the 1951 elections, to nominate Faye alone to attend the Festival of Britain celebrations. As the most senior unofficial member in the Legislative Council, Small was of the view that Faye should have deferred to him and should not have accepted the nomination. Disgruntled, he decided not to withdraw from the elections and give his support to Faye, but to contest again as the flag-bearer of his latest creation, the catch-all Gambia National League. It may be recollected that Small obtained only 45 votes (2 percent), well behind the other three candidates competing for the seats in the offing.

The other two major parties tended to be more "political" in the sense that they adjusted their positions on issues in line with their interests, personal and organizational. In this regard, the evidence shows that this was truer of Garba-Jahumpa whose success in this "game" is seen in the fact that he and his party were aligned to different parties at different points in time and in that he survived as a politician well into the 1970s. This was unadulterated realpolitik!

One field of party rivalry was that of local politics which mainly revolved around elections to the BTC. Here, Faye had been weaker than the other two leaders and, rather than contest seats directly, left it to his lieutenants. This compared with Garba-Jahumpa, for example, who attached much importance to municipal politics and, indeed, often stood for elections at this level. He was right, as party performances in BTC elections were indicative of the health status of a party. On the side of the electorate, it was an opportunity to demonstrate concretely where their support lay and to rekindle their enthusiasm for the party. This was of especial importance in between elections at the national level.

By the late 1950s the UP was growing in strength and asserting its dominance in Bathurst. As evidence, in the BTC elections in October 1959 it won three out of five seats and even defeated Garba-Jahumpa himself in what was considered by many as his fief; it also gave active support to the NP candidate who won, meaning that 80 percent of the constituencies were "won" by the UP. The MC won one and the DP no seat.[53]

Though from 1955 Faye and NJie had occasionally worked on constitutional and other reforms, they had no intention of merging their parties, nor did they agree on close collaboration in other areas. The distrust between these two personalities remained as strong as ever and, at the party level, a spirit of healthy competition was encouraged, such as in the rivalry in the BTC elections in 1957 and 1958.

The rise of the PPP was particularly difficult for Faye. His worst fears had been realized. Behind it all, for him, were the visible and invisible hands of the colonial government. The position it had taken on many constitutional issues affecting the Protectorate, and its influence over some of the stronger and more vocal chiefs, had finally borne fruit!

Faye had always prided himself on being an adopted son of the Protectorate, with his impressive record of educational and pastoral work in the area. Indeed, this was an advantage which none of the other Bathurst political leaders or the trade unionists had. Throughout the length and breadth of the country he was known by the chiefs; he had much faith in them, notably Chief Karamo Sanneh and Chief Moriba Krubally. Not infrequently, they consulted him on the complexities of politics and sought his advice even on internal chieftaincy matters. Similarly, the leading lights of the PPS/PPP had been in sustained consultations with Faye, seeking advice on their politics and on strategies their party should adopt.

In this regard, one memorable event was that, during the visit of the Duke of Edinburgh in 1957, the Kombo and Niumi Society wanted to join with Faye and his DP in the construction of an arch on Allen Street. Faye, as chairman of the government committee responsible for the programme, disagreed with Sanjally Bojang of the PPS; he insisted that the PPS must have its own independent arch as this was one means of asserting their identity and claiming a place in the sun. This advice was adopted; the arch was mounted in Albion Place by an expert recommended by Faye, and he himself showed it to the Duke during his tour of the arch exhibitions, explaining that it was sponsored by the Mandinka population in Bathurst.

The likelihood that some of Faye's supporters who originated from the Protectorate would leave the DP to join the new PPP party was very real. Apart from Faye, very few of those in the DP leadership had had any meaningful contacts among the chiefs or would be effective in canvassing votes in this area. Another consideration was that the DP and the older party machineries were already aging; their efficacy had not been tested since 1954 and in BTC elections. The PPP, on the other hand, was young and full of vitality, hungry and aggressive. It had a clear purpose and ambition—to acquire power and transform the homeland.

Faced with this situation, the DP turned to work closely with the MC; from late September 1959 they frequently held joint rallies and attempted to coordinate their campaigns. On 7 April 1960, a few weeks before the national elections, the two announced the formation of the Democratic Congress Alliance (DCA). It was to be:

> a national non-sectarian Alliance, to unify and strengthen their political aims and to fight the forthcoming General Elections in May this year. The main aim of the Alliance is to secure complete Self-Government for The Gambia now and to lead the country to independence at an early date. A Manifesto setting out in full the Policy of the Alliance will be published shortly.[54]

According to Faye, this was "an act which, in one fell swoop, has stamped out religious sectarianism and discrimination in Gambian politics—a blessing to the country, one and all would admit."[55] At the inaugural meeting of the promoters of the new party, held at the BTC on 26 March 1960, the positions on the Executive Committee were filled: Mohammed El Bashiru Jagne as President, Faye as Leader, and Garba-Jahumpa as Secretary-General. The other positions were divided as follows: Elhadji Ousman Ndure and Momadou Ceesay (Vice-Presidents); Alieu Jack and Alieu Cham-Joof (Assistant Secretaries General); Louis Cherry (Treasurer); Crispin Grey-Johnson (Financial Secretary); Henry Forster and Kebba Baboucar Foon (Auditors).[56]

In terms of the imminent elections, this alliance could attract votes as it brought together the long-standing leaders of the Christian and Muslim communities; Faye's support in the Protectorate, particularly in the URD, would also be helpful. But, history was unambiguously clear that if ever there was a marriage of convenience it was this one.

Two giants of Gambian politics who had flowered in earlier days were now struggling. The personal rivalry between them went back over a decade and was known to the colonial authority and the electorate at large. In earlier times, Faye's gain was popularly seen as coming at Garba-Jahumpa's expense, and *vice versa*. In the hustle and bustle of Gambian politics, opponents alleged that, since Garba-Jahumpa's departure from the DP in 1952, he had been determined that Faye would not succeed in politics. It was claimed that Garba-Jahumpa seized any and every opportunity to undermine Faye and that, as discussed in

Chapter 5, during the crisis over the meeting with Oliver Lyttleton in 1952 he had been quick to confirm to Governor Wyn-Harris that Faye had indeed stated that he had lost confidence in the Governor at the Mohammadan School rally; this is what had led to Faye's first suspension from the Executive Council.

Some of these claims were undisputed, while others were unsubstantiated allegations and part and parcel of the struggle for power in the context of the competitive politics of decolonization. Politics was conceived in zero-sum terms and every single practitioner of the art got back as much as he gave.

Without a doubt, the facts showed that Garba-Jahumpa had closely identified with the colonial Governor from the early days of Wyn-Harris and welcomed the 1954 Constitution against which Faye fought so hard. The MC leader had also supported the government-favoured inputs to the 1959/1960 discourse on the constitution and declared his opposition to some of the fundamental positions taken by Faye in the constitution-making process.

It was also known that Garba-Jahumpa had sought to align himself with the chiefs and was, at one time, on their side on the crucial issue of restricting the franchise and the qualifications of candidates for Protectorate seats. Knowing all this and more, some of the diehard Krio/Aku backers of the DP could not appreciate Faye's agreement to the merger. For them, was it not the same MC that advocated sectarianism and expressly set out to neutralize the power and influence of the Krio/Aku in government and business? In the light of these realities, these Krio/Aku critics were compelled to break ranks with their leader and gravitated slowly towards the PPP. It is probable that some activists from the MC also resigned because of this merger and joined the UP.

It could be said, obviously, that it was out of desperation that Faye agreed on the merger of the two parties. This desperation had arisen from the realities on the ground. The UP was slowly monopolizing the electoral space in the Colony Area whilst the PPP was daily sinking its roots deep in the Protectorate. It was this same motivation that compelled the NP leadership to establish close working relationships with the UP; by the beginning of 1960 it was virtually absorbed into the UP. Jones, one of the leading lights of the party possessed highly sophisticated political skills which were recognized by the other party leaders; he was therefore a much-targeted person. Particularly when his relationships with NJie and the UP took a turn for the worse after the 1962 elections, the other parties attempted to woo him over. Faye and his DP/DCA pursued him vigorously. Even as late as the end of 1964 Faye directed R. K. O. Joiner, a trusted party organizer, thus:

> I think you, Crispin Jones, (Matarr) Silla, and Cham Joof should try and get Senami (Jones) into the Party. You should not let him drift back into the UP. Tell them that I have said that this is the time for gathering and not scattering. Besides, this will bring the Creoles (Aku) together once again.[57]

These senior party members were to first meet informally and discuss the matter with Jones and then a bigger group could meet to put the seal formally on Jones's membership of the party. However, it appears that they did not succeed in convincing Jones.

As if the political landscape was not complex enough, Sanjally Bojang, the architect, financier and chief organizer of the PPP, supposedly acting in the name of the party, and in the declared interest of forming a common front in dealing with the colonial authorities, had hatched a plan to merge the infant PPP with the other parties to form a Gambia Solidarity Party (GSP). Sanjally had not discussed the matter with the other PPP leaders; as the standard bearer, kingpin and national president of the PPP he saw himself as having the right to speak and act in its name.

P. S. NJie soon denounced the plan and refused to be part of it. Sanjally had been one of his staunchest supporters and financiers in the early years of the UP, but they had fallen out subsequently. There was no way they could sit under the same roof. Faye and Garba-Jahumpa, on the other hand, gave Sanjally's project their active support. In the company of Sanjally they undertook extensive broadcast tours of the capital and its environs jointly addressing the crowds.

For Bojang, this plan would see the end of the PPP, and he said as much in picturesque language throughout their tours. The other members of the PPP leadership were not long in acting. They pulled all the stops and convened a meeting of the rank and file in Brikama, down the road from Bojang's residence at Kembuje. After heated debate, the meeting decided to expel Sanjally. The baby GSP died an early and natural death. Sanjally was to return to the PPP fold later in 1968.[58]

Thus, with these alignments and realignments, there were now three dominant political parties in The Gambia, namely the UP/NP, the DCA (DP/MC), and the PPP. Arguably, this consolidation of parties was very much a positive response to the preoccupations of some civic and religious leaders. A bridge-building meeting of leaders of the UP, DP, and MC was convened at the Ritz Cinema on Fitzgerald Street, with Imam Momodou Lamin Bah as Chairman. This was followed by another at Albion Place, presided over by Ebrima Ndow, the Deputy Imam, and the last at Dobson Street.

After the deadlock, a Committee of Youths was formed; its mandate was to undertake political education through mobile night broadcasts in different parts of Bathurst. Its was to pressure the parties "to consider the possibility of merging into one great unit to be able to lead the territory to independence along with the other West African countries".[59] It gave an ultimatum to the political leaders that any of them who refused to join the Unity Van would be challenged at the elections. This is why, in the elections a formidable candidate, Alieu E. Cham Joof, was nominated by the DCA in the New Town East constituency against P. S. NJie.

Summary Observations

The period covered in this chapter was another one of the high points in Faye's political career and in the political evolution of The Gambia. It began with the launching of a new Constitution in 1954, in which changes were more cosmetic than radical. New forces were soon to emerge which would upscale the debate on the way forward. The landmarks were the constitutional conferences in Bathurst and in London, the visit of the Secretary of State to Bathurst, and the various stages in the constitution-making process leading to the 1960 Constitution. The situation was to change dramatically in the months and years to come, bringing dark clouds to the political career of John Colley Faye.

Gracée Faye

J. C. and Cecilia Faye

Faye at the Empire State building, New York.

Faye and some grandchildren.

Axel Faye

Colley Faye

Cecilia Faye in traditional outfit with Governor's wife.

Cecilia Faye with family member.

Grandpa John Charles Faye

Grandma Gracée Faye

John Charles Faye with son John Colley Faye.

Cecilia Faye, State Certified Nurse, (UK).

Adele Faye in Girl Guides uniform.

Kristi-kunda "family"

Faye with workers at Kristi-kunda.

Opening of the AVTC, Farafenni.

Parsonage Nursery School

At Southampton University College, with fellow students.

Graduate of Southampton University College.

At the opening of the Trans-Gambia road.

Democratic Party symbol

African Conference, 1948

DCA/PPP Alliance

(L-R) Kalilou Singhateh, A.B.Njie, Rev.J.C.Faye,Sherrif Ceesay,SM
Dibba & Nfamara Wassa Touray,President of PPP

St. Mary's Cathedral, Banjul.

Bishop John Daly

Bishop Regal Elisée

Reverend Hunter

Rev. Faye at his ordination service.

Ordination as a deacon.

Faye being introduced to the Archbishop of Canterbury.

At the ordination.

Installation as Provost.

At reception after installation as Provost.

Reverend J.C. Faye in London.

The coffin lying-in-state.

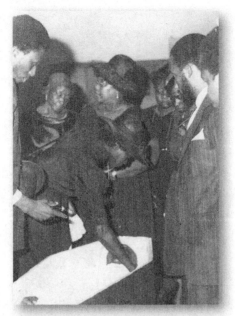

Family members around casket.

Reverend J.C. Faye Funeral

The Very Reverend John Colley Faye.

CHAPTER 7
POLITICIAN: THE SKIES DARKEN

The 1960 Elections and Outcomes

Elections had not taken place in The Gambia since 1954. But, in the meantime, massive changes had taken place in the political landscape of the country, especially as regards political actors; they had multiplied over time and cultivated sharper political skills. Constitutional advancement was the pivot around which political competition revolved; much had been achieved in this sector but, perhaps more important, the outcome of the competition would determine the fate of the politicians and their parties. In this sense, the 1960 elections were a major turning point in Gambian politics; there was much more at stake than in the previous three elections to the central legislative and executive bodies. As one observer stated:

> The recent decisions to enlarge the House of Representatives and to extend universal suffrage to the protectorate are radical innovations which have altered the whole balance of political power in the country, and make this election particularly important.[1]

For one thing it meant that there was a much bigger territory to cover; parties would have to expand their organizational structures which implied a larger and more robust resource base. This became a factor limiting the effectiveness of some of the parties which were less endowed than, say, the PPP and the UP. As a consequence, they had to

200

be very selective as to the constituencies in which they had candidates. This was especially so for Faye and the new DCA.

Faye contested the Kombo West seat. Candidates were nominated for the DCA in five constituencies in Bathurst: Alieu B. NJie (Joloff/Portuguese Town), Alieu Cham-Joof (New Town East), I. M. Garba-Jahumpa (Half Die), Crispin Grey-Johnson (Soldier Town), and Momodou Sallah (New Town West). The party may also have supported S. J. Oldfield (Kombo East).

As always, campaigning was a "do or die" affair. To quote a contemporary observer:

> In the past few weeks the people of Bathurst, and even parts of the Protectorate, have been bombarded with political slogans, door-to-door canvassing and party manifestos. Gambia may be small and poor but its politicians are second to none when public meetings, party rallies and all the usual excitement of the hustings have to be arranged. Songs, drumming, dancing, and the incessant blare of political propagandists, with magnificently effective loudspeaker-vans, ensure that every voter knows that the election campaign is under way. To the observer the candidates' aims may appear obscure and their propaganda crude, but all must admit that they are enthusiastic—and that they are passionately aware of their opponents' shortcomings.[2]

Campaigning revolved around differences on constitutional issues; though there was actually a constitution already in place there was always the possibility of it changing till after the elections.[3]

Election Results (1960)

The results of the elections were dramatic. The PPP topped the group with 25,490 votes out of a total of 69,048 votes cast (36.92 percent), the UP obtained 12,497 votes (18.10 percent), the DCA had 3,526 votes (5.11 percent), and Independents obtained 27,535 votes (39.88 percent). The UP figures did not include candidates not officially belonging to the party but supported by it. On the distribution of seats the PPP had 9 seats with 8 in the Protectorate and one in Kombo East. The UP got 5 seats with three in Bathurst; the DCA won one seat and the Independents four seats.

As noted, Faye stood in the Kombo West constituency where, in the four-cornered race an Independent candidate, Howsoon Semega-Janneh, won with 562 votes; Ebrima D. NJie of the UP followed with 415 votes; Faye came third with 289 votes, and M.A. Jobe, Independent, secured only 70 votes. Garba-Jahumpa also lost to Joseph H. Joof (UP) in the Half-Die constituency in Bathurst South, with 943 votes to Joof's 1,009 votes; the third candidate, I. A. S. Burang-John, Independent, obtained a miserable 42 votes. Joof was the same UP candidate who had defeated Garba-Jahumpa in the earlier BTC municipal elections. Alieu B. NJie of the DCA won the party's only seat, in the Jolof and Portuguese Town constituency in Bathurst. The situation was vastly different as regards the other two party leaders. P. S. NJie won a decisive victory over Alieu Cham-Joof of the DCA with 1,017 votes as against 687 votes for Cham-Joof. Jawara, leader of the PPP, was unopposed in the Kombo constituency.

The results were devastating for Faye and the DCA. It was the first defeat that he had suffered since he formally entered politics in 1947. Both he and Garba-Jahumpa, the two leaders of the DCA, had no place in either the Legislative Council or the Executive Council. The tide was against them.

Faye had been interested in standing in a Protectorate constituency, notably in the URD, but was barred from so doing by the existing constitutional provisions. He was convinced that he could have stood anywhere in the Protectorate and won—definitely so in any constituency in Niumi or anywhere in the URD, but particularly in Kantora District. In the latter, he regarded successful Independent candidates, such as his "sons", Michael Baldeh and Andrew Camara, as his "stand-ins", and contributed to their campaigns in cash and kind. The two could not stand under the DP banner simply because the party did not exist in the Protectorate.[4] The claims that Faye could have stood in any constituency in the URD and won, and that Baldeh and Camara saw themselves as his surrogates, have been confirmed by Camara.[5]

Indeed, as demonstrated in other chapters in this biography, Faye had a thorough knowledge of the Protectorate: few from this part of the country were as conversant with its history, sociology, culture, politics and economy as Faye. He had personal direct contacts and relationships with many of the chiefs inside and outside the URD. In the latter, in 1945, Faye had been allocated an area of 50 acres by the Alkali and village elders of Jawo-kunda in appreciation of the good neighbourliness existing with the KK village and the benefits they had derived from the presence of Faye and the KK community. The chief and elders offered to provide young men to tend the herds and to weed and look after Faye's farm, if he needed such assistance.

The farm was turned over to the Anglican mission but as it was unable to provide resources for an initial investment in the property Faye was compelled to resort to his own; this was not only because of the potential economic benefits but so as not to hurt the feelings of the kind neighbours. Faye and his advisers from the mission decided to clear only 10 acres of the land and there establish the village of "Sinchu Faye" between Koina and Kenneba and about four miles east of KK. Villages from around vied with each other in rendering help in supplies and workmanship to raise up the village and make it operational.[6]

Besides the argument that Faye had chosen the wrong constituency there were suspicions in his inner circles of a conspiracy against him, notably from within the DCA itself. Faye had brought up M. A. Jobe (the fourth candidate in the Kombo West constituency) and he considered him his ward; he had taught Jobe at school and assisted him in every way in his younger days. Even from within Jobe's own family there was strong opposition to his running against Faye, to no avail. As for the other candidate, E. D. NJie, Faye believed that he also had been imposed on the constituency just to prevent him from winning in a straight fight with Howsoon Semega-Janneh. Faye therefore concluded: "I was the villain of the piece as far as the powers that be were concerned. I must be removed [from the legislature and executive] and I was removed."[7] His election petition against Janneh was dismissed, with costs, and Janneh was declared duly elected.

There is little doubt that Faye would have won if he had stood in Soldier Town constituency which was heavily populated by Krio/

Aku, and was where he had his home and where he had always been unchallenged. He had agreed to give up this safe constituency to an old-time friend and DCA stalwart, Crispin Grey-Johnson, who polled 496 votes as against 644 votes for Melville B. Jones (formerly the leading light in the NP). Jones stood as an Independent but, with strong UP backing and access to the large UP money-chest. As it happened, Grey-Johnson and Jones had contested the same ward in the earlier BTC elections, which Jones had won. All the indications were that in a second contest within the year the results would not be any different.

Augusta Jawara, the wife of the PPP leader, stood in the same Soldier Town constituency and obtained 232 votes. As a Krio/Aku it was likely that she would attract votes away from the DCA candidate rather than from Jones, this because he already had sizeable support which mainly came from voters disgruntled with the DP for political and personal reasons. Obviously, in the light of these realities it was in the best interest of both Faye and the party that a very strong candidate, in the person of Faye himself, should be fielded. But, Faye stubbornly maintained that he was well known in Kombo West, that the family had landed property and other connections in the area, and that he would have a surprise victory.

For the parties and for politics in general, the old order was on its way out and a new era beckoning. A different type of party, the PPP, now had a massive presence in the organs of government and new youthful men with access to power; in all respects there was a huge gap between the old and new guard. This was a positive development for the country; it was appropriate in that it was entering a different stage in its constitutional development which, inevitably, would lead to the end of British colonialism.

Faye and the DCA were in a quandary. Obviously, they were in a position of weakness. If the party was to continue to have a presence in Gambian politics it was imperative that new alliances be forged. The UP was excluded, for obvious reasons. The only remaining card, therefore, was the PPP, and soon overtures were made for a cooperation agreement. Happily, the two crises outlined below had the effect of bringing the two parties closer and to strengthening the foundations for intense collaboration.

Crises in Power Distribution Arrangements

All was not to be plain sailing in the new order. First, there was the crisis over the allocation of ministerial portfolios central to which was the Governor's decision not to appoint any of the UP legislators as ministers; rather, he selected one each from among the chiefs, the PPP, the DCA and the Independents. NJie had, in fact, been appointed a minister without portfolio but he denounced the offer as not befitting his political and personal status. The administration stuck to its position, influenced, apparently, by the fact that NJie was entangled in serious legal battles which, in the end, led to his disbarment from the local bar.

Reactions from both the UP and the Bathurst electorate were that the appointment to an inferior ministerial position was insulting to their leader's pedigree, qualifications and standing in society. Subsequently, the party entered into extended negotiations with the administration which were unproductive. Demonstrations, a boycott of the House of Representatives, appeals to the Colonial Office, and other forms of protests did not produce any change in the situation. This crisis left a bitter taste in the mouths of the die-hard devotees of the UP supremo.

The second crisis, over the appointment of a Chief Minister, saw the shoe on the other foot. As decided by the Governor, the major criteria for selection were that the appointee should be able to command a majority following in the House and that his colleagues must acknowledge his leadership. In March 1961, after further delicate consultations with wide-ranging stakeholders, the Governor appointed P. S. NJie as Chief Minister, as he "commanded the greater measure of support".[8] In reaching this decision, the Governor was convinced that most of the chiefs were behind NJie. For him there was convincing evidence that most of them did not support Jawara and the PPP and were, in fact, suspicious of the party; this was truer among those who were uneducated. Similarly, some extremists in the PPP were extremely critical of the chiefs and even the institution of chieftaincy.

NJie and his party saw the appointment as a vindication of the position they had adopted over the allocation of ministries and an admission that the executive, as then constituted, had not reflected popular support for the UP. In reaction to this development, the PPP and DCA members of the Executive Council resigned. They organized rallies up and down the country and advanced well-reasoned arguments in support of their claim to the office of Chief Minister; in the process, the chiefs came in for hard knocks, given that their support was seen as having balanced the scales in favour of the UP.[9]

Faye was convinced that the chiefs in the Executive Council favoured him and would have declared for him if he had been elected; with the chiefs, A. B. NJie, Andrew Camara, Michael Baldeh, and himself, the DCA would have obtained 13 votes to the PPP's nine votes. And he, Faye, would have been appointed Chief Minister. But, with his absence from the House, and their opposition to the PPP, the chiefs had no option but to throw their weight behind NJie. Faye also hinted in an interview that Jawara had requested him to intervene with the Governor but he, Faye, would have none of it, ostensibly because Jawara's party was a Protectorate party and the non-Protectorate-born Faye did not qualify to be a member. The chiefs informed the Governor about this move on the part of Jawara, which counted against him.[10]

Whilst NJie and his team settled down to the business of government the aggrieved parties (mainly the PPP and DCA) sustained the campaign against them, especially on the issue of legitimacy. To clear the air, and in recognition of the need for further constitutional progress, Governor Windley announced arrangements for a local constitutional conference to be held in May 1961.

Bathurst Constitutional Conference (1961)

Like its predecessors, the Bathurst Constitutional Conference (4-11 May 1961) was meant to obtain views on revision of the Constitution. On this occasion, the approach was different, that is, a draft revised Constitution was made available and delegates were to give their comments on and criticisms of it. The draft dealt, inter alia, with size and composition of the legislature, the role of chiefs, relations with Senegal, size and composition of the Executive Council and its transition into a cabinet; full internal self-government and independence preceded by elections.[11]

The conference was opened by the Earl of Perth who was the Minister of State for Colonial Affairs. Representation of the parties was as follows: J. C. Faye, Garba-Jahumpa, and A. B. NJie for the DCA; D. K. Jawara, Sherif Sisay and Paul Baldeh for the PPP; P. S. NJie, James E. Mahoney, and S. B. Gaye for the UP; and Omar Mbake, Karamo Sanneh and Landing Sonko for the chiefs. There were three Independents—Rachel Palmer, M. E. Jallow of the GWU, and Henry Madi.

The main recommendation of the conference was that a new constitution should be introduced in which the country would be granted full internal self-government after elections. During a period of about nine months the Governor would preside over the Executive Council and only the Attorney General would be an ex-officio member. A Premier would be appointed from among the elected Legislative Council members; he would be the leader of the majority party. At the end of this first phase the Premier would become the Prime Minister and take over the chairmanship of the Executive Council from the Governor. The Prime Minister would be granted special powers and take responsibility for internal security, defence, external affairs, and the civil service. Independence would follow after another nine-month period.

There were variations in opinions on the question of the composition of the legislature but all—except the UP—agreed that the disqualification of chiefs from registering as voters should be lifted; they would then be eligible to run as candidates for elections. Views differed marginally on the issue of the electoral units but all agreed on the overarching principle that all constituencies should be single-member. The DCA, PPP and Rachel Palmer recommended that there should be a House of Chiefs or Senate, with the DCA recommending that it should be composed of not less than 12 members elected by all chiefs. The PPP argued that, in addition to the chiefs, the Governor, on the advice of the Premier, should have the authority to nominate an unspecified number of other members. On this, the Independent members of the committee had their own combinations and permutations. The PPP and DCA were also in agreement as far as the jurisdiction of the House of Chiefs was concerned.

Concerning another previously controversial topic, that is, qualification of candidates, the Independents, the DCA, PPP and chiefs proposed that, in addition to literacy in English, candidates should be certified as being able to play an effective part in the proceedings of the House. The conference actually settled on literacy in English up to old standard IV whilst the UP advocated the old standard VI. All except the UP supported the position that academic qualifications should be tested by a panel of three; the UP was of the view that this should be left to the Registering Officer. Jallow preferred that candidates for the Upper House should be of at least Standard IV level. On the related matter of the language to be used in the proceedings of the House there was agreement that it should be English; those who supported a House of Chiefs agreed that vernaculars could be used but the records should be in English.

It was agreed unanimously that a Speaker should be appointed by the Governor on the advice of the Premier after consultations with the legislature; a Deputy Speaker should also be appointed by the House from among its members. Unanimously favoured was the retention of the name "House of Representatives" for the legislature; for the second chamber the PPP and DCA proposed House of Chiefs whilst Rachel Palmer recommended "Upper House" and Jallow went for "Senate". The life of all parts of the legislature was to be five years.

Turning next to the executive, the conference decided on the composition, powers and duties without any disagreements; the subjects of internal security, external affairs and defence were reserved for the Governor. The PPP and DCA proposed, and the conference generally agreed, that, after a nine-month period the Governor should cease to attend Council which responsibility would be exercised by the Premier-turned-Prime Minister. The powers under the Governor's purview would be exercised through the Prime Minister. All except the UP agreed that, at this stage of the Governor's withdrawal, the name of the body should be changed to "Cabinet"; the view of the UP was that this should only be after the attainment of full independence.

In his letter to the Secretary of State for the Colonies conveying the report of the Bathurst Conference, the Governor, as was usual practice, indicated his own opinions on the major issues.[12] For example, he asked for caution as concerns the creation of a House of Chiefs, mainly because it would be an administrative and financial burden:

> With a population estimated at only 300,000, administrative
> overheads are already a most serious burden and there would
> have to be very positive advantages in favour of a bicameral
> system to justify its obvious disadvantages.[13]

He expressly consented to, or did not strongly oppose, all of the other recommendations of the conference.

Fortunately, whilst the report of the Conference was under consideration in London, the delegates to the Bathurst Conference held several meetings locally to iron out outstanding issues. They agreed that the idea of a second chamber should be dropped; that the number of chiefs in the legislature should be four and they would have full equality as other members including voting rights; that there should be a Minister of Finance; that the Attorney General would have a seat in the House but without a vote; that elected members should be 36, of which 7 would be from the Colony Area, 25 from the Protectorate and four chiefs; and that elections would not be conducted before May 1962.

The two outstanding issues were a date for independence and the procedures for selecting a Prime Minister if no party had a clear majority in the legislature. On the first, P. S. NJie's position was that this should be left to the government that would emerge after the expected elections. Jawara, Faye and Garba-Jahumpa proposed January 1963 as the date for independence; they also proposed that a firm commitment to full independence must be one of the outcomes of the Conference. Jallow and Sisay also insisted on a definite date. Mbake and the other Independent delegates argued that the present Conference should not go beyond the attainment of internal self-government even though independence remained a fundamental objective. In his final decision the Secretary of State leaned more to this last view, that is, that independence would be a matter for consideration in the next stage of constitutional advance, after the new Constitution had been in force for a while.

The Secretary of State, in acknowledging receipt of the report and the stand of the Governor on its various recommendations, also decided that:

In the light of the wish of the conference that discussions should be resumed in London very shortly and your own support for this, I agree at once that these discussions should take place. I should, therefore, be happy to hold a conference in London during the week beginning Monday, the 24th July.[14]

London Constitutional Conference (1961)

At the London Constitutional Conference, 24-27 July 1961, the Governor was accompanied by his Financial Secretary as adviser. The PPP was represented by D. K. Jawara and Sherif Sisay, the DCA by J. C. Faye and Garba-Jahumpa, the UP by P. S. NJie and Michael Baldeh, and the chiefs by Omar Mbacke. As for the earlier Bathurst conference, Rachel Palmer, M. E. Jallow and Henry Madi attended as Independents. The United Kingdom delegation, led by Honourable Ian Macleod, Secretary of State for the Colonies, and the Earl of Perth, also included seven senior officials from the Colonial Office and advisers.

As stipulated by the Secretary of State, the aim of the talks was:

> to work out arrangements which will in due course provide the Gambia with a fully representative government based upon the expressed will of the people, which can face up to the problems, political and economic, which will have to be resolved if the interests of the people are to be furthered in the years to come.[15]

The final outcomes of the London Constitutional Conference which were to be the key elements of a new 1962 Constitution can be summarized as follows:[16]

Executive Council

1. The Executive Council should consist of the Governor as president, a Premier and not fewer than eight ministers drawn from the legislature.

2. There should be a Minister of Finance.

3. The Financial Secretary should attend meetings of Executive Council as appropriate.

4. The post of Civil Secretary was abolished and a post of Deputy Governor created. He would administer the government in the absence of the Governor and assist him in matters for which he remained responsible.

5. The Instruments should permit the Premier to preside should the Governor (or Deputy Governor when administering the government) be absent.

6. The Attorney General should receive papers and normally attend Executive Council in an advisory capacity.

Governor's Special Responsibilities and Reserved Powers

1. Internal security, external affairs and defence should be the responsibility of the Governor.

2. The Governor should be responsible for the public service (the Public Service Commission remaining advisory).

3. The Governor should act in accordance with the advice of Executive Council except on the subjects referred to in (1) and (2) above, but he should retain full reserved executive and legislative powers.

Appointment of the Executive Council

1. The Governor should appoint as Premier:

   (a) the elected member of the House of Representatives leading the party commanding the support of the majority of the House; or failing this:

   (b) in the absence of such a person, the elected member of the House who, in the Governor's judgement, seemed likely to command the support of the majority. In the last resort if no such person could be found able to command a majority, there would no doubt have to be a further general election.

2. Other Ministers would be appointed by the Governor on the advice of the Premier.

The Legislature

1. The legislature should consist of:

    (a) A Speaker elected by the House. A Deputy Speaker should be elected by the House from among its members;
    (b) Elected members—7 from the Colony, 25 from the Protectorate;
    (c) The Attorney General, but without a vote;
    (d) Not more than two members nominated by the Governor after consultation with the Premier, and without votes;
    (e) Four chiefs elected by the chiefs in assembly.

2. The Governor should have the right to address the House.
3. Suffrage:

    (a) The qualifications for registration should be reduced from 12 to 6 months residence.
    (b) As the chiefs were to have special representation, they should not vote in the ordinary constituency elections.

4. Candidates:

    (a) The requirement that candidates for Protectorate seats should be born or registered in the Protectorate should be removed.
    (b) Chiefs should not be allowed to stand as candidates for the constituency elected seats.

5. Electoral procedure:
    The arrangements should provide for a secret ballot.

Elections

A general election should be held under the new Constitution not later than May 1962, if administratively possible, and new executive and legislative arrangements were to come into force thereafter.

The 1962 Elections: Campaigning

It was under a formal PPP/DCA pact that the May 1962 elections were contested. Ever since Alieu B. NJie, the DCA member on the Executive Council, had resigned at the time of the appointment of P. S. NJie as Chief Minister (March 1961), the two parties had been coordinating their positions on issues. At the London Conference they worked closely together, with the blessings of Faye and Jawara. In the legislature they also cooperated. Notably, in the BTC elections in 1961 the two parties formed an electoral pact which led to the DCA winning four out of the five wards, at the expense of the UP. Faye also saw this pact as additional proof of the commitment of the DCA to national unity which was a *sine qua non* for political development: "in fact and in deed we have already started to effect this in the merger known as 'The Alliance', from 1960 to date and in our collaboration with the Progressive Peoples' Party since February 1961 for the good and progress of The Gambia."[17]

The manifesto of the DCA stressed the urgency of unity "of all progressive persons and patriots of this land", which had been exemplified in the agreement to collaborate as closely as possible with the PPP. This, it was anticipated, would:

> provide for The Gambia a stable, capable and competent government which could and would creditably utilize the internal self-government now conceded, and subsequently gain for The Gambia independence and sovereignty within the Commonwealth by January 1963.[18]

The manifesto explained that smallness of physical size or population was not peculiar to The Gambia and had little to do with the right to autonomy. In fact, "the smallness of this our country could even be

213

of some advantage . . . our strength as a nation would in many ways lie in the quality of what The Gambia would produce in the days to come." Economic viability could only come about if free and sovereign countries acquired the right to exploit untapped natural resources, mineral and otherwise.

The manifesto continued that given these perspectives, the two parties would work hard to achieve a majority government of sons and daughters "who would carve-out for this land the peace, prosperity and dignity that would render her a state of no mean stature and standing". With such a majority government, the PPP/DCA would proceed to implement a host of programmes in the fields of economic development, education, social and cultural development which the document outlined. Respect for the dignity and independence of the judiciary, the integrity and impartiality of the public service, and the freedom and rights of the individual, were principles the party promised to uphold.[19]

The pact required that the PPP support the DCA candidates in four of the Bathurst constituencies and in Serre-kunda whereas the DCA would support the PPP in all 25 Protectorate seats and in two seats in the Colony Area. Alieu B. NJie, Garba-Jahumpa and Cham Joof each stood in the same constituencies as in the 1960 elections. This time Faye decided to run on terrain that was not the most ideal but more familiar: New Town West in Bathurst. Importantly, the constituency had gone to the UP in the 1960 elections though by a small majority.

There was the usual excitement and party atmosphere. One commentator, like others quoted during other elections, noted again:

> During the last few weeks The Gambia's renowned calm has been disturbed by blaring loudspeakers, political songs and, for a short while, even the rhythms of a jazz band imported from Ghana to help raise funds for the smallest party—the Democratic Congress Alliance of Mr. Garba-Jahumpa and the Rev. J. C. Faye.[20]

But the campaign was also fierce and vicious; personal verbal abuse and character assassinations were at a level never before witnessed in the country. So threatening was the campaign that the administration had to strengthen legislation to prevent violent conflicts between opposing forces and to prevent fraud and bribery. As the Governor warned:

> In a small country such as this there is a great need for unity of purpose, and if we are to see deep divisions fomented by irresponsible electioneering tactics [and] bitter dissension growing between party and party, between tribal groups, and even within families it can only retard the progress of this country and lead us to an unhappy future. The electorate must be given a fair chance to choose their representatives free from the duress or intimidation or the misleading tactic of falsehood or misrepresentation.[21]

There were the usual allegations of vote-buying, bribery, undue influence, intimidation, corruption, and other malpractices. There was also the issue of imbalances in financial resources, with the UP accused of obtaining money from suspicious sources. Faye pointed out, for example:

> Our antagonists had the [colonial] government in their hands and did everything fair and foul to retain their hold thereon. They were heavily financed by a neighbouring state as well as by commercial circles and the rich Lebanese community. They had 16 vehicles to our (PPP/DCA) joint effort of seven for instance; so we had to attack vigorously what the UP deem their stronghold for them to concentrate their poison there (i.e. the urban and sub-urban areas).[22]

NJie, in a party broadcast was, perhaps, most vitriolic in describing the PPP as an "organization of the devil . . . Here is a gang of political upstarts operating on the well-known totalitarian principles of terrorism and coercion." He also claimed that the PPP was "compelling their lukewarm supporters into taking secret and frightful oaths of allegiance to the party".[23]

As regards policy differences, there was not much distinguishing the parties. All agreed on the urgency of improving the socio-economic conditions of the mass of the population, and particularly those in the Protectorate. Unity was fundamental for the future well-being of the country and, in this context, tribalism must never be allowed to take root in Gambian society.

But, there was disagreement on policy toward Senegal, on which the PPP and DCA advocated a cautious gradualist approach and the UP favoured a more integrationist stance. Then, also, on the subject of independence, the DCA/PPP actively pressured for accelerated action towards this cherished goal and, for the DCA, membership of the radical Casablanca group of African states; the UP opted for indefinite postponement of independence, depending on how the situation evolved in implementing the new constitutional order. Finally, there was the matter of chieftaincy—some elements in the PPP were consistently critical of chiefs, some characterizing them as "tools of imperialism" and "exploiters of the people". For the UP these chiefs were the bastions of local government, close to the populations and, as such, deserved recognition, especially in the organs of government.

The obvious reason for this ferocious electioneering was that whichever party won was going to lead the country to self-government, would have increased ministerial posts and its leader would eventually be elevated to the exalted position of Prime Minister. Given the clout that went with all this, it was also likely that he would lead to country to independence.

Election Results (1962) and the Aftermath

In terms of share of the total votes, the distribution was as follows. Out of the total of 97,647 votes cast, the PPP had 56,343 votes (57.70 percent); the UP scored 37,061 votes (37.91 percent); the DCA had 4,180 votes (4.28 percent); and the Independents won 108 votes (0.11 percent).[24] Translated into parliamentary seats for each the outcome was: 18 for the PPP, 13 for the UP and one seat for the DCA.

Again, the results were disastrous for Faye and his DCA. Though the party obtained one-third of the total Colony Area votes it won only the same single seat, that of Alieu B. NJie. Again, Faye and Garba-Jahumpa lost. Faye lost in the New Town West constituency to Ishmael B. I. Jobe of the UP, with 824 as against 893 votes (69 votes difference). Garba-Jahumpa lost to his old nemesis, Joseph Joof of the UP, who obtained 1,205 votes as against Jahumpa's 1,194 votes; this was an even smaller majority of 11 votes.

For the other two major leaders, again the results were more favourable. P. S. NJie repeated his victory over Cham Joof, though by a smaller majority—1.221 to 907 votes. On this occasion, Jawara had an opponent from the UP (Bakary Jabang) whom he defeated by the largest majority—4,073 to 721 votes.

Jawara, who by virtue of his party's clear-cut majority was now the Premier, appointed Alieu B. NJie, the successful DCA member, a minister not only by virtue of the electoral pact between the two parties but also because NJie was more experienced than all of the PPP members. According to various sources Jawara had also intended to have Faye and Garba-Jahumpa appointed as "Nominated Members" in the legislature so they could be appointed to ministerial positions. However, the Governor, John Paul (March 1962 to February 1966), refused the request arguing that it was neither in the spirit nor in the letter of the new Constitution.[25]

Some of the other leaders of the DCA benefitted from the alliance with the PPP in that they were appointed to positions in the House of Representatives. Faye was appointed to head the Gambia Liaison Office in London. Sallah, who had to give up the New Town West constituency for Faye, became a Nominated Member, and Alieu Jack was elected Speaker of the House with PPP support.

On the other hand, Garba-Jahumpa was bitterly disappointed that he was out of the House and saw the alliance with neither the DP nor the PPP of any use. Therefore, in October 1962, he bolted to form the Gambia Congress Party (GCP); some of his top members such as A. S. Jack, stayed on with Faye and the DCA. With the wave of popularity enjoyed by the UP in Bathurst, the MC then switched loyalties to the UP. Garba-Jahumpa, as the candidate of both parties, contested and won one of the seats in the Bathurst municipal elections the very next month.[26]

As was becoming normal in Gambian politics, the 1962 elections were followed by a Constitutional crisis; this time it revolved around three issues, namely: the wide-ranging and bold initiatives taken on cooperation and integration with Senegal; the validity or invalidity of the voters' registers; and the demand for elections before independence.[27] On all these, the UP, joined later by the CP, launched a massive onslaught on the new administration. One consequence of the upheaval created by the politicking over these issues was a decision by the colonial administration to work out a detailed programme for accelerating Constitutional progress.

The first stage of the process would be the granting of internal self-government. Essentially, this implied that the Premier would become Prime Minister and the Executive Council would be the Cabinet. The Prime Minister would preside over the Cabinet and some aspects of external affairs would be delegated to Gambian ministers; internal security could also be delegated to a minister on behalf of the Governor. This meant a significant measure of autonomy for the country, only slightly short of full sovereign independence. The Premier discussed the subject with both the Governor and the Colonial Office after the April 1963 annual conference of the PPP and DCA at which a resolution was adopted on internal self-government and eventual independence. Action on the Order-in-Council and related legalities led to the formal granting of internal self-government on Friday 4 October 1963.

Independence: Constitutional Conference, London (1964)

The second stage was the holding of another Constitutional Conference in London, starting on 22 July 1964, at which "the date and form of Gambia's independence would be discussed and settled". This was preceded by the publication of Sessional Paper 12 of 1964, which outlined the issues to be discussed at the Conference as formulated jointly by the colonial government and the Jawara government. Therefore, at the Conference itself there was little dissension, apart from the matter of elections before independence—which was rejected—and that of association with Senegal, two issues raised by the UP/CP opposition. The decision of greatest import was that independence would be granted to The Gambia on 18 February 1965.

Faye was not at the final London Constitutional Conference as a political leader but as an agent of the government in Bathurst. He had played a dominant role in the heated controversies preceding all such earlier events, whether in Bathurst or in London, and had been intensely involved in mobilizing opinion in support of Constitutional change. Now, at the last such conference he was performing advisory functions to other politicians as a member of a conference secretariat. Paradoxically, all of his contemporaries as political leaders continued in their active political roles as before—Jawara, as Premier and official leader of the Gambian delegation, and NJie and Garba-Jahumpa as opposition delegates.

The *dénouement* of Faye's political career was on the horizon. The signs pointed in the direction of the end of a distinguished political career. He had played his part in the political drama of the 1950s and was slowly moving towards the exit.

The euphoria generated in the planning for independence and other factors compelled the UP and CP to cooperate with the government in the celebration of this momentous occasion. Over a period of time, discussions were held between the parties and in December 1964 it was announced that the UP and the PPP/DCA had agreed in principle to form a coalition in order to foster "the best interests of the Gambian people at large and in furtherance of our desired aims of political stability and unanimity of purpose".[28] As an immediate demonstration of their sincerity the parties would jointly support the nominee of the PPP/DCA for the post of Chairman of the BTC and that of the UP for the post of Vice-Chairman. At the central government level the principle of a coalition was accepted; the precise terms were to be negotiated in due course.

In one action, the political divide between Colony and Protectorate appeared to have been bridged—even if only temporarily.

Summary Observations

The emergence of the Protectorate as a political force and the subsequent birth of the PPP considerably complicated the political scene; ultimately, with even more complicated bargaining over a new Constitution, inter-party alliances, mergers and splintering resulted. There were also the elections of 1960 and 1962, which sounded the death knell for Faye and some of the old original leaders but heralded victory and the crown for a new generation. The formal accession to self-government and independence merely confirmed that in many senses there was a new dawn in Gambian politics.

Perhaps more that any of the politicians of the day, Faye had been deeply immersed in this history-making enterprise. Either, like a symphony conductor, he was separating the parts and then bringing them into a whole, or he was in the trenches fighting against the enemies of progress in the country. In terms of winning the ultimate prize, that is, leader of a politically independent Gambia, he had not been victorious. But, it can safely be said that without his deep involvement it is not likely that things would have been the same. He had been there at the beginning (1947) and was yet there at the end (1965).

Still on the agenda was the transition which Faye and The Gambia were to experience, after which he moved on to the greener pastures offered by the church.

CHAPTER 8

POLITICIAN: THE VICISSITUDES OF POLITICAL AND PERSONAL TRANSITIONS

Commissioner of The Gambia

Faye was appointed Commissioner of The Gambia to the United Kingdom in early October 1963 and assumed office the month following after the celebrations of internal self-government. It was suspected that his appointment was a strategic move by Jawara, on the advice of Governor Paul, to get Faye away from the scene as, for one thing, this would reduce his influence on the younger and less-experienced ministers. Other sources indicate that, among the conditions for the creation of the PPP/DCA Alliance, was an agreement that one of their members who had sacrificed the opportunity to contest the 1962 elections in order to make room for another member would be nominated as Speaker of the House; other senior party members who stood and lost would be appointed to the posts of Chairman of the Gambia Oilseeds Marketing Board (GOMB), Commissioner to London, and other such positions. This agreement had been negotiated in secret at a joint meeting of the Executive Committees of the two parties.

In principle, Faye was opposed to such an agreement, specifically as concerned positions in the legislature. After the announcement of the 1962 election results, Jawara invited him and Garba-Jahumpa to a private meeting to discuss the Speakership. For this position there were a few names, including those of Faye and Garba-Jahumpa. However, Faye argued that from his understanding of what had been agreed upon between the PPP and DCA, preference should be given to Alieu S. Jack,

JEGGAN C. SENGHOR

who had been magnanimous enough to stand down in the Half-Die constituency in Garba-Jahumpa's favour. Faye reasoned:

> A fact is a fact, and that is that we have not been elected to the House. The people have decided that I am not eligible to go there, then what would they think if you (Jawara) now decide that I should go there by appointment after being rejected in the elections? They have rejected me going into the House through the front door why should I go in by the back door? This is not correct so let [Alieu] Jack be.[1]

In the event, Jawara saw the wisdom in Faye's reasoning and A. S. Jack was appointed Speaker.

There was a near-hitch with the processing of Faye's letter of appointment to London which could have resulted in its withdrawal. After the 1962 elections, accompanied by A. E. Cham Joof, Faye travelled to London for meetings with businessmen keen on investing in the country. While he was away, the letter from the Prime Minister on the appointment to the Commissioner's post was delivered at Faye's residence in Bathurst. For over a week the Prime Minister did not receive a reply and there was talk of revoking the appointment. Fortunately, in one of Faye's telephone conversations with his wife, she mentioned the letter and Faye requested her to open and read it. He then promptly prepared an acceptance reply and despatched Cham Joof to Bathurst to deliver it by hand to the Prime Minister and to explain the circumstances for the delay in responding. To Cham Joof's immense pleasure he was received, in person, by the Prime Minister who thanked him for his patriotism and for all the support he was giving to his mentor, Rev. J. C. Faye. The announcement of the appointment was made on the radio that same evening.

On the eve of his departure for London Faye organized a farewell get-together for his political supporters, friends, associates, and those who had stood by him through the years. He advised them to maintain their unflinching support to the PPP/DCA government.

222

Preoccupations in London

Originally a Liaison Office, the Commission's headquarters were small and primarily intended to maintain contacts with and supervision of the growing body of Gambian students in the United Kingdom. In 1962, the title of the post of the head of office was upgraded from "Liaison Officer" to "Commissioner for The Gambia" and it moved to more dignified premises. Staff strength was increased and included a new post of Assistant Liaison Officer.

The welfare of Gambian students in the United Kingdom remained the basic function of the office, in which area Faye registered significant achievements. Through various activities he was able to bring them together and promote a sense of oneness. For this purpose, his open-door policy contributed greatly. Having himself been a student in England he was able to empathize with them and to identify with the apprehensions, insecurities, loneliness, and trials and tribulations of daily living.

Strengthening the Gambian Students Union was one of Faye's commitments. In this regard, even as far back as the early 1950s he had sympathized with the idea of forming a Gambia Students Union, which would qualify for British government subvention. Faye encouraged the prime mover, H. L. O. George, a Gambian ex-student and secretary of WASU, to form the union as WASU affiliate. Faye also appeared to be more interested in Gambians who had originally gone to Britain to study as private students but, for one reason or the other, had dropped out. He specifically pressured for the Government to sponsor their training and encourage them to return home as, if not, they might be attracted to radical and undesirable ideologies.

More generally, as regards the Gambian community at large, Faye was equally supportive. Even where he did not know the persons concerned he visited Gambians in their homes, attended their funerals, involved himself in resolving problems with the authorities, and gave moral support as required. One of his countrymen attested:

> I was in London during the tenure of Rev. J. C. Faye as Gambia Commissioner to the United Kingdom, and I remember him as a warm and affable person who reached

out to the Gambian community in London and was very
much liked, respected and appreciated.[2]

Faye quickly expanded his responsibilities to take on representational functions. In carrying out this role he had to build relationships with relevant structures in the British Government and with other diplomatic representatives. One area of particular importance was that he had to develop strategies for attracting business investments and for marketing the country. Here, in a short period, Faye registered some successes. For example, for the tourism sector the Lyndhurst Brothers showed clear interest and incorporated a company, the Gambia Development Company, in Bathurst. Faye was also involved in the establishment of Jac Sieber Consortium—a mining company—and Bafa-Adripêche Limited, a fishing enterprise. He was a shareholder in both companies and for as long as they operated the dividends turned out to be a welcomed element in the family budget.

With Faye's strong dedication to education, and given the importance he attached to providing opportunities to the younger generation, securing scholarships for Gambian students featured prominently on his agenda. A case in point is that he took advantage of the Commonwealth Scholarship scheme for undergraduate studies in different Commonwealth countries: it was during his stewardship that the very first group of Gambians undertook university studies in Canada which opened the way for many others to follow, both in Canada and other Commonwealth countries.

Over time, the workload in the office increased significantly. As he complained to a friend: "The trouble with our Commission is that its work has increased fourfold but the staff is still the same . . ."[3] The workload included not only official demands but enquiries such as where to purchase a doll dressed in the Gambian national costume; Faye replied that they were not sold in shops but could be made on request and that his wife could be contacted in Bathurst for help.[4] Perhaps more demanding were invitations to address organizations such as the United Nations Association (Salisbury Branch) on what Africa can do to acquire full recognition and respect in the world.[5]

In all this Faye's motivation was to advance the development of his country. As he noted in a letter to R. K. O. Joiner, "I really want to bring something to The Gambia that will help build our country and help all my friends who have suffered with me in the struggle. God grant my prayer would be answered and my efforts blessed; then we shall all laugh."[6]

Unfortunately, because of impolitic deportment on his side there was not enough latitude for Faye to achieve his goals. This lay in the fact that, though he was the government's diplomatic representative in London, Faye did not hesitate to express opinions critical of its policies and programmes to whoever cared to listen. As a young student in London, this author was subjected to many hours of "education" as to the countless errors of the PPP regime. The Prime Minister had himself been receiving reports on the "disloyalty" of his Commissioner; for this and other reasons he then decided to recall Faye to Bathurst in September 1964. Faye had barely spent one year in post.

Republican Referendum, 1965

In May 1965 the government announced its proposal for The Gambia to become a republic on the first anniversary of independence, in February 1966, with an Executive President. The proposal, together with an Emergency Powers Bill, would be subjected to debate in the legislature and, in line with the Constitution, be submitted to the electorate in a referendum.

Despite the unwelcome development regarding their leader, in his recall from the position in London, the DCA remained active alongside an even livelier PPP. The fact that its sole House member continued to hold ministerial office in the PPP government and was becoming a very trusted confidant of the Premier helped the party maintain some presence on the political scene. At every opportunity both parties adopted positions opposed to the UP. As evidence, the DCA gave its fullest backing to PPP candidates who had submitted election petitions to the courts and, in turn, the PPP threw its weight behind DCA candidates in the elections to the BTC. Even on the republican proposal of the PPP government, as a party the DCA did not openly oppose it. This was vital as all the other parties and other powerful opinion-moulders were ranked against the government; together, they were, indeed, a force to be reckoned with.

It was not surprising that this oneness in all things resulted in the agreement to merge the PPP and DCA into one organization bearing the PPP name, and with Jawara as its leader. This was in August 1965 and it was a crowning achievement for the PPP. The party had been growing in strength, especially with the mass "crossing of the carpet" by many former UP members of the House; by the end of 1964, eight of the 13 UP representative had defected to the PPP or the DCA.[7] The PPP was now at the head of a one-party dominant system and was impregnable.

Faye actually returned to Bathurst in January 1965. He signed the merger agreement between the DCA and the PPP in August, because he considered it in the future interest of the party. But, at heart, he was not in support of some of the policies of the PPP, amongst them the decision to introduce a republican Constitution. Consequently, the very next month, on 30 September 1965, he announced that he was resigning from the enlarged PPP:

> I, the undersigned, Rev, J. C. Faye, of 46 Gloucester Street, Bathurst, do hereby declare that I am no more a member of the People's Progressive Party as I cannot conscientiously subscribe to, support or condone a policy designed to shape the Gambia into a Republic with an Executive President.[8]

He convened a mass meeting of supporters the weekend following at which he spoke at length on the reasons for his resignation. Some in the DCA leadership, such as Louis Cherry, wanted to join Faye but he, Faye, advised that, because of their superior experience, the PPP stood to benefit from their continued membership and loyalty. They stayed on with the PPP.

Referendum Campaign (1965)

Faye joined the motley band of anti-republicans (the UP/CP, GWU, and leading independent newspapers) and launched "a mission of enlightenment" to different parts of the country to inform the populace of the dangers inherent in a republican constitution; his case was clearly articulated in a broadcast talk titled "The Referendum and You." Like the other opponents, his grounds for rejection of republicanism were as follows. First, that the PPP's ulterior motive was to consolidate its position, especially in the light of the decline in the popularity of the UP, as reflected in its relatively poor performance in the Bathurst 1964 municipal elections; this last had been one of the reasons for the termination of the PPP/DCA/UP coalition arrangement in June 1964. Further, the intended delimitation of electoral boundaries was likely to result in a reduction of Bathurst parliamentary seats and, therefore, the UP's representation in the legislature.

Second, the timing was inappropriate—it was too soon after independence and more of a guise for some to arrogate more power to themselves; the people in government were young and needed more experience in the art of governance.

Third, republicanism could not be said to be better understood by the African; in fact, it was also very foreign, having been introduced by France in francophone Africa. It resulted in highly centralized and monolithic structures which were foreign to the British parliamentary system of government.

Fourth, this move was not in the best interest of the country; an Executive Presidency would not necessarily promote socio-economic development and a better life for the masses of people. Retaining the status quo would mean greater access to financial and technical assistance from Britain and the Commonwealth of Nations.

Fifth, the new Constitution must not be modelled on existing ones such as those of the United States of America or Nigeria.

Finally, the anti-republicans felt that the PPP government wanted to avoid another general election; its tenure of office was to end in 1967 and it wanted to side-step the right of the people to vote it out of office.

These and several other arguments were trumpeted in joint and individual political rallies throughout the country by the UP, MC, the GWU and smaller opposition groups. To these were to be added the loud voice of Faye. What a coincidence that this was the same set of actors whose fierce in-fighting in the previous decade had contributed so significantly to the electoral ascendancy of the PPP.

Faye held numerous meetings all over Bathurst and travelled as far as he could in the Protectorate to propagate his message; sometimes he had to hire private taxis in order to keep his campaign appointments. He narrated that when one chief, Kantara Jawara of Wuli, heard of Faye's rallies in Brikama, he approached P. S. NJie and requested that a vehicle be put at Faye's disposal as he was no longer a member of any political party and was short of resources. NJie was not keen on the idea. Nonetheless, by Faye's reckoning, the fact of having very limited means did not affect his effectiveness;[9] except that without any means of transportation he could only campaign over eleven days instead of the 20 days he had originally planned.

Referendum Results

The referendum was conducted on a phased basis from 18 to 26 November 1965. The final results were as follows: 31,921 "No" votes, and 61,568 "Yes" votes. This was a majority of 29,647 votes, which was neither two-thirds of the total of 93,789 votes cast nor one-half of the 154,626 registered voters, as required by the Constitution. Therefore, the republican constitution was not approved.

However small his input may have been, Faye had contributed to the failure of the government to meet the statutory requirements.

General Elections, May 1966: Campaign, Results

In reaction to the referendum results, and in order to demonstrate the popularity of his government, the Prime Minister announced, soon afterwards, that general elections would be held from 17 to 26 May 1966.

Gambian electors had not lost their verve for political campaigns and this one was as intensive as earlier ones. The PPP government highlighted its achievements since assuming office—independence and international recognition, and economic, social and infrastructural developments. New orientations in relations with Senegal were also included in the list of achievements of the PPP government. On the other hand, these were the same areas in which the opposition parties criticized the performance of the governing party. Not much was heard from Faye.

Of the total 124,492 votes cast, the PPP obtained 81,313 votes (65.31 percent), the UP had 41,549 votes (33.37 percent) and the Independents obtained 1,630 votes (1.31 percent).[10] These votes translated into 24 seats for the PPP, 7 seats for the UP and one seat for the DCA. With no party behind him, Faye chose to stand as an Independent candidate in the Bathurst Central constituency. In a three-man contest John R. Forster (UP/GCP) obtained 1,564 votes, Melvin Jones (PPP) scored 941 votes, and John C. Faye (Independent) only 104 votes (4 percent).

As regards the other party leaders, NJie comfortably won the Bathurst North seat with 2,449 votes as against 688 votes for M. Harley NJie (PPP) and 115 votes for the trade unionist M. E. Jallow (Independent). Garba-Jahumpa (CP/UP, Bathurst South) defeated a new PPP candidate, Abdoulie M. Drammeh, by 2,118 to 541 votes. Jawara polled 4,515 votes as against 589 votes for Sillah Bojang his UP rival.

Thus, NJie and Garba-Jahumpa continued to maintain a presence in front line politics. But, for Faye, the circumstances had changed considerably since the early fifties when Soldier Town/Bathurst Central constituency was the bastion of his support and that of the DP. Now, it was an uphill task for him to make any headway. In the earlier elections, due mainly to misjudgement and miscalculation, he had bypassed this safe and personal fief to go and stand in two other "foreign" constituencies (Kombo West and New Town West) where his support base was comparatively fragile. Naturally, during the period of absence opposing politicians had planted roots which had proved very fruitful.

Faye's two historic rivals, NJie and Garba-Jahumpa, had been realistic enough not to make such a mistake; throughout his political life Garba-Jahumpa had stood only in the Half-Die/Bathurst South constituency whether in local government or national elections. Much the same for NJie, who permanently stuck his roots in the New Town East/Banjul North constituency. Again, Faye was not helped by the

fact that, in this last contest, the other two candidates (J. R. Forster of
the UP and M. B. Jones of the PPP) were of Krio/Aku stock. Both had
stood in the same constituency before, in national and local government
elections; they were also very experienced at the hustings.

To all intents and purposes J. C. Faye's active political career was
at an end.

J. C. Faye on Independence

Since his earliest days in politics, and definitely since the mid 1950s,
Faye had set his sights on independence as a natural objective. This, for
him, was his ultimate purpose for participating in politics. Commitment
to independence also explains Faye's perennial conflicts with those
responsible for perpetuating the colonial system, in the persons of
colonial governors and other officials. Additional evidence is to be seen
in his leadership role in the heady days of the struggle for constitutional
progress throughout the 1950s, but particularly in the post-1955 period,
as amply discussed in several places in this biography.

In a broadcast talk just before the 1962 elections, Faye had reasoned
that:

> The watchword of the Democratic Congress Alliance
> being "Peace and Prosperity", we realize that the nation we
> would and must build should enjoy peace both internally
> and externally. With this in view, our party aims for
> independence for The Gambia not later than January 1963.
> Under the colonial system the shackles of dependency do
> not fully allow Gambian brains and brawn to imprint their
> stamp on the land of The Gambia, and bring into it all the
> improvements and development that would help eradicate
> unemployment, frustration, backwardness, defeatism,
> disappointment and poverty. These, in turn, fetch in their
> wake unrest and irascibility to any country under subjugation,
> especially when other partners in trouble have loosened the
> hands of servility and are rapidly making advancement all

around, as is the case of a Gambia that grovels under colonial
status, still.[11]

As noted in this quotation, for Faye independence was not for its
own sake but, rather, for the socio-economic benefits it would bring to
the Gambian peoples. At the PPP/DCA Annual Delegates Conference
(April 1963) he added:

> We are asking for independence . . . There are countries
> smaller than us which are independent. We must have
> confidence, sweat and work to build it [an independent
> Gambia]. If we do this then The Gambia can become a great
> force in West Africa and a great country in the future.[12]

Faye's personal commitment to independence for The Gambia also
throws light on his perspectives on relations with Senegal, summarized
in his plea:

> I have a message for President Senghor. We are swimming
> for our lives and if Senegal is a blood relation she will send
> us a lifeline to land us on dry ground more quickly.[13]

This was very much in line with nationalist thinking and action in
the West African region, particularly in Kwame Nkrumah's Ghana.
The record shows that the DCA developed close relations with, and
received assistance from, the government of Ghana, both financially
and materially. In June 1961 Garba-Jahumpa paid a ten-day visit to
Accra as an official guest of the Ghana government; he returned with
offers of scholarships and funds for the party.

At the conference of dependent African states in Accra, in June
1961, a follow-up to that held in Addis Ababa the previous year, Faye
was a member of the delegation of five Gambian politicians and trade
unionists who attended. He was selected to chair the Constitutional
Crises Committee whilst Garba-Jahumpa chaired that on African Unity.

In his post-conference briefing to party leaders on his return to
Bathurst, Faye declared that in his opening statement Nkrumah had

stated that the aim was to discuss the shortest possible way to gain independence and how to bring about mutual understanding and dignity and form one solidarity front to achieve a United States of Africa. The continent would become one nation only after independence had been won by the dependent African countries. Faye then went on to refer to Garba-Jahumpa's earlier expressed view that, after independence, Gambia would join the Ghana/Guinea/Mali bloc, for which statement Garba-Jahumpa had been severely criticized. There and then, Faye confirmed that he himself fully agreed with his colleague. After all, Chief Awolowo of Nigeria had also declared at the conference that Nigeria would join the bloc too if he ever became Prime Minister as "it was through them that Africa has a voice in the world".[14]

The month following, during the visit of Kofi Batsa, editor-in-chief of the *Voice of Africa*, a leading newspaper of the Ghana Bureau of African Affairs, he addressed a public meeting of the PPP/DCA and implored Gambians to regard Faye, Jahumpa and M. E. Jallow of the GWU as heroes, and to vote for them in the coming 1962 elections.

It was in this same context that Ghana had provided the services of some legal experts to assist in the petition cases against some of the DCA and PPP candidates who had won in the courts after the 1962 elections. These included the Attorney Kaw Swanzy, and a senior Ghanaian counsel, Alex da Costa. At the same time the Ghana Government seconded an expert to occupy the post of principal veterinary officer which had been vacated by Jawara when he decided to enter politics. All of these were at no cost. Scholarships were also offered to other staff of the veterinary department at the Ghana Veterinary. Assistants School.

For the DCA, so significant was this connection with the Ghana government that, following the resignation of Garba-Jahumpa from the party, it was decided to inform President Nkrumah and to provide him with a copy both of the resignation letter and the reply accepting it from the party. Cham Joof, the Secretary General, argued in the letter that:

> Though presently we cannot predict Mr. Garba-Juhumpa's
> political leanings yet we deem it fair to state that anyone in
> The Gambia today who is anti-PPP/DCA is either in league
> with, or an indirect aid to, the United Party (UP), which

party, to say the least, is reactionary and a collaborator with imperialist and neo-colonialist agents in this country . . .

We are resolved to work with the PPP and press forward until independence is gained for The Gambia in the shortest space of time. The DCA sees nothing but the emancipation of this much-maligned but nevertheless dear land of ours. Admittedly, any splinter movement at this momentous hour of the Gambia's political growth would split the people, sap their solidarity and prove a direct sabotage of this country's independence.[15]

Before the merger of the DP and the MC, Faye issued a manifesto in which, inter alia, he called for a Federation of British West Africa and the retention of the regional functional institutions such as the currency, military, and research institutions. Speaking specifically of the West African Examinations Council, he had declared: "After independence it would be advantageous to keep such links. England is our old friend and The Gambia should remain in the Commonwealth after independence."

Such commitment to West African cooperation attracted the attention of regional political leaders such as the highly respected Nigerian nationalist, Nnamdi Azikiwe; in fact, Azikiwe sent Faye a personal invitation to his inauguration as Governor General of Nigeria in 1960, which Faye honoured. It was during this visit that Faye was invited to give a lecture on Africa and African affairs. So impressed were some members of the United States delegation "for his eloquence and knowledge" that, subsequently, they requested him to go on a lecture tour of a number of American institutions.

From various sources it appears, though, that there were occasions of wavering, or even turn-around, in Faye's dedication to independence. A case in point is that, at the May 1961 Bathurst Constitutional Conference, Faye had supported Jawara's general demand for independence but when it came to fixing a date, he was of the opinion that it should be after a period of nine months. Jallow maintained that a date should be determined there and then, whereas Jawara argued that the date must be fixed at the subsequent London Conference which was to consider the proposals of this Bathurst confab.

According to the report of the follow-up London talks, Jawara combined his recommendation of January 1963 as the independence date with the request that:

> A firm indication should be given at this conference that The Gambia would achieve full independence. He added that the question of association with other countries should not be linked with the question of independence. Any negotiations for such association could only properly and successfully be carried out by a fully representative and independent Government.[16]

The report records that both Faye and Garba-Jahumpa supported Jawara's views. Given Faye's own earlier position on the independence date, it is more likely that his support of Jawara related more to the question of independence and association with Senegal than to the independence date proposed by Jawara. Another possible explanation of this foot-dragging is that Faye's move was strategic, in that an emphasis on an independence date might jeopardize the achievement of the more immediate objective of self-government. On the other hand, astute and realistic a politician as Faye was, it must have been palpably clear to him and everyone else that the new-born PPP was growing rapidly and had a good chance of leading the country to independence if an early date was agreed on.

J. C. Faye on Senegambian Integration

In his broadcast campaign talk to the nation on 17 May 1962, Faye laid out the details of his Africa policy; it deserves to be quoted in some detail because it encapsulates the thinking of the man on the subject:

> We would strive to maintain friendly relations with all our neighbours, especially the British West African territories with which we have had close and inseparable bonds, and Senegal next door as well as Mali and Guinea our other near neighbours. As touching Senegal, however, we would like

to develop closer cultural and economic relationships as and when independence is attained by The Gambia. We believe and hold that it is only equals who could and should parley or negotiate fairly with each other. Whenever we can call a government here ours, then and only then could we speak with the Senegalese on equal terms, and the boundaries between ourselves and our cousins [be] broken down even as those between Ghana and Haute Volta are at Paga. Let no one kid us. Senegal needs our river as we need freer trade with them. But as we give away we must receive also, we must know our economy would be sapped and its vital cord snapped. May The Gambia be delivered from such tomfoolery.

We wish our neighbours well and do long for our river to fulfil the purpose for which it was ordained and destined, namely, not only to serve The Gambia but Upper Senegal, Mali and Upper Guinea also. However, we want to be free first . . . The Gambia's role in West Africa must be that of a palm of olive branch, a bearer of peace; but The Gambia must be firm to keep her identity immaculate and independent till when other states in this corner of Africa are prepared to work in a greater political set-up (confederation or federation) which would prove a power in Africa and in the great forum of the world.[17]

The first official contacts between the governments of Senegal and The Gambia took place in December 1958 in the form of a visit by Premier Mamadou Dia and senior officials. The purpose was to test the waters, through interactions with a wide spectrum of persons to collect information on latest developments in the country and, in particular, sound out feelings on relations with Senegal. In as delicate a manner as was possible, the delegation also advanced the case for integration, emphasizing the socio-cultural bonds between the two peoples; this was, for them, a solid basis for building a future Senegambia. Gambian legislators and officials endorsed, in general terms, the arguments made, especially as concerns the socio-cultural commonalities. But, the differences in institutions and systems called for a cautious approach.

As was to be expected Faye took a very active part in the deliberations, both in his personal capacity and as a government minister. His guiding principle was: "You must count one before you go to two." But, at the same time, he recognized that:

> France and Britain have become friends from the Entente Cordiale despite the Hundred Years War. We can, in their example of reason, unite ourselves. And we are sure of their support in this endeavour because Senegal and The Gambia form the same people with the same language, the same blood and same traditions.[18]

Inevitably, this reality of the strong unities that exist between the two countries took on a life of its own and became the framework for policy-making on options for cooperation and integration between the two countries. Equally relevant was the assumption that, with its small geographic size, its paucity of natural and other resources, its fragile institutions and limited political development, Gambia would not be able to stand on its own feet.

Merger with Senegal was only one option. Another was autonomy, but with some type of close links with the United Kingdom. Garba-Jahumpa, in a 1953 interview, expressed interest in this: "I don't know whether we should be represented in the House of Lords or the House of Commons but [there] should be one."[19] He saw interactions with Senegal in competitive terms such as building a local airport better than the one in Dakar.

Faye, on the other hand, was vociferous in his opposition to any such arguments for a "permanent alignment" with Britain. And this was for two reasons. First, lessons from similar arrangements in French-colonized Africa indicated that Gambian legislators would be easily manipulated by the majority British legislators. Second, representation in metropolitan parliamentary institutions would prevent Africans from acquiring appropriate skills for running their affairs seeing that the contexts were so different.

At this stage Faye's preference was, ideally, that the country should unite with other British West African territories to form a Federal British West Africa, on condition that Gambia would have full internal autonomy, and that foreign affairs, external communications, and defence and currency would be shared responsibilities.

In the Legislative Council Adjournment Debate, in November 1959, Faye and his party colleagues were more decisive in that they now preferred links with Sierra Leone but with guarantees such as those noted above. The stated reason for this was that the two countries had a similar "political and cultural mosaic", a common official language and a tradition of elite interactions and commercial relations. Historically, also, The Gambia had been administered from Freetown twice, from 1821 to 1843 and 1866 to 1888; between 1947 and 1948 a system of joint administrative departments was tried out. There was, in other words, some foundation on which the proposed linkage could be built.

Allied to this was the likelihood that the Krio/Aku, the backbone of support for the DP, would be an influential factor as far as the party's position on Senegambian relations was concerned. They were firm in their opposition to close association with Senegal. Faye was speaking on their behalf when he declared:

> She [The Gambia] does not want, nor does she intend, to sever her connections with the British Commonwealth of Nations. Her 300 odd years of apprenticeship therein she cherishes and will not throw away lightly.[20]

The UP stuck to its support for very close relations and even integration with Senegal. This was consonant with NJie's desire to revive the ancient Saloum state as a unifying force for Muslim/Wolof and Catholic/Wolof alike; they, in turn, were predominant in the Bathurst electorate and constituted the greater proportion of the UP leadership.

Garba-Jahumpa and his MC rejected the position of Faye and his DP on the grounds that tiny Gambia would be swallowed up in a British West Africa Federation; the costs involved would be prohibitive anyway. By 1959, Garba-Jahumpa had shifted dramatically to favour Gambia's joining Senegal and, *ipso facto*, the Mali Federation between Senegal and French Soudan.[21] He was even more vocal in his crusade in favour of full integration with Senegal. For the other leaders the only explanation for this somersault was that it was in response to the fundamental interests of Garba-Jahumpa's core support group and, more generally, he was playing to the voting public.

In the 1960 to 1962 period, relations with Senegal took on greater urgency; it was second only to the question of how soon constitutional reforms would lead to self-government and independence. Activities bearing on Senegambian integration were rapidly stepped up after the appointment of P. S. NJie as Chief Minister, from March 1961 to the demise of his government after the May 1962 elections. These included the path-breaking official visits to Dakar by NJie, the identification of specific functional areas for cooperation, and the establishment of joint institutions for managing cooperation.

For Faye, this was not unexpected as it was precisely because NJie was ready to endorse and implement the position of the colonial administration that he had been selected as Chief Minister in the first place. Besides, Britain's real intention was to sell the country to Senegal, which accounts for its reluctance to fully grapple with the declining performance of the economy and to finance major development projects such as the airport. These claims were to be repeated ad nauseam in the months following.

Alarmed at the pace at which substantive moves were being made on Senegambian integration by the NJie government, under "manipulation" by the colonial authority, Faye and the DCA leadership agreed with their PPP partners to bring this to the attention of the London Constitutional Conference of July 1961. It was done in the form of a press statement, signed by Faye and four others, which detailed their concerns, especially the suspicions of many Gambians that Britain intended to "teleguide" The Gambia into full union with its neighbour. Faye's preference, and that of both the other signatories and their parties, was that all such policy actions must be suspended until after the country was fully independent.[22]

Faye was also among the five-man delegation that subsequently met in private with the Secretary of State to consider these grievances. They were able to obtain assurances that the government emerging from the scheduled general elections would be empowered to "exercise responsibilities in the major field of internal affairs . . . and foster relations with Gambia's neighbours".[23]

As expected, in the May 1962 elections which followed, the subject of relations with Senegal was more prominent in the debates. The Day of Judgement (that is, independence) was very much in view and it was imperative that the final stance on the subject be clarified once and for all. Faye seized every occasion to re-state his long-held views and was ferocious in his criticisms of the initiatives the UP had embarked on with the Senegalese. At one public rally he said of the UP leader: "Having failed to govern the country, he now wants to sell it to Senegal." Continuing, he cautioned the electorate that "as P.S. NJie is giving you gifts of Senegalese rice so he will give you up to Senegal later." He repeated the warning that the colonial administration was pushing the UP government to integrate with Senegal as this was the only way to rid itself of The Gambia, an unwanted child:

> The aim of England is to edge us around to Senegal. The British do not want to free us even now. They are starting to call us an enclave of Senegal although we were never that under colonial rule.[24]

On assuming power after the 1962 general elections, Jawara embarked on a systematic orderly approach to relations with Senegal. The invitation of the United Nations to provide independent experts to review the situation and recommend alternatives to association was an excellent strategic move for the PPP, for it provided a basis for evidence-based policy-formulation. But, for Faye, it was not even necessary for the UN to send a team of experts to investigate the matter, given that the views of the vast majority of Gambians were well known as were his own, as leader of a political party.

Faye sent a memorandum to the PPP/DCA Executive Committee on the risks involved in inviting the UN. He took advantage of every opportunity to repeat his long-standing conviction that relations with Senegal should focus on fuller exploitation of the sub-region's resources short of a full customs union, but should not venture into the political arena. He also favoured initiatives to foster socio-cultural links, in recognition of the strong bonds between the two peoples. Faye's appointment as Commissioner in London did not deter him from communicating his dissenting views, and he did this to British colonial officials such as John Tisch, who was in charge of the West Africa Department in the Colonial Office. As if all this was not bold enough, when the final report of the UN mission was released, Faye carefully dissected it and proffered extensive critical comments on specific issues.

During the UN mission the political parties and other groups were extremely vocal in their opposition to close association or integration with Senegal. And this influenced the work of the experts, their analysis of the issues, and their final recommendations. In no small measure, Faye's opposing voice was just what the anti-Senegal forces wanted. Though at this time his party, the DCA, was in an informal alliance with the PPP, on this issue there was no compromise.

Faye worked assiduously to keep his views on the public agenda, especially during the bilateral negotiations on the UN report in May 1964. As he was now in London as Commissioner for the Gambia, his agents operated through the younger members of the Gambian delegation and encouraged them to resist any form of close links with Senegal. It is reported that so strident were these Young Turks that, at one point in the negotiations when the Senegalese delegation became overly aggressive, these Turks threatened to walk out. Since they came from a man of such experience and stature in society as Faye, there is no doubt that the memorandum and his position on the whole business of policy towards Senegal made an impression on the younger politicians in the PPP/DCA leadership.

Given Faye's personal and extended family connections in Senegal and his deep-rooted historical and current attachments, it would have been natural for him to strongly advocate close association, and even integration, with that country. Like NJie and Garba-Jahumpa, Faye had qualities and competences that would have guaranteed him prominent roles (political or non-political) in an integrated Senegambia. Nevertheless, throughout his days of active politics, Faye supported sectoral economic cooperation with the neighbour but without any expectations of integration or absorption of The Gambia into Senegal. Through the ups and downs of political life in his home country and the swings in the politics of Senegambian cooperation and integration, he remained as doggedly principled as on other matters. Unlike NJie and Garba-Jahumpa, Faye never wavered on this issue.

In terms of the bigger picture this position of Faye was, perhaps, surprising. He was acutely aware of the movement for political emancipation in West Africa and beyond, and of the pull of Pan-Africanism at the time—as is suggested in the preceding paragraphs. During his formative years he had closely followed the activities of the Bathurst branch of the NCBWA and came under the influence of a dynamic activist like E.F. Small. Faye also closely followed Nkrumah's ideas and the massive efforts he was making to promote African unity; but though he admired and respected the man he was hesitant about his socialist ideological orientations.

Ironically, and as illustrated in Chapters 5 and 6, in the local politics of the day Faye cut an image of a radical, someone who was always questioning the status quo and wanted rapid transformation. It was for this reason that he played a leading role in organizing opinion against piecemeal changes to the existing reactionary constitutional order which was favoured by some other politicians. Could all these be reconciled with Faye's stance on a unified Senegambia?

An explanation for this is that Faye cherished The Gambia very highly; it was his country of birth, regardless of its shortcomings. Especially when compared to the other British colonies in West Africa, The Gambia had rather little to offer. But still he was very proud of the British inheritance, in terms of its traditions and institutions, its culture and values, and its history and systems. This was particularly so when he juxtaposed it with what he saw of French colonization as practised in Senegal. As he had clearly stated in his intervention at the 1948 African Conference:

> I agree with Mr. [E. F.] Small when he mentioned, in effect,
> that the British must watch French designs on The Gambia.
> We in The Gambia do not want French rule. We are British
> and want to remain so. But it does not gainsay the fact that

our affairs are so wrapped up and linked up with Senegal that a commercial understanding with the French is as relevant as it is salient to the economic development of The Gambia.[25]

He was to elaborate further on the last part of the above quotation when he explained:

But The Gambia today, and since 1948, had never lost sight of the mutual advantage and economic benefits that would stem from a sensible economic agreement that could be effected between herself and her next door neighbour. The readiness of The Gambia to cooperate with Senegal in this connection has already been manifest in The Gambia's conceding to Senegal the privilege of evacuating Upper Casamance nuts from the river ports of Basse, and in the existence and operation of the Trans-Gambia Road. Such economic and cultural association (not customs union for that is rather complicated) would create a closer relationship between the peoples of the two territories. More than this should not now be sought.[26]

This was the essence of Faye's pragmatism. His many private and official visits further reinforced his questioning attitudes towards the neighbour and made him want to guard jealously what The Gambia had to offer.

Summary Observations

With the move of Faye to London, his political career practically came to an end. Among all the other doyens of Gambian politics—indeed, all the other political leaders of the day—he was the only one to drop out of the scene, with ambitions unfulfilled. The campaign over the proposal for a republican constitution was his last hurrah; he savoured the failure of his erstwhile comrades-in-arms to succeed in this venture.

Thus, the Rev. J. C. Faye bowed out of politics with grace and dignity, ready to return to a more sedate life in the search for lost souls.

CHAPTER 9

CLERGYMAN: IN THE QUEST FOR SOULS

The Setting

The Gambia has always been predominantly Muslim with over 95 percent of the population adhering to the religion. This has been so both in the country as a whole and, separately, in the Protectorate and the capital area. Christianity can be traced back to the Portuguese, who arrived in 1456. James Island was their initial base but they built churches in several other towns in the vicinity. The religion spread to other parts of the country as their trading expanded into other areas. By the middle of the sixteenth century the number of Christians had grown significantly, though concentrated around specific trading stations. With the "foundation" of Bathurst in 1816 and its settlement, the Christian population increased, with arrivals from Senegal, Freetown and from among colonial officials. In January 1821 the Society of Friends (Quakers) first explored possibilities of setting up a mission in The Gambia and had actually established one by the end of that year.[1] However, they were confronted with a range of difficulties and withdrew in 1824.

The Wesleyan Methodist Mission (WMM) soon followed in February 1821, and established a base in Bathurst; 70 percent of its adherents were in this area and 30 percent on McCarthy Island in the Protectorate. The Catholics made initial ventures in Bathurst in 1823 and set up a permanent presence in 1849. Through aggressive proselytizing by the 1930s they outnumbered the other denominations, both in Bathurst and the rest of the country. By 1944 they were estimated to be almost 50 percent of Bathurst's Christian population, the Methodist were one-third, and the Anglicans the rest.[2]

Christians were relatively few in the Protectorate in the early part of the twentieth century. According to the 1911 census, Muslims made up 85 percent of the population; of the rest, 14 percent belonged to traditional African religions, and 0.6 percent were Christians. In 1931 the figures for both Muslims and traditionalists increased slightly but that of the Christians dropped to 767 (0.4 percent). Of this 421 were Catholics, 216 Methodists and 130 Anglicans.[3]

Given the high mortality among European clergy, due mainly to malaria and other tropical diseases, the Catholic Church embarked on training a core of local priests who would also serve the growing population of local adherents. Towards this end, a bold step taken was the training and ordination of Father Charles Mendy in 1922 and Father Edwin Paul and Father Gregory Thomas Jobe in 1933. Regrettably, Paul died in 1934 followed by Mendy in 1935.

The Call: True or Not for Now?

John Colley Faye decided to go into the church quite early whilst a teacher. Encouraged by Rev. Hunter, who was his boss at St Mary's School, and Rev. S. F. W. During, the pastor at St Mary's Church, he had started reading up on theology and church history. Faye was further motivated by Bishop Daly, whose first words to him when he arrived to assume his responsibilities in the diocese, on Ascension Day in 1935, were: "I have something more for you than school mastering." This was a very profound message for Faye, who read something spiritual in it. He became a lay reader and leader of the Prayer, Example and Action (PEA) youth group in the church. His lieutenants were Henry Mensah (who was to become Archdeacon in Ghana), then an employee in the Education Department, and A.S.C. Able-Thomas, a school teacher.

So caught up was Faye in matters spiritual that as early as March 1936 he took the bold step of writing to Bishop Daly offering himself "as a candidate for the sacred ministry of God's word".[4] He further noted that the call to the ministry had intensified since the very first sermon given by Daly after which he had appealed:

> for the prayers of the old and the zeal and support of the young I have felt and realized an urging I cannot stifle, for, from that time, I have discovered that, do as I may, no other vocation than that of the ministry can satisfy the spiritual longing and unrest that have become a part of myself.[5]

By mutual consent it was decided that Faye's request should be put off till the Bishop had more fully acquainted himself with his new church and its people. Faye was encouraged to continue with the variety of services he was offering at St Mary's, and especially with the youth.

As detailed in other parts of this biography, in the 1930s and 1940s there were many other preoccupations occupying the attention of Faye, particularly in connection with his teaching career and the challenges of managing KK School. But, there were also two contending forces that impacted on Faye's decision as to whether or not to pursue the priesthood or continue as a lay worker.[6]

First, the push factor. This related to the fate of a number of Gambian clergy from different denominations (Rev. Father Mendy, Father Jobe, and Rev. Hunter) who were on the move, allegedly in unsavoury circumstances. Reverend Father Mendy, the first Gambian Roman Catholic priest, was believed by many Christians in the country to have died due to maltreatment and harassment by some foreign colleagues. Then also it was believed that Reverend Gregory Thomas Jobe went into self-exile due to provocation bordering on persecution from some of the non-African clergy. Jobe was renowned for such daring moves as conducting the Sung Mass in Wolof and for his dynamism in spreading Catholicism; he was very popular among the congregations and took advantage of whatever opportunities arose to do things his own way and not in line with the dictates of the European priests. Together with Fathers Meehan and Whiteside, he established schools and experimental agricultural farms and was highly successful in winning converts.

In 1944, Jobe's relationship with Father Meehan deteriorated over allegations of racism and he moved to Casamance to join Monsignor Faye.

But here he found the prelate having extremely difficult relationships with the French priests under him, to such an extent that he, Jobe, had to move on to Paris in 1947 to run an anti-colonial journal. As for Monsignor Faye, shortly afterwards, he himself gave up his bishopric and retired to a teaching position at a seminary in Senegal. In the case of Reverend Canon Henry Newman Hunter he also had to undergo some trying times with his European fellow clergy and had to leave to serve in the Lagos Diocese and later the Nigerian Army.

Owing to these unfortunate experiences of Gambians in the priesthood, Faye, after consultation with his wife, decided that it was better to remain in The Gambia and function as a lay worker rather than become a priest and eventually be forced to leave the country, as had happened to other Africans. He also decided to give up his theological studies and instead continue as a lay worker.

The Power of Dreams

The dominant factor that pulled Faye towards the ministry took the form of the dreams of three key personalities—Faye himself, his wife Cecilia, and Bishop Daly. As recorded by Faye,[7] at the end of 1945 he was admitted to hospital in Bathurst suffering from acute dysentery. Towards the end of his recovery, he had a strange dream. In his own narration:

> It was as if I was in the Serre-kunda area and, as it was my wont, I visited a little Jola hamlet. But as I approached the village the usual noise of Jola children playing round and about the village was not heard. Another strange thing is that I was robed in a white cassock. Doubting what would have caused the silence, I doubled up my steps and entered the village and there I found my young friends, the Jola lads and lasses, all sitting round a Koranic teacher and [they] were being taught the Koran. Then it was as if something within me questioned me—"What will you do about it?"[8]

The following morning he wrote a letter to Cecilia recounting the dream. At the same time, she had also had a dream and had written to Faye about it. Obviously, their letters crossed. His reportage continues:

> She was sleeping in her room in Kristi-kunda at midday when she heard a knock on the front door. She accordingly went to see who was there. She found a personage dressed in biblical clothes. She complimented the stranger and asked him who he was. He too returned her compliments and declared, "I am John." Cecilia then added: "Do you mean John the Baptist in the Bible?" He answered, "Yes, I mean John the Baptist in the Bible, get me John. Cecilia then came to the room and woke me up with the words "John the Baptist in the Bible is calling you." With that, as she related it, I got up and wearing my Fula sandals went straight to meet the waiting stranger.
>
> As soon as I reached where John the Baptist was standing, he simply turned round and the two of us started going towards Fatoto, the river port of Kristi-kunda. Cecilia too summoned courage and followed us until we reached a hillock on which another person, similarly robed as John the Baptist, was standing looking towards the east. St. John and I went on and on until we arrived at the top of the little hill where the other person was standing. And, as soon as John [the Baptist] and I came up to him, John said to me: "I want you to preach to these people." Thereupon, I too took two steps forward and started to preach.
>
> Then she [Cecilia] woke up.[9]

Three days after Faye received his wife's letter, and while still in hospital, he received another letter from Bishop Daly in which he informed Faye that he had seen him in dreams, three times, fully attired in clerical apparel and celebrating the Holy Sacrament at the altar.

With these experiences, Faye and his family were convinced that he was being called to the ministry. The Bishop then decided that Faye should undergo more structured training for the ministry and concentrate, in particular, on Comparative Religions, Pastoral Theology, some New Testament Greek, the Common Prayer and Church Teaching, "What a Christian believes and Why", Church History, and the Art of Sermon Making. This course of study, designed by the Bishop, was similar to that of the Church of England for its ordinands. The Priest-in-Charge was Faye's direct supervisor and the Bishop in overall charge.[10]

The Bishop had a well-laid-out plan for Faye's early career in the Church. This was that after he had been made a deacon in 1947 he would spend the next two years at KK. He would then give up his responsibilities there and spend 12 to 18 months preparing for ordination into the priesthood. The first few months of this period would be spent visiting the Church in West Africa and the rest in England, where he could build a prayerful life and learn the workings of a good English parish.[11]

The Bishop assured Faye—and his wife—that he was aware that one of the factors that had influenced his decision on whether or not to join the ministry was their concern that it might lead to their having to leave the diocese, as had happened to other Gambians of the Anglican and Roman Catholic faiths. Daly reassured Faye that "I value your work as a layman so highly that I should only have offered ordination had I believed that in holy orders you will be able even better to serve the Master in building His Kingdom in your own land."[12]

Deacon: Complications in Abundance.

Rev. J. C. Faye was made a deacon in the Anglican Church on 2 February 1947. The ceremony, which took place at the Pro-Cathedral of St Mary in Bathurst, was attended by many of his students at KK. In fact, some were baptized and others confirmed after the ordination ceremony, including Teacher Arthur Cates, who was originally a Methodist. Faye then served his curacy at St John's Church in KK and later moved back to Bathurst to be Honorary Curate at St Mary's Pro-Cathedral and Christ Church, Serre-kunda, from 1949. During his stint as Commissioner to the United Kingdom he was Honorary Curate at Holy Trinity Church, Finchley Road, in Hampstead, North London.

Faye's roles as deacon and politician brought to the fore five matters arising which occupied the attention of the church in the 1950s, namely, his political activities, his formal training in theology, his court cases, his designation, and his emoluments.

Matters Arising 1: Politics or/and Priesthood?

The first issue—Faye combining his political activities and his responsibilities as a deacon—was problematical. It has already been noted that Bishop Daly was not in opposition to Faye's appointments to the Executive and Legislative Councils and to his early involvement in politics. However, both from among his fellow clergy and from the Church Body—a congregation of the membership at large—there were fears about conflict of interest, and worse. This was so much so that in May 1949 the Priest-in-Charge of the Pro-Cathedral was obliged to explain to the Church Body that Faye was a curate serving under him and that the Bishop had given Faye permission "to continue his political activities on the understanding that these shall diminish and, of course, that he would not introduce politics into his teaching or preaching". Besides, Faye had been assigned specific responsibilities which he was compelled to execute regardless of any other commitments. These included oversight of the Sunday School, religious instruction at St Mary's School, special care for Christ Church, Serre-kunda, and care of the sick ensuring that they receive the Blessed Sacrament regularly.[13]

The matter could not be easily laid to rest, as other clergymen, especially those from England, became increasingly concerned about the repercussions on the mission of Faye's stepped-up political activities. From February 1949 until his departure two years later Bishop Daly engaged Faye in exchanges (sometimes acerbic) on the matter. In one detailed letter, Daly noted that in February 1949 he had asked Faye to make a break with official politics and give his full attention to the work of the Church. Faye had responded that as a Christian Gambian he felt an over-riding call to continue to work for the good of his country, through the Legislative Council, for another year. Daly recognized the sense in Faye's argument but felt that one year was too long and categorically decided that "by the end of 1949 you should have broken with politics".[14]

Daly also pointed out that in discussions with Faye one year later, in February 1950, he had "warned you [Faye] again that I wanted to see this break made at once". Faye had then asked Daly for an extension of 18 to 24 months, which was rejected out of hand. Daly had then cautioned:

> Unless you have sent in your resignation from the Legislative
> Council before Easter this year I shall not feel it my business
> to make any further arrangements for your training for the
> Sacred Ministry and I shall not be able to continue your
> employment as one of our clergy beyond the end of 1950.[15]

Still according to the Bishop, Faye had promised not to hold political office after ordination to the priesthood, but he could not avoid exerting political influence so long as he was in his country; his people went to him for advice on political matters and he had no choice but to speak out "in the face of wrong". This the Bishop appreciated, though he thought it would be more important to see how it would work out in practice. Faye's training in England would be suspended till 1952—"by then we shall be able to see whether we agree on what is meant by this permissible political activity". Daly had concluded:

> West Africa needs Christians who will care for the political,
> commercial and social welfare of its people. West Africa
> also needs spiritual leaders, and spiritual leadership is a
> whole time job: at least I require a team who will regard it
> as a whole time job.

In his combative reply to the Bishop's letter, Faye first emphasized that he had never committed himself to leaving politics at the end of 1949 but that he would try to influence a friend to become politically active and by then and, over time, he, Faye, would hand over to the friend all the work that he had started "for the well-being and advancement of this country". At the end of 1949 Faye would review his involvement in politics and decide on future directions.[16]

In the same reply Faye recalled that at a meeting in February 1950 the Bishop had declared that "he had no reason to believe that politics was tainting me"[17] and that:

> the official mind has interpreted me and my political activity as sincere and true but that [the Bishop] would not have me, as a clergyman, to be looked upon more as a politician than a clergyman as some High-Ups would continue to regard me, inasmuch as I am so heavily engaged in politics.

Faye was "particularly non-plussed" by the statement of the Bishop which ran counter to the glowing tributes that he, the Bishop, had previously showered on him on the eve of his departure from KK for the inaugural meeting of the Legislative Council in November 1947:

> You then said, inter alia, that you were about performing a duty you felt long overdue, in that you had never thanked me before in KK where I had laboured so outstandingly, but that it was not you who were thanking me but God Himself had done so. For, at the beginning of that year the King honoured me by adding M. B. E. behind my name, and then in February of that year (1947) God showed you that I was to be a priest and "Rev." was added before my name, and that we both were to go down to Bathurst because my country had honoured me by making me a member of Council and so "Hon." was added to the "Rev." before my name. That I was no more just "Uncle Faye" as heretofore, but "The Rev. and Hon. John Colley Faye, M. B. E." and that was how God rewarded a faithful worker.

Faye quoted Daly as having concluded that "if I [Faye] were to be diligent in the work of my country, as I was in that of the mission, then The Gambia would soon be shot right up."[18] It was in this spirit that he, Faye, entered politics, "determined to purge same (politics) and create a healthier atmosphere therein".[19] If not, he reasoned, why would he, a clergyman, have anything to do with politics?[20]

Faye was unequivocal on the pivotal question of his quitting politics if he wanted to continue to serve in the diaconate:

> My answer to your letter of 8 February 1950 is that at present I feel myself called to fill a gap in the life of our people and I am prepared to go through thick and thin until such be achieved. I do not see in any way how politics is hindering my steps to the priesthood. Circumstances beyond my control have made my staying here for at least two years more a *sine qua non*, and while here as a deacon I feel I can do useful service for the Church and for my country. *I therefore cannot withdraw from politics now* [Italics added]. You rightly said, my Lord, that my country needs Christian leadership. I agree with that part of your statement but do maintain that Christian leadership cannot be better given than by the clergy. Hence, Archbishop Langton led England against the evil rule of King John and gave to the world "the Keystone of Liberty", and Archbishop Damaskinos of Greece held sway in Greece during the interregnum. Also, hence Archbishop Lang withstood the desire of King Edward VIII in 1936-1937.[21]

Faye accepted with grace the decision of the Bishop to remove him from the pay-roll of the Church after 1950. For him:

> I am prepared to face darkness again even as I did in 1934 when I left my headmastership of the Methodist Senior School for the second (deputy) headmastership of St. Mary's, and then again in 1942 when I left all that the Colony held out to me for the work of the mission field. A clergyman I am and that I will remain. Politics will never be my career and a civil servant, I pray, never to be. If I should find myself without a means of livelihood after 1950, I would have to roll my sleeves and do farming in the Kombo South area.

. . . My Lord, may it be plain to you that I am . . . [not] engaged in politics because of finance but because I see my people's need in these spheres and God has given me the grace of helping in the matter.[22]

. . . Whether in the Church employment or not I shall continue to help in the Pro-Cathedral should I be allowed to do so.[23]

Further written communications and several meetings brought to the fore the options for Faye as presented by the Bishop. He had raised the first option in a letter of 20 February 1950, to the effect that "long before the end of the year (1950) if you decide that you have no overruling vocation for the priesthood, we will discuss at length how under the new direction of your life's work you will be of maximum benefit to God and His Church".[24] Faye's reaction was direct: "under the very peculiar circumstances in which I am placed I have to remain a deacon."[25]

Linked to this was the general issue of training in England. Faye was far from excited. First, from past experience there was no guarantee that further down the line during his training he would not be told that there was no money. Second, given the way he had been treated at the end of his long sojourn in KK, and the disillusionment experienced by his wife, it was not likely that she would support him on this new venture. Third, life in a theological college in England could be "smooth and cozy . . . assured and soft", followed by return to "a safe and assured income". But "my going to England now will mean to me a betrayal of the trust of my people and my smashing all the great things that I have planned to do for them."[26]

Despite these drawn-out exchanges, the Church had to take into account Faye's readiness "to render service in the parish in the way and manner I am doing and more if permitted", and to recognize the range and quality of the services he had provided from the 1930s. The final compromise position taken by the Bishop was that:

At the end of this year (1950) Mr. Faye ceases to be on the payroll of the Diocese. He does not however cease to be a

> Deacon. So long as he does not engage in work that I should
> deem contrary to his profession as a Minister of Religion he
> is available for part-time employment by the Church.[27]

Thus, Faye could now freely practise politics whilst giving service to the Church, as and when required. He continued to wear the clerical collar and to be addressed by the title "Reverend".

Nevertheless, in January 1951, the St Mary's Church Body adopted a unanimous resolution reiterating its desire for a full-time curate; some members expressly opposed Faye being employed in church services because of his other employment and they requested that a full-time clergyman be recruited. The Bishop, in response, emphasized that, world-wide, there was a massive shortage of candidates for the cloth and the situation in The Gambia merely confirmed this. He regretted that Faye was unable to go forward with his training for the priesthood and, as things were, he did not have the time, the qualifications, or the Orders necessary to function as a full-time curate. In support of his final position, as quoted above, the Bishop explained that, historically, it was not unusual for someone in Deacon's Orders to have a secular occupation and work part-time in the Church. Besides, Faye had himself assured the Bishop that his other occupations had not stood in the way of his carrying out his Church responsibilities.[28]

With this, on 29 January, the same Church Body passed another resolution which read:

> That the Church Body decided to engage Rev. J. C. Faye
> in view of the Bishop's definition of a deacon's position,
> provided that Rev. Faye's past services are specially defined
> by the Bishop in agreement with the St. Mary's Church
> Body.[29]

At a meeting at the end of March 1951 between Canon Macauley, Father Coote, and Rev. Faye the precise functions to be undertaken by Faye were agreed upon; the list was to be adjusted on a monthly basis.[30] The functions included:

1. To be responsible, normally, for the services of Morning Prayer in Christ Church, Serre-kunda, and for the flock there generally.
2. To preach in St. Mary's, Bathurst, once a month, and to take part in Evensong on Sundays.
3. To visit the members of the Church in Bathurst, especially the sick, and to report to Canon Macauley any who required Holy Communion.
4. When necessary, to take the reserved Sacrament to the sick, as directed by Canon Macauley.
5. To assist Canon Macauley with funerals, particularly on occasions taking the grave-side prayers when Canon Macauley takes the prayers in Church.
6. Mr. Faye expressed his willingness to assist in the administration at mass and in reading the Epistle whenever present.

Besides these tasks, Canon Macauley felt he could use Faye's services in other areas provided the Church Body was ready to remunerate him; the additional areas would be:

a) Taking Men's Class and Women's Class on occasions.
b) Prison visiting.
c) Week-day evensong.
d) Giving instructions in Religious Knowledge in the day schools.
e) Assisting the activities of the servers, to ensure that they keep up to scratch.

These clearly-defined arrangements were easy to follow throughout the decade of the 1950s as the two Bishops who came after Daly—Roderic N. Coote (1951 to 1957) and St. John Surridge Pike (1957 to 1963)—were already serving in the Diocese as Priests at the time Daly reached his decision on Faye, his Church obligations and his politics. More likely than not, the two priests had participated in the decision-making process and/or been consulted by Bishop Daly.

Matters Arising 2: Faye's Professional Training for the Priesthood

Concerning Faye's professional training for the Christian ministry, it has already been noted that whilst preparing for his teaching certificates he also studied theology privately in Bathurst and continued whilst at KK. As also pointed out above, Daly had already raised the possibility of Faye joining a religious community in England in order to develop a prayerful life before ordination into the priesthood. Now the Bishop had taken concrete action. He had approached the Reader Missionary Studentship Association, which trained licensed Readers for Holy Orders for service in the mission fields overseas, and Faye was accepted; fees and books were paid for.

Faye did not accept the offer. First, as he saw it, the Bishop was going to spend almost 1,000.00 pounds on his training but, at the same time, he had turned down Faye's earlier request for 400.00 pounds to further the work of the KK mission. Second, they had both agreed that Faye should spend a period of three years in service to the people of the Upper River and this had not yet expired. Third, the Bishop had indicated to him that some senior colonial officials were very uncomfortable with his extremely critical postures in discussions in the Executive Council.[31]

Whilst Faye pursued his political career, this issue of professional training was irrelevant. But it came to the fore again after he retired from politics and applied for the holy orders of the priesthood in 1972. Initially, whilst a Chaplain to Bishop Jean Rigal Elisee and an Assistant at the Cathedral he resumed his studies in theology and related subjects under the Bishop. Nevertheless, this was considered inadequate as, in the view of the Bishop and his colleagues, some formal training was most necessary before ordination into the priesthood.

In May 1972, soon after receiving the formal application from Faye for the priesthood the Bishop wrote to the Archbishop of the Province of West Africa, based in Freetown, requesting placement in a suitable local training institution. In his reply the Archbishop noted that the Bible Training Institute in Bo, Sierra Leone, was inappropriate for Faye as the academic standards were very low and, in any case, the Institute was on the way to being closed down; possible alternatives were Trinity College, Legon, Accra, or Emanuel College, Ibadan, Nigeria. Regarding funding, the Archbishop regretted that the Province had no scholarship funds for training of candidates for the ministry; he suggested that, as in the past, the SPG be approached.[32]

Bishop Elisee then decided to go directly to the Rev. Canon Harry Sawyer, Principal of Fourah Bay College, University of Sierra Leone. His request was not for a degree course but for Faye to audit courses on pastoral theology, dogmatics, history, Old and New Testament, and liturgies. The Bishop explained that, after this exposure, he would obtain books for Faye to continue his studies after ordination, under his guidance and monitoring. The Bishop proposed that Faye join the college in October 1972 but spend only six months in residence; he would undertake some parish work under the watch of the Principal and visit Bo for evangelical practice. The Church in Bathurst would grant him 40.00 pounds monthly plus round-trip air fares.[33]

Sawyer's response was very positive and, indeed, flexible: Faye would be given a place on the course for the Licentiate in Divinity but he would be in residence for only two terms (six months), as requested, and then withdraw. Sawyer promised to take a personal interest in Faye who, at the suggestion of the Archbishop, would also be attached to St George's Cathedral.

After all this effort, Faye could not take up the offer for a period as long as six months. According to Elisee, Faye was willing to go to Bo for three months and on his return would teach catechists and evangelists.[34] Interestingly, the Principal was even more accommodative: he proposed that Faye join the college under the same terms as earlier proposed but for a period of only three months, i.e. from October to December 1972: "He would find much to stretch his mind even in that time . . . I feel three months at Fourah Bay will be useful."[35]

But even with this degree of good will from the Principal Faye did not accept the place at Fourah Bay. Officially, this was because of the complexity of his family and personal problems, as interpreted by Bishop Elisee.[36] However, the real reason was that Faye was convinced that there was nothing much he could gain from any such training in theology; from his one-on-one private training with Bishop Daly in the 1940s, from his extensive private reading and tuition, and from the lessons of life, he was as good a professional as any. The Archbishop knew this and was himself convinced from the outset that Faye would not go for any training.

Matters Arising 3: Faye's Appearances in Courts of Law

A somewhat slippery area in Faye's relationship with the Church during this period was that of his appearances in various courts of law. One such instance, discussed in Chapter 5, was that of the Pilot Produce Syndicate on whose behalf, and as a trustee, Faye had borrowed an amount of 20,000.00 pounds, and which had become bankrupt. Wisely, Coote recognized that: "It has happened chiefly because he was surrounded by rogues in these commercial undertakings. I think his sin has been that of foolishness rather than theft, but the Anglican Church will suffer whichever it is."[37]

In these and several such cases it was difficult for the Bishop and his senior clergy to determine what action to take. Perhaps more than anyone else, he was acutely aware of the dilemma for the Church; as he observed "He [Faye] is Number One in the African political world in Gambia, and has considerable popularity. Even now the people will put the blame elsewhere and feel sympathy for him, with a few exceptions."[38] Coote sought direction from the Archbishop who prescribed the following possible lines of action:

1. If he [Faye] is convicted in Civil Court and sentenced to imprisonment we could declare him, under the Clergy Discipline Act, deprived of any right to exercise his ministry and incapable of holding a clerical appointment, though the Act provides a way back, if necessary.
2. He could be tried in the Bishop's Consistory Court with the same result.
3. He could be put under Ecclesiastical Discipline without any trial, thus he could be inhibited by the Bishop from exercising his ministry.

He further maintained that the line of action actually taken would partially depend on the degree of publicity and scandal arising from a particular case; it was sometimes better to deal with such matters pastorally than officially, he warned.

In the event, it was not necessary to resort to any drastic action on the occasions when Faye had to appear in court: as soon as a case was mentioned in court, either his licence to perform the work of a clergyman in the diocese was suspended, or he was given orders not to robe or officiate in the Church, or his services were just not used until the case was terminated.

Matters Arising 4: Faye's Designation

On the subject of Faye's designation, either "worker priest" or "supply priest" for Bathurst (a part-timer) were the preferred designations. One reason for this was that he would not have to depend on a salary from the church to meet a growing family budget but benefit from his other sources of income such as dividends from Jac Sieber Ltd. and Bafa-Adripêche Ltd., in which he had interests, and the Parsonage School.[39] However, in the official letter from Bishop Elisee informing Faye of his acceptance of his application for the priesthood, he noted that: "there is no category of priests in the Church of God. It is just a matter of functioning. You will be ordained a Priest of God, but you will work for some time as an 'Auxiliary Priest' in the Diocese, as you requested."[40]

In July 1974, Faye wrote to Elisee informing him that he would be available for full-time service as a priest, as from 1 September 1974.[41] The Bishop, in reply, noted:

> This is not a surprise to us, knowing that you are already working as a 'full-time Priest' at St Mary's, but without promising to do so and without getting the right stipend paid to a 'full-time Priest' of the Diocese.

Elisee accepted the application instantly and upgraded Faye from "Auxiliary Priest" to "Diocesan Priest" in accordance with the laws and discipline of the Diocese.[42]

Matters Arising 5: Faye's Emoluments.

On his emolument, after Faye's eventual break with KK in February 1949, it was agreed that he would continue to work as a deacon earning 250.00 pounds per annum as salary and wife's allowance. However, after the matter of his status had been settled, as discussed above, he ceased to be on the pay-roll of the Diocese. It was agreed that, as he was a deacon, the Vicar (Canon Macauley) would determine when his services would be required. For any extra services the Church Body of the parish concerned would recommend a suitable rate of remuneration agreeable to Faye and confirmed by the Bishop.

Despite this, within the Church there continued to be a vocal minority who felt that Faye should not be rewarded financially, since he spent much of his time in politics. To avoid further complications Faye decided that for the time he was in government (1951 to 1960) he would give up all allowances from the Church and offer his services free of charge; he continued to do the same up until the early 1970s when he was granted a token allowance. In a letter to Bishop Coote he explained:

> As such an appointment [as member of government without portfolio] would carry with it an allowance on which I can subsist, I do not feel personally justified to hang on to the stipend which I had been receiving from the mission . . . this does not mean that I propose in any way to stop operating as Curate of the Pro-cathedral; . . . I would continue my work in the Church as at present, but without any emoluments attached thereto.[43]

Summary Observations

From the early days, even as early as his school days, Faye had had an inclination for service in the Church. This led to an active life in Church organizations whose purpose was to socialize youth in the ways of the faith. By the time of the creation of the diocese in 1935, his mind was made up. But, as is usual in such matters, there was doubt and apprehension, borne out of the experiences of others who had opted for a religious vocation. However, once the decision had been made, Faye proceeded with being made a deacon, a status he was to hold for almost three decades.

Quite unusually, during this period Faye was able to combine the seemingly conflicting roles of pastor and politician, giving rise to controversies with the hierarchy in the Church. It appeared as if controversy was Faye's namesake. But, as discussed in this chapter, he was able to surmount the controversies and advance in his career.

CHAPTER 10

CLERGYMAN AND PHILANTHROPIST: UP THE LADDER AND OUT

Priest: Catching Up with the Gap Years

Faye retired from active politics after the first referendum in 1965 and the general elections of 1966. He resumed his career in the Anglican Church as a curate at the pro-Cathedral from 1965 to 1973, and then consecutively as Priest (1973-1974), Priest-in-Charge (1974-1977), and Provost (1977-1980). The hands of Bishop Elisee were behind all of these moves. As he noted from the outset: "This 'deacon' as you call him has been working so hard in this place there is no reason why we should not make him priest."[1]

Nonetheless, Faye's ordination into the priesthood followed very stringent procedures, to ensure that his intentions were purely godly, and that he had been a worthy follower of Christ, deserving of a position as shepherd in the earthly Kingdom.

On 25 February 1972, his birthday anniversary, Faye informed the Priest-in-Charge, Venerable Mathias George, of the "burning desire in me being received into the Holy Order of Priesthood . . . Hereby, I do confirm in writing this ardent and unrelenting urge . . ." He requested that Venerable George should transmit his application to the Bishop "so that he would know that by our Saviour's help and cleansing I still say 'Here am I, send me'".[2] In March 1972, just a month after the new Bishop, The Rt. Rev. Jean Regal Elisee (1972-1986), was consecrated, Faye verbally informed him of his desire to be ordained into the priesthood after decades in the diaconate.

Rev. George dutifully transmitted Faye's application to the Bishop. In a brief assessment, the Reverend outlined Faye's historic role in the Church and the contributions he had made towards its development; he also noted Faye's political activities. Rev. George's concluding observation was: "Should he be risen to the Priesthood, I have no doubt that he will be able to contribute more to the welfare and progress of the Church in this land. I have no doubt in recommending this 'burning desire', as he expressed it, to you for your consideration."[3]

In his response, the Bishop proposed that, instead of going through the Priest-in-Charge, Faye should apply directly to him as his Diocesan Bishop, and include a detailed account of his life and work, paying particular attention to elements that qualified him for the life of a priest. To this Faye replied with a letter dated 28 April 1972 in which he gave a comprehensive biography.

Later in the year, Elisee sought from Archbishop Scott, his "paternal advice", approaching him as "your son of God".[4] In reply, whilst observing that "you will have to be the best judge because you have the man and know the immediate situation", Scott suggested that Elisee proceed along the following lines:

a) Draw out from him what he thinks has been the cause for his being so long a Deacon.

b) If the cause was from his side you will check if he is now convinced a change will help.

c) If the cause was from without, then check on the likely after-effects of the ordination.

d) You need also to check if the community will accept him as a clergyman.

e) Help him to see that a true disciple cannot offer Christ split loyalty.

f) His wife has a part to play—is she prepared to cooperate?

g) Two clergymen will be needed to testify to his integrity and fitness—and the Archdeacon should have had the opportunity to assure you that he would present him "having examined him and found him so to be".[5]

Similarly, advice was sought and obtained from Elisee's immediate predecessor, Rt. Rev. Timothy Olufosoye, who was then Bishop of Ibadan, Nigeria.

All the documents obtained from Faye and other sources were then submitted by the Bishop to the Chancellor of the Cathedral, S. H. A. George, for study from both legal and spiritual viewpoints. The Chancellor found these documents satisfactory and in order, and advised, "I can find no impediment why he should not be ordained a Priest."[6]

With this assurance, the Bishop proceeded with his soundings of the opinions of some senior-level hierarchy who had worked with Faye. First, testimonial letters were solicited and obtained from three former Bishops with whom Faye had worked, who had now returned to England, namely, the Rt. Rev. John C. S. Daly, the Rt. Rev. R. N. Coote and the Rt. Rev. St. John Pike. All were glowing in their assessment of Faye's character and of his dedication to service to the church and humanity at large; they strongly recommended him for the appointment which was long overdue.

Another required action was for Faye to obtain two/three testimonials:

> of his good life from three priests of whom one at least must be beneficed, who have had personal knowledge of his life, work, and doctrine during his Diaconate; whose signature shall be countersigned by the Bishop of the Diocese where the said priests are respectively either beneficed or licensed.

These confidential references were obtained from Rev. Jacob Williams and Rev. Canon A. C. Agyemang. The following quotation from Rev. Agyemang's reference reflects the thrust of all the others:

> He (Faye) is a deeply spiritual Christian, devoted and scholarly, with wide and sympathetic understanding of others.
>
> He possesses a uniquely intimate knowledge of the Church of England, both as regards the personnel of the

Clergy, and the problems of the Parishes. He possesses also the friendship and affection of all and sundry.

I can vouch that he is a staunch and Godly Deacon who, if ordained Priest, will be a great asset to St. Mary's parish, in particular, and the Diocese in general, as far as his devotion to duty is concerned.[7]

Based on the wealth of material and testimonials received from diverse quarters, the Bishop formally informed Faye that "after long prayers and intercessions on your behalf to Almighty God, I have accepted to ordain you Priest on Sunday 21 January 1973, in conformity with the Constitution and Canons of the Church of the Province of West Africa."[8] The ordination would coincide with the commemoration of the first anniversary of the consecration of Bishop Elisee as the fifth Bishop of the Diocese of The Gambia.

The next stage in the procedures was a canonical oral examination before a Board of Examining Chaplains, "to test his ability". This was held on 12 January 1973 about ten days to the scheduled ordination; the Board comprised Bishop Elisee as Chairman and the Reverends George and Williams as members. Alongside was the important requirement that the Church Body should discuss and endorse all aspects of the ordination and write to inform the Bishop of their acceptance of Faye to work with them; they were also to state the monthly stipend and transport allowance they would be able to pay him. These were duly done.

There remained the reading of the *si quis* by an officiating minister to the full congregation, at least ten days before the scheduled date of the ordination. It announced that Faye intended "to offer himself as a candidate for the Holy Office of a Priest" and that "if any person knows any cause or just impediment why the said John Colley Faye ought not to be admitted into Holy Orders, he is now to declare the same or to signify the same forthwith to the Lord Bishop of the Gambia and Rio Pongas." The Priest-in-Charge and two Church wardens certified that this was done on 7 January 1973 and "that no impediment was alleged".[9]

On 21 January 1973 during the Sung Solemn High Mass at the St. Mary's Pro-Cathedral, Bathurst, John Colley Faye was ordained

Priest by Bishop Elisee. The Reverend G. L. O. Palmer, the Dean of St. George's Cathedral in Freetown, Sierra Leone, delivered the sermon; the Bishop had previously invited Rev. Harry Sawyer of Fourah Bay College who, unfortunately, had other long-standing commitments. Nevertheless, Palmer rose to the occasion, especially in that he focused on one of the major preoccupations of Bishop Elisee's, that "Christianity in The Gambia needs very badly to hear the voice of African theologians to help kick it out to die and rise again an African Christianity for Africa."[10]

At the Mass the Venerable Mathias George was the celebrant, Father Willie Macauley, the deacon, and Father Williams the sub-deacon. The Diocesan Registrar also witnessed and recorded the event. In attendance were over 600 members and non-members of the faith, including a large delegation of relatives from Senegal.

Provost: Recognition None Too Late

Faye was the first Provost of the Cathedral Church of St. Mary's after the church was upgraded from its Pro-Cathedral status in 1977. He was installed on 11 September 1977 at a service of collation.

The post was established in Article 18 of the Diocesan Constitution which was to be discussed and approved by the Provincial Synod of the Church of the Province of West Africa. Faye's appointment was effective from 1 September 1977 for one year, renewable every twelve months by the Bishop. This arrangement was to last until the constitution was approved by the Synod.

In terms of seniority, the office of Provost is next highest to that of Bishop and the holder is accorded the title "Very Reverend". Faye was responsible for all aspects of the Cathedral's life and worship. He also assumed superintendence over St Andrew's, Lamin; the Joint Anglican-Methodist Mission, Mansakonko; St Cuthbert's in Basse, and the Farafenni Mission Station.[11]

The service was most solemn and dignified. Leading the group of senior clergy from all Christian denominations was Bishop Elisee. Supporting clergy included Rev. Willie Macauley, and Rev. S. Tilewa Johnson, who was chaplain to the Bishop on that day. At the reception that followed several old colleagues, such as Matarr Sillah, outlined the great achievements of Provost Faye, especially at KK.

Retirement: Thanks be to God.

The subject of the retirement of Faye from the service of the Church arose in 1979, by which time he had served two terms of one year each as Provost and the renewal of his tenure for a third term was under consideration. On this, a key factor was that in February 1980 Faye would attain the age of 72 years, and the general age for clergy retirement in the Church in the Province of West Africa was between 65 years and 70 years, with the maximum being 72 years. For the Bishop it appeared that the guiding consideration on a further extension of Faye's appointment was more moral than bureaucratic:

> My concern is that I could not ask Provost Faye to get ready for retirement in February 1980 without making provision for another post for him where he can continue to work for the Church and earn a living. It is a fact that there is no pension scheme yet in the Diocese. My question is what could we offer to this man?[12]

The question was directed to some senior advisers who counselled that the shortage of clergy and the heavy workload in the Cathedral were two parametric factors of direct relevance in reaching a decision.[13] To this the Bishop also added Faye's own heavy Church-related responsibilities, which included the following: Provost of the Cathedral; Chairman of the Board of the Parsonage Nursery School; Chairman of the Management Committee of St Mary's Day School; Member and Convenor of the Cathedral Chapter; Chairman of the Cathedral Council; Chairman of the Board of Governors of the Anglican Vocational Training Centre; and member of the Gambia District Standing Committee. Outside the Church, among many others, Faye was Vice-Chairman of Opportunities Industrialization Centre and held memberships in many non-governmental organizations.[14]

To ascertain that Faye's physical and mental health were good enough for him to continue to perform full time the functions of Provost, at the same time as all the above-listed extra responsibilities, a thorough medical examination was organized. The results were positive; Faye's appointment was consequently renewed for another year ending December 1980.

Faye's age remained an outstanding issue. As stipulated in Article 19, paragraph 2 of the Cathedral Constitution:

> Every Clergyman or Catechist shall retire at the age of seventy years provided that he may be permitted by the Bishop to continue for further periods of one year at a time if on each occasion the Bishop and the appropriate District Church Council consider it to be in the interest of the Church that permission should be granted.[15]

There was, therefore, little room for manoeuvre for Faye, assuming that he was, in fact, interested in staying on. This turned out not to be the case, as in a letter to Bishop Elisee written soon afterwards, Faye formally requested "that I go into full retirement at the end of February 1981, which would almost synchronize with my 73rd birthday."[16]

A parting piece of advice was that "the foundation laid for the resuscitation of our beloved St Mary's during these toilsome but happy six years, would grieve me sore if smashed to smithereens through any choice of a successor without due consultation with the Cathedral congregation through its chosen leaders." [17]

Faye's retirement service was held in the Cathedral Church on 26 April 1981; he was succeeded as Provost by Willie Macauley, a former teacher at KK. As with his ordination into the Priesthood and his installation as Provost, the valedictory service for Faye was pitched at a very high level. Again, the Bishop of The Gambia and Guinea, the Right Reverend J. Rigal Elisee, was the celebrant, attended by all available clergy of the mission—Rev. J. J. Williams, Rev. Levi Akuna, and Archdeacon William Macauley. The renowned choir from the Roman Catholic Cathedral, the *Baati Linguere,* graced the occasion with beautiful lyrics set to melodious African music.

The service was followed with a reception to which the whole congregation was invited and at which various parishes, church groups and organizations presented a range of gifts to the outgoing luminary. Representatives from the Catholic and Methodist missions and from the Muslim community made speeches extolling the extensive contributions that Rev. Faye had made to his country in diverse fields. His Excellency, Mr. Assan Musa Camara, the Vice-President of the Republic, on behalf of the KK Old Students, gave a detailed account of the origins of the KK project and the sacrifices that Rev. Faye and his family had been called upon to make, living and toiling "in the bush", in service to the underprivileged and deprived.

From within the church the Archdeacon of the Cathedral and Provost Designate (William Y. Macauley), the President of the Mothers' Union (Dr. Florence Mahoney), the Peoples' Warden (J. Wole Coker), the Principal of the Anglican Vocational Training Centre, and delegates from the parishes of Christ Church at Serekunda, St Paul's at Fajara, St Andrew's at Lamin, St Cuthbert's at Basse, made speeches highlighting the work Faye had accomplished in their parishes during his long years of service to God.

On the same day as his retirement, and with the approval of the 18th session of the Gambia District Council, Elisee appointed Faye Consultant to the Bishop for the Development of Church Properties and for the Organization and Supervision of Church Schools (crèche, primary, secondary and vocational) in the Gambia District. He was to go on three-month paid leave from the day of his retirement and the new appointment was to become effective on the day following the last day of the leave. Thus, there would not be any break in service.[18]

Rev. Faye did indeed have some knowledge of Church properties and was very protective of them. There was a document which vested ownership of such real estate (e.g. St Mary's Church building itself, St Mary's School, the Parsonage, and later House of Transformation, St Paul's and Christ Church) to the St Mary's Church Body; Faye and Crispin Grey-Johnson, a senior Church leader, guarded and protected this document diligently to avoid it falling in the hands of any authority who might want to tamper with the ownership. One possible usurper was the church in Sierra Leone which had exercised oversight over the church in Bathurst before it became autonomous; but there was always the possibility of an errant Bishop attempting to take personal control over these properties.

It is an interesting co-incidence that the first non-Gambian bishop Daly (from Britain) and the last Elisee (from Haiti) demonstrated such profound concern about the professional and private life of Faye. Regarding Daly, the supporting evidence is scattered in this biography. Elisee had worked consistently for Faye's advancement into the priesthood and as Provost of the Cathedral, even though he lacked formal theological education. Like Daly, he tried very hard to arrange for Faye's training. Both failed. But, as Daly would most probably have done, Elisee succeeded in providing the means for Faye's smooth transition into retirement.

Faye's Sermons

A final word relates to the sermons of Rev. Faye, on which he built quite a solid reputation. He was known only to jot a few themes on a small piece of paper, usually an envelop, and develop them as he went along in the pulpit. This he enjoyed doing, but at the expense of his congregations whose attention spans were not known to be very extensive. He combined the teacher, the politician and the preacher in delivering his sermons, which concoction led to long, winding and disjointed speeches. It was not unusual for worshippers to first enquire as to whether or not Faye would be preaching at a particular service before deciding whether or not to attend; if the answer was positive they would then postpone their attendance or go to the Methodist Church.

From time to time, through the effective medium of members of the congregation falling asleep and even some snoring coming from the choir stalls, the Reverend would be reminded that he was neither in the classroom nor on a soapbox. On one occasion the sermon was on the significance of different parts of the body of Christ from the top of his head to the soles of his feet. It lasted almost an hour. After the service, a fellow clergyman was over heard whispering to another that Faye should have stopped at the middle of the body and leave the rest for another sermon or, better still, for another preacher!

Philanthropist: Service to Humanity Writ Large

Rev. Faye's concern for the well-being of humanity and the need to do something about it went back to his schooldays. It is said, for example, that even in those early times he showed concern for his schoolmates from the Protectorate who were compelled to attend school in Bathurst and lived in conditions that were far from ideal. Faye never hesitated to share his school lunches with some who appeared hungry, sleepy or not able to concentrate on their school work. He would even invite them home where his mother provided food and drinks.

Faye was to build on this sense of caring in his later life. Despite his many and varied public and professional responsibilities he found enough time to render service to different categories of his fellow citizens, particularly the young and deprived. In August 1937, Bishop Daly opened the House of Transfiguration at 2, Pignard Street in Bathurst, property which had been bought by the Church. As explained by Daly: "it was to house boys who had from time to time been entrusted to me by their parents whom I had met during my travels in the diocese."[19] In their own home Faye and his wife also had a group of boys for whom they were responsible. The Bishop therefore requested the Fayes to move into the House of Transfiguration and take full charge. Even with Faye's high status as Headmaster of St Mary's School, the two lived there with the boys and catered to their needs.

The House was dedicated on the Feast of the Transfiguration which was one reason for its name; the Bishop also hoped that "the boys living there would be changed into His likeness by the Lord".[20] Basically, it was to be a foster home for young men from the rural areas, many of whom had come to Bathurst to attend school and were without any relatives with whom they could stay. Some of the residents were also from Bathurst and there were not a few Muslims. Altogether, some 24 boys lived in the house over the five years the Fayes were in charge. Among the residents were: Andrew (Assan Musa) Camara, Samuel Palmer, Andrew (Dentist) NJie, Willie Macauley, John Jawo, Amang Kanyi, Saer Gueye, Doudou Faal, Modou Samba, John and James Baker, Jeremiah Harding, Ebrima Jarra, Modu Duks, Bokari Fofana, George

3333

Sagnia, James Campbell, Sammy Johnson, Abraham, Paul Sajaw, Pa Sara Bah.

Where possible each resident had his own room; meals and pocket money were also provided by the Church. They stayed at the residence till they completed their education and got employed. Naturally, the boys brought in many friends who were influenced by the culture of the place; they also benefitted from extra lessons that Faye offered free of cost. Here, it is worth noting that "Uncle" and "Auntie" became a very popular way of addressing the two house parents. With the turnover of students, the "nephews" increased in numbers.

Indeed, Faye believed strongly in fostering, as opposed to adoption as favoured in Western culture, and was a foster father to many. His opposition to adoption came out clearly in a debate on a bill on the subject in the national legislature in the 1950s. Based on his rich experience he argued that in the African perception of things, the child always belonged to his/her original family and there should always be a possibility of him/her returning to the family. Adoption might involve a change of surname, to which any African family would strongly object, given the importance of continuity of the family surname in the African psyche. On both scores, fostering was therefore a preferred option.

In the Church too Faye was at the beck and call of any and every one. For example, the Mothers' Union at St. Mary's promoted Christian marriage and tried to help families experiencing difficulties. Father Faye willingly contributed to its work and turned out to be an effective counsellor in promoting family life and family values. As Florence Mahoney, the long-term President, recalled:

> He was very helpful. Whenever it was reported to me, as President, that there was any family having problems I would go to Father Faye and the Union Worker and they would go visit and try to sort things out. Many families were rescued through these interventions.[21]

In another area of action, Faye was assisted by one of the staff at St Mary's School, C. S. Modu-Coker, to found and commission the 3rd Bathurst Group of Scouts and Cubs (1940-1942) and the Bishop's Own

272

Scout Troop, Kristi-kunda (1943-1948). Together with Crispin R. Grey-Johnson, a former troop leader of the first-ever troop of Scouts in The Gambia, they organized the first company of Rover Scouts—making the 3rd Bathurst Group complete, with a three-tier structure of Rovers, Scouts and Cubs (1939-1942). It may be remembered that, from 1921-1925, Faye had himself been a Scout Second Patrol Leader and then Patrol Leader—after having gained the Tender Foot, 2nd and 1st Class badges with the Bushman-thong; from 1926-1930 he was Assistant Cub-master and then Cub-master.

Faye also organized evening classes at St Mary's School at which he himself gave lessons, supported by faithfuls like Matarr Sillah; they received no remuneration for this service. Initially, the lessons were free of charge but small fees were charged later, mainly for purchase of teaching aids and supplies. Among others, junior members of the police force and the civil service took advantage of the opportunity to study for the proficiency bar and for promotion examinations. Earlier, in KK, Faye had run similar adult literacy classes in the evenings, mainly for herd boys and, on Saturday afternoons, for ex-soldiers from the Burma campaign and other adults.

When serving in Kantora District (Kristi-kunda) Faye was concerned about the hungry season, which he referred to as "the Dreadful Monster".[22] This was the annual period when the planting season was over and weeding under way, when farmers and farm labourers found themselves with relatively little food. Faye came up with a possible solution, which he shared with the chief through one of his local students who served as his interpreter:

"Chief," he began, "as you know better than I do, this season of hunger is doing havoc among our peoples."

"Yes, indeed," replied the chief. "If there is one problem that gives me sleepless nights it is this one, for I hate to see how our peoples suffer till the time for harvesting. As you know, we have discussed the subject in Council many times; the effect of the food shortages on families, especially the children and women, is what is of particular concern."

"Yes, Chief," Faye answered. "I am really angry at the way the agents of these big commercial firms take advantage of the situation, offer loans and credit to the poor farmers against future produce.

Sometimes the 'interest' is really exorbitant and our people are left with so little. Can you please convene a meeting of the District Council to discuss the subject again? I have some important ideas I would like to share with them."

"That we shall do immediately," the Chief said, aware of the importance of the subject. "You who are educated may have other ideas on the matter."

At the meeting, after introducing the subject, the Chief invited Faye to address the gathering.

"Our Chief and members of Council," Faye began, "You all know very well that at the peak of the rainy season, when the food reserves in the store are depleted and families are reduced to one meal a day or even only four meals a week. We must fight this wolf. Earlier I was discussing this problem with the Chief, a problem which our people face every year at this time when there are shortages of food as we wait for the harvest. To combat this menace I want to propose the following actions which must be taken immediately:

- "All villages in the district must have a labour organization which will be composed of the young men and women of each village;
- "I myself am going to raise a loan for purchasing foodstuffs and seeds for the farms; each village will pay back after the rainy season;
- "Each village will work or produce two farms, one for subsistence crops such as millet, maize or sorghum and the other for groundnuts. This, of course, will have nothing to do with their private farms;
- "At the end of the rainy season, the produce from both farms will be sold in the presence of the Chief and elders and the proceeds will be deposited to the Commissioner of the district;
- "This amount will be used to pay the food aid loan and to purchase more food. These will then be distributed to the villagers at the beginning of the rains before the hungry season begins;

- "Each village compound will receive food according to the number of young men and women it had in the labour organization;
- "Only groundnuts are sold for cash, the other food crops grown on the communal farms will be distributed."

After prolonged discussions, the meeting accepted these proposals and promptly established the *Kantora Kafo*. Key to its success was the fact that the loans from the trading agents were repaid from the proceeds from the groundnuts produced on communal farms whilst the foodstuffs were stored for distribution to members at the beginning of the rainy season. In a sense the village *kafo* were meant to function along the lines of producer cooperatives.

Faye did not confine his involvement just to theorizing and discussing the requirements for a buoyant agricultural sector in the country. As a practical person, as far back as the late 1930s, he had resurrected his father's farm, "The Rest-Rust", at Serre-kunda and became a poultry and cassava farmer in his spare time. In 1937 he bought "Sahayai" farmstead opposite Christ Church, Serre-kunda and established a piggery, a poultry run and vegetable garden.

Faye also had a model farm on the outskirts of Sukuta which he named "*Bulen-bagn*" ("Never Refuse"), and where he spent his spare time. He advocated diversification and multi-cropping in the country at large, in order to escape from dependence on groundnuts as a single commercial produce; this would also keep the farmers productively employed during the off season. Promising crops, about which Faye talked a lot, included castor-oil seeds, cashew nuts, palm kernels from which animal feed could be obtained, and palm oil extracted for export.

Similarly, it was in the common interest of his compatriots that Faye went into the Produce Pilot Syndicate, discussed in Chapter 5.

Besides his political positions, Faye held many top offices in both the private and public sectors in The Gambia. These included:

- Founder Member, Commonwealth Parliamentary Association, Gambia Branch.
- Member, Gambia Oilseed Marketing Board (1949 to 1952).

- Vice-President, Gambia Family Planning Association (1970 to 1976).
- Vice-President, Gambia Horticultural Society (1950 to 1985).
- Founder and Manager of the Parsonage Nursery School (1976 to 1985).
- First Vice-Chairman of the President's Award Scheme for youth training and citizenship.
- Chairman, Board of the Anglican Vocational Training Centre.
- Member of the national Scout Council and of its Executive Committee.
- Manager of Anglican Schools.
- Member, Gambia United Nations Association.

Summary Observations

The resumed career of Rev. J. C. Faye in the Church saw a series of promotions, from Deacon to Priest, from Priest to Priest-in-Charge, and then to Provost. In the circumstances surrounding his career in the Church he could not have done better. Indeed, as pointed out by several interviewees, if from the outset he had decided to devote his whole life to the Christian ministry, if he had decided to give up politics in the early days, or if he had accepted one of the offers for formal theological training, he would soon have risen to the high position of Bishop of the diocese. In that he failed to meet all of these conditions and yet rose to be the first Provost of the Cathedral he had again lived up to his reputation.

Faye's philanthropic work, from the very early days, was of varied character and in different ways touched the lives of people and provided them with opportunities for a better life.

CHAPTER 11
CLOSURE: THE STRIFE IS O'ER

The Very Reverend John Colley Faye died on Tuesday 10 December 1985.[1]

Surviving him was his wife of many decades and fellow combatant, Cecilia Priscilla Faye (née Taylor), whom he married on 7 September 1933 at Bethel Methodist Church; he was only 25 years old then, rather young even for those times. As noted in Chapter 1, at MBHS it was practice for the brightest among the students preparing for the Cambridge Senior School Certificate to be recruited to teach in the lower levels at both MBHS and the Methodist Girls High School (MGHS). Faye was one of these pupil teachers; he gave classes in various subjects at the MBHS and in art at the MGHS. But for a young man like him, this was not all that was on his mind at MGHS: aside from his lessons he kept an eye for the young charming ladies, amongst whom was Miss Cecilia Taylor. She was to become Mrs Cecilia Faye. At the wedding his boyhood friend, Jacob Mahoney, was his best man and his cousin, Mary Chapman, the chief bridesmaid. Their marriage weathered many storms, particularly from the school, the church, and politics. Nonetheless, these cemented rather than undermined the marriage, which lasted 52 years, a record by any standards.

For her primary schooling Cecilia had attended the St. Mary's Anglican Day School, like her husband, and subsequently won a scholarship to the MGHS for her secondary education. She was an accomplished seamstress with a clientele cutting across social classes; some young Christian girls learnt the art of sewing from her. Whilst in KK, and even in Bathurst, she was struck by the high infant and maternal mortality rates. Thus, on her return to Bathurst from KK, she worked as a midwifery nurse in a private clinic in Bathurst; she later went to England where she qualified as a State Certified Midwife. On her return she continued the outstanding work with expectant mothers.

For much of her working life Cecilia was a Girl Guider and one of the lieutenants of the wife of the Governor, Lady Southorn, in the "Busy Bees," a voluntary organization of women and girls. When at KK, she organized the five girls who were under her care into a Lone Girls Company and later rose to become Honorary Assistant Guide Commissioner of The Gambia. As a true helpmate to Faye she was matron of the KK, a teacher in the junior section, and an instructor in the domestic science programme which she organized for girls from the neighbouring village of Jawo-kunda.

"Auntie" Faye herself passed away on 4 February 1991. Part of a tribute to her read:

> Aunty Faye, as she was commonly known, was a warm, tolerant and generous person. John Colley Faye could not have accomplished so much without her continuous support and presence. She created a conducive environment for the children they fostered. She was indeed instrumental in both his political and personal life.[2]

Also surviving Rev. Faye were the three children, Adele, Axel, and Colley, and numerous grandchildren and great-grandchildren (see Appendix 2). He saw a strong family unit "as a good foundation for the nation and the extended family as a gift from God. The family home must create an atmosphere where mutual respect, trust and constant love and dialogue are always present."[3]

Outside the areas discussed in more detail in Chapters 2 to 10 above, there were many others to which the versatile Faye made contributions. Only a few will be mentioned herebelow.

Interest in Languages

Faye had a thorough knowledge of Wolof culture and his competence in the Wolof language was pure and unadulterated. As mentioned in the opening chapter, he often subjected family members and friends to a language test of Wolof names of objects; invariably, the answers were corrupted by French or English. He, of course, knew the original equivalent in Wolof. This was one motivation for his co-authorship of a publication (with Matarr Sillah) titled *The Orthography of Gambian Languages—Wolof and Mandinka*,[4] It was the product of the period he spent as researcher on the subject—with Eliman Bah—under the late Dr. Ida Wood at the School of Oriental and African Studies (SOAS), University of London (1938). His knowledge of orthography led to his decision to adopt "Faye" in the spelling of his name instead of "Fye".

Other outputs of the period at SOAS were two double-sided records and material issued under the title *A Short Phonetic Study of Wolof (Jolof) as Spoken in The Gambia and in Senegal*. The study was published in the renowned *Africa: Journal of the International African Institute,* volume 12, no. 3, 1939.

Indeed, generally, Faye was very keen to reproduce Gambian languages using the Roman script. As he once admitted: "I am very keen to see the day when there is literature in our own languages in Roman letters and, in fact, I have done some translation of them." He recognized, nevertheless, that several questions must first be confronted head-on. These included: Should one adopt a strictly phonetical means for reducing Gambian languages to writing? Is the Western alphabet adequate to represent all the sounds in Gambian languages? Is it advisable to use diacritical signs and/or accents? Would the use of phonetical characters not involve extra expense? These and other issues Faye and Silla sought to grapple with in the *Orthography of Gambian Languages,* as far as the Wolof and Mandinka languages were concerned.

Faye introduced the teaching of Mandinka in the Protectorate when he was based in KK. He bemoaned the fact not only that transliteration had not been done but that there was an inadequacy of literature in indigenous languages. This, for him, was part of the liberating tonic accompanying political independence which had been ignored. He argued: "Even in the great meetings in the Mother country, at first the official language was Latin and then Norman French. It was not till when the English language developed that English took over."[5]

National Anthem of The Gambia

In the same sector, during his posting in London Faye composed a poem titled *Gambia* (1 July 1964) which was transcribed and the music arranged by Richard Arnell. The three stanzas read as follows:

GAMBIA

1. On Afric's western sky,
   Set by the deep blue sea,
   Amid lands large and long,
   Small thou art, small may be;
   Bless'd thou art! For by thee
   Borne shall be "Branch of Peace"
   To countries far and nigh.
   Gambia! Good-will land, "Neu Terre-wul a gen"*;
   Gambia! Gambia! God bless our Fatherland!

2. Thy river gently flows,
   Palms feath'ry fronds do wave,
   Wafted by breezes soft,
   Small thou art, small may be;
   Bless'd thou art! For from thee
   Days gone by greater lands
   Bless'd were they through thy toil.
   Gambia! Good-will land, O Koras sweetly ring;
   Gambia! Gambia! God bless our Fatherland!

3. Kambi's daughters and sons
   From pleasant sandy shores
   Join Afric's freedom band.

Few you are, few may be;
Bless'd you are! For of you
Shall be asked service true
By mankind and our land.
Gambia! Good-will land, pledge we ourselves to thee:
Gambia! Gambia! God bless our Fatherland!

Paucity debars not from greatness

Faye submitted this poem to the National Anthem Selection Committee when the competition was open. The poem rightly extolled the virtues of the country and its peoples. For Faye smallness was not a handicap as The Gambia had always been a model of peace, which could be exported to bigger and more endowed countries throughout the world. He deeply appreciated the natural beauty of the country, linked to the vastness of the contributions that Gambia's children have made to the richness of other bigger lands. The Gambia, through its freedom and its membership of the comity of nations, would in the future enlighten others and her children would make significant contributions to the betterment of their country and others. Looking back from the vantage point of today, the dreams of Faye, the poet, have indeed come to reality.

Altogether, there were three submissions, two of which were rejected by the Cabinet because they were not of the required standard. It was acknowledged that the content of Faye's submission was superb but it was not accepted because it was considered too long; the Committee preferred something which was to the point and easy to memorize.[6]

The words of the winning entry, *For The Gambia our Homeland*, were written by Virginia Julia Howe and the music composed by Jeremy Frederic Howe from a traditional Mandinka song, *Foday Kabba Dumbuya* by Jali Nyama Susso. Julia Howe was the spouse of Jeremy Howe and a university-trained composer of music. Jeremy Howe was in the Gambia colonial service (1954-65), an Administrative Officer in the Ministry of Local Government; he was also the Chairman of the Selection Committee. According to Howe he was invited by the Cabinet to submit both words and music of the Anthem and both entries were accepted.[7]

Though his entry had not won the competition, according to Alieu Cham-Joof,[8] Faye was benevolent enough to be involved in the translation of the winning entry into Wolof, as follows:[9]

Gambia mede sunyu rewe.
Nyu nge jaim di liggaye de nyan
Ndakh nyun nyep nyu bolloh nek a bena
Am sunyu affier ak jama base bu neka.

Na degga sama sunyu jefye
Nyeal jef yu bakh ye ngu digalleh
Tay bolleh sunyu girr ye
Ndakh wonneh ni dom adama wara nekeh bena.

Nyunge tailleh Sunyu degga deggi nangu
Tei essal sunyu diggeh
Yalla mu maggame omba askanwe
Sahal nyu chi Gambia beh fau.

Honours

Some of the awards received by Faye included the Insignia of Member of the Order of the British Empire (MBE, January 1947) for his pioneering work in the Protectorate, especially in the education field; also, the Insignia of Officer of the National Order of the River Gambia (ORG, April 1976) awarded by the President of the Republic for Faye's significant contributions to the emancipation and political advancement of The Gambia and his distinguished service in the educational and religious fields. He had a street named after him in a surburb of Serre-kunda, to complement that named after his father, John Charles Faye Street, in Banjul.

Uncle lived a full life. Perhaps what was most pronounced about it was his dedication to public service, a quality that he inherited from his father. From teaching in Bathurst and the Protectorate, to the complex world of independence politics, and back to church and school, service was his watchword. The 1950s were the most turbulent period in Gambia's political evolution, given that the aim was to confront and dismantle the colonial system, in which process one had to contend with powerful opposing political forces. Faye was fully enmeshed in this struggle, again in service to his country and people.

Fond Remembrances

Uncle was a simple and modest man. He had a unique sense of humour and laughed at his own jokes even if his listeners did not find them funny. He enjoyed the company of the young ones and never hesitated to wrestle them to the ground in fun. He had time for people from all walks of life, not just for political purposes but because of a genuine interest in the well-being of the human being. Many there were who benefitted from his generosity, in cash or in kind, often without any member of his inner family knowing.

Perhaps the indelible image of Uncle Faye is of a man in long white flowing cassock with the bottom flaps tucked under his front belt, and riding a ladies' bicycle. More often than not, he did not have his clerical collar on. He rode slowly to his destination, often humming hymns or psalms softly to himself. He had two cars at his disposal but he used them only on very special occasions. This, not because he did not have a driver's licence, but because with the bicycle he could get some physical exercise and, very important, it was so much easier to stop and talk to people. When appointed Provost, the residence at the Parsonage and a car were put at his disposal but, he declined both, on the grounds that "when I retire I will have to go back to my bicycle and to my house on Gloucester Street so I might as well stay with things as they are."

Last Days

Uncle's last days were spent in full communion with his Maker. With close members of family around his hospital bed he led them in reciting Psalm 23 in the Holy Bible. His voice was weak throughout but it became bold and strong when he got to the declaration:

> Yea, though I walk through the valley of the shadow of death,
> I will fear no evil:
>> for thou art with me; thy rod and thy staff, they comfort me.

Indeed, in his lifetime he had walked through many valleys of the shadows of death, some very deep, but his Lord and Shepherd had always lifted him up, given him comfort and guided him onward.

To the consternation of all, on three consecutive days, as he lay on his deathbed, the Very Reverend would from time to time raise his hands, with fingers clasped, and murmur something to himself. Not until he repeated the same on the fourth day did it dawn on the family members present that it was the body of His Lord and Saviour that he was consecrating, for communion with his people. He was still in service to his congregation and to the people of his beloved Gambia, even at the moment of death.

The strife was o'er and the battle won, in the name of Christ!

The Obsequies

Given Reverend Tilewa Johnson's excellent relations with Reverend Faye, and in Johnson's new office as Priest-in-Charge, he was made responsible for organizing the vigil, the laying-in-state, and the requiem mass. The vigil was held in the church and, for the first time, tributes were allowed from the public. Also, for the first time in many years the casket of the deceased was laid in state in the nave of the Cathedral from late morning of the day of the funeral, so well-wishers could pay their last respects to this illustrious son of the soil. It was then transferred to the sanctuary and, contrary to usual practice, the top end of the coffin was made to face the congregation instead of the bottom end. The message here was that Faye was a man of the people; his life had been dedicated to serving them and, in death, he still belonged to them. He was their "*Goor Gayndé*" (meaning "fearless and strong"). As put even better by Bishop Tilewa Johnson in an interview on 17 October 2012: "Man, this was Rev. Faye! We had to do something different for him."

The funeral and requiem mass, on Sunday 15 December 1985, were again presided over by Bishop Elisee with all the Anglican clergy present. Rev. Jacob Williams read the Epistle, from I Thessalonians chapter 4, verses 13 to 18; Rev. S. Tilewa Johnson read the Holy Gospel, from John chapter 11, verses 21 to 27; Rev. Alex Yorke and Rev. Malcolm Millard joined in reading the burial sentences. Representative Ministers from the other denominations participated, such as Rev. E. B. Stafford, Chairman of the District and Superintendent of the Methodist Church; he read the first lesson, from Revelation, chapter 7, verses 9 to 17. Bishop Elisee gave the address.

Not forgotten was the favourite hymn of the deceased:

O Holy Spirit, Lord of grace,
Eternal fount of love,
Inflame, we pray, our inmost hearts
With fire from Heav'n above.

As Thou in bond of love dost join
The Father and the Son,
So fill us all with mutual love,
And knit our hearts in one.

All glory to be Father be,
All glory to the Son,
All glory, Holy Ghost, to Thee,
While endless ages run.

Attending the funeral were people from all walks of life and constituencies. The government of The Gambia was represented by Louise NJie, the then Minister of Health. Again, his long-time trench-mates and confidants, Matarr Sillah and Alieu E. Cham Joof, gave eulogies; Sillah on the subject "J. C. Faye, the Man" and Cham Joof on "J. C. Faye, the Politician".

Perhaps one of the greatest honours done to Faye was that a delegation from KK was present. They had come to pay their respects to one who was part and parcel of their inheritance and had laid the foundations for the development of their communities.

The Sereer community was, of course, not to be left out. They believe that when a person dies his departure should be celebrated and not mourned for three reasons: namely, because he would have completed his time on earth; because life on earth is burdensome; and because he is proceeding to a place of peace and rest. Closely associated with these is the further belief that death is a mere extension of life, as the dead person is leaving behind children and grandchildren (very broadly defined) who are of his own flesh and blood. Before departing this world, therefore, the dying person must indicate who in the family should sing his praises and the ritual observances the family must perform when he dies; these requests are never denied.

Whether or not Faye held these beliefs, and respected them, the Sereer community had no option but to celebrate this giant of a son in grand style. Unlike former President Léopold Sédar Senghor of Senegal, himself a Sereer, whose praises at his funeral in 2001 were to be sung by Yandé Codou Sène (*la griotte* de Senghor), it is not known if Faye had selected the person to undertake this function. In any case, as his corpse lay in state at his house, Fara Junjun, the master-drummer and king of the Sereer Griots, appeared with his ensemble from Njongon and performed the last rites. For hours they continued with ceremonies associated with the death of a royal son of Siin.[10]

Long before Faye's death, at a dinner on 8 July 1968 in honour of Bishop John Daly, first Anglican Bishop of The Gambia who was on a courtesy visit to the diocese, this Bishop paid tribute to Rev. Faye, his partner in various endeavours in the course of 16 years' sojourn in the country. Daly said:

> I want to pay tribute to this remarkable friend known as "J.C." or "Uncle" throughout The Gambia. I often find myself receiving the praise which is due to him. This is especially so in connection with St. Mary's School, the old House of the Transfiguration on 2 Pignard Street, and the Secondary School of the Transfiguration at Kristi-kunda. The greatness of that work in the Kantora and the fruits of that work are due under God to Uncle J. C. I may have been ultimately responsible and we had many other fine workers

at KK—both Gambian and expatriates—but initially most of the inspiration and drive came from J. C. Faye.[11]

Additional Testimonials

This biography can fittingly end with a series of quotations by a few people whose lives were touched by The Very Reverend John Colley Faye.

> Uncle had no ambition to be Head of State of the Gambia. He was so much more interested in the lives of people, in national problems which he thought he could handle better. Even in his early days he was interested in the problems of the people and how he could solve them. This is also why he went into politics and wanted to be in the legislature. He wanted to be well-placed in order to help people. He was a simple man, a very genuine man. He had no enemies. He put everybody ahead of himself. Day and night he was involved in other people's problems. He loved young people. He only saw good things in people and tried to help as many people as he could. He was not interested in any personal gains. Altogether, he was a man for whom I had the greatest respect. He was more than a father to me.
>
> *Assan Musa Camara,*
> *former Vice-President of the Republic of The Gambia*

> I have spoken about Uncle's generosity of spirit. Rightness for him was something to aim for and one must be seen to be trying one's best to walk down the path of righteousness. He was so conscious of his human frailty that for him to apologize and to seek to make amends was not something difficult to do. He had strong views. He stood firm in his convictions because he must have thought through them before coming to such conclusions; one had to work very hard to persuade him otherwise.

Uncle was a true leader whom we looked up to. The fact that he immersed himself in the lives of the people made a big difference. Uncle also had the intelligence, the aptitude, the mastery of spoken and written English—at a time when this was of extreme importance in society. All these could have made him much greater than he actually was.

On a personal note I cannot deny the fact that he contributed immensely to laying the foundations for my pastoral ministry; he sponsored my candidacy for the Ordained Ministry. It was as early as in my second year as a theological student that both the Principal of the college and my Bishop decided that I should be made a deacon. This I attributed to the solid foundation Uncle had given me. I am so pleased that in my first sermon as a deacon I was able to spend some time thanking him.

Rt. Rev. Dr. S. Tilewa Johnson, Bishop of The Gambia

Father Faye was a committed Christian and really devoted to the Anglican Church. There were many pillars of the Church but he was one of the most outstanding. He loved St. Mary's . . . He was a great adviser to all of the bishops, from Daly to Tilewa Johnson. Of course, he disagreed with them sometimes but always stuck to his advice convinced that it was in the best interest of the Church. Father Faye was definitely someone to be reckoned with, generous and friendly, he certainly liked people.

Dr. Florence Mahoney,
senior church member and historian

I believe that the way Uncle Faye has been treated in the political history of this country is nothing short of a disgrace. I speak of him all the time—in church and outside. Young people need to be reminded that we had great nationalists like Uncle who gave their all for the progress and prosperity of our people. The newcomers to politics ought to know this too.

St. George Ade Joiner,
former Judge, High Court of The Gambia

J.C. had interest in people and helped a lot of people, especially young people. He was generous to a fault but never made his many gifts to others known to his family or anyone. He paid the school fees of so many young persons. He was very sociable and had many friends. He was always the life of any party and liked those around him to be happy. He was involved and did well in any sporting activity and was ready to participate at a moment's notice.

The late Mary Jarra-Chapman,
first cousin, retired teacher

In both the conceptualization and overall implementation of the AVTC project Rev. Faye was a good leader. His experiences in the field of education and of life in the Protectorate were major assets in the early days. Without a doubt he was the right person to lead the Board. Some members, quite advanced in age, would put up with the bad roads and the ferry crossing to get to Farafenni just because they were inspired by the leadership qualities of Rev. Faye.

Delphin Carroll,
educationist, founding member of the Board of AVTC

Uncle Faye was a visionary. He was involved in so many things. He had many dreams, all of which he could not achieve during his lifetime. J. C. Faye Memorial School is his making as is the Anglican Vocational Training Centre.

We lost a great man. For me if only he had stayed on in the Church instead of going into politics there is a lot he would have achieved for all us Christians and for Anglicans in particular.

A simple, warm and charming personality, he was true to himself and never hesitated to speak his mind. But perhaps what I admired most about him is that he was not a greedy man, he was ready to die for others, to sacrifice himself for others.

Theophilus W. George, former organist and choirmaster,
St Mary's Anglican Cathedral, and AVTC Board Member

Growing up he was the grand-uncle we could make jokes with, he ran after us and, generally, felt at home with him. I was just as close to him as I was to my father . . . I have seen the man at different times and all throughout have been impressed with his even-tempered composure; every time you see him with people something beaconed from his eyes. Faye was the sort of person who can swim with the ordinary people, dance with the intellectuals and hold hands with the clergy. That was the type of person he was . . .

I drank from every pearl of wisdom that fell from his breath . . . All throughout the 1960s I eavesdropped on conversations both with his allies and his adversaries and these have left a significant dent on my understanding especially on the varying perspectives on pan-Africanism and the horrors of disenfranchisement. In fact, when Ivan Illich and others were coining the phrase 'liberation theology' Faye had already practised and mastered its methodology and reduced it to a fine art . . . I have learnt a lot from him.

Baaba Sillah, grand-nephew,
author, When the Monkey Talks, *Acknowledgements*

When Rev. J. C. Faye arrived in London as the Gambian Commissioner, he quickly became acquainted with my father, Antoine Mendy (better known as Pa Mendy or Uncle Mendy), who was well-known in the Gambian community for his social welfare activities. The Reverend was "famous" for tirelessly attending to Gambians with family problems or in trouble with the law, visiting those in prisons and the sick in hospital. In recognition of my father's community activism, Rev. J. C. Faye recommended him to be invited to the Queen's Garden Party, an important event which also recognizes the accomplishments of the invited guests. My father was deeply appreciative and fond of narrating this unique experience; he always talked about J. C. Faye with great admiration and immense esteem.

Peter Karibe Mendy, Professor (USA)

No doubt Uncle was truly a giant in Gambian politics and deserves a bust or statue in his memory. He had vision combined with an unrelenting fighting spirit, yet a caring and humble man. But, boy, did he go through some rough times; however, never did he waver in his commitment. The man had a superb command of the English language, wow!

Ransford Cline-Thomas,
senior churchman at St Mary's and
former United Nations official

There are lots of things one can say about Rev. J. C. Faye. He was a fighter, he had always been a fighter; he fought for the voiceless, the powerless, and always putting himself last. A nationalist at heart he made so many sacrifices all for the better of the people. He loved children. One of his attributes was that he was so open. He had a way of not imposing himself but because of his personality and the respect people had for him he usually got what he wanted. He was well-connected, well wired-up.

Rev. Faye had little regard for wealth-accumulation; an example is that it was he who donated to the community the land where the Serre-kunda police station presently stands. He left an indelible mark on people and made an impression on the very first meeting [with] him. There was nothing in life that was complicated to Uncle; he made every problem simple. These are some of the things for which I would like to remember Father Faye.

> *Francis Jones, senior Anglican Church official and, inter alia, Board Member of the J. C. Faye Memorial School and the Anglican Vocational Training Centre*

Rev. Faye was a man of ideas and also a man of action. He always wanted things done and could not stand bureaucracy and rules and regulations which he saw as hampering the achievement of his goals. Sometimes, this gave rise to problems, especially with donors and their agents. With his death the Church lost a great man.

> *Wilmot John, senior Anglican Church official and Board member, Anglican Vocational Training Centre*

I looked upon Uncle Faye as my dad. He was everybody's dad. When I paid tribute to him on his death, in my capacity as People's Warden at St. Mary's Cathedral, I described him as the intrepid father, the courageous leader, the honest worker and, above all, the loyal and trusted servant of his people. This, I remembered when I stood at his coffin in St. Mary's Cathedral.

Uncle Faye died and left a legacy that is incomplete, in the sense that he knew St. Mary's Church better than anybody who was alive. He knew the history of the Church inside-out. He lived his life regardless of the political shadows which were slowly creeping in. He did his best for society and helped so many individuals regardless of who they were and where they came from.

> *Femi Peters, senior Church member and close family friend*

CHAPTER 12

CONCLUDING REMARKS: REVEREND J. C. FAYE AND THE LEADERSHIP QUESTION

Much of what can be said about Rev. Faye and the leadership question has already been raised in different parts of this book; thus this section merely highlights some of the more prominent leadership qualities demonstrated in the life of Reverend J. C. Faye.

Speaking from her own personal experience Ellen Johnson Sirleaf, President of the Republic of Liberia, says of "leadership":

> Leadership requires a whole lot of acceptance, the ability to remain committed to your cause and to have the courage of your convictions. It requires understanding that sacrifices will have to be made—and the willingness to make them again and again and again.
>
> The greatest sacrifice is putting everything important— the challenges, the needs, your own ideals and sense of responsibility—ahead of yourself. In effect, to be a great leader is to sacrifice oneself, because if you ever stop to think about your own preservation, your own safety and your own survival, you will immediately become constrained. You will cease to act, or to act in the best interest of those you are leading. To be a great leader means to get to a place where personal considerations and needs become secondary to the achievement of your goal. That is the greatest sacrifice that you can make, but that is precisely what leadership demands.[1]

Leadership in Education

Undoubtedly, in relation to these standards Faye was a leader *par excellence*. In the different professions in which he served, he was invariably accepted as the leader, especially in his careers in education and in politics. In education he had an impressive pedigree dating back to his senior years at Methodist Boys' High School and his stint as Headmaster of the St Mary's School. Kristi-kunda was the pinnacle of his training in leadership which was to stand him in good stead in his future professional life. Here he learnt the rudiments of institution-building, management of people and other resources, building relations with people from all walks of life but particularly the teaching and support personnel, the students, and the community at large. Even today, the fondness with which those who went through "the Kristi-kunda experience" continue to reminisce about "those days" is very much a testimony to Faye's outstanding leadership qualities. The award of the insignia of Member of the British Empire and his appointment to the Legislative and Executive Councils are enough evidence of his successful leadership of the Kristi-kunda community and the district at large.

In the education sector Faye was undaunted by the unbecoming manner in which he had departed Kristi-kunda. Rather, he turned to projects involving the establishment of the Parsonage Nursery School and the Anglican Vocational Training Centre. By their very nature both were very demanding hands-on projects, especially in the infant stages. Again, with determination, Faye saw both institutions take off and, against all odds, the School and Centre have survived and continue to fulfil their missions and to offer service to their clientele.

Leadership in Politics

The period spent by Rev. Faye in politics also richly illustrates his leadership qualities. He founded and led the Gambia Democratic Party throughout its existence; it was the first political party in the country. Especially in the early 1950s this party was at the centre of politics. As a pioneer party, it produced men who subsequently proceeded to launch their own parties to challenge Faye and his party; they cut their teeth in the Democratic Party.

With Faye at the helm, the party became a model of organization, mobilization, and campaigning. Further, throughout the decade the party played a dominant role in the politics of decolonization, with Faye firmly in the saddle; his leadership was unchallengeable, not for want of other competent and capable people but because of his charisma, intellectual prowess, and political skills. In that he was always ready and willing to stand up to the colonial authorities, he attracted younger people and radical elements to the party.

Functioning in the context of the colonial order brought out certain qualities in Faye which could have led either to advancement in his political career or to his demise. Perhaps the most striking is that he was in sustained conflict with the colonial administration, particularly during the tenure of Sir Percy Wyn-Harris; Faye pitted himself squarely against the colonial order and, unlike some of the other parties, never wavered. He saw himself and his party in the likeness of other anti-colonial movements across West Africa and in the British colonies globally. They were in the vanguard of the struggle against foreign domination and there was little room for compromise. The fact that, unlike Governor Barkworth Wright, the Governor of the day, Sir Percy Wyn-Harris, was rather cautious about rapid constitutional progress merely strengthened Faye as to the rightness of his cause.

Faye was truly national in outlook and in spirit. In fact, given that he belonged to a small minority ethnic group and minority Christian religion he could not have practised "narrow nationalism" and been successful. That is, only if he had belonged to a sizeable ethnic or religious group would he have attempted to be "tribal" and expect to be victorious. The composition of the leadership and the following of the party he led were reflective of this bridge-building mission; as in other areas, here also there was a distinct difference between his Democratic Party and the other political parties.

Elaborating further, in terms of Faye's nationalist outlook the most notable observation was his personal connections with the Protectorate, the traditional leadership and the rural people. The experience at Kristi-kunda provided convincing evidence, if any were required, to which can be added his genuine efforts to bridge the gap between the Colony and Protectorate in the later half of the 1950s. Faye waged a battle against any designs to accentuate the differences between the two, not only as regards social and economic development but also political arrangements. His was a mission to promote understanding. He resisted any and every move that would keep the two parts of the country apart. As ever, he saw many of the colonial officials working assiduously for the opposite—to divide and rule.

Faye's Readiness to Make Sacrifices

In line with the convictions of President Ellen Johnson Sirleaf, as quoted above, another mark of leadership exemplified in the life of Rev. Faye was a readiness to make sacrifices for the well-being of others. In 1942, he chose to give up a successful and prestigious career in the educational field in Bathurst to set up a new institution in the far-off eastern part of the country, with all the risks involved, not only as concerned the environment but also the management of a virgin settlement. Even after he had been the victim of machinations of others and had had to depart from Kristi-kunda he was ready to help in a significant way when discussions on the revival of the institution came up in 1966. Then also, it is to be remembered, he gave up a university place at Fourah Bay College to another student when requested to stay at home and assist with teaching at the Boys' High School. To these and other items of evidence must be added the evening classes he conducted for "mature" students both during his stay in Kristi-kunda and on his return to Bathurst.

Perhaps the best examples of this spirit of selflessness were the two occasions, in 1960 and 1962, when Faye gave up his safe Soldier Town constituency in Bathurst to other party diehards who went on to lose the elections to opposition candidates. These particular sacrifices were of tremendous consequence in that they led to Faye's electoral defeats and, eventually, to his exit from politics. Faye also made sacrifices in the matter of the Pilot Syndicate and in the debts he incurred on behalf of other people—matters which landed him in court on numerous occasions.

In the Church similar sacrifices where made by Faye for the benefit of others. One such is the running of the House of Transfiguration in Bathurst; no remuneration was paid to Reverend Faye or his wife, even though they shouldered a number of heavy family and other responsibilities. In the same vein, during his period in government he did not accept any remuneration from the Church; again the list of his regular assignments was quite lengthy.

Professionalism

Faye was well-qualified for the leadership positions he held and was well-equipped to perform creditably. He was appointed to positions purely for reasons of proven competence and ability and his performances confirmed this. In teaching, he devoted much time and resources to preparing himself privately and succeeding in various professional examinations. The period spent at Southampton University was one of his proudest achievements. It was because of his professional standards that he was appointed to the leadership positions at Kristi-kunda, in the Democratic Party and in the Democratic Congress Alliance; it was for the self-same reasons that he was able to attain the rank of Provost at St Mary's Cathedral.

Many who worked closely with Rev. Faye admit to having been highly inspired and motivated by his personal and professional qualities. This came out in the interviews conducted during the research for this biography and also in the testimonials quoted in the previous chapter. He had a clear vision of what was to be done (as seen in his many projects) and pursued his goals with commitment and sense of purpose.

Conclusion

In all these different spheres Faye served as a role model. Looking back over his life and times, it is difficult not to conclude that perhaps a main point of criticism is that he sought to do many things at the same time; he was actively involved in a multitude of professions and aimed to lead in all. The argument continues that if he had remained in one profession—education, politics, or the Church—he would have attained more than he did and would have contributed more meaningfully to the development of his country. That is to say, he would perhaps have been the first Gambian Director of Education, the first Prime Minister, or the first Gambian bishop. In the event, though Faye never achieved such heights, the record reveals that in many different ways he laid the foundations on which others who came after him were able to build.

Further, as Florence Mahoney has suggested, to make a great impact on society do we necessarily have to be at the pinnacle? Do we necessarily only leave a mark when we reach the top as a Prime Minister or Bishop? Even in lowly positions one can make a difference in the lives of people.[2] For Faye, this biography speaks for itself.

> Don't judge each day by the harvest you reap but by the seeds you have planted.
>
> *R. L. Stevenson*

APPENDICES
AND
NOTES AND REFERENCES

APPENDIX 1

MAJOR BIOGRAPHICAL MILESTONES

Year	Event
1908	Birth of J. C. Faye on Tuesday 25 February.
1913	Started school at St Mary's Anglican Day School.
1921	Progressed to (Wesleyan) Methodist Boys' High School (MBHS).
1924	Passed Junior Cambridge School Certificate.
1925	Appointed Pupil Teacher and Tutor, MBHS.
1926	Passed Senior Cambridge School Certificate.
1927	Obtained Certified Teachers' Certificate, First Class.
1930	Associate of the College of Preceptors, United Kingdom.
1932	Headmaster, Methodist Central Junior Secondary School.
1933	Faye married Cecilia Pricilla Taylor.
1934	Assistant Headmaster, St Mary's Anglican Day School.

1937   Attended University College of Southampton (England) where he obtained the Cambridge Certificate of Proficiency in English, First Class, Special Mention.
House of Transfiguration opened by Bishop Daly, at 2 Pignard Street, Bathurst; it was to serve as foster home for boys from the Protectorate but also took in those from Bathurst. Faye and his wife, Cecilia, were charged with responsibility to manage the home.

1938   Headmaster, St Mary's Anglican Day School.
Formation of the Gambia Teachers' Union with Faye as Liaison Officer relating to the colonial administration.

1940   Kristi-kunda project, Phase One.

1942   Kristi-kunda Phase Two. Faye appointed Headmaster of Transfiguration School, Kristi-kunda. He set out to build an institution with high standards in terms of academic performance, comportment, values, etc.

1947   Faye appointed to both the Executive and Legislative Councils of The Gambia by the Governor.
Awarded insignia of the Member of the Order of the British Empire (MBE) for services to education, especially in the rural areas.
J. C. Faye made a Deacon of the Anglican Church; he served his deaconate first in KK and then at St Mary's Church in Bathurst.

1948   Faye represented The Gambia at the African Conference, London.

1949   End of the Faye era in Kristi-kunda and his return to Bathurst. Governor Barkworth Wright, who highly appreciated Faye's abilities, left The Gambia for Cyprus, on transfer.

1951   Faye represented The Gambia at the Festival of Britain.

Formation of the Motor Drivers' and Mechanics Union, many of whose members were taxi drivers. Faye played a prominent role.

Formation of the Gambia Democratic Party, led by Faye. It was the first political party in The Gambia.

New Constitution introduced.

Elections. Faye defeated all the other candidates and became the First Elected Member of the Legislative Council. He was appointed minister—without portfolio and, thus, a member of the Executive Council.

Faye played a leading role in the establishment of the Pilot Produce Syndicate.

1952   Formation of the Gambia Muslim Congress, under the leadership of I. M. Garba-Jahumpa.

Selected by members of the Legislative Council to represent them at a conference of the Commonwealth Parliamentary Association, in Ottawa, Canada.

Faye's first suspension from the Executive Council and his subsequent reinstatement.

1953   Advisory Committee of 34 constituted to come up with proposals for a new Constitution.

Faye's second suspension from Executive Council and his reinstatement.

Faye's third suspension from the Executive Council and his non-reinstatement.

New Constitution allowing for direct election of seven members of the Legislative Council.

1954   Formation of the United Party led by P.S. NJie.

Elections in which Faye came second to NJie. Garba-Jahumpa was third.

Faye appointed by the colonial administration as minister without portfolio responsible for works and communications.

1956   Gambia Workers Union established under the leadership of M.E. Jallow.

1957   National Party formed, under a collective leadership troika. Initially, it maintained an independent stance from the other parties but later moved close to the UP.

1959   Protectorate People's Party (PPP) formed; later renamed People's Progressive Party. David (later Dawda) K. Jawara led the party. Bathurst Constitutional Conference to make proposals on the next phase of constitutional advance.
Visit of Alan Lennox-Boyd, Secretary of State for the Colonies. Organized mass agitation for more rapid constitutional progress led to "Bread and Butter" demonstration.

1960   DP and MC merged to form the Democratic Congress Alliance (DCA).
New Constitution providing, inter alia, for universal adult suffrage.
First national elections. Faye stood in Kombo West and lost. His party, the DCA, won only one seat.

1961   P.S. NJie appointed Chief Minister.
Bathurst Constitutional Conference to prepare draft new Constitution.

1962   London Constitutional Conference, focusing primarily on items outstanding from the earlier Bathurst Constitutional Conference. Second national elections. Faye lost in New Town West, his newly-adopted constituency. DCA retained its one seat.
Garba-Jahumpa lost and resigned from the DCA to form the Gambia Congress Party.
New Constitution providing for full internal self-government.

1963   Full internal self-government.
       Faye appointed Commissioner of The Gambia to the United
       Kingdom.

1964   London Constitutional Conference to finalize and adopt the
       Independence Constitution.
       Faye recalled to Bathurst for his divergent views on government
       policy on various matters.

1965   Faye returned to Bathurst from London.
       The Gambia became an independent and sovereign state.
       Absorption of the DCA into the PPP retaining the PPP name.
       Though Faye signed the merger agreement he appears to have
       done so only in the interest of party unity.
       Faye resigned from the PPP basically because of his opposition
       to the proposal of the PPP government to adopt a republican
       form of government for the country.
       Government defeated in referendum on republican constitution.
       Faye had campaigned very actively against republicanism.

1966   General elections. Faye finally came "home" to the Bathurst
       Central constituency but he was defeated again. This marked
       his exit from the political scene.
       Faye resumed his career in the Anglican Church as curate at St
       Mary's Pro-Cathedral.

1973   Ordained Priest at St Mary's Pro-Cathedral.

1974   Advancement to position of Priest-in-Charge.

1976   The Parsonage Nursery School opened. Faye developed the idea
       and saw it through to fruition.

Awarded the Insignia of Officer of the National Order of the River Gambia (ORG) by the government of The Gambia.

The Anglican Vocational Training Centre legally registered. Faye initiated the project and served as Board Chairman up to 1983.

1977   Elected Provost of St Mary's Anglican Cathedral, Banjul.

1981   Retired from position in the Church.

1985   Demise of the Very Reverend J. C. Faye on Tuesday 10 December. Funeral and burial rites took place on 15 December.

1986   Name of Parsonage School changed to "Rev. J. C. Faye Memorial School".

APPENDIX 2

GENEALOGICAL TREE

SAMUEL JARRA (SAMBØU) MARRIED LISA CHAW (SISTER OF TEHDEN CHAW)

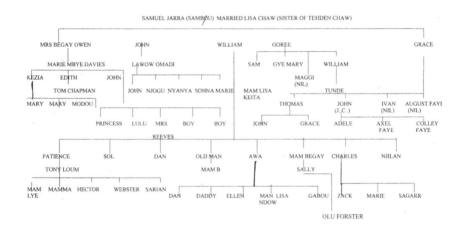

APPENDIX 3

NOTE ON THE GAMBIA LEADERSHIP PROGRAMME (GAMLEAP)

Context

Like many colonies in Africa The Gambia negotiated its way to self-government and independence. Initially, progress towards political independence was complicated by the perception that the country was too small, economically weak and geographically artificial to survive as an independent state. For the most part, the British colonial authorities treated it as a temporary outpost whose future would be decided by the willingness of France to incorporate it into Senegal in exchange for another territory. Even when negotiations to the effect failed, the policy favouring exchange of The Gambia for French territory remained, albeit mutedly.

In the 1950s the question of Gambia's ability to manage statehood resurfaced, against the backdrop of increased agitation for independence in the African colonies. The question of integration with Senegal reared its ugly head again. It subsequently led to discussions on modalities for cooperation and integration between the two countries, guided by the findings and recommendations of a United Nations team of experts. With this matter resolved the long-drawn-out and multi-faceted process of political change culminated in the declaration of independence on 18 February 1965.

The collective yearning for freedom embodied a powerful narrative for a peoples' agitation for self-rule. As in other African countries, the struggle to attain self-rule and independence in The Gambia was channelled through many movements which provided the rallying points for anti-colonial agitation. By the 1940s and 1950s, the resentment towards colonial rule in Africa was so strong that anti-colonial movements in some countries mutated into violence and warfare, as happened in Kenya, Algeria, Zimbabwe, Guinea Bissau, Sudan, Mozambique and Angola. Happily, decolonization in The Gambia was fairly orderly and peaceful, meaning that advancement to self-rule was secured without the resort to massive violence, organized or spontaneous. In the midst of these decolonization initiatives, there were personalities with incredible foresight, resilience and ambition. And although their individual ideological orientations differed, there was a certain sense of uniformity in their mission in so far as the attainment of self-rule and independence were concerned.

The Gambia was also no exception to the fact that the decolonization leadership comprised a good mix of people from different walks of life. Many abandoned lucrative professions to dedicate time, resources and emotion to a national cause. This was in large part due to the calibre of the country's nationalist leaders and the strong culture of dialogue that characterizes its people. With their visions and energies, dedication and persistence, an impassionate campaign was formulated and pursued culminating in the attainment of independence.

Justification

The statehood question instituted considerable strain on the minds of Gambia's nationalist leaders. Yet the ability to tackle it with maturity bespeaks of a country with a strong tradition of the practices of mediation, compromise and conciliation. The social tenets upon which Gambian society is constructed provide the avenues through which a peaceful existence is negotiated. In the march to independence, these became useful tools and common denominators that allowed for an orderly post-independence transition. But a great part of this *entente cordiale* and its contribution to a peaceful Gambia owes as much to the calibre of nationalist leaders as it does to the maturity in which they conducted themselves. They provided guidance where it was required, pacified when the need arose, and above all, compromised when it was critical. In short, they led by example.

Of course, the Gambian nationalist leadership disagreed on the key fundamentals underpinning their respective individual political ideologies. They had personal feuds, broke up ranks and bitterly fought for political dominance. But despite all the tension, they remained united on the need for a peaceful, inclusive and prosperous Gambia. It is perhaps this unity in purpose that led to a peaceful post-independence transition.

Unlike some other African countries, where the lives and times of nationalist leaders have been adequately documented, celebrated and, in some instances, immortalized, those of The Gambia still remain largely unknown. It is an obvious reality that the dominance of Gambia's immediate pre—and post-independence history by these personalities constitutes a significant part of the nation's political history. Yet, with the exception of Sir Dawda Jawara, who recently published his memoirs, no memoirs of the other leaders have thus far been done. Only relatively short accounts of the careers of some appear in publications such as *The Historical Dictionary of The Gambia* and the new *Dictionary of African Biography,* and in various secondary sources such as *A Political History of The Gambia.* What this means is that the lives, sacrifices, political battlegrounds and major contributions they have selflessly rendered to The Gambia remain unrecorded and so outside the public domain.

Thus, the absence of extensive biographies or documented studies on these personalities is a serious chasm in the country's institutional memory. In light of their selfless devotion and contributions to the construction of political and governance frameworks in The Gambia this ought to be rectified. Without such biographies the political history of The Gambia cannot be recovered, reclaimed and celebrated; after all, history accounts for the past, contextualizes the present, and provides a preview of the future.

Particularly critical, also, is the fact that unlike other African countries the Gambian school curriculum is remiss in its rendition of national political history. Thus far, what is taught in these schools provides little or no initiation into the lives and services of its pre—and post-independence personalities. The absence of a university for most of Gambia's recent history meant that there was no recognized platform of public discourse which would have encouraged enquiries on the country's political history and the place of the political leadership of yesteryear. The University of The Gambia, set up as recently as 1999, remains in its infancy and therefore largely unable to expand beyond its demarcated priorities.

The upshot of these combined factors is that a generation has grown up, or is growing up, with little knowledge of the national political history and the prominent actors that shaped it.

Concerned about this state of affairs, in July 2011 the Gambian Leadership Programme (*GamLeaP*) was launched by a team of researchers based in The Gambia, the United Kingdom and the United States of America. The immediate and medium-term ambitions of the programme are:

- To undertake extensive research on leading political personalities in pre—and post-independence Gambia; this would primarily be in the form of biographies.
- To celebrate the lives and contributions of these Gambian personalities to the social, economic and political development of The Gambia; including exhibitions of their speeches, writings, interviews and personal mementos.
- To organize debate on the struggles, political activities and ideological persuasions of the leading political personalities in pre—and post-independent Gambia, mainly in the form of workshops, seminars and public lectures.
- To create scholarships and other schemes in honour of the personalities as a way of keeping their legacies alive.
- To promote the incorporation of the biographical outputs of the programme into the Gambian school curriculum and introduce special collections on them in the Gambia National Archives.

As seen above, one of the major project elements in this programme aims to promote research and document the biographies of some of the more prominent Gambian political personalities whose lives were dedicated to the country's pre—and post-independence nationhood.

These include such luminaries as Edward Francis Small, Rev. John Colley Faye, Pierre Sarr NJie, Ibrahima M. Garba-Jahumpa, and Sir Dawda Jawara. Of an earlier era is Sir Samuel Forster whose own biography would, in many ways, demonstrate the generational shift that had taken place in politics in The Gambia through the decades.

This Gambia Biography Series Project will serve an important purpose by providing biographies of such individuals while also presenting new and previously unpublished material on each. The studies will be published under the overall theme, *The Gambia: Leading Political Personalities in the Decolonization and Early Post-Independence Era.* A separate collection of short portraits of other leading Gambians, past and present, will serve as an introduction to the more detailed main biographies.

This is only one of the projects in the Gambia Leadership Programme; other projects will be built around the above-mentioned immediate and medium-term programme ambitions. Some of the above programme components will feature prominently during the triennial celebrations of an official National Heroes Day which the government will be invited to declare; mass popular involvement would be emphasized in these celebrations. In time, the appropriate authorities would also be encouraged to erect monuments honouring these personalities and to name prominent streets and public buildings after them

Implementation Modalities

The *GamLeaP* will be a programme of the Centre for Research, Development and Social Justice Advocacy (CreSpsa); whilst awaiting its physical establishment in The Gambia, it is planned that the Centre functions as an on-line facility.

The general objective of the institution is to undertake high-quality innovative research directly linked to development, policy-making and implementation in The Gambia and other African countries. In an increasingly globalized world, research alone is unable to deal adequately with the challenges faced by individuals, communities and nation-states. Therefore, CreSpsa's goals and approaches will involve a strong advocacy dimension with a view to shaping effective and relevant policies, shifting individual and collective mindsets to issues related to socio-economic development, poverty and justice as well as generate practical results and outcomes.

The preparation of the biographies is seen as the responsibility of Gambian and non-Gambian researchers with different professional and academic backgrounds. Coordination and management of the whole programme is the responsibility of Jeggan C. Senghor (jeggancsenghor@gmail.com), University of London. He will ensure that the researchers work as a team and take responsibility for quality control; further, he will manage all matters related to editing, publishing, and marketing, and ensure that the biographies are consistent.

Data-collection Methodology

The methodology for collecting material for the biographies will largely involve the use of primary sources such as archival materials through existing public records in national research centres and institutions. In this connection the National Records Services in Banjul and the National Archives at Kew, London, are rich sources of information. Other more specialized entities are the National Museum in Banjul and the Oral Archives (the Mango Tree), in Fajara, which store a collection of taped interviews. It is anticipated that private records held by the families of some of the personalities will be consulted.

Allied to this are interviews with the contemporaries of the concerned personalities, including surviving family members. Regrettably, the pool of such potential interviewees and living witnesses is depleting rapidly; in itself this gives additional urgency to the organization and implementation of this project if the outputs are to be of the desired quality and value. The initiative will generate sufficient interest to entice a level of public participation that will ultimately establish the project as an authentic and authoritative public and academic reference point.

In addition, oral history constitutes an important medium of historical memory, information retrieval and dissemination. To the extent necessary this instrument will also be employed. There is, of course, a danger in relying on this source as the recollections may well be distorted by intervening factors such as amnesia and the lapse of space and time. It is also possible that events could be skewed by an overzealous oral historian running the risk of substituting facts with opinions.

It is hoped that using these various instruments quality material will be generated to do justice to the biographies of these great Gambians.

Outputs

Without a doubt it will take time for comprehensive stand-alone biographies to be completed and published at regular intervals. Thus, for mainly practical reasons, the project will produce two outputs. First will be an edited volume comprising chapters on each personality, tracing their lives, family lineage, education, professional activities, and their politics in particular. Second, there will be comprehensive full-length, detailed stand-alone biographical accounts; as far as possible they will follow a similar overall structure so that they are seen as companion volumes. Again, a separate set of portraits of other "second-tier" Gambian leaders in different works of life, past and present, will accompany the other two sets of project outputs.

NOTES AND REFERENCES

Preface

[1.] Legally, the Colony Area comprised Bathurst, the capital, the nearby Kombo St Mary, the stretch of territory across the Gambia River known as the Ceded Mile and MacCarthy Island, some distance up the river. In practice "Colony" referred only to the first two areas. The Protectorate was created in 1889 through the gradual expansion of British suzerainty in areas adjoining the Colony Area. With the Soninke-Marabout Wars and open French incursions in the area, it became necessary for the British to get involved in the local politics. The subsequent demarcation of the boundaries between (British) Gambia and (French) Senegal led to the consolidation of British administration in the area. Several Protectorate Ordinances defined the arrangements for local administration of this comparatively vast area, chieftaincy matters, legal and fiscal matters and relationships with the Colony Area.

Introduction: The Foundations

[1.] Communication from Baaba Sillah, Norway, dated 17 April 2012.
[2.] Interview, Adele Faye, Banjul, 19 November 2010.
[3.] Ibid.
[4.] See, Hughes, A. and Perfect, D., *A Political History of The Gambia,* Rochester, New York: University of Rochester Press, 2006, Table 1.5 on p.12, Table 1.6 on page 13, and Table 1.7 on page 14.
[5.] See Sonko-Godwin, P., *Ethnic Groups of the Senegambia: A Brief History,* Banjul: Book Production and Materials Resources Unit,

1985; Mwakikagile, Godfrey, *Ethnic Diversity and Integration* in *The Gambia; The Land, the People and the Culture,* Dar-es-Salaam: Continental Press, 2010, pp. 217-238.

6. "Letter from John C. Faye to Rt. Rev. Jean Rigal Elisee, Bishop of The Gambia, dated 28 April 1972," Banjul: Anglican Diocesan Archives, File 84/207, p. 1. Also, "Gambia Mourns J. C." in: *Programme for Funeral and Requiem Mass for the Late Very Reverend John Colley Faye.* Bathurst: Government Printer, 1985.

7. Hughes, A., and Perfect, D. *Political History of The Gambia,* op.cit., p. 27-28.

8. Letter from John C. Faye to Bishop Elisee, op. cit., p. 1.

9. Ibid., p. 2.

10. On the College of Teachers see: www.college of teachers.acuk/about/what-we-do.

11. See: CPE, hppt://en.wikpedia.org/wiki/Certificate of Proficiency in English.

Chapter 1: Educationist: Planting Institutions

1. On education in the early days of settlement see Mahoney, Florence, *Government and Opinion in The Gambia, 1816-1901,* doctoral dissertation, School of Oriental and African Studies, University of London, 1963, Chapter 4.

2. Ibid., p. 171.

3. Hughes and Perfect, *A Political History of The Gambia,* op. cit., p. 27.

4. Initially, the name was given to re-captives from among the Yoruba peoples of south-western Nigeria and the Ibos of eastern Nigeria who had been rescued from slavery and settled in The Gambia; in time, it was extended to include the Westernized Christian descendants of these re-captives, and free slaves, particularly those from Sierra Leone, who migrated to The Gambia. As to the meaning of the word, some authors claim that it was derived from "Eko", a Yoruba greeting; there is also the view that it came from "Acoo" an Ibo word meaning "wealth" with which local Ibos settlers identified this group.

    A few references include the following: Mahoney, F., *Government and Opinion,* op. cit., chapters 4 and 5; Mahoney, F., *A Creole Saga: The*

Gambia's Liberated African Community in the Nineteenth Century, 2006; Fyle, C., and Jones, E., *Krio-English Dictionary,* New York: OUP, 1980; Sonko-Godwin, P., *Ethnic Groups of the Senegambia: A Brief History,* Banjul: Book Production and Materials Resources Unit, 1985; Mwakikagile, Godfrey, *Ethnic Diversity and Integration in The Gambia,* op. cit. pp. 238-262; Porter, A., *Creoledom,* Oxford: O.U.P., 1966.

5. Mahoney, *Government and Opinion,* op. cit., p. 192.
6. Hughes and Perfect, *A Political History of The Gambia,* op. cit. p. 28.
7. Letter from John C. Faye to Bishop Elisee, op. cit., p. 2.
8. Quoted in: Jones, S. H. M., *The Diocese of Gambia and the Rio Pongas, 1935-1951. Its origins and Early History,* Banjul: BPMRU, 1986, pp. 37-38.
9. Daly, J., *Four Mitres: Reminiscences of an Irrepressible Bishop,* Parts I and II, London: n.p., 1983, p. 25.
10. Jones, *The Diocese of The Gambia,* op. cit., p. 29.
11. Daly, *Four Mitres,* op. cit., Part II, p. 4.
12. Laughton, J., *Gambia: Colony, People and Church in the Diocese of Gambia and Rio Pongas,* 2nd Edition, London: SPG, 1949, p. 37.
13. Letter from Colonial Office to SPG, June 1942, quoted in letter from SPG to Sir John Paul Governor, Government House, Banjul: Anglican Diocesan Archives, File: Anglican Mission. Also Jones, *The Diocese of The Gambia,* op. cit., p. 43.
14. Daly, *Four Mitres,* op. cit., Pt. II, p. 39.
15. Letter from N. M. Asheton, Commissioner, Upper River Province, to the Bishop of Gambia, dated 29 January 1942, Banjul: Anglican Mission Archives, file 84/127.
16. Letter from Archdeacon Cyril Mudford to Bishop Daly, dated 14 January 1944, Banjul: Anglican Diocesan Archives, file J. C. Faye, loose document.
17. Jones, *The Diocese of The Gambia,* op. cit., p. 44.
18. Letter from John C. Faye to Bishop Elisee, op. cit., pp. 5-6.
19. Letter from SPG to Governor John Paul, 1962, Banjul: Anglican Diocesan Archives, file 84/127, p. 1.
20. Letter from John C. Faye to Bishop Elisee, op. cit., p. 6.

21. Report of the Bishop of The Gambia on his Visit, Banjul: Anglican Diocesan Archives, file 84/127.

22. Letter from John C. Faye to Bishop Elisee, op. cit., pp. 8-9.

23. Ibid., pp. 8-9.

24. Letter from Bishop Daly to the Senior Education Officer, dated 4 January 1949, Banjul: Anglican Diocesan Archives, file 84/127.

25. Laughton, J., *Gambia: Colony, People and Church,* op. cit., p. 37.

26. Ibid., p. 40.

27. Ibid., loc. cit.

28. Jones, *The Diocese of The Gambia,* op. cit., p. 46.

29. Ibid., p. 45.

30. Letter from J. Baylcy to Honourable Colonial Secretary, dated 20 July 1943, Banjul: Anglican Diocesan Archives, file 84/127.

31. Ibid., loc. cit.

32. Letter from E. R. Ward, Colonial Secretary to Bishop Daly, dated 19 May 1949, London: National Archives, file 879/189.

33. Jones, S. H. M., "My Visit to Kristi-kunda," 1955, Banjul: Anglican Diocesan Archives, loose document, p. 1.

34. Jones, S. H. M., "My Visit to Kristi-kunda," op. cit., p. 2.

35. Letter from SPG to Governor John Paul, op. cit., p. 2.

36. Ibid., p. 2.

37. Letter from Brooke to Bishop Olufosoye, 15 March 1966, Bathurst: Anglican Diocesan Archives, loose document.

38. Letter from Alex Yorke, Headteacher, to Bishop Olufosoye, 21 September 1966, Banjul: Anglican Diocesan Archives, File: Anglican Mission.

39. Bishop to Yorke, dated 28 September 1966, Banjul: Anglican Diocesan Archives, file Anglican Mission.

40. A. C. Andrews, Education Officer, Primary, "Inspection Report on Kristi-kunda School, U. R. D.: A School run by the Anglican Mission", Banjul: Anglican Diocesan Archives, October 1966, p. 1.

41. Letter from James Baker to the Minister of Education, dated 4 November 1966, Bathurst: Anglican Diocesan Archives, file Anglican Mission, p. 1.

42. Extract from report of "Director of Education's tour of Schools in the Upper River Division, 20-25 February 1967", Banjul: Anglican Diocesan Archives, file Anglican Mission.

43. Record of Meeting of Ad Hoc Committee on Kristi-kunda, 12 July 1968, Banjul: Anglican Mission Archives, file Anglican Mission, loose document.

44. Roberts, G. J., "Tour of Provincial Schools, 7-11 January 1969", Banjul: Anglican Diocesan Archives, file Anglican Mission, loose document.

45. Sourced from a paper by Head Teacher James Baker, "The Close down of Kristi-kunda School, November 1969", Bathurst: Anglican Diocesan Archives, file Anglican Mission.

Chapter 2: Educationist:
Planting Institutions—The Seed Multiplies

1. "Bishop's Address at the Official Opening of J. C. Faye Memorial Nursery School—24 June 1992", Banjul: Anglican Diocesan Archives, file J. C. Faye Memorial Nursery School, mimeo p. 3.

2. Interview with Francis Jones, Banjul, 8 October 2011.

3. "Anglican Diocese of The Gambia, Rev. J. C. Faye Memorial Nursery School, School Bus Project", Banjul: Anglican Diocesan Archives, file: J. C. Faye Memorial Nursery School, p. 1.

4. "Bishop's Address for the Official Opening of J. C. Faye Memorial Nursery School—24 June 1992", op. cit. p. 1.

5. Letter from Rev. Johnson to Mrs. C. Faye, Anglican Diocesan Archives, Banjul, file: J. C. Faye.

6. Letter from Permanent Secretary, Ministry of Education, dated 2 June 1875, Banjul: Anglican Diocesan Archives, file AVTC, 1972-73-74.

7. Memorandum on "Present State of the Project and the Next Steps to be Taken", Banjul: Anglican Diocesan Archives, file Anglican Church of Canada, p. 4.

8. Address of Bishop Elisee at the Ground-breaking ceremony of the AVTC, Banjul: Anglican Diocesan Archives, 27 March 1977, file Anglican Mission AAVTC, p. 1.

9. "Ground-breaking Ceremony for the Anglican Vocational Training Centre, Farafenni", Banjul: Anglican Diocesan Archives, file Anglican Mission.

10. Minutes of Twelfth Board Meeting, 12 November 1977, Banjul: Anglican Diocesan Archives, file Anglican Mission.

11. Address at the Ground-breaking Ceremony for the AVTC, Banjul: Anglican Diocesan Archives, file: Anglican Mission, p. 2.

12. Board Minutes of the Eleventh Meeting, 11 October 1977, Banjul: Anglican Diocesan Archives, file AVTC.

13. Letter dated 29 January 1973, from Nora Cleaver to Bishop Olufosoye, Banjul: Anglican Diocesan Archives, file African Training Centre 1972-73-74.

14. Letter from Permanent Secretary, dated 25 January 1973, Banjul: Anglican Diocesan Archives, file Anglican Vocational Training Centre, 1972-1973-1974.

15. Anglican Church of Canada, Request for Programme Development Assistance to CIDA, Banjul: Anglican Diocesan Archives, file: Anglican Training Centre, 1972-73-74.

16. Anglican Church of Canada, Request for Programme Development Assistance to CIDA, op. cit., p. 2.

17. Letter from George Cram to Bishop Elisee, dated 28 May 1975, Banjul: Anglican Diocesan Archives, file AVTC 1972-73-74.

18. George Cram, Memorandum on "Present Status of the Project and the Next Steps to be Taken", dated 30 May 1975, Banjul: Anglican Diocesan Archives, file: Anglican Church of Canada, p. 2.

19. "Report of the Fourth Review Commission, Anglican Training Centre", pp. 5-14 December 1984, Banjul: Anglican Diocesan Archives, File: Anglican Training Centre.

20. Letter from George Cram, Development Projects Officer, PWRDF, to Faye, Chairman, Board of Governors, AVTC, dated 31 January 1977, Banjul: Anglican Diocesan Archives, file AVTC.

21. "Final Review of the Anglican Vocational Training Centre", PWRDF and CIDA, 1988, Banjul: Anglican Diocesan Archives, file Anglican Church of Canada, p. 8.

22. Letter from Romeo Maione, NGO Division, CIDA to Rev. R. D. MacRae, Secretary, Anglican Church of Canada, Toronto, Canada,

dated 22 March 1977, Banjul: Anglican Diocesan Archives, file AVTC.

23. Letter from George Cram, Development Projects Officer, Church of Canada to Rev. J. C. Faye, Chairman of the Board, dated 31 January 1977, Banjul: Anglican Diocesan Archives, file Anglican Mission, AVTC, pp. 2-5.

24. M. E. Millard, "Minutes of an emergency meeting of the Board of Governors of the AVTC", 24 June 1977, Banjul: Anglican Diocesan Archives.

25. "Final Review of the Anglican Vocational Training Centre", PWRDF and CIDA, 1988, Banjul: Anglican Diocesan Archives, file Anglican Church of Canada, p. 12.

26. Ibid., p.1.

27. Minutes, Board Meeting, 8 March 1980.

28. Interview, Serre-kunda, 16 October 2001.

29. See: Peter Hawkins, "Report for Period December 1st 1976 to April 1st 1977", dated 5 April 1977, Banjul: Anglican Diocesan Archives, file AVTC, p. 1.

30. Interview with Rev. J. C. Faye conducted by Bakary Sidibe, 16 December 1982. Private collection.

Chapter 3: Politician: Blazing the Path

1. Hughes and Perfect, *Political History of The Gambia*, op. cit., p. 78.

2. Hughes and Perfect, *The Political History of The Gambia*, op. cit., pp. 447-48, quoting Newbury, C., *British Policy Toward West Africa: Select Documents, 1786-1874,* Oxford: Clarendon Press, 1964, pp. 47-48.

3. Ibid., Table B.1, Legislative Council election results, p. 298.

4. On the process of selection of the Protectorate members, see: London: National Archives, file 87/260/2.

5. See "Legislative Council Representation", Letter from Senior Commissioner N. A. C. Weir to Colonial Secretary, dated 15 June 1947, Banjul: National Records Services, file 84/25; Legislative Council Nomination of Members under the 1946 Instruments. Letter reference no. S1526A.

6. Letter from Governor Barkworth Wright to Secretary of State for the Colonies, dated 27 September 1947, Banjul: National Records Services, file 84/27, Subject: "Legislative Council: Nomination of Members under 1946 Instruments", Reference S1526A, para. 4.

7. Letter J. C. Faye to Bishop Jean Elisee, op. cit., p. 7.

8. Loc. cit., p.7.

9. Letter from Governor Barkworth Wright to Secretary of State for the Colonies, dated 27 September 1947, op. cit., para.5.

10. Hughes and Perfect, *A Political History of The Gambia,* op. cit., pp. 45-46.

11. See *Gambia Outlook and Senegambia Reporter*, GOSR, 11 October 1947, p. 3.

12. Letter from A. B. Wright to A. B. Cohen, Colonial Office, dated 5 April 1948, London: National Archives, file 847/38/5.

13. Confidential letter from A, B. Cohen, Colonial Office, to Barkworth Wright, Governor, dated 12 April 1948, London: National Archives, file 847/38/5.

14. Confidential letter from Barkworth Wright to A. B. Cohen, Colonial Office, dated 1 May 1948, London: National Archives, file 847/38/5.

15. "The African Conference 1948", London: National Archives, file CO 847/38/5.

16. "African Conference in London 1948" (http://www.colonialfilm.org.uk/node/1007).

17. Ibid.

18. Letter from J. C. Faye to Bishop Elisee, op. cit.

19. All of the above quotations in telegram dated 12 May 1949, file CO 554/422.

20. Resolution passed at the Extra-ordinary Meeting of Council, held on Monday 16 May 1949, London: National Archives, file CO 554/422.

21. "Petition to The Right Honourable Arthur Creech Jones", dated 18 May 1949, London: National Archives, file CO 554/422.

22. Personal letter from J. C. Faye to Arthur Creech Jones, Secretary of State for the Colonies, dated 18 May 1949, London: National Archives, file CO 554/422.

23. Ibid.

24. Petition to the Rt. Hon. A. Creech Jones, Secretary of State for the Colonies, London: National Archives, file CO 554/422.

25. Letter dated 16 May 1949, London: National Archives, file CO 554/422.

26. Note from Creech Jones to Governor Wright, dated 16 May 1949, London: National Archives, file CO 554/422.

27. Confidential memo. No. 137, "Departure of Sir Andrew Wright", from Secretary of State to Governor A. B. Wright, dated 30 May 1949, London: National Archives, file 554/422.

28. Detailed treatment of this subject in Berg, E. J. and Butler, J., "Trade Unions" in: Coleman, J., and Rosberg, C., *Political Parties and National Integration in Africa*, Berkeley: University of California Press, 1970, pp. 340-381.

29. Gambia Teachers Union, Rules and Regulations, Banjul: National Records Services, file Gambia Teachers Union.

30. Letter from Wilson Plan, Superintendent of Education to Honorary Secretary, Gambia Teachers Union, dated 13 July 1937, Banjul: National Records Services, file Gambia Teachers Union.

31. See Perfect, D., "Organized Labour and Politics in The Gambia, 1920-1984", Ph.D. dissertation, University of Birmingham, 1987, pp. 117-121.

32. West African Youth League (1937) Constitution of Rules, Regulations and Bye-Laws, Etc, and Obligations and Benefits, Accra.

33. Interview with Rev. J. C. Faye conducted by Bakary Sidibe, Banjul, 22 December 1982. Private collection.

34. Ibid.

35. "Mass Meeting held at the Catholic Mission Schoolroom, Hagan Street, Bathurst, on Thursday, 22 February 1951", confidential report prepared by the Superintendent of Police, dated 24 February 1951, London: National Archives.

36. See: "The Gambia's Amiable Example" *West Africa*, 30 August 1952, p. 803; Nyang, S., "Historical Development of Gambian Political Parties", *Africa Research Bulletin,* vol. 5, no. 4, 1975.

37. Perfect, "Organized Labour", op. cit., p.117.

38. Senghor, Jeggan, C., *The Politics of Senegambian Integration: 1958-1994,* Oxford: Peter Lang International Academic Publishers, 2008, p. 76.

39. Cham-Joof, *History of the trade union movement in The Gambia,* mimeo, n.d., n.p.

40. Hughes, A. and Perfect, D., *Political History,* op. cit. footnote 37, p. 372; "Changes in Gambia's Executive Council", *New Commonwealth,* October 1951, p. 309.

41. Hughes, A. and Perfect, D., *Political History of The Gambia,* op. cit., Table B2 Appendix B, p. 299; "The Gambia Has Elections, Ministers and a Speaker", *West Africa,* 24 November 1951, p. 1095; "Elections to The Gambia's Legislative Council", *New Commonwealth,* December 1951, p. 473.

42. See: "Democratic Party Programme", *Gambia Echo,* 10 September 1951 and 24 September 1951.

43. H. R. H. Rowland, "Gambia—Election manifestos, 1951", 8 October 1951, London: National Archives, file CO 554/536.

44. See: "M. M. NJie", *West Africa,* 3-19 August 1990, p. 272.

45. Letter from Colonial Secretary E. R. Ward to H. R. H. Rowland of the Colonial Office, dated 17 November 1951, London: National Archives, file CO 554/536.

46. Letter from E. R. Ward, Colonial Secretary, to H. R. H. Rowland, Colonial Office, dated 17 November 1951, London: National Archives, file CO 554/422.

47. Letter from H. R. H. Rowland, Colonial Office to E. R. Ward, Colonial Secretary, Bathurst, dated 23 November 1951, London: National Archives, file CO 554/536.

48. Appointment Letter from Colonial Secretary E. R. Ward to Faye and Garba-Jahumpa, dated 14 November 1951, London: National Archives, file CO 554/575.

Chapter 4: Politician: Beginnings of the Struggle for Power

1. Hughes, A., and Perfect, D., *Historical Dictionary of The Gambia,* op. cit., p. 121.

2. See *The Hibar,* organ of the Muslim Congress, January 1954, Issue 1.

3. "The Gambia's First Minister" *West Africa*, 12 December 1952, p. 1157.

4. Cham-Joof, A. E., *History of the Trade Union Movement*, op.cit.

5. See: "P. S. NJie", *West Africa*, 3 May 1958, p. 411; and "Man of The People", *West Africa*, 29 July 1961, p. 823.

6. Senghor, Jeggan, *The Politics of Senegambian Integration*, op. cit., p. 56.

7. Communication from Baaba Sillah, 17 April 2012.

8. Alieu E. Cham-Joof, *History of Trade Unionism in The Gambia*, op. cit.

9. "Our Election Campaign", Banjul, *The Vanguard*, 9 April 1960, p. 2. See also "Politics in the Gambia", *West Africa*, 21 May 1960 and "Dragon's Teeth," *Vanguard*, 17 May 1960, p. 2.

10. Extract from The Gambia Political Intelligence Report, dated April 1953, London: National Archives, file 554/221.

11. On its composition, deliberations and recommendations see: "Public Announcement", *Gambia News Bulletin*, 29 April 1953 p. 1; "Proposed new constitution for the Gambia as put forward by the Consultative Committee", *Gambia Outlook and Senegambia Reporter*, 8 August 1953, p. 1.

12. Gambia: Political Intelligence Report, January 1952, dated 23 February 1953, London: National Archives, file CO 554/382, p. 1.

13. "Constitutional Reform—The Gambia," Report from Governor Wyn Harris to Secretary of State, dated 22 May 1953, London: National Archives, file CO 554/250, p. 1.

14. Ibid., loc. cit.

15. See: Hughes and Perfect, *Political History of The Gambia*, op. cit., pp. 122-23.

16. See also: Letter from Wyn-Harris to Gorsuch, Colonial Office, dated 9 May 1951, London: National Archives, file CO 554/250.

17. Ibid.

18. For a more detailed commentary on this report by Wyn-Harris see: Letter from P. Wyn-Harris to Sir Thomas Lloyd, Colonial Office, dated 7 March 1952, London: National Archives, file 554/250.

19. "Note of a meeting in the Colonial Office on the 9th October 1952", London: National Archives, file CO 554/250.

20. J. C. Faye, "Gambia's New Constitution", *West Africa*, 17 October 1953, p. 971.

21. Ibid., loc. cit.

22. Ibid., loc. cit.

23. Ibid., loc. cit.

24. Ibid., loc. cit.

25. For more see: Wyn Harris to Gorell Barnes, 14 November 1953, London: National Archives, file CO 554/251; Wyn-Harris to Lyttleton, 31 October 1953, London: National Archives, file CO 554/422; Lyttleton to Wyn-Harris, 23 November 1953, London: National Archives, file 554/422; *Gambia Echo*, 7 December 1953.

26. "New Constitution" in Supplement to Gambia News Bulletin, 9 June 1954.

27. Letter from Wyn-Harris to Gorell-Barnes, dated 14 November 1953, London: National Archives, file 554/250, p. 5.

28. "Summary of Gambia Constitutional Proposals", London: National Archives, file CO 554/250.

29. Letter from Governor Wyn-Harris to Secretary of State Oliver Lyttleton, dated 12 June 1953, London: National Archives, file CO 554/250, p. 3.

30. See: "The Gambia's General Elections". *West Africa* 6 November 1954, p. 1036 and "Three Ministers Appointed in The Gambia", *West Africa*, 4 December 1954, p. 1143.

31. Interview with Rev. J. C. Faye conducted by B. K. Sidibe and K. Saplaha, 10 November 1982. Private collection.

32. "Legislative Council Election Results", Bathurst: *Gambia News Bulletin*, 20 October 1954.

33. See: Chapter 5 below; also Waddell to Williamson, 21 March 1953 and Wyn-Harris to Lyttleton, 31 October 1953, London: National Archives, file CO 554/422.

34. See, for example, Hughes and Perfect, *Political History of The Gambia,* op. cit., pp. 123-127 and footnotes.

35. On this and related issues see: "Three Ministers Appointed in The Gambia", *West Africa*, 4 December 1954, p. 1143.

36. The selection process is discussed in: Wyn-Harris to Secretary of State, 4 November 1954, London: National Archives, file CO 554/801.

Also, Wyn-Harris to Secretary of State, 20 May 1952, London: National Archives, file CO 554/250.

37. Letter from J. C. Faye to Bishop Elisee, op. cit, p. 3.
38. Ibid., p. 11.
39. Ibid., p. 12.

Chapter 5: Politician: Contending with the Colonial Order

1. Interview with J. C. Faye conducted by B. K. Sidibe, 21 December 1982. Private collection.
2. Letter from J. C. Faye to Bishop Elisee, op. cit., p. 10.
3. "Moral Re-Armament", wikipedia.org.
4. Ibid.
5. "John Colley Faye", Secret Report, Special Branch, dated 29 November 1952, London: National Archives, file CO 554/422.
6. "Gambia Students' Union", *Gambia Echo*, 24 November 1952, p. 4.
7. "John Colley Faye", Secret Report, Special Branch, op. cit.
8. Letter from Colonial Secretary to Colonial Office, dated 29 November 1952, London: National Archives, file CO 554/422.
9. Memo from Rowland in file CO554/422.
10. "Note of a Meeting between the Secretary of State and the Unofficial Members of the Gambian Legislative Council, Bathurst, The Gambia, Thursday, 12 June 1952", p. 1. London: National Archives, file CO 554/422.
11. Ibid., p. 2.
12. Ibid., loc. cit.
13. "Note for the Secretary of State", from Wyn-Harris to Secretary of State, dated 7 June 1952, London: National Archives, file CO 554/250.
14. "Note for the Secretary of State", op. cit., p. 2.
15. "Report of Sir Gorell Barnes on a discussion with the three Elected members of the Legislative Council—the Hon. and Rev. J. C. Faye, M. B. E., The Hon. Henry Madi, The Hon. Garba-Jahumpa", dated 20 June 1952, London: National Archives, file CO 554/250, p. 1.
16. Ibid., p. 2.
17. Ibid., p. 3.

18. The Gambia: Political Intelligence Report, January to June 1952, dated 15 July 1952, London: National Archives, file CO 554/382, p. 2.

19. Ibid., loc. cit.

20. Ibid., loc. cit.

21. Letter from Faye to Wyn Harris, dated 30 June 1952, London: National Archives, file CO 554/422.

22. Letter from Wyn-Harris to Faye, dated 1 July 1952, London: National Archives, file CO 552/422.

23. Letter from Faye to Wyn-Harris dated 2 July 1952, London: National Archives, file CO 554/422.

24. Letter from Wyn-Harris to Faye, dated 4 July 1952, London: National Archives, file CO 554/422.

25. Letter from I.M. Garba-Jahumpa to Wyn-Harris, dated 1 July 1952, London: National Archives, file CO 554/422.

26. Letter from Madi to Wyn-Harris, dated 29 June 1952, London: National Archives, file CO 554/422.

27. Letter, Wyn-Harris to Gorell Barnes, Assistant Under-Secretary of State, dated 10 July 1952, London: National Archives, file CO 554/422.

28. Letter from Romford to Hopkinson, dated 31 March 1953, National Archives, London, file CO 554/422. Also in same file, Wyn-Harris to Secretary of State, memo dated 16 August 1952.

29. Political Intelligence Report, January to June 1952, London: National Archives, file CO 554/382, p. 2.

30. "Announcement", Supplement to the *Gambia News Bulletin*, 28 July 1952, London: National Archives, file CO 554/422.

31. Letter from Wyn-Harris to Gorell Barnes, dated 26 July 1952, London: National Archives, file CO 554/422.

32. Ibid.

33. Letter Wyn-Harris to Faye, dated 25 July 1952, National Archives, London, file CO 554/422.

34. Letter Faye to Wyn-Harris, dated 26 July 1952, London: National Archives, file CO 554/422. Full details of these events given in "Rev. Faye asked to resign", *West Africa*, 19 July 1952, p. 659.

35. Copy of telegram, dated 5 August 1952, London: National Archives, file CO 554/422.

36. "The Gambia's Amiable Example," *West Africa* 30 May 1952, p. 803.

37. Copy of telegram, dated 5 August 1952, loc. sit.

38. Letter from Wyn-Harris to Oliver Lyttleton, dated 16 August 1952, London: National Archives, file CO 554/422.

39. Letter from Faye to O. C. NJie, Clerk of Council, dated 23 March 1953, London: National Archives, file CO 554/422.

40. Letter, A. S. N. A. Waddell, Colonial Secretary, to Faye, dated 28 March 1953, London: National Archives, file CO 554/422.

41. Letter from Faye to Colonial Secretary, dated 7 April 1953, London: National Archives, file CO 554/422.

42. Political Intelligence Report for April 1953, dated 12 May 1953, file: CO 554/ 382, p. 2.

43. "Report of the circumstances surrounding the vacation by the Honourable and Reverend John Faye, M. B. E. of his seat on the Executive Council of the Colony and Protectorate of The Gambia", Enclosure to Gambia despatch No. 562/53 dated 31 October 1953, London: National Archives, file CO 554/422.

44. Letter from Governor to Secretary of State, dated 21 April 1953, London: National Archives, file CO 554/422.

45. The Gambia: Political Intelligence Report, September 1953, London: National Archives, file CO 554/382, p. 1.

46. Telegram from OAG to Secretary of State for the Colonies, dated 21 September 1953, London: National Archives, file CO 554/422.

47. Internal Memo, dated 24 September 1953, London: National Archives, file CO 554/422.

48. These and other quotations below from: Letter from Faye to Oliver Lyttleton, dated 30 September 1953, London: National Archives, file CO 554/422.

49. Letter accompanying petition from Alieu Cham Joof, dated 3 October 1953, London: National Archives, file CO 554/422.

50. "Report of the circumstances surrounding the vacation by the Honourable and Reverend John Faye", London: National Archives, file CO 554/422.

51. Letter from Oliver Lyttleton to Wyn-Harris, dated 23 November 1953, London: National Archives, file CO 554/422.

52. Letter from Governor Wyn-Harris to Secretary of State Oliver Lyttelton, dated 31 October 1953, London: National Archives, File CO 554/422.

53. Letter from Oliver Lyttleton to Wyn Harris, dated 23 November 1953, London: National Archives, file CO 554/422.

54. Letter from J. C. Faye to Bishop Elisee, op. cit., p. 10.

55. Letter from T. B. Williamson, Colonial Office, to A. N. A. Waddell, Colonial Secretary, dated 8 December 1952, London: National Archives, file CO 554/422.

56. The Gambia: Political Intelligence Report, December 1952, dated 30 December 1952, London: National Archives, file CO 554382, p. 1.

57. Letter from Waddell, Colonial Secretary, to Williamson, Colonial Office, dated 6 February 1953, London: National Archives, file CO 554/422.

58. Political Intelligence Report, February 1953 dated 4 March 1953, file CO 554/382, p. 2.

59. Letter from Colonial Secretary to T. B. Williamson, Colonial Office, dated 21 March 1953, London: National Archives, File CO 554/422.

60. Letter from Williamson (Colonial Office) to Waddell (Colonial Secretary) dated 7 March 1953, London: National Archives, file CO 554/422.

61. *Gambia Echo*, 18 May 1953. In parenthesis, P. S. NJie was the counsel for C. R. Page, the judgement creditor.

62. Letter from Colonial Secretary to Williamson, Colonial Office, Dated 6 January 1953, London: National Archives, file CO 554/422.

63. Letter from Secretary of State Oliver Lyttleton to Governor Wyn-Harris, dated 23 November 1953, London: National Archives, file 554/422.

64. Letter from Colonial Secretary to Williamson, Colonial Office, dated 6 January 1953, London: National Archives, file CO 554/422.

65. Letter from Gorell Barnes to Wyn-Harris, dated 20 April 1953, London: National Archives, file CO 554/422.

66. Memo from Hopkinson to Rowland, both in Colonial Office, dated 31 March 1953, London: National Archives, file 554/422.

67. Letter from Romford to Hopkinson dated 31 March 1953, London: National Archives, file CO 554/422.

68. Ibid.

69. Letter from Colonial Secretary Waddell to Williamson (Colonial Office) dated 6 January 1953, London: National Archives, file CO 554/422.

70. Letter from Governor Wyn-Harris to Gorell-Barnes, Colonial Office, dated 14 November 1953, London: National Archives, file CO 554/251.

71. Political Intelligence Report, January-June 1952, London: National Archives, file CO 554/382, p. 1.

72. Interview with J. C. Faye conducted by Bakary K. Sidibe, 22 December 1982. Private collection.

73. See "Police Report, 1958", London: National Archives, file: CO 89/39.

74. For an even more damming assessment see: "Periscoping the Administration of Sir Percy: Forecasting Future Trends in Gambian Affairs", Bathurst: *The Vanguard*, 26 April 1958, pp. 1, 6.

75. "Exit Sir Percy" by Mr. Gambia, Bathurst: *The Vanguard*, 29 March 1958, pp. 1, 6.

Chapter 6: Politician: A Bumpy Political Terrain

1. Rev. J. C. Faye, Party Political Radio Speech, 1962, mimeo. Bathurst, p. 2.

2. Hughes and Perfect, *A Political History of The Gambia,* op. cit., pp. 128-29.

3. "Note for Windley", London: National Archives, file CO 554/1513.

4. Crowder, M., "The Gambia Political Scene", *West Africa*, 2 November 1957 p. 1035.

5. See Perfect, "Organized Labour and Politics in The Gambia, 1920-1984"; "Organized Labour and Politics in The Gambia", *Labour, Capital, and Society*, vol. 19, no. 2; Hughes and Perfect, "Trade Unionism in The Gambia," *African Affairs*, vol. 88, no. 353, October 1989.

6. See "Behind the Gambia Strikes", *West Africa*, 19 March 1960, p. 321.

7. "Politics in The Gambia", *West Africa*, 21 May 1960, p. 563.

8. See: Windley to Eastwood dated 29 February 1960, London: National Archives, file CO 554/2498.

9. "Summary of Proceedings of the Fifteenth Conference of Protectorate Chiefs, held at Brikama, Western Division, from the 18th February to 21st February 1958", Bathurst: Government Printer, Sessional Paper 4/58, p. 23.

10. See "Sir Percy sees a Revolution", *West Africa*, 15 March 1958, p. 251.

11. See: Crowder, M., "Chiefs in Gambia Politics: 1", *West Africa*, 18 October 1958, p. 987 and "Chiefs in Gambia Politics: 2", *West Africa*, 25 October 1958, p. 1017; "Constitutional Changes Discussed", *Africa Digest*, vol. 6 no 3 1958, pp. 119-120.

12. See: Crowder, M., "Chiefs in Gambia Politics: 1", *West Africa*, 18 October 1958, p. 987.

13. Ibid., loc. cit.

14. Interview with Rev. J. C. Faye conducted by Bakary K. Sidibe, 22 December 1982. Private collection.

15. See: Senghor, Jeggan C., *Politics of Senegambian Integration*, op. cit., pp, 58-61.

16. Special Editorial Commission, *The Voice of the People: The Story of the PPP, 1959-1989*, Banjul: Baroueli publications, 1992.

17. Gambia Government, *The Gambia, 1958 and 1959*, Bathurst: Government Printer, 1960, p. 3.

18. On the Georgetown Conference see: Windley to Eastwood, London: National Archives, 27 February 1959, file: CO 879/189.

19. "Summary of Proceedings of the Sixteenth Conference of Protectorate Chiefs, held at Basse, Upper River Division from 10th to 14th February 1059", Bathurst: Government Printer, 1959, p. 20.

20. See: Chiefs Annual Conference, *Vanguard*, 21 February 1959; 'Gambia's Protectorate Parliament," *West Africa* 28 March 1959, p. 295.

21. "Record of Meeting of Chiefs . . .", *Gambia Echo*, 9 February 1959.

22. Clark, A., "Constitutional Problems in The Gambia", *West Africa*, 31 May 1958, p. 511. See also: "Exit Sir Percy", *Vanguard*, 29 March 1958, p. 6; "A Testing Time," *Gambia Echo*, 24 February 1958, p. 4.

23. See: "Report of Meeting of All-Party Committee", *Gambia Echo*, 5 May 1958, p. 4; also: "The Gambian Political Scene", *West Africa*, 2 November 1957, p. 1035.

24. See: *Gambia Echo*, 2 November 1958.

25. See: "Our Political Parties and Party Government", *Vanguard*, 17 May 1958.

26. See: "How far do we go by the New Constitution?", *Gambia Echo*, 11 August 1958; "Our Political Parties and Party Government", *Vanguard,* 17 May 1958, p. 4.

27. "Chiefs' Annual Conference", *Vanguard*, 21 February 1959, op. cit.

28. See: "Record of Constitutional Conference Held in Bathurst," March 1959, Sessional Paper 3 of 1959, Bathurst: Government Printer.

29. "Constitutional Conference," *Gambia News Bulletin,* Banjul, 6-13 March 1959.

30. See "Record of the Meeting", enclosure to letter from Windley to Macleod, 3 November 1959, London: National Archives, file: CO 554/1518.

31. "Georgetown Constitutional Conference", *The Gambia Echo,* 9 February 1959, p. 8.

32. See: Perfect, "Organized Labour and Politics in The Gambia", op. cit., p. 160; also, Letter from Windley to Eastwood, dated 15 June 1959, London: National Archives, CO 554/1518 and CO 879/189; record of the meeting with Lennox-Boyd, 5 June 1959, file: CO 554/1518.

33. Same sources as for footnote 32.

34. Cham-Joof, "Note on Meeting", op. cit., p. 9.

35. Ibid., p. 10.

36. Despatch No. 366/59 of 15 June 1959, from the Governor to the Secretary of State, in: "Constitutional Development in The Gambia", Bathurst: Government Printer, Sessional Paper No. 4 of 1959. All footnotes, from 37 to 44, are from this source.

37. Ibid., paragraph 4.

38. Ibid., paragraph 10.

39. Ibid., paragraph 11.

40. Ibid., paragraph 11.

41. Ibid., paragraphs 12, 13.

42. Ibid., paragraph 13.

43. Ibid., paragraph 16.

44. Ibid., paragraph 18.

45. Confidential letter No 389, from Alan Lennox-Boyd to the Officer Administering the Government of The Gambia, dated 8 September 1959, Bathurst: Government Printer, Sessional paper 4 of 1959, page 9.

46. See: Memo from Windley to Lennox-Boyd, 7 May 1959, London: National Archives, file: CO 879/189; Windley to Eastwood 13 November 1958 and Windley to Eastwood, 24 March 1959, in same file.

47. See memo from Windley to Eastwood, 24 March 1959, London: National Archives, file: CO 879/189; Windley to Eastwood, 7 May 1959, same file; and Eastwood to Windley, 13 April 1959, same file.

48. Letter from Windley to Macleod, 3 December 1959, file: CO 879/189.

49. List of Committee members given in *Gambia Echo*, 2 November 1959.

50. See Memo Windley to Eastwood dated 27 October 1959, London: National Archives, file: CO 554/1518; also, Windley to Macloud 3 November 1959 and Macloud to Windley, 20 November 1959 in the same file. Both rejected the proposals in the petitions. See also Memo from Windley to Eastwood, dated 15 June 1959, file: CO 879/189.

51. "The Chiefs Conference: A special sitting", *Gambia Echo*, 3 February 1958; "The Gambia's darkest day", *Gambia Echo*, 24 February 1958; "A testing time", *Gambia Echo*, 24 February 1958.

52. See Perfect, "Organized Labour and Politics in The Gambia," op. cit. pp. 117-19.

53. See: *Gambia News Bulletin*, 16 October 1959, p. 1, for the results.

54. "Announcement: The Democratic Congress Alliance", *The Vanguard*, 9 April 1960, p. 2.

55. Broadcast talk by Rev. J. C. Faye, Party Leader, Democratic Congress Alliance, 17 May 1962, loose memeo.

56. "Announcement: The Democratic Congress Alliance", op. cit.

57. Letter dated 21 September 1964, Banjul: National Records Services, file EXA2/5, letter ref. GHC/166.

58. Jawara, D., *Kairaba: The Autobiography of Dawda K. Jawara,* Burgess Hill, West Sussex: Domtom Publishing, 2009, pp. 213-14.

59. *The Vanguard*, 12 March 1960.

Chapter 7: Politician: The Skies Darken

1. "Politics in The Gambia", *West Africa*, 21 May 1960, p. 563.
2. Ibid., loc. cit.
3. See: "Politics in The Gambia", *West Africa*, 21 May 1960, p. 563; "The Dragon's Teeth", *Vanguard* 17 May 1960, p. 2; "Our Election Campaign", *Vanguard*, 9 April 1960; "General Elections in The Gambia", *New Commonwealth*, July 1960, p. 468; "A Model Election", *Vanguard*, 28 May 1960.
4. Interview with Rev. J. C. Faye conducted by Bakary K. Sidibe, 22 December 1982. Private collection.
5. Interview with Assan Musa Camara conducted by the author, Banjul, 18 October 2011.
6. Letter from J. C. Faye to Bishop Elisee, op. cit., Schedule 2.
7. Interview with Rev. Faye conducted by Bakary K. Sidibe, 22 December 1982. Private collection.
8. Senghor, J. C., *The Politics of Senegambian Integration,* op. cit., p. 97.
9. On both crises much more detail and analysis given in ibid., pp. 92-98.
10. Interview with Rev. J. C. Faye conducted by Bakary K. Sidibe, op. cit., 22 December 1982. Private collection.
11. On the Conference see: "Record of the Constitutional Conference held in Bathurst from the 4th to 11th May 1961 with the Rt. Hon. The Earl of Perth's Opening Address", Bathurst: Government Printer, Sessional Paper No 6 of 1961, pp. 4-16.
12. See: "Despatch No. 302/61 of the 31 May 1961 from the Governor to the Secretary of State", Bathurst: Government Printer, Sessional Paper No. 6 of 1961, pp. 1-3.
13. Ibid., p. 1.
14. Ibid., p. 3.
15. "Report of the Gambia Constitutional Conference", London: Her Majesty's Stationary Office, August 1961, p. 2.
16. Ibid., pp. 4-6.

17. Broadcast Talk by Rev. J. C. Faye, Party Leader, Democratic Congress Alliance, 17 May 1962.

18. Democratic Congress Alliance, manifesto. 18 May 1962, mimeo, p. 1.

19. Ibid., p. 4.

20. "Campaigning in The Gambia", *West Africa*, 19 May 1962, p. 535.

21. "Address of H.E. the Governor Opening the Budget Session of the House of Representatives on 12 December 1961", Banjul: National Records Office, file: 87/13.

22. Faye, Letter to Overseas Friends, dated 12 July 1962, mimeo, Banjul: National Records Services, p. 1.

23. Quoted in: People's Progressive Party, *Voice of the People: the Story of the PPP, 1959—1989*, Banjul: Baroueli, 1992.

24. Hughes and Perfect, *A Political History of The Gambia*, op. cit., Table C.2, p. 306.

25. See letter from Governor Paul to Maudling, 7 June 1962, London: National Archives, file CO 554/2148.

26. BTC Election Results, *Gambia News Bulletin,* 27 October 1964.

27. Senghor, Jeggan C., *The Politics of Senegambian Integration*, op. cit., pp. 129-134

28. "Joint Statement, PPP-DCA and UP", *Gambia Echo*, 28 December 1964, p. 1; "Gambia Coalition Agreement", *Africa Digest*, 12.4, 1964, p. 115.

Chapter 8: Politician:
The Vicissitudes of Political and Personal Transitions

1. Interview with Rev. J. C. Faye conducted by Bakary K. Sidibe, 16 December 1982, op. cit. Private collection.

2. Peter Mendy, personal communication, 29 March 2011.

3. Letter to Mrs. E. H. Amoo-Adare, dated 19 June 1964, Bathurst: National Records Services, file: GHC/166.

4. Letter dated 1 July 1964 from R. D. Frith and Faye's response, Bathurst: National Records Services, file: GHC/166.

5. Letter from United Nations Association, Salisbury Branch, dated 9 July 1964, Bathurst: National Records Services, file: GHC/166.

6. Letter from Faye to R. K. O. Joiner, Banjul: National Records Services, file: GHC.

7. See "Gambia Intelligence Report", December 1964, London: National Archives, file: DO 195/382.

8. "Announcement", *Gambia News Bulletin*, 30 September 1965, p. 3.

9. Interview with Rev. J. C. Faye and Bakary Sidibe, op. cit., 16 December 1982. Private collection.

10. Hughes and Perfect, *A Political History of The Gambia*, op. cit., Table C.3, page 310.

11. "Broadcast talk by Rev. J. C. Faye, M. B. E., Party-Leader, Democratic Congress Alliance", 17 May 1962, mimeo, p. 2.

12. P/DCA Annual Conference' Gambia News Bulletin, Supplement, 9 April 1963.

13. Report of the PPP/DCA First Annual Conference, 9 April 1963, mimeo, p. 1.

14. "Report on Gambians Visiting Ghana" by Assistant Superintendent of Police, to the Civil Secretary, dated 7 July 1961, London: National Archives.

15. Letter, 22 September 1962, mimeo.

16. Report of the Gambia Constitutional Conference, 1961, London: Her Majesty's Stationery Office, August 1961, p. 3.

17. "Broadcast talk by Rev. J. C. Faye, M. B. E., Party-Leader, Democratic Congress Alliance", 17 May 1962, mimeo, pp. 2-3.

18. Senghor, Jeggan C., *The Politics of Senegambian Integration*, op. cit., p. 71.

19. Ibid., footnote 51, p. 73.

20. "Gambia's relations with Senegal and Mali", *Vanguard,* 5 December 1959, p. 2, Quoted in Senghor, op. cit., p. 77.

21. See: Senghor, Jeggan C., *The Politics of Senegambian Integration*, op. cit., footnotes 64 and 65 on page 78.

22. "Telegraphic Statement", in GPRO (Archives), file: 2/2369A.

23. "Constitutional Advance", *Africa Diary* 5-11 August 1961, pp. 64-65; "Fears of Gambian Delegates", *The Times*, 29 July 1961.

24. See Dunayevskaya, R., "In the Gambia during elections", *Africa Today*, vol. 9, no. 6, 1962.

25. Senghor, Jeggan C., *The Politics of Senegambian Integration*, op. cit., p. 75, footnote 54.
26. Ibid., p. 75, footnote 58.

Chapter 9: Clergyman: In the Quest for Souls

1. Gray J. M., *History of The Gambia,* Cambridge: Cambridge University Press, 1940, pp. 311-313.
2. Hughes and Perfect, *A Political History of the Gambia*, op. cit., p. 26.
3. Colonial Office, "Annual Report on the Social and Economic Progress of the People of The Gambia, 1931", Colonial Reports No. 1572, London: HMSO, 1932, Table 9.
4. Letter from Faye to Daly, dated 25 March 1936, Bathurst: Anglican Diocesan Archives, file: Anglican Mission.
5. Ibid.
6. Letter from J. C. Faye to Bishop Elisee, op. cit., Schedule 1.
7. Ibid., loc. cit.
8. Ibid., loc. cit.
9. Ibid., loc. cit.
10. Ibid., loc. cit.
11. Letter from Daly to Faye, dated 28 November 1946, Banjul: Anglican Diocesan Archives, file: 84/127.
12. Ibid., loc. cit.
13. Letter, Bishop to Priest-in-Charge, dated 9 May 1949, Banjul: Anglican Diocesan Archives, file: 84/127.
14. Letter from Bishop Daly to J. C. Faye, dated 8 February 1950, Banjul: Anglican Diocesan Archives, file: 84/127.
15. Ibid., loc. cit.
16. Letter from Faye to Daly, dated 2 May 1950, Banjul: Anglican Diocesan Archives, file: 84/127, para.2.
17. Ibid., paragraph 3.
18. Ibid., paragraph 4.
19. Ibid., paragraph 5.
20. Letter from Faye to Daly, dated 2 May 1950, Banjul: Anglican Diocesan Archives, file: 84/127.
21. Ibid., paragraph 6.

22. Ibid., paragraph 8.

23. Ibid., paragraph 9.

24. Letter Bishop Daly to Faye, dated 20 February 1950, Banjul, Anglican Diocesan Archives, 84/127.

25. Letter, Faye to Daly, dated 4 May 1950, Banjul: Anglican Diocesan Archives, op. cit., para. 3.

26. loc. cit.

27. Letter from Bishop Daly to Canon Macauley, 24 June 1950 (St. John's Day), Banjul: Anglican Diocesan Archives, file: 81/274.

28. Letter from Bishop Daly to Canon Macauley, dated 8 January 1951, Banjul: Anglican Diocesan Archives, file: J. C. Faye, p. 1.

29. Letter from A. C. Able-Thomas, Hon. Secretary, to Bishop, dated 22 March 1951, Banjul: Anglican Diocesan Archives, file: J. C. Faye.

30. "Conversation between Canon Macauley, The Rev. J. C. Faye and Father Coote", March 29, 1951, Banjul: Anglican Diocesan Archives, file 84/127.

31. Letter from J. C. Faye to Bishop Elisee, op. cit., p. 9.

32. Letter from Archbishop's Chaplain to Bishop Elisee, dated 10 May 1972, Banjul: Anglican Diocesan Archives, file 84/127.

33. Letter from Elisee to Sawyer, dated 18 July 1972, Banjul: Anglican Diocesan Archives, file: 84/127.

34. Letter from Elisee to Sawyer, dated 25 August 1972, Banjul, Anglican Diocesan Archives, file: 84/127.

35. Letter from Sawyer to Elisee, dated 5 September 1972, Banjul: Anglican Diocesan Archives, file: 84/127.

36. Letter, Elisee to Sawyer, dated 28 November 1972, Banjul: Anglican Diocesan Archives, file: 84/127.

37. Letter from Coote to the Archbishop of West Africa, dated 26 November 1952, Banjul: Anglican Diocesan Archives, file: 84/127.

38. Ibid., loc. cit.

39. Letter from J. C. Faye to Bishop Elisee, op. cit., p. 12.

40. Letter Elisee to Faye, dated 27 December 1972, Banjul: Anglican Diocesan Archives, file 84/127.

41. Letter from Faye to Elisee, dated 10 July 1974, Banjul: Anglican Diocesan Archives, file: J. C. Faye.

42. Letter, Elisee to Faye, dated 26 August 1974, Banjul: Anglican Diocesan Archives, file: J. C. Faye.

43. Letter Faye to Bishop Coote, dated 25 November 1951, Banjul: Anglican Diocesan Archives, file 84/127.

Chapter 10: Clergyman and Philanthropist: Up the Ladder and Out

1. Interview, Florence Mahoney, Fajara, 5 April 2013.

2. Letter from Faye to George, dated 7 March 1972, Banjul: Anglican Diocesan Archives, file: 84/127.

3. Letter from George to Elisee, dated 8 March 1972, Banjul. Anglican Diocesan Archives, file: 84/127.

4. Letter dated 16 November 1972, Banjul: Anglican Diocesan Archives, file: 84/127.

5. Letter from the Archbishop of the Province of West Africa to Bishop Elisee, dated 23 November 1972, Banjul: Anglican Diocesan Archives, file: 84/127.

6. Letter from George to Elisee, dated 27 November 1972, Banjul: Anglican Diocesan Archives, file 84/127.

7. Letter from Canon Agyemang, dated 8 January 1973, Banjul: Anglican Diocesan Archives, file: 84/127.

8. Letter from Bishop Elisee to Faye, 27 December 1972, Banjul: Anglican Diocesan Archives, file: 84/127.

9. "SI QUIS" in: Banjul: Anglican Diocesan Archives, file: 84/127.

10. Letter Elisee to Sawyer, dated 28 November 1972, Banjul: Anglican Diocesan Archives, file: 84/127.

11. Letter from Elisee to Faye, dated 24 August 1977, Banjul: Anglican Diocesan Archives, file: J. C. Faye.

12. Letter from Elisee to Sam George, Chancellor of the Cathedral, dated 11 August 1979, Banjul: Anglican Diocesan Archives, file: J. C. Faye.

13. Letters from Sam George to Elisee, 20 August 1979, Banjul: Anglican Diocesan Archives, file: J. C. Faye.

14. Letter from Bishop Elisee to Faye, dated 10 September 1979, Banjul: Anglican Diocesan Archives, file: J. C. Faye.

15. Quoted in letter from Elisee to Faye, dated 13 September 1980, Banjul: Anglican Diocesan Archives, file: J. C. Faye.
16. Letter from Faye to Elisee, dated 8 November 1980, Banjul: Anglican Diocesan Archives, file: J.C. Faye.
17. Ibid., loc. cit.
18. Letter from Elisee to Faye, dated 26 April 1981, Banjul: Anglican Diocesan Archives, file: J. C. Faye.
19. "The Four Mitres Pt. II", op.cit., p. 43.
20. Ibid., loc. cit.
21. Interview, Fajara, 5 April 2013.
22. Cham-Joof, A. E., "Cooperative Activities in The Gambia," op. cit., n.d., pp. 6-7.

Chapter 11: Closure: The Strife Is O'er

1. "J. C. Faye is dead", *Gambia News Bulletin*, Bathurst, 11 December 1985, p. 1.
2. Faye-NJie, Adele and Cham-Joof, Alieu, *A Pictorial Biography of the Very Rev. J. C. Faye, MBE, ORG*, p. 2.
3. Ibid., p. 3.
4. Banjul: Government Printer, 1956.
5. Report of Meeting with the Secretary of State for the Colonies, Alan Lennox Boyd, op. cit., p. 11.
6. Interview with a member of the Committee, 5 March 2013.
7. See: "Ex-British administrator discloses origins of Gambia National Anthem", Banjul: *The Observer*, 27 February 2012.
8. Interview with Hassoum Ceesay, Banjul, 28 March 2013.
9. Gambia Government, Independence Ceremonies Programme, 17 and 18 February 1965, Banjul: Government Printer, 1965.
10. Communication from Baaba Sillah, 17 April 2012.
11. Quoted in "Gambia Mourns J.C", Funeral and Requiem Mass Programme, Banjul: Government Printer, p. 4.

Chapter 12: Concluding Remarks:
Reverend J. C. Faye and the Leadership Question

1. Johnson Sirleaf, E., *This Child will be Great, Memoir of a Remarkable Life,* New York: Harper, 2009, p. 309.
2. Florence Mahoney, in an interview, Banjul, 5 April 2013.

INDEX

Printed in Great Britain
by Amazon

11567628R00220

IMPROVE YOUR
PRESENTATION
TECHNIQUE

IMPROVE YOUR PRESENTATION TECHNIQUE

EDITORIAL
MagBook Contributor Tommy Melville
MagBook Design billbagnalldesign.com
Digital Production Manager Nicky Baker

MANAGEMENT
MagBook Publisher Dharmesh Mistry
Production Director Robin Ryan
MagBook Advertising Director Katie Wood (katie_wood@dennis.co.uk)
MD of Advertising Julian Lloyd-Evans
Newstrade Director David Barker
MD of Enterprise Director Martin Belson
Chief Financial Officer Brett Reynolds
Group Finance Director Ian Leggett
Chief Executive James Tye
Chairman Felix Dennis

CONTENTS

How good are your
presentation skills?

If you're reading this as a presentation is looming, take heart! This book will help you conquer your nerves, get your message across, and give a great performance. Start here by answering these questions and reading the guidance points.

HOW DO YOU FEEL ABOUT PUBLIC SPEAKING?
a) I hate it.
b) I prepare very carefully to avoid nerves.
c) I always enjoy it and never get too stressed.

HOW DO YOU DEAL WITH NERVES?
a) I don't really. I just have to get on with it.
b) I try to take it in my stride. I think being a bit nervous helps me to perform.
c) Although I do get nervous, I always pretend that I don't and bluster my way through by playing a role.

DO YOU PRACTISE?
a) Yes. I often try to improve my presentation at the last minute.
b) I rehearse four or five times but when I feel I have got it right, I don't tinker with it.
c) I don't bother to rehearse. I know I'll be fine.

HOW GOOD ARE YOUR PRESENTATION SKILLS?
How long do you usually make your presentations?
a) I keep it as short as possible.
b) As long as it takes to cover all the necessary ground.
c) As long as it takes—I really enjoy public speaking.

HOW DO YOU DELIVER YOUR PRESENTATION?
a) I often fiddle with my hair or props as I get so nervous.
b) I stand up straight and make sure I address my audience directly throughout the presentation.

c) I tend to sit down and relax.

DO YOU CATER YOUR PRESENTATION TO YOUR AUDIENCE?
a) No, not really—I just want to get my point across.
b) Yes. I try to find out as much about them as I can beforehand.
c) Yes. I tend to aim it at the most senior people.

HOW LONG DO YOU ARRIVE BEFORE YOU ARE DUE TO GIVE A PRESENTATION?
a) I'm always a few hours early.
b) I like to leave enough time to check my equipment.
c) I'm often late.

WHAT WOULD YOU DO IF EVERYTHING WENT WRONG?
a) If I'm honest, I'd completely panic.
b) I'd keep smiling and try to keep calm.
c) I don't think I'd be too bothered. I'm not likely to see the audience again.

a = 1   b = 2   c = 3.
Now add up your scores.

8–13: The very thought of presenting makes you nervous, so take some action to calm your nerves. Chapter 3 will help with this particularly, but chapters 1 and 2 feature lots of practical tips on planning and research that will help make your life easier too. They'll help you work out your objectives, so that you know exactly what message you want to get across. Read Chapter 7 and find out that you can survive if things don't quite go to plan!

14–19: Well done—you've realised that practising is the key to a great presentation! Chapter 4 will show you how you can take your performance up a notch further still by boosting what you say with the way you say it. Chapters 5 and 6 offer lots of advice on how you can further enhance your message with the clever use of visuals and images; chapter 5 is particularly useful if you're having to present 'virtually'.

● **20–23:** It's great that you enjoy presenting; it's a really useful skill to have and will stand you in good stead as you move up the career ladder. Try not to be over·confident, though, and take the time to tailor what you say to your audience—you'll really grab their attention then. Chapters 1 and 2 are particularly helpful here.

Preparing great
presentations

G iving a presentation can strike fear into the heart of even the most experienced business people. It takes some courage to stand up in front of an audience and deliver a well-structured and interesting talk, and most of us at one time or another have experienced the panic, sweaty palms, blank minds, and wobbling voices that sometimes accompany this.

Being able to cope with presentations is a very valuable skill, though, whatever your job. Presentations are useful in many situations, such as pitching for business, putting a case for funding, addressing staff meetings, or even as part of the application procedure for a new job. Few people like speaking formally to an audience, but there are many real benefits and as you gain experience in giving presentations, you'll probably find that it becomes less of a worry, and even enjoyable.

This chapter offers you help on the first step of your journey towards a great presentation: preparation. It will give you some suggestions for preparing the content of what you're going to say, looking at your objectives, gearing it to your audience, and getting your points across well.

STEP ONE WORK OUT YOUR OBJECTIVES

Clear objectives are the starting point for all great presentations. Start by working out your objectives—ask yourself why you're giving the talk and what you want your audience to get out of it. Think about whether using speech alone is the best way of communicating your message, or if your message might benefit from using visual aids and slides to further illustrate its main points.

When you're planning and giving the presentation, keep these objectives in mind at all times—they'll focus your thoughts. Having an objective for giving the presentation will ensure that you're not wasting anyone's time, either your audience's or your own.

For example, let's say that you're presenting a new product to your company's sales reps at your annual sales conference. Your objectives in this case may be to:

 Introduce your product to them positively and enthusiastically.

 Talk them through the benefits of your product.

 Point out the many advantages it has over any competition.

 Explain why the target audience would want to buy it.

TOP TIP!

It's very important that you believe in what you're going to be talking about. This is particularly the case if you have to deliver a difficult message, such as one related to change or what others are likely to perceive as bad news. These situations are bound to be uncomfortable, and if you don't wholeheartedly believe in your message, others will be able to pick this up. It won't necessarily be as a result of anything you say, though; your body language may give it away without you even noticing. See the next chapter for more information on this.

STEP TWO FIND OUT WHAT YOU NEED TO KNOW ABOUT YOUR AUDIENCE

Before you plan your presentation, try as best you can to find out who is going to be in your audience, and their expectations. For example, the tone and content of a presentation to the managing director of another firm will be very different to one addressed to potential users of a product, or to one directed at people you know well. It's important that you know the extent of the audience's knowledge about the topic you'll be discussing, as their familiarity with the subject will determine the level at which you pitch the talk and the language you use (see below).

Whatever the interests of your audience, try to appeal to what will motivate and interest these people. For example, if you're talking to senior people in your company about a new product, you might want to include information about how it can be produced cost-effectively; if you're talking about a new way of doing things, stress how much more effective it will make your team. If you're talking to reps who'll be selling the product for you, you need to highlight how much better it is than the competition. As you can see from these examples, you need to 'tune in' as far as you can to your audience's needs. A few hours doing the groundwork is time very well spent.

STEP THREE MAKE SURE YOU'VE GOT YOUR FACTS STRAIGHT

Once you know why you're speaking and who you're talking to, you can firm up your ideas about what you're going to say.

Get back to basics by checking that you have all the main facts straight. For example, if you're talking about a product or service, make sure you know:

- Its current name (remember that this may have changed many times!).

- Its price.

- When it will be ready.

- What it's meant to do.

- How it works, if appropriate.

- Benefits.

- What the competition is.

If you're talking about a new process, find out about:

- Why you're changing from an existing way of doing things.

- What the changes are.

- When they'll take effect.

- What benefits they'll bring.

> ## TOP TIP!
> If you're giving your presentation just after you've come back from holiday or a business trip, take a few moments to check a few key facts with colleagues before you speak. Some key elements of your presentations (such as prices, names, delivery dates) may have changed while you've been away, and the last thing you need is to have someone pipe up from the back to correct you. It will boost your confidence to know that you're on top of things!

STEP FOUR BEGIN WRITING YOUR SPEECH

When it comes to presentations, there's no substitute for detailed preparation and planning. While everyone prepares in different ways, all of which develop with experience, here are a few key points to bear in mind while you're preparing.

Start by breaking up the task of preparing your speech into manageable units. Once you know the length of the presentation—let's say 15 minutes—break up the time into smaller units and allocate sections of your speech to each unit. For example, you might want to give two minutes to a general introduction, six minutes to a discussion of your main theme, two minutes to sum up key points, and five minutes to take questions. All of this will depend very much on your topic and audience, however, so don't try and shoe-horn your presentation into a very rigid format—keep things fluid if you need to.

Note down all the points you want to make, and order them logically. This will help you develop the framework and emphasis of the presentation.

Keep your presentation short and simple if you possibly can, as it will be easier for you to manage and remember. A shorter presentation is usually more effective from the audience's point of view, too, as most people dislike long presentations and will not necessarily remember any more from them.

TOP TIP!

If you need to provide more detail, it's a good idea to supply a printed handout to your audience at the end of the presentation. This is the best time to do it, as otherwise you'll be fighting to make yourself heard against the rustling paper.

Avoid overloading your talk with facts and figures; a few well-placed numbers can help illustrate a point, but it can be hard to maintain an audience's interest if they are being bombarded with figures. Instead, use some graphs or charts to illustrate what you're saying. Aim to identify two or three key points, and think about ways you can get these across creatively.

Don't use too much jargon. It may be tempting, especially if you work in a technical industry, but bear your audience in mind at all times—if you've followed the steps above and done some research on them, you'll know how familiar they are with your theme, and not everyone will be a specialist. If you do need to use abbreviations or acronyms, explain early on what they mean so that everyone can follow you. You can always recap on your handout, if you provide one, or list them on your website.

STEP FIVE THINK ABOUT USING VISUAL AIDS AND EQUIPMENT

Some presentations may benefit from the use of visual aids of some type, such as acetates for an overhead projector (OHP), or a computer presentation package such as PowerPoint. Remember that visual aids should only be used as signposts during the presentation, to help the audience focus on the main point you're trying to make.

✓ If you do decide to use them, try not to cram too much information onto one slide or screen, as you'll lose your audience's attention while they try to read everything on it. Make sure the audience can see the information by using big, bold, simple lettering, and bear in mind that images are often far more effective than words.

Turn to Chapter 6 for step-by-step advice on this topic.

STEP SIX PRACTISE!

OK, so you know what you want to say, who you're aiming it at, and your slides are ready. It's time to put everything together and practise.

✓ Practise as much as you need to make sure that you're very familiar with your speech—allow plenty of time for rehearsal before the event. Even if the presentation has been sprung on you with very little notice, run yourself through it at least three or four times. Don't panic if your mind goes blank when you start off; keep calm, go back to the beginning, and start again. At points you may feel that you'll never get it right, but you will and you'll find a rhythm that swings you along.

TOP TIP!

Once you're confident that your presentation is right, don't tinker with it! You may have heard it many times, but your audience won't have. Changing things at the last minute is just giving you more stress that you don't need.

Also practise your speech using the equipment you intend to use; slide projectors and video machines should be tested in advance to make sure you know how to operate them, and your laptop or PC should be checked out to make sure that it hasn't developed some dreadful problem.

Have a contingency plan to cope with any unforeseen mishaps. For example, you might want to print out copies of your slides so that if the computer breaks down and there's an OHP to hand, you can show them that way. If the worst comes to the worst, you can distribute them as handouts at the end of your talk. See Chapter 7 for more help on what to do if things don't go to plan.

TOP TIP!

Using cards rather than pieces of paper has lots of advantages. You can move through the cards much more easily (and quietly, especially if your hands shake!) than you can do with sheaves of paper, and you can also add notes to yourself to help you speak more confidently. This can be anything from 'breathe!' to 'emphasis here' to 'pause here'— whatever works best for you.

Time your speech during rehearsals to make sure that your speech is taking the time you'd estimated. Remember that you'll probably need to allow time at the end for a question-and-answer session. Don't bring all your notes into the presentation, but instead list the main points on numbered cards, known as cue cards, to provide reminders.

STEP SEVEN THINK ABOUT THE VENUE

✅ If you're giving your presentation on home turf, book or arrange an appropriately-sized room as soon as you know you're going to have to speak. Make sure there's enough seating for your audience, and that lighting, ventilation, and heating are all working properly.

✅ Organise some refreshments for participants such as tea, coffee, and water. You also need to make sure there will be no interruptions, for example by phone calls, fire drills, or people accidentally entering the room. Put a sign up on the door that states the time the meeting is due to begin and how long it will go on for. If your talk has a title, such as 'Motivating your sales team', or 'New products for ABC Ltd', you could add that too.

✅ Whether you're presenting at your own office or elsewhere, you must make sure that any equipment or props you need are available and set up properly before the presentation starts. If you're presenting away from your office, for example, at a conference or a client's premises, it's a good idea to visit the site beforehand to make sure it has everything you're expecting. It's even a good idea to check out where the switches or plug points are, so that you don't get caught out on the day.

TOP TIP!

If you've saved your talk onto a CD-ROM that you're going to run from a computer on-site, it's a good idea to also e-mail the file to an e-mail account that you can get into wherever you're giving the presentation. This could be your work e-mail address if it allows remote access, or an Internet-based e-mail provider such as Hotmail, AOL, or Yahoo. This means that if the CD-ROM goes haywire for any reason, you can download the presentation from your e-mail to the computer you're using, and carry on as normal.

TOP TIP!

Ask a colleague to stand at the back of the room in which you're going to speak so that you can make sure you're speaking loudly enough. If the room is very big (a boardroom in a large organisation, say) or even a small one with poor acoustics, it might be worth finding or asking the company to invest in a microphone. They're inexpensive (from £10 upwards) and can be used time and again.

COMMON MISTAKES

 YOU DON'T FIND OUT ABOUT YOUR AUDIENCE

A good knowledge of the audience is absolutely crucial in finding the correct pitch. It's no good blinding your audience with technical jargon if they only have a basic grasp of the subject. Similarly, a very knowledgeable audience will soon switch off if you spend the first few minutes going over the basics.

YOU TALK FOR TOO LONG

If your presentation absolutely has to be longer than 20 minutes, insert some breaks so that your audience remains fresh and interested and you can have a sip of water to keep you going.

YOU DON'T CHECK THE ROOM AND EQUIPMENT

This can be disastrous! Imagine, for example, arriving and finding that there's no facility for delivering PowerPoint presentations, and you have no other method of showing slides. Make sure you're familiar with the environment in which you'll be presenting.

STEPS TO SUCCESS

✓ Make sure you have clear objectives for your presentation. Know what you want to say and why.

✓ Believe in what you're saying; if you're unsure of or unhappy about your message, the audience will pick up on it.

✓ Find out about your audience. This will help you 'pitch' the presentation well.

✓ Make sure you're up-to-speed about all the basic facts relevant to your presentation, such as prices, deadlines, specifications, benefits, competition, and so on.

✓ Prepare, plan, and practise thoroughly.

TOP TIP!

If your company has a receptionist, it's a good idea to let him or her know that there'll be an influx of guests on the day. He or she can then point them in the right direction and let you know when they start to arrive so that you can be ready to greet them.

USEFUL LINKS

● **Mind Tools:**
www.mindtools.com

● **SpeechTips.com:**
www.speechtips.com/
preparation.html

● **PublicSpeakingExpert:**
www.publicspeakingexpert.co.uk

● **Presentation skills training:**
www.businesstrainingdirect.
co.uk/index.php

Delivering
great presentations

A presentation is an ideal environment for you to promote your ideas, your products, or your services. You have a captive audience, are able to provide them with relevant information, and can answer any questions they may have on the spot. For a presentation to be a success you must be able to hold the attention of the audience and leave them wanting to know more.

Some people are natural presenters, while others find it more difficult. If you fall into the latter group, don't worry; practice and feedback from previous audiences will help you develop all the necessary skills. In Chapter 1, we found out about how to get ready for the presentation; this chapter will help you deliver it with confidence and style.

STEP ONE LOOK AT THE STRUCTURE OF YOUR PRESENTATION

Structure is essential for any presentation. There should be an introduction, a main body, and a conclusion. You can be witty, controversial, or even outrageous if the mood of the presentation allows, but whatever approach you try, your chief aim is to arouse the audience's curiosity, and to get your message across.

1 Introduce your presentation

The introduction to your presentation needs to attract your audience's interest and attention.

A good opening will also boost your own confidence, because if you start well, the rest should follow easily. Plan your opening words carefully for maximum impact: they should be short, sharp, and to the point.

✅ If appropriate (that is, if you're speaking externally at a conference or internally to people you've never met before, such as prospective customers or suppliers), introduce yourself briefly. There's no need to go into too much detail; just tell them your name, job title, and the broad subject you're talking about.

✅ Let your audience know how long your presentation will take, as this will prepare them to focus for the period of time you expect to speak.

✅ Summarise the contents of your presentation, so that your audience can work out how much information they'll need to absorb.

✅ Explain how the presentation will work in terms of the audience's interaction with you; tell them if you'll be taking questions at the end, or if you're happy for them to pipe up as you go along.

> **TOP TIP!**
> Explaining the key points in the first few sentences will also help your mind to focus on the task in hand, and refresh your memory on the major points of your presentation. It sometimes helps to get started if you can learn your first few sentences by heart.

2 Make an impact in the main section of the presentation

It goes without saying that the main section of your presentation will be driven by the points you want to make.

✅ For maximum impact, use short, sharp, and simple language that will keep your audience's attention and also make sure that your message is being understood.

✅ While you do need to be precise in what you say, make sure you don't sound too stilted or as if you're reading something out of a book—it's good to give the impression of spontaneity.

TOP TIP!
Include only one idea per sentence and pause after each one, so that you make a mental 'full stop'.

✅ However nervous you feel, stick to your original plan for your presentation, and don't go off at a tangent on a particular point and miss the thread. Why not try using metaphors and images to illustrate points? This will give impact to what you say, and help your audience to remember what you've said.

3 Conclude your presentation

Close by summing up the key points of what you've covered. The closing seconds of your presentation are as crucial as the opening sentence as they give you an opportunity to really hammer home your point. To make the most of this, think about what action you'd like your audience to take after the presentation is over and then inspire them to do it.

For example, let's say you've been presenting your new star product to your company's most loyal customers. You want them to love the product as much as you do, to buy it in large numbers, and to sell it with gusto. Remember that this is where your enthusiasm for, and belief in, your message can truly make a difference, so:

 Be brief, but speak clearly without rushing.

 Quickly restate the product's advantages or benefits.

Emphasise your hopes for the product (for example, you believe it will be the market leader in X months' time).

 If it's in your gift, offer them an incentive, such as if they buy early, an X % discount or a multi-buy offer.

STEP TWO THINK ABOUT YOUR POSTURE AND DELIVERY

Now that you know what you'll be saying, it's time to think about how you can say it best and definitely make a splash.

 Maintain eye contact and address your audience directly throughout your presentation.

Be aware of your stance, posture, and gestures without being too self-conscious. Don't slouch, as you'll look unprofessional. Standing up straight will make you appear more confident and will also help you to project your voice better.

Remember that your audience has come to learn something. Try to sound authoritative, sincere, and enthusiastic. If you don't sound as if you believe in yourself, this will come across to the audience.

Think about the way in which you're speaking. Most people need to articulate their words more clearly when addressing an audience. There's usually no opportunity for the audience to ask you to repeat a word they've missed, so aim to

> **TOP TIP!**
> Always stand, rather than sit, when you're doing a presentation. Don't fiddle, for example with a pencil or a piece of paper; try to keep still and avoid moving around excessively. All these things are distracting for an audience, and will mean that they're missing important points you're trying to get across.

sound the vowels and consonants of words clearly.

✓ Think about the expression in your voice too. Try to vary the volume, pitch, and speed of delivery to underline your meaning and to keep up your audience's interest.

STEP THREE ANSWER ANY QUESTIONS

Some people prefer to take questions at the end of a presentation rather than have their flow of concentration interrupted while they're speaking. This is a good strategy if you're nervous or if you're talking about a complicated or very technical subject—it's all too easy to lose your way.

TOP TIP!
Think about your facial expressions too. Obviously, if you're talking about a contentious issue or have to tell a group of people bad news, you're not going to be all singing, all dancing as you take the podium, but if your presentation is a more general one, or sales-orientated, it's good to smile! Smiling at your audience will give the impression that you're at your ease and that you're looking forward to talking to them.

✓ If you do take questions at the end of a talk, give your audience an idea of how much time you have to spend on it; this may be an issue if you're just one of a number of people speaking in a particular session, as if you run over, everyone will start running late.

✓ If someone asks you a question and you don't know the answer, be honest and tell the other person that you'll find out what they need to know and get back to them separately. This will save time, and also prevent you from giving an incorrect answer.

✓ Encourage interesting discussions between members of the audience by throwing general discussion points open to the floor once you've said your piece (or even if you haven't!). This tactic may be appropriate if you're speaking to an audience made up of your peers or of specialists in a certain subject; you may all learn something from it.

STEP FOUR MAKE A DIGNIFIED EXIT

Once the question and answer session is over, you're just about done. All that remains is for you to say thank you to the audience for listening. If you have handouts to circulate, now is the time to do it. It's a good idea to include your contact details on these handouts so that people can get in touch with you about questions that occur to them later, or hopefully to indicate some interest in what you've been talking about. Thank them for their feedback and keep in touch if you can; giving presentations is a great way to network and build up your contact list.

> ## TOP TIP!
> Watch where you're going! If you've been nervous about doing your presentation, you're bound to be heartily relieved that it's all over. In your eagerness to take your seat elsewhere, don't rush off stage in case there are tricky steps to negotiate. Also keep an eye out for cables, leads, plugs, or even chairs in the way that you don't want to bump into and ruin the great impression you've made.

COMMON MISTAKES

YOU'RE NOT ENTHUSIASTIC
If you're not interested in what you have to say, don't expect your audience to be. Listening to a single voice for 20 minutes or more can be difficult for an audience, so you have to inject some enthusiasm into what you're saying if you are to keep them with you (and awake!). To help keep things going, activities or discussion with your audience, as mentioned above, can help a great deal.

YOU SPEAK TOO QUICKLY
Don't rush your presentation; it's important to take your time. It's

hard not to rush, especially when you're nervous and want the whole thing over with as soon as possible, but the audience will find it difficult to understand you, or to keep up, if you talk too fast. Make sure you summarise your main points every five minutes or so, or as you reach the end of a section. This will help to pick out the most important issues for your audience, and it's then more likely that they'll remember the central issues long after you've finished your presentation. As discussed in Chapter 1, practising with a colleague or friend will help a lot here, as he or she can tell you how you're doing in terms of the speed of your delivery.

❌ YOU DON'T CHECK THE EQUIPMENT

There's nothing more irritating for an audience who have all made an effort to turn up on time, than to have to sit around and wait while you struggle to get your laptop to work, or sort your slides out. Make sure everything is exactly in place well before your audience begins to arrive. A technician should be on hand if you're planning to use sophisticated technology.

❌ YOU DON'T INTERACT WITH THE AUDIENCE

Be careful not to look at the floor during your presentation, or to direct your speech at one person. Try and draw your whole audience into the presentation by glancing at everyone's faces, in a relaxed and unhurried way, as you make your points. Keeping in tune with your audience in this way will also help you judge if people are becoming bored. If you do detect that people are glazing over, you could try to change the tempo of your presentation to refocus their attention.

❌ YOU'RE LATE!

We all have days when absolutely everything seems to go wrong, but turning up late to your own presentation is the last thing you want to have to worry about. So leave yourself twice as much time for your journey than you think you'll need. This will allow for getting ost several times en route. If you're driving or taking the train, check your local news before you leave to see if there are any hold-ups. If the presentation is more than a few hours' drive away and you're on quite early, see if your company will foot the bill for you staying overnight nearby.

USEFUL LINKS

BusinessTown.com:
www.businesstown.com/presentations/index.asp

iVillage.co.uk:
www.ivillage.co.uk/workcareer

SpeechTips.com:
www.speechtips.com/delivering-a-speech.html

PublicSpeakingExpert:
www.publicspeakingexpert.co.uk/

TrustyGuides.com:
www.trustyguides.com/public-speaking4.html

Fighting back
against nerves

Being overcome by nerves can be a completely debilitating experience that sabotages our ability to communicate well and to demonstrate how well we can do our job. If you're prone to feeling nervous, presentations are probably one of the most stressful situations you can be placed in. The body's nervous reaction to speaking in public, whether it's making a presentation to customers or colleagues, or even making an intervention during an internal meeting can, if left unchecked, rob us in just a few seconds of the confidence and experience built up during the course of our career.

If you do suffer from nerves in some work situations, take comfort in knowing that you're not alone and that with the help of a few simple techniques, you can kick nerves into touch. It's always tempting to think that a problem will just go away, but tackling nerves will offer a range of positive results, including being able to be yourself, contributing to events in the way you know you can deep down, and getting the amazing next job you deserve. Overcoming nerves is a great first step on the journey to full confidence.

STEP ONE START OFF WITH SOME POSITIVE THINKING

TOP TIP!

Don't let negative images or words creep in and get in the way of your preparation; if you feel your positive attitude starting to slip, take a short break and start again.

It's always hard to be objective when you're very worried about something, but it really is the first step on the road to taking charge of yourself. If you see yourself failing at something in your mind's eye, you're much more likely to end up with a disaster on your hands. Try to get your imagination under control and instead of seeing yourself getting it all spectacularly wrong, see yourself succeeding brilliantly. Your body will follow the cues from your mind, so train your mind to be positive and to 'invite' success for yourself.

STEP TWO **BREATHE!**

When people get nervous, they panic and speak before they've thought things through. If you're worried that your mouth may run away with you, manage your breathing. Most people aren't particularly good at doing this, but it's the key to giving yourself space to observe and hear what's going on. This is an important technique to learn if you have to participate in meetings or if people will be asking you questions as part of your presentation—being sensitive to the needs of others and different situations is an important part of being able to say the right thing at the right time.

> **TOP TIP!**
> If you're in an important meeting that you want to contribute to, give yourself time to take in the information you need and formulate what you're going to say. Don't rush in, but breathe calmly and don't worry about short silences.

STEP THREE **DON'T LET SHYNESS BE A BARRIER**

If you're naturally a shy person, then public speaking can seem a huge barrier to overcome. Strangely, though, some of the best presenters are introverts and many have severe bouts of nerves before taking the stage and delivering a polished performance.

One good way of lessening the fear of public speaking is to think of it as having a conversation, rather than giving a talk. It also helps to break the ice by meeting a few people from your audience first; this will help you make a connection with them that you can use and build on while you're on the platform. Be friendly, smile, look people in the eyes, ask questions if appropriate, and take the listening time to breathe, relax, and enjoy the experience if you can.

STEP FOUR UNDERSTAND THE PHYSICAL EFFECTS OF WORRY

Although the effects of a bout of nerves show themselves physically, it's actually our state of mind that triggers them. Fears that we'll make a fool of ourselves or that we won't achieve our aims commonly drive our nervous reactions, which are often known as the 'fight or flight' response.

Thousands of years ago, when we were surviving in a physically hostile world that was populated by human predators or enemies, our fight or flight response enabled us to fuel our strength and overpower a beast or build our speed and outrun a something that was threatening us. In the moment of need, adrenalin would be released, our hearts would pump faster, our blood would be super-oxygenated, and our muscles would be fed to achieve higher levels of performance. This is what enabled human beings to survive and build the (relatively) safe, sophisticated, and cerebral world that we enjoy today. However, in spite of our successful emergence from the primitive world, our bodies still react to fear— whether it be real or imagined—in the same way.

When we're giving a presentation, our fear of failure gives rise to the fight or flight response along with its characteristic bodily reactions, but these now have nowhere to go. We don't take flight and neither do we fight, but instead stand still, tell ourselves not to be so silly, and try to combat the panic. By this stage, there's no point in trying to use our mind to control the effects of fear as our body has taken control. The fact that we can't do anything about it gives rise to further feelings of anxiety and sends a message to the body to try harder because the threat has not disappeared and there's still work to be done. More adrenalin . . . faster heart beat . . . busy muscles . . . and so it goes on. Trying to break this cycle is the challenge of overcoming nerves and it can be tackled in two ways; through the mind and through the body.

1 Overcome nerves through the mind

Use visualisation as a technique for removing fear. Imagine your audience receiving your information enthusiastically, being interested in what you're saying, and applauding when you've finished. Enhance this image with feelings of satisfaction, achievement, and pride. Watch yourself leave the spotlight feeling confident and happy to acknowledge people who come up to you afterwards to congratulate you on your performance.

Think through your presentation or performance beforehand so that you're both practically and mentally prepared. If you're likely to be asked questions on your presentation, imagine what these might be and prepare some answers. If it helps, write them down, read over them a few times and tick them off your 'checklist' of things to prepare.

Get as much information as possible. This will help you target your talk appropriately and demonstrate that you understand your audience's perspective and needs well. Being able to show that you've taken the time to do this will help win them over and put them on your side.

Working through the exercises above will help remove the perceived threat you fear and will fill your mind with positive images. Cancelling out the threat in any given situation means that you're a lot less likely to have an adverse physical response to it.

2 Overcome nerves through the body

Some of these well-known relaxation techniques will help prevent your body from triggering the 'fear response'.

✓ Spend a few minutes to calm your breathing and to take attention away from the impending performance. Breathe deeply into your stomach, hold your breath for a few seconds, and breathe out again. Do this several times in a quiet spot away from the action.

✓ Relax your body. Sit in a chair and concentrate on each muscle group one by one. Working from your feet to your forehead, contract and then relax your muscles. Feel the difference. If you find yourself becoming tense again, go back to the problem area and try again, breathing deeply and steadily as you do so.

✓ Have some water before your performance to prevent you from drying up and keep another glass beside you so that you can refresh your mouth as you go.

TOP TIP!

Overcoming nerves is hard work, but it's well worth spending the time to do it. Succeeding means that you'll be able to express yourself well and with confidence in any situation. This will help you in all areas of your life.

CHAPTER 3

COMMON MISTAKES

YOU PUT YOURSELF UNDER TOO MUCH PRESSURE

It's completely counter-productive to beat yourself up about getting nervous. What is the point? The best thing to do is to set yourself reasonable goals, take things one step at a time, and give yourself an opportunity to celebrate each small success and build upon it incrementally. If you challenge yourself by putting yourself in extreme situations, you run the risk of failing in those extremes and it can be very difficult to recover from that. Be gentle with yourself and try to build your confidence steadily and soundly.

YOU PRETEND YOU DON'T SUFFER FROM NERVES

When people want to appear confident and competent, they often won't own up to suffering from nerves and end up playing a part, rather than being themselves. This is a common mistake which at best makes it seem as if you're suppressing the real 'you', but at worst, can make you seem arrogant. Putting on masks can be helpful in some situations, for example, if the real you is hidden somewhere in the role that you've decided to act out, but removing who you are by 'being someone else' isn't a good way to overcome nerves. Hiding yourself away won't help and in fact sometimes it's just better to acknowledge your perceived short-comings and turn to someone who can help you find an appropriate way through.

YOU THINK THE PROBLEM WILL GO AWAY

Many would-be presenters who are overcome by nerves avoid dealing with them, thinking that they just have to get through their ordeal and somehow arrive at the other side. This is perfectly true, but it can be life-enhancing to face your fears and find a dignified way through. Often when we look our fears in the face, they begin to subside, especially if we practise techniques to master them. Rehearsing is extremely helpful, whether it's in front of friends, family, or even the mirror. If you're able to video yourself rehearsing, so much the better; you'll learn a lot.

USEFUL LINKS

● **businessknowhow.com:**
www.businessknowhow.com/

● **Total Success:**
www.tsuccess.dircon.co.uk/

● **Mind Tools:**
www.mindtools.com/

Boosting your message
with your body language

We all know that real communication is not just a matter of making a noise. But did you realise just how little impact what we actually say has on people we're speaking to? In a face-to-face situation, like a presentation, between 55 and 65 per cent of your meaning is communicated by your body language—your posture, movements, and facial expressions—and 38 per cent comes from your tone of voice. That leaves just seven per cent to be conveyed by the words you use!

In addition, researchers also agree that the verbal part of the communication is used to convey information, while the non-verbal part is used to convey values, feelings, and attitudes— the things that build rapport.

It's obvious, then, that if you can learn to understand and control body language in a conscious way, you can make an enormous difference to the impact you have on your audience. This chapter will help you to use the different forms of non-verbal communication to help get your message across effectively and to build rapport with your listeners.

STEP ONE MAKE A GOOD ENTRANCE

People, like animals, are territorial and instinctively perceive new spaces—like an unfamiliar presentation room—as hostile territory. As a result, it's natural, if you have not been in the room before, to decrease your speed as you enter it, and this can make you look as if you lack confidence. There are a number of things you can do about this:

 Be in the room first, before your audience arrives, so that you already 'own' the space.

Familiarise yourself with the room before the presentation, so that when you do enter you are more relaxed and in charge.

 Make a point of going into the room at an even speed, or even stopping at the door before entering.

STEP TWO USE POSITIVE POSTURES

One of the biggest giveaway indications of nerves is your posture. And interestingly enough if you look nervous, rather than getting people's sympathy, you tend to make your audience inclined to feel hostile towards you. Self-defence teachers know this: they teach their pupils to carry themselves in a self-confident and upright manner, as people who walk in a timid or frightened way are much more likely to be victims of attack.

To make sure that your posture doesn't betray your nerves as you speak:

Stand up straight with your feet slightly apart; keep your head up, and think generally about taking up as much space as you can. It might help to keep in mind the saying, 'think tall and you'll be tall'—this will automatically help you to adopt a much more confident posture.

Don't hold your arms in front of your body too much. People feeling nervous or unsure of themselves will often 'protect' themselves: in other words, they adopt a posture that protects a vulnerable area. Men might stand with their hands clasped in front of their genitals, and women tend to fold their arms across their chests.

> **TOP TIP!**
> If you can avoid it, don't have any piece of furniture or other object between you and your audience— it can act as a barrier and create a distance between you. However, if you find you have a tendency to shuffle your feet nervously, you could try positioning a table behind you where you can lean back on the edge of it.

Nothing can make you look more nervous than standing in front of a presentation audience with a folder clasped to your front!

STEP THREE BE NATURAL WITH GESTURES

It's easy to worry too much about gestures. With a few exceptions, most gestures are fine—providing they feel natural to you. After all, for most people, gestures are an extension of their personality and it can make you feel uncomfortable and unnatural if you try to repress them.

Neil Kinnock, the former leader of the Labour Party, gave an intriguing example of someone trying to repress his natural gesturing habits during the 1992 general election campaign. His tendency to wave his arms around was interpreted by some as a sign of impetuousness, when in fact his aim was to show he could be trusted to run the country and command the respect of other world leaders, so campaign organisers advised him to grip the sides of the rostrum. Camera shots from the rear, however, show clearly how he slid his hands up and down and gripped the edges during his speeches as he tried to keep a grip on his enthusiasm. It clearly wasn't comfortable for him to have his natural exuberance restrained in that way.

Having said this, there are a few useful things to remember about gestures:

 Never make a rude one, obviously!

 Try not to make the same gesture too many times, or it will turn into a mannerism that will distract your audience. They might find it tempting to count how many times you wag your forefinger, rather than listening to what you're saying.

Be on the look out for distracting habits you acquire only when you're under stress, such as foot shuffling or lip licking. If you know what these are, you might be able to eliminate them, or at least minimise them.

If you find it difficult to know what to do with your hands, you could try using a 'prop'. Many people use props to reinforce their messages, the most common being extensions of the hand such as a pen or pointer. Using a prop extends the space taken up by your body—and hence your territory—and you are perceived as more confident and powerful.

> **TOP TIP!**
> No matter how nervous you are, try to avoid hand-to-face gestures such as touching your nose or rubbing your eye. These often mean you're not entirely comfortable with your subject matter, and can signify that you're not being completely honest about something. Even if your listeners don't know this consciously, they will pick up on your discomfort.

STEP FOUR KEEP UP EYE CONTACT

It's true of all human interactions to say that the more eye contact we have with someone, the closer we tend to feel to them—and they to us. Often we will avoid eye contact with someone we don't like, and if we do make it, we will adopt an unemotional stare, rather than a friendly gaze.

When you're giving a presentation, keep your eye contact with people as normal as possible. Look at everyone in the room, not just person in the middle at the front who you feel is on your side. That way each member of your audience

> **TOP TIP!**
> There are two useful things to remember about eye contact. Firstly, lowered eyes make you look shy. Secondly, people will naturally follow your gaze and if you keep looking at the ceiling, so will they.

will begin to feel that they have forged some sort of personal bond with you, and will be more receptive to your message.

STEP FIVE KEEP AN EYE ON YOUR TIMING

In normal conversation, another element that conveys information (often unconsciously) is the speed at which you talk. Speaking slowly can sometimes indicate that you're uncertain of what you're saying; speaking quickly may show that you're anxious or excited. These rules still apply to some degree when you're making a presentation, which may make you feel as if you're stuck between a rock and a hard place. As ever, though, going for the middle ground is much the safest option.

Although it's important to speak slowly enough to enable your audience to hear what you're saying, don't overdo it or you'll sound hesitant. Conversely, you also need to guard against gabbling—it's a natural tendency to speak faster than usual if you're nervous and if you're normally a fast talker anyway, you can completely lose your audience!

STEP SIX WATCH YOUR TONE AND MANNERISMS

The manner in which you speak during your presentation is almost more important than anything else. If you think about it, even a simple word like 'hello' can have multiple different meanings—friendly, hostile, surprised, suspicious, offhand, and many others—depending on how you say it, so you need to be careful about what tone of voice you use. There are a number of things to think about here.

Try to sound friendly, but not so casual that you lose your authority.

 At the same time, don't be too bossy—this is a presentation, not a lecture.

It's better to be too loud than too soft: nothing is more trying for an audience that a mumbling presenter.

Ask someone you trust to listen to you and check that you are not swallowing words (easy to do when you're nervous)—in other words, that the ends of your sentences don't die away and become inaudible. To a listener, this makes it seem as if the presentation is repeatedly grinding to a halt.

Bear in mind that too many 'ums', 'ers' and hesitations make you sound unprofessional and can be irritating to listen to. Plenty of rehearsal should solve this issue.

> ## TOP TIP!
> As with physical gestures, most catchphrases—'as I say', 'basically', 'you know', for example—are fine unless they're used too frequently, when they become a distracting mannerism. Again, when you practise, ask someone to keep an ear out for things like this. You'll be so used to saying them, that you won't notice you're doing it!

STEP SEVEN REMEMBER YOUR FACIAL EXPRESSIONS

As with eye contact, people's emotions towards us are influenced by our facial expressions. In fact, this is so much the case that if someone continually shows the 'wrong' facial expressions, or doesn't change their expression at all, we find it hard to warm to them.

While this doesn't mean you should grin manically at your audience throughout your presentation, it does mean that you don't have to be too guarded in your expressions—and it won't ruin your image or make you appear unprofessional if you smile occasionally. In fact, smiling will help put you and your audience at ease. It's not appropriate at all times, of course—if you're delivering bad news of some type, for example—but in the normal run of things, it does no harm.

STEP EIGHT MATCH YOUR CLOTHES TO THE OCCASION

According to the experts, people form 90 per cent of their opinion about someone within the first 90 seconds of meeting them, which means that your audience will be making judgments about you long before you even open your mouth.

What you wear is therefore your first means of communicating something about yourself, and will help your audience to relate to you . . . or not. As a rough rule of thumb, people tend to like people who are like them—so it's best to dress in the same sort of way as those you'll be presenting to. If you're presenting informally to a group of colleagues, for example, you can wear normal office attire, while a more formal suit might be better for a meeting of government bureaucrats.

If in doubt, it's probably best to err on the side of restraint. That way, the worst you can do is to present a blank canvas that doesn't distract your audience from what you have to say. After all, you want your message to be the point of focus in your presentation, not your personality.

COMMON MISTAKES

YOU LACK 'CONGRUENCE'

Because body language is something that occurs naturally, whether or not we are conscious of it, it's impossible to control every last aspect of it. This means that if you are talking about something you don't really believe in, or if you're not entirely comfortable with what you are saying, your body language will subtly 'leak' this somewhere along the line. This lack of 'congruence' between your words and your body language will be picked up on by your audience, and they are likely to feel suspicious and distrustful of you and your message. The only answer is to be authentic in what you say and your body language will reinforce that message naturally.

YOU OVER-DO THINGS

When you become conscious of all the ways in which you communicate non-verbally with others, it can suddenly become terribly easy to over-do them . . . your eye contact is a little too intense, your posture a little too confident, your gestures a little too controlled, and so on. And, just as is the case with a lack of congruence, this can make you come across as insincere and inauthentic and may turn your audience against you. To be effective, body language must be subtle and seem completely natural—and the only way to achieve this is to practise over and over again. Try watching yourself in a mirror as you rehearse your presentation, or ask someone you trust to observe you and give you honest feedback. Eventually, if you practise enough, controlling your body language will become second nature to you.

STEPS TO SUCCESS

 Make a positive entrance so that you 'own' the space.

 Adopt a confident posture that will reduce any inclination in people to be hostile towards you.

 Be natural in your gestures, while taking care that no individual gesture becomes a mannerism through being used too frequently.

 Regular eye contact with your audience builds rapport.

 Speak at the right speed—not so slowly that you sound hesitant, but not so fast that you gabble.

 Your tone must be friendly and accessible, while authoritative.

 Don't worry about being too guarded in your facial expressions, or you may come across as odd.

USEFUL LINKS

Culture at Work:
www.culture-at-work.com/
nvcnegotiation.html

NLP training and resources:
www.altfeld.com/

PPI Business NLP:
www.ppimk.com

Rider University Clinical Psychology Department:
www.rider.edu/

Mind Tools:
www.mindtools.com

Creating
virtual or online
presentations

Online or virtual presentations are rather different creatures from the type of presentation that you would deliver in person. Their purpose is the same—to convey information in a concise way that makes a real impact—but they raise many other issues that need to be thought about carefully.

There are many reasons why people choose to, or must, present virtually or online. You may want to add something to your company's website that new customers can visit to find out exactly what you do, for example. Or you may want to showcase an idea or a service to a partner based overseas; you may not be able to justify a business trip to see them, or perhaps the time difference doesn't allow for 'real-time' presentations via the Web.

Whatever the reason, the crucial point is that you yourself will not be there, and so your presentation will need to compensate for this in a number of ways. It must reinforce the image, brand, and overall message of your company; it must engage the audience's attention; it must answer as many of their potential questions as possible, and it must be easy to use.

You'll need to consider how your presentation looks and 'feels', how you can involve the people reading it, and what technology or software you use to create it. The guidelines below will help set you on the right path.

STEP ONE THINK ABOUT THE LENGTH AND FORMATTING OF YOUR TEXT

As with a face-to-face presentation, the first and most important things to decide are who your audience will be, exactly what you want to say to them, and how to split this into sections to present as slides.

However, there is one big difference: because you won't be there to explain the slides, visuals, or screens, each will have to contain all the explanation necessary. In other words, instead of simply being the written back-up to your speech, this presentation must stand alone.

As a result, it will be very tempting to write yards and yards of text to explain everything properly. Don't go there!

> # TOP TIP!
> Web page designers work on the premise that reading speeds are more than 25 per cent slower from computer screens than from paper. But that doesn't mean you should write 25 per cent less—you should write 50 per cent less.

How you *structure* your text is also important, as people rarely read screen pages word by word; instead they scan the page, picking out individual words and sentences. To cater for this, your copy needs to be very clear and easily readable in order to get the message across quickly.

Here's a list of pointers:

 Keep your sentences short and punchy.

 Make sure that each line is no more than about 12–13 words long.

TOP TIP!

To get the amount of copy roughly right, write out your presentation text as if you were going to deliver it to an audience in person. Then cut it in half. Then cut it in half again. That way you will be left with the important essence of what you want to say, and none of the extra 'fluff'.

 Highlight important keywords so that they catch the reader's eye.

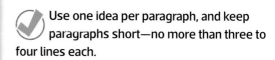 Use one idea per paragraph, and keep paragraphs short—no more than three to four lines each.

 Break up the text wherever appropriate with sub-heads, bullet points, and numbering.

Make sure your spelling and grammar is top-notch. Many people adopt a friendlier or more casual tone in virtual communications than might apply to other business materials, but spelling mistakes and grammatical howlers are a step too far.

STEP TWO GET THE LOOK AND FEEL RIGHT

As with other kinds of presentation, it is important that the look and feel of an online or virtual presentation are consistent with the rest of your company image, so that your audience receives the same key messages from it as they would from any other contact with your business (see Chapter 6 for more information on this). In fact, it's even more important in this case as, once again, you won't be there in person to reinforce the impression it creates.

In addition to this, there are other considerations when designing the look of a virtual or online presentation. Because reading on screen is much harder on the eyes than reading on paper, you need to:

Avoid cramped text and use as much white space as possible.

 Use a light background with dark text.

Be careful in your choice of colours. Although these should complement your corporate colours and logo, bright tints like reds and yellows can be dazzling on a screen and difficult to read; paler shades or dark colours are easier on the eyes.

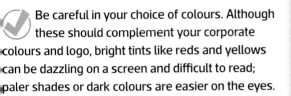

TOP TIP!

Inconsistency or poor quality design will detract from your image, and may even lose you business. Attention to detail, on the other hand, will automatically ensure you come across as professional and even compensate for small shortcomings in content.

 Choose a simple, non-serif font (like Arial) and a standard font size of 10–12 pt.

 Illustrate and enhance key points with tables or simple graphics.

 Aim to keep each page to one screen in length, as most people prefer not to have to scroll too much.

STEP THREE THINK ABOUT ADDING SOME 'DRAMA'

A big advantage of online and virtual presentations is that you can use all sorts of effects to make your information more dramatic and interesting, and thereby catch your audience's attention.

While the important rule here is not to over do it—less really is more!—here are some ideas:

EFFECT	DESCRIPTION
Orchestrating of information	Use of a pointer to guide the viewer: this could be an ordinary screen pointer, or an animated character of some kind. Try not be too cutesy with this type of thing, though—it might be a good idea to use a character if it ties in with your company logo, for example, but don't go overboard with cuddly toys.
Reveals	This technique allows one piece of information at a time to be presented to the audience, frequently by using a 'grey-out' facility that hides content and reveals it in gradual stages.
Build-ups	Similar to the reveal, this technique allows information to be added in stages.
Overlays	This usually involves the complete image being presented but each 'overlay' highlighting or expanding on the initial image. It can be used to highlight paths through complicated diagrams.
Variety	While all your slides should have a uniting look and feel, it could become boring for the viewer if every screen looks identical. Make sure that there's some variety between them, such as colour coding for different subjects.

STEP FOUR BE USER-FRIENDLY

When you're creating your presentation, it's important to keep the needs of your audience in mind. They are probably busy people with limited time, so you need to make it as easy as possible for them to access the information you're providing.

Explain clearly what your presentation is about on the front page. There's nothing more annoying for people—or anything more likely to lose attention— than having to hunt around to find out what you are talking about. Think perhaps about beginning with a summary of the information you are presenting, with links that click directly through to the different sections so viewers can go straight to areas of interest.

> ## TOP TIP!
> Give your presentation a human feel, perhaps by including information about, or a photograph of, yourself. This will make your audience feel they are receiving information from an individual, rather than just wading through another piece of anonymous material.

As with a good website, your presentation should be easy to navigate. Try to give readers more than one way to access the information—for example, by having navigation buttons down one side as well as links at the bottom of each page, and cross-reference hyperlinks within the text. If there's a lot of material to get through in your presentation, you might even want to include a simple search facility.

If your presentation requires a lot of detailed information—such as technical specifications, for instance—think about putting it in separate appendices rather than in the main body of the text. That way anyone who needs the in-depth information can find it, while at the same time your main pages remain uncluttered.

Make it easy for readers to contact you should they have questions or require further information. Make sure your phone number or e-mail address can be read clearly and is prominent.

STEP FIVE THINK ABOUT COMMON QUERIES IN ADVANCE

Try to anticipate likely questions that people might have after reading your material. Providing the answers in a separate section of your presentation—perhaps in the form of frequently asked questions—will show you're ready to help and may encourage them to contact you. And it may also save you time and money by nipping some basic queries in the bud, such as requests for your opening hours, or prices of the products you're promoting.

Providing an e-mail facility for queries and audience feedback can be useful, but if you do this you must make sure you check your messages regularly and respond promptly or you'll undo all your good work and undermine your professional image.

STEP SIX INVOLVE YOUR AUDIENCE

One disadvantage of not presenting your information in person is that it is much harder to make your audience feel involved. However, there are various techniques you can use to hold their attention.

● **Interactivity**. Interactivity is one of the greatest strengths of online technology, and it's a good idea to make your presentation as active as possible. Consider if you can offer online tools such as calculators or quizzes viewers can fill in. These help them feel involved and—if they're useful—will also encourage them to return to your presentation.

● **Changing content.** If your presentation is featured on your website somewhere, you can extend its shelf-life considerably by adding visibly new content on a regular basis. Perhaps you could offer a new tip each day or provide a weekly news service to give visitors a reason to return. This is what is known as 'sticky content'. Remember, to do this you will need to be able to access the presentation to make changes; it will also take a certain amount of time and effort on your part.

● **Freebies.** People are more likely to remember your presentation, and return to it, if they got something useful or free out of their last visit. Is there something you can include that will add value—such as a set of document templates, or a printable poster they could put up on the wall? Perhaps you could even consider providing an incentive such as free entry to a prize draw for giving you feedback?

> ## TOP TIP!
> It is essential that your material is up to date— readers will be put off immediately if there's something obviously obsolete on your presentation, such as an old date at the foot of it. If the material needs to last some time, consider removing anything time-sensitive from it and keeping dates as vague as possible, perhaps restricting them simply to the year of publication.

COMMON MISTAKES

YOU GET CARRIED AWAY
There are so many exciting tools, effects, gadgets, and gizmos that can be used in electronic documents, it can be very easy to overdo it and make your presentation far too busy. Always remember that less is often more and that the main point of your presentation is the information you are trying to convey, not your artistic skills or technical wizardry.

YOU DON'T MAKE YOUR PRESENTATION EASY TO ACCESS
One vital thing that's easy to forget is how your audience is going

to access this presentation of yours. Are you going to e-mail it out, or will you put it on CD and post it? Or do you plan to put it up on the Internet? If it's too complicated or cumbersome, or involves technology that readers don't possess, you will lose them straight away.

As ever, the answer lies mainly in knowing your audience, but generally speaking it's best to keep things as simple as possible. Word documents, for example, are accessible to most PC users, and the files tend to be a manageable size for sending electronically. PowerPoint presentations can be enormous, and very trying to download for anyone who doesn't have a broadband connection. On the other hand, PDF documents require people to have Adobe Acrobat in order to read them: are you sure your readers possess the right software, or can you send out a copy with the presentation? If you want to use the Internet, do you have the right skills to make your presentation look effective and work properly?

If in any doubt, get expert advice—either from your IT department, or from someone experienced in such matters. It would be a pity to fall at the last fence and waste all your hard work!

STEPS TO SUCCESS

 Keep your text short, snappy, and punchy.

 Check that the look and feel matches the rest of your corporate image, and that it works when displayed on screen.

 Add some drama—though judge it carefully.

Be sure that your presentation is user friendly and easy to navigate.

 Try to anticipate and answer likely queries arising from your material.

 Use clever techniques to involve your audience.

 Don't get too carried away with snazzy or unnecessary details and effects.

 Make sure that your presentation is not too complicated or high-tech to be easily accessible.

USEFUL LINKS

● **Businesslink:**
www.businesslink.gov.uk

● **e-Learning Centre:**
www.e-learningcentre.co.uk

● **Web Style Guide:**
www.webstyleguide.com

6

Using slides and visuals
in your presentation

I t's a very common mistake—particularly for those who are new to presenting—to feel that it's necessary to produce a huge number of slides or overheads, containing all the information being discussed, as well as all sorts of complicated and sophisticated diagrams and visuals. You'll be relieved to know that, thankfully, this isn't the case!

In fact, the golden rule is: all written or visual material is only there to back up and give emphasis to what the presenter is saying. That's it. If the audience requires reference material or detailed information, it is far better to produce this as handouts and give them to people at the end of the presentation, to be taken away and mulled over at leisure. Otherwise, the watchwords are simplicity and clarity.

This chapter provides a series of rules and suggestions which, if followed, will help you to create a presentation that has all the impact necessary, but which may also save you considerable time and effort.

STEP ONE THINK ABOUT 'BRAND CONSISTENCY'

Whether you're creating slides, visuals, or any other kind of presentation material, it's important to make sure that your audience receives the same key messages from it as they would from any other contact with your business. In other words, the presentation needs to portray the same brand as your website, stationery, sales and marketing materials, offices, signage, or any other promotional literature you might have. If it is not consistent, it may well have a negative impact on how your audience perceives your image in general, so it's worth spending the time to get it right.

Think about the following factors when designing the overall look of your presentation:

- A specific typeface.

- Your logo and letterhead design.

- A particular colour or palette of colours.

- Any text that needs to be included on every slide— perhaps your website address or business slogan, for example.

STEP TWO CREATE TEXT SLIDES

When creating text slides, there are five main rules to bear in mind. Get these right and you're well on the way to having an effective presentation.

1 Make it BIG

You need to choose a font size that's big enough for everyone to read—even from the back row. As a rough rule of thumb:

 For text in bullet points use a font that's at least 24 pt in size.

 For any added detail, use text of at least 18 pt.

> ## TOP TIP!
> Even if you're not representing a company or organisation, you still need to create a consistent, professional 'brand' for your presentation. Choosing or designing a particular template as the basis for each slide or overhead is a great place to start and will save you time in the long run.
>
> If you're using PowerPoint, use the 'Slide Master' page to design your overall look right at the start. By setting up your fonts, sizes, and colour scheme here, and inserting any logo you want, they'll appear on every slide and you won't have to format each one individually.

2 Keep it simple

Most people tend to put too many words on a slide, and it's important to get rid of all unnecessary text. You don't want your audience's attention to be fixed on trying to read a long slide rather than listening to you. The guidelines are:

 No more than six lines of text per slide.

 No more than seven words per line of text.

 Use colour to attract attention to important points—for example, keywords could be highlighted in a different shade.

3 Make it clear

Choose a clear, non-serif font (like Arial) and write in upper and lower case—text that's all in capitals is difficult to read. You also need colours that enhance the readability of your slides. Most of PowerPoint's default font sizes and colour schemes work well; if you decide to experiment with your own, be sure that you don't reduce readability in the process.

TOP TIP!

If in doubt, for printed slides, dark colours on a light background tend to be the easiest to read; for projected slides, light colours on a dark background work best.

4 Follow a logical sequence

In order to clarify your message for your audience, the stages of your presentation and the slides you use need to follow a logical sequence. Here are a couple of useful ideas:

Begin and end the presentation with an identical pair of slides, which summarise your main points. At the beginning, this gives the audience a notion of what to expect and helps you conquer last-minute nerves by reminding you of what you want to say. At the end, it provides a way to recap your arguments and also gives the audience the sense that you've come full circle, completing the 'story' you promised them at the beginning.

Create 'signpost' slides, or slides that remind the audience at intervals where you've got to in the presentation, and how each part fits into the whole. This is a very good way of keeping people's attention— particularly if the presentation is a long one.

> **TOP TIP!**
> Your audience must be able to get the point of a slide within five seconds of seeing it. When you put up a new slide, don't say anything for a few moments—let people absorb the information. Then, when you have their undivided attention, expand upon what the slide has to say.

STEP THREE DECIDE ON THE RIGHT VISUALS

A picture is worth a thousand words, they say—and it's certainly true that a verbal message which is reinforced with a visual one is stronger than the verbal message alone. So visual aids, which in this case means any sort of illustration, graphic, graph, or diagram that you might want to use, are certainly an important part of most presentations.

However, there's a problem: while a good visual gives a huge boost to a presentation, a poor one leaves it worse off than no visual at all. At best, it distracts the audience; at worst, it baffles them. So if you're going to use visuals, it's essential that you use them well.

Your first question, then, when planning your presentation shouldn't be 'what visuals do I need?', but 'do I need any visuals at all?'. Here are three benchmarks to help you decide whether a visual is necessary or not:

1 **Does it back up your argument?** Any visual that doesn't reinforce what you're saying will simply distract the audience.

2 **Does it clarify a tricky point?** Using a picture is sometimes the only effective way to explain something complicated, for example how a machine works, or how different statistics compare with one another.

3 **Does it make an impact?** If there is just one important message you want your audience to take away from your presentation, can it be summed up in a single image?

A GOOD EXAMPLE

One presenter was talking to an audience about 'good corporate governance' in their organisation—in other words, getting the whole company into the right mindset to comply with a series of government regulations. There could hardly be a drier subject! But instead of using a series of organisation charts, workflow diagrams, or illustrations of departmental responsibilities, the presenter used just one visual: a picture of the company chief executive, with a set of prison bars superimposed over his face. This certainly got the message across: non-compliance with the regulations could result in big trouble. You could have heard a pin drop.

STEP FOUR DESIGN VISUALS

1 **Use pictures, not words.** The best question to ask yourself when designing a visual is, 'what does this show?' (rather than 'what does this say?'). In other words, use as little text as possible. If you do need to add words—labels on graphs, titles on organisation charts, stages on workflow diagrams, for example—make sure:

● They're still in a decent font size (18pt minimum, preferably).

● They're horizontal wherever possible, for ease of reading.

● Even if they have to be vertical (along the bottom axis of a graph, for instance), the letters are horizontal.

2 **Try some icebreakers.** Sometimes it can be helpful to use a visual early on as an icebreaker that will warm up the audience and to get you over the jitters. Presenters often make this a 'funny', which is fine, but you do need to be a bit careful: if you're not a natural joke teller, it can be embarrassing all round if your funny falls flat. Cartoons can also do the job for you, but again, make sure the content and implications of the cartoon suit the rest of the presentation.

3 **Titles for visuals.** Too often, presenters make the mistake of putting a general label, such as 'Sales in 2009' at the top of a visual. However, it's much better to come up with a very specific label that tells people what you want them to look at in that visual. Instead, if you wrote 'Sales in 2009 reverse previous downward trend', your audience would know instantly why they're being shown this slide. The key message here is: make the title of a visual the same as its message.

4 **Choose the right kind of chart.** Charts are the ideal way to convey information instantly. However, different charts are appropriate for different kinds of information. Here's a quick checklist:

PURPOSE	CHART TYPE AND DESCRIPTION
Showing change over time (e.g. share prices)	**Line charts.** The slope of the line instantly tells viewers the direction of the trend.
Direct comparisons over time (e.g. how manufacturing costs have risen faster than manufacturing costs over three years)	**Vertical bar chart.** The height of the bars shows the comparative costs; and because people naturally associate left-to-right with the movement of time, vertical bars work better than horizontal ones when there's a time element involved.
Direct comparisons at one time (e.g. the building society with the lowest interest rate in March)	**Horizontal bar chart.** The length of the bar gives its ranking; the label on it identifies the item.
Comparing parts of a whole (e.g. the percentage of government budget spent on education)	**Pie chart.** This is the simplest way to show proportions, as long as there aren't too many slices (five maximum is ideal).
Comparison by geographic location (e.g. sales by region)	**Map.** Distinguish among regions by using different colours, shadings or symbols.

5 **Build up an image.** If you have a complicated concept to communicate, it can be very effective to break your image up into stages and introduce them one at a time. PowerPoint is the ideal medium for doing this, but you can do it with acetates and flipcharts too.

Say, for example, you're showing an intricate organisational design. You could start with the top executives, then add the directors who report to them, then the group managers, then the departmental heads, and so on. You could do this in a number of ways:

- Sequentially—separate diagrams for each part, which you show one at a time.

- Build-ups—where each new layer is added individually, one on top of the next.

- Reveals—where you start with the whole diagram, but most of it is covered up to begin with and sections are exposed gradually.

Remember that you may not need to include every single detail of the new organisation in the diagram; just make sure it contains the bits your audience will be interested in.

STEP FIVE BOOST YOUR MESSAGE!

Once you have your visuals, you need to make the best use of them during the presentation to reinforce what you're saying.

Unless a visual is completely obvious or self-explanatory, you need to discuss it—or at least refer to it. It's amazing how many presenters put up a visual and then don't even mention it!

Make sure you don't block audience's view of the visual; you could even step aside for a moment and let people look at it properly.

 Once the visual has made its point, take it down— otherwise it might become a distraction.

COMMON MISTAKES

YOU OVER-COMPLICATE THINGS

'Keep it simple' is the implicit message throughout all the guidelines above, but it's worth reiterating here. It's extraordinary how many people forget it. Sometimes this is due, ironically, to lack of time—it can take longer to think through a point and boil it down to its essentials than simply to slap down all the available material. It can also be easy to fall for lovely software and graphics packages that tempt you to create fancy effects and animations. Don't! If you bewilder your audience or distract people from your main message, all your efforts will be wasted.

YOU FORGET TO CHECK FOR ERRORS

This is one of the commonest ways to shoot yourself in the foot. Your presentation looks lovely, your arguments are sound, your visuals are punchy and effective, BUT . . . you misspell the chief executive's name, or the first word on the title page. Zap goes your credibility, and you'll have to work very hard to build it back up!

TOP TIP!

A visual doesn't always have to be a design on a slide or overhead: it can also be a prop—a 3-D object that you pass round, for the audience to examine. If you're enthusing about your company's new design of paper clip, for example, there's nothing like letting people handle a real one for ensuring that they remember it.

STEPS TO SUCCESS

 Make sure everything looks consistent and professional, and fits with your business image or brand.

 Use big font sizes that can be read from the back row.

 Cut out all but essential text.

 Check that all fonts and colours are clear and readable.

 Follow a logical sequence throughout your presentation.

 Decide whether visuals are really necessary.

 Make sure all visuals are well designed and appropriate to the rest of your presentation.

 Think about using props in addition to your visuals.

 Be careful not to get too complicated.

 Check for errors!

USEFUL LINKS

● **Advisory Group on Computer Graphics:**
www.agocg.ac.uk/brief/ppt.htm

● **Awesome Powerpoint Backgrounds:**
www.awesomebackgrounds.com

● **Business Link:**
www.businesslink.gov.uk

● **KU Medical Center, on-line tutorial series:**
http://library.kumc.edu/

● **Warwick University e-learning guides:**
www2.warwick.ac.uk

● **Presentation Skills:**
www.presentation-skills.biz

Surviving
worst-case scenarios

n an ideal world, everything would always go as planned. Sadly the world is anything but ideal and as a result, hardly anything ever does! This can be pretty disconcerting, particularly if you're in a situation where you're 'on show', such as giving a presentation. However, there are very few circumstances which are completely irredeemable, unless you panic.

It's well worth spending some time thinking through all the things that could possibly go wrong and (if possible) taking preventive action, or (if not) planning what to do in the event. This chapter lays some ground rules . . .

STEP ONE MAKE SURE YOU CAN HANDLE THE TECHNOLOGY AND EQUIPMENT YOU NEED

Technology is a potential problem for every presenter. Even the best designed presentation will fail if the technology you use to deliver it goes wrong, so it's really important to check everything beforehand.

1 Technology

Unless you're using your own equipment, make sure that your presentation will work on what's provided.

- Have you checked that you can load your presentation onto the computer (does it have a CD drive, for example)?

- Does this machine run the same software version that you use? You may be able to run newer presentations under older versions of PowerPoint, for example, but extra features (such as animations or links to other applications) may not work. Check that they do.

- If you need to link to the Web, can you get Internet access?

- Is the projector a relatively new one? Older projectors may be dim and/or have fewer colours.

- Are there enough power points, of the right kinds and in the right places? Will you need extension cables or extra plug sockets, or do you need to rearrange the room?

- Do the connections between different pieces of equipment—from the computer to the projector, for example—work properly?

- If at all possible, run your presentation through from beginning to end in situ.

2 Other equipment

- Make sure you have spares of everything you could need—back-up disks, spare bulbs, spare batteries, extra handouts, pens, and so on.

- Check that any lectern or stand is at the right height for you.

TOP TIP!
Be prepared! If you're presenting on home turf, do a practice run-through the day or a few hours before your presentation, so you can check everything mentioned above. If you're presenting elsewhere, liaise with your contact at the venue to find out as much as you can about what equipment is available and what you'll be expected to bring. Arrive at the venue in plenty of time so that you can practise there too.

- Confirm that people will be able to hear properly from all parts of the room, particularly if you're using sound effects or a microphone.

- Have a spare copy of your notes in your briefcase, stapled together and numbered so they can't get mixed up.

- Familiarise yourself with how to operate all the lights, air conditioning, heating, and so on.

● Make sure you know where all the amenities are—coffee rooms, toilets, reception areas, phones, for example— not just for your own information, but so that you can answer if asked by an audience member.

STEP TWO MANAGE THE AUDIENCE

1 Arrange the seating sensibly

There's nothing worse, when presenting, than facing an audience that is scattered all over the room or, even worse, huddled into the back rows of seats leaving a great gulf between you and them. Even the greatest speaker will have difficulty building energy or creating rapport in such circumstances. There are a couple of ways you can prevent such a situation arising.

● If at all possible, find out how many people are coming and put out just enough seats, plus a couple of extras. Arrange them in an arc facing you.

● If you have no idea of, or control over, the numbers attending, tape off the back row of seats and put a 'Reserved' sign on them. Once the front rows are full, remove the sign and let the last arrivals sit at the back.

2 Think about the staging

There are a few other tips for staging the presentation which will also help things run smoothly and enable you to engage with your audience.

Make sure you're not standing with your back to a window, or you'll appear as a silhouette to your listeners.

Check that you have somewhere—like a table—to put your papers, notes, handouts, briefcase, and anything else you have with you.

If you need to darken the room, make sure you know where light switches are and how curtains or blinds close.

Try sitting in different parts of the room to check that all members of the audience will be able to see properly.

If possible, make sure there's nothing—like a desk or table—between you and your audience. Psychologically it will act as a barrier, and you will have to work that much harder to create rapport.

TOP TIP!
Audiences have a very short attention span— most adults cannot concentrate for more than seven to ten minutes. To prevent people from wriggling, chatting, or switching off, it's a good idea to break your presentation into easily digestible sections and change the pace or create a diversion at regular intervals.

STEP THREE DEAL WITH DISRUPTIONS

Interruptions can put you off your stride, so take preventative action before your presentation begins:

Make sure the room is booked well in advance—you don't want another group of people arriving at the same time expecting to have a meeting there!

 Arrange for any phones in the room to be diverted for the duration.

Put a sign on the door to stop people from barging in unintentionally.

 Check that there's no regular interruption planned, such as a fire drill. If there is, plan a break around it, or at least tell the audience what will be happening beforehand.

 Fill the seats from the front, as described in the previous section; this has the added benefit of preventing late arrivals from walking all the way to the front and climbing across other people to find somewhere to sit.

 If the presentation is likely to be a long one, make sure you schedule plenty of breaks—preferably on the hour, every hour. This helps to eliminate surreptitious escapes to the toilet, and maintains people's concentration.

A DIFFICULT SITUATION

Possibly the most difficult disruption you might encounter is if several people in the audience start a side conversation while you are speaking. If this happens, in the following order:

- Ask if anyone has any questions

- Ask the talkers if you can do anything to clarify

- If they carry on, move closer to them

- If they still don't stop, lower your voice, or pause in what you're saying and look at them

- If all else fails, call a halt to the presentation and ask the whole group whether a new session should be arranged

STEP FOUR SURVIVE UNEXPECTED TIME ISSUES

Uncertainty about or problems with the time available can throw a presenter completely. Say, for example, the meeting before yours overruns and cuts your time severely . . . what do you do then? The two scenarios below cover most contingencies.

1 **You find you have 20 minutes instead of the hour you planned on.** Talking quickly isn't the answer! Decide swiftly what proportion of the 20 minutes each part of your presentation should take. Is there any section that could be omitted altogether? Then keep your eye on your watch as you speak and limit yourself to the key concept in each portion.

2 **A vital member of the audience has to leave before you've reached your key points.** Say the finance director, who has ultimate say over whether his company buys your products, tells you he has to leave early. This could be disastrous. However, there's an old rule regarding presentations: tell people what you're going to tell them, tell them, and then tell them what you told them. If you follow this rule when creating your presentation in the first place, you won't get caught out this way.

✓ Always mention your main point and major supporting points within the first few minutes of any presentation.

✓ If you're using slides or overheads, always have one that contains the main point and the key points.

If, however, you've made the fatal error of trying to save the best for last,

TOP TIP!
You can never expect to eliminate all kinds of interruption, so the golden rule, if you are interrupted, is to acknowledge it rather than trying to carry on regardless. If you pause and laugh while a jet plane thunders overhead, for example, the audience will probably laugh too, and the whole episode will actually work to your advantage by creating a bond between you.

ask the decision maker for a moment to summarise (anyone will give you a moment if you ask nicely). Then state, in one sentence, the single point you want the decision maker to remember and, if you have a chance, the two concepts that best support that point.

STEP FIVE ANSWER DIFFICULT QUESTIONS

Some presenters dread questions from the audience more than anything else, as it's impossible to know what might come up or whether someone might have a particular agenda attached to the question they ask. However, most tricky questions tend to fall into one of only a few categories, and if you recognise these, it will help you know how to answer.

TYPE OF QUESTION	BEST RESPONSE
The concealed objection—e.g. 'How come the price is so high?'	● Don't get defensive. ● Ask them to clarify the objection— e.g. 'What makes you feel that the price is too high?' ● Put it in perspective—e.g. 'It's only a few pence more expensive than its nearest rival . . .' ● Give the compensating benefits— ' . . . and the quality is much higher, so it's actually better value for money.'

TYPE OF QUESTION	BEST RESPONSE
The test question, designed to test your knowledge— e.g. 'What are the research findings on side effects for this new drug?'	● Don't bluff. ● Call on an expert colleague if you have one there. ● If you don't know, say so—but offer to find out later, make a note, and then keep your promise.
The display question, often intended to demonstrate the questioner's own expertise	● Play along and don't be afraid to acknowledge how clever they are publicly. 'Of course you're right—I didn't mention it, simply because I thought it might be too technical for this occasion.'
The challenge question, which usually means you've trespassed on someone else's area of knowledge	● Back down straight away, concede all territorial rights, and perhaps consult their opinion. 'I'm sorry, I meant the transport policy in the West Midlands, not in the whole of the UK—which of course you know more about than I do. Would you say it's the same across the board?'

TYPE OF QUESTION	BEST RESPONSE
The defensive question, which tends to mean something you've proposed is a threat to the questioner—e.g. 'Do you really think it's a good idea to let managers train their own staff?'	● Try to question the questioner. 'Could you explain your concerns further, perhaps?' ● Throw the question open to the floor . . . do other people feel managers aren't qualified to train their staff? ● If it's not within your remit, refer the questioner to someone who can provide answers.
The question you plan to discuss in detail later	● Provide a brief answer, then say that you plan to cover the subject properly later. ● Don't ask the questioner to wait until you reach the point at which you originally intended to discuss the subject, or everyone will focus on the unanswered question instead of listening to you. ● In a meeting setting or small presentation, don't ask people to keep their questions for the end as this suggests that you're not confident enough to deal with interruptions.

STEP SIX DON'T LET NERVES GET TO YOU

Almost everyone, even those with lots of experience, suffers from nerves to some degree when they have to present to a group of people. And nerves can make you prone to accidents and stumbling.

> # TOP TIP!
> If nothing else, making sure that you know your stuff and keep calm will usually be enough to deal with most questions that you might face.

However, the one key to solving almost all of these is understanding what causes an attack of nerves: fear, usually of what could possibly go wrong. This is why you generally feel better once you've got going: your equipment's working OK, the audience hasn't booed you off the stage, you haven't made an idiot of yourself, and so on.

The more you pre-empt your fear, then, by doing your preparation thoroughly and taking preventive measures against things that could go wrong, the less nervous you will feel, and the less you'll be to come a cropper. However, even with all the preparation in the world, things can still sometimes go awry. If they do, don't panic—you can still win through. Here are some of the most common nerve-induced pitfalls, and what to do about them:

1 **You lose your train of thought mid-sentence.** Smile, say 'excuse me' or 'I'm sorry', and start again. Try not to panic or get flustered: it's not the end of the world and everyone in the room has lost track of an idea at least once in their lives. People want you to succeed and are generally sympathetic. Keep smiling.

2 **Your throat dries up.** Actors have a good trick for dealing with this. Roll a tiny piece of paper into a small ball and place it between your gum and the inside of your cheek at the back of your mouth. It will stimulate the flow of saliva, just like that little roll of cotton wool the dentist uses. Try this in private first, however, so you are sure you are comfortable.

3 **You drop your overheads on the floor.** Make a joke about your clumsiness, pick them up and take a few moments to put them in order. (Now is the time to be grateful you have numbered them.)

COMMON MISTAKES

✖ YOU DON'T REHEARSE

Almost every piece of advice in this actionlist points to one thing: you MUST PRACTISE! With plenty of rehearsal, your confidence will be sufficient to see you through just about any disaster. It's not enough to say your presentation over to yourself in your head, as it's very different when you have to get up and do it in front of an audience. Choose a friend or colleague who you trust, and ask them if they will watch you and give you honest feedback. As an absolute minimum, stand in front of a mirror and run through the presentation, checking yourself as critically as you can.

STEPS TO SUCCESS

 In order to pre-empt disasters with equipment, check thoroughly that everything works, in situ, before the presentation starts.

 Arrange the seating and staging in the best way to help build rapport with your audience and to maintain their concentration.

Take pre-emptive measures to avoid interruptions.

 Have contingency plans in case the time available alters significantly.

 Learn to handle difficult questions.

 Manage your nerves by addressing the fear behind them.

 Practise, practise, practise.

USEFUL LINKS

● **Business Link:**
www.businesslink.gov.uk

● **KU Medical Center, on-line tutorial series:**
http://kumc.edu/

Where to find more help

DON'T SWEAT THE SMALL STUFF AT WORK
Richard Carlson
London: Hodder Mobius, 1999 284pp ISBN: 0340748737
This is a best-selling comprehensive guide to combating stress in your life at work. The book is full of useful advice for dealing with a range of panic-inducing situations, including presentations and meetings.

POINT, CLICK AND WOW!: A QUICK GUIDE TO BRILLIANT LAPTOP PRESENTATIONS: 2ND ED.
Claudyne Wilder, Jennifer Rotondo
Chichester: Jossey-Bass Wiley, 2002 240pp ISBN: 0787956694
Aimed at business people of all levels, this book offers a practical guide to using technology in effective presentations. The authors explore how to balance on-screen activity and human interaction, how to deal with software and hardware issues, and how, when, and where to practise. The book includes checklists and illustrations.

PRESENTATION ZEN DESIGN: SIMPLE DESIGN PRINCIPLES AND TECHNIQUES TO ENHANCE YOUR PRESENTATIONS
Garr Reynolds
New Riders, 2010 264pp ISBN: 0321668790
Presentation master Garr Reynolds shares his knowledge on designing effective presentations containing text, graphs, colour, images, and video by applying time-honoured design principles to presentation layouts. After establishing guidelines for each of the various elements, he demonstrates how you can achieve overall harmony and balance using the tenets of Zen simplicity in order to make a stronger, more lasting connection with your audience.

Index